# COMPUTERS IN BUSINESS

## AN INTRODUCTION

**McGRAW-HILL BOOK COMPANY**
New York  St. Louis  San Francisco  Auckland
Bogotá  Düsseldorf  Johannesburg  London  Madrid
Mexico  Montreal  New Delhi  Panama  Paris
São Paulo  Singapore  Sydney  Tokyo  Toronto

# DONALD H. SANDERS

M.J. Neeley School of Business
Texas Christian University

**FOURTH EDITION**

# COMPUTERS IN BUSINESS

**AN INTRODUCTION**

**COMPUTERS IN BUSINESS an introduction**

234567890   VHVH   7832109

This book was set in Optima by University Graphics, Inc.
The editors were Charles E. Stewart and Edwin Hanson;
the cover was designed by Nicholas Krenitsky;
the production supervisor was Leroy A. Young.
New drawings were done by Allyn-Mason, Inc.
Von Hoffmann Press, Inc., was printer and binder.

Library of Congress Cataloging in Publication Data

Sanders, Donald H
    Computers in business.

    Includes bibliographies and index.
    1. Business—Data processing.  2. Electronic digital computers.  I. Title.
HF5548.2.S23   1979        658'.05        78-17877
ISBN 0-07-054645-2

*To my family:* Joyce, Gary, Linda, and Craig

# contents

# preface

In recent months, a number of articles have appeared in information system and data processing periodicals with titles such as "The Primacy of the User" and "The Age of the End User." Many of these articles stress the importance of having those who must use the output of information systems participate in the planning and development of such systems. But there is really nothing new in this recognition of the importance of users. In fact, this edition of *Computers in Business,* like the three previous editions, is written with the needs of future users specifically in mind. Such students probably accept the fact that in their future work they will need a basic understanding of computerized information processing and a familiarity with computers, but they have not chosen to become computer scientists or information system specialists. Rather, they are preparing for management or staff positions in such functional areas of business as accounting, finance, marketing, personnel, and production, or they are planning to become administrators in government, health, or educational organizations that make use of business procedures.

As future end-users (rather than as designers) of information systems, then, these students have needs and objectives that will eventually differ from those of students who expect to work more closely with computers. But at the introductory course level, the needs of end-users may not differ significantly from the needs of those students who may be thinking of embarking on a career in business data processing. Initially, both types of students will need to understand basic computer hardware concepts, and both will need to learn the concepts relating to system/program development and implementation. Furthermore, if we are now in "the age of the end-user," an understanding by specialists of the broad implications that *their* future efforts may have on business management and on society may be as important to them in their dealings with users as it is to the users themselves. (If both users and specialists had had a better understanding of the consequences of their actions in the past, perhaps Robert Townsend would not have written in *Up the Organization* about "managers drowning in ho-hum reports they've been conned into asking for and are ashamed to admit are of no value.")

In summary, then, *the purpose of this book* is to introduce both future users and data processing beginners, at an early stage in their college programs, to many of the important common topics that are likely to be relevant to them in their future careers. More specifically, *the objectives of this edition are to provide students with* (1) some of the fundamental concepts of (and developments associated with) computerized information processing; (2) a general orientation to the computer—what it is, what it can and cannot do, how it operates, and how it may be instructed to solve problems; and (3) some insights into the broad impact that computers have had, are having, and may be expected to have on businesspeople, on the environment in which they work, and on the society in which they live.

**REVISION FEATURES AND TEXT ORGANIZATION**

There have been more changes made in the organization and content of this version of *Computers in Business* than in any previous edition. There were 18 chapters in the third edition. The contents of nine of these earlier chapters have been reorganized, rewritten, and condensed into five present chapters; three of the earlier chapters have been dropped; and the remaining six chapters have been thoroughly reviewed and updated. Six new chapters have been added. Although the net effect of these changes has been to reduce the size of the book by nearly 200 pages, the essential material needed for a balanced presentation of a broad range of topics has been retained, and much that is new and relevant has been added.

New opening pages containing *learning objectives* and *chapter outlines* are presented at the beginning of each chapter. The review and discussion questions at the end of each chapter support the learning objectives of the chapter. Finally, *cartoons* have been inserted in a number of places in the text to help maintain student interest and to reinforce important points that are presented. (This approach differs from some books where cartoons and inserts are randomly placed in such a way as to cause distraction rather than reinforcement.)

To achieve the book objectives that were listed above, this edition is divided into *five parts*. Each of these parts is introduced by a brief opening statement. *A brief summary of these five parts, along with a more specific outline of the significant revisions made in this edition, is presented below.*

PART I: INFORMATION AND COMPUTERS: SOME INTRODUCTORY THOUGHTS

The chapters included in Part I (which is aimed at the first objective of the book) are

1. *Information and Information Processing: Concepts and Historical Developments.* Materials previously covered in the first two chapters have been updated and condensed into this single chapter.

2. *The Information Revolution in Perspective.* Although it combines some of the material previously found in Chapters 3 and 4, this chapter has several entirely new sections. For example, much of the material presented on adapting to the information revolution is new.

## PART II: BASIC COMPUTER CONCEPTS

The chapters included in Part II (which focuses on the hardware aspects of the second objective) are

**3.**  *Introduction to Computers.* A new introduction and updated examples of computer capabilities and limitations have been added, and the material on overlapped processing and buffer storage previously found in Chapter 7 has been moved to this chapter.

**4.**  *Input and Output: I.* This chapter (and the one which follows) has been completely reworked and reorganized. The introductory section on data organization concepts has been greatly expanded to include discussions of logical data structures, physical structures, and file organization approaches. Sections dealing with character recognition equipment, printing and microfilm equipment, and direct-access storage devices have been repositioned in this and the following chapter. The material on punched cards and punched paper tape has been condensed.

**5.**  *Input and Output: II.* In addition to being reorganized, this chapter has new sections dealing with magnetic bubble storage and with the latest online terminal devices. Much of the material on data communications is new.

**6.**  *The CPU: Concepts and Codes.* The section on computer numbering systems has been condensed, and the supplement on hexadecimal numbers has been deleted.

**7.**  *The CPU: Components and Comparisons.* A new section on the types of CPU storage elements has been included, much greater emphasis has been placed on the discussion of semiconductor storage devices, and a new section that compares some of the characteristics of CPUs of different sizes has been added.

## PART III: USING COMPUTERS TO SOLVE PROBLEMS

The chapters found in Part III (which focuses on the software aspects of the second objective) are

**8.**  *Information System Development: Overview and Analysis.* This is a *new chapter* that first outlines the general procedure to be followed in using computers to solve problems. The remainder of the chapter is then devoted to the system-analysis stage of the system development effort.

**9.**  *Information System Development: The Design Stage.* Another *new chapter,* this one deals with the system-design stage of a system development project.

**10.**  *Programming Analysis.* This chapter has been modified somewhat because of text reorganization.

**11.**  *Program Preparation and Programming Languages.* Combining elements found in Chapters 11 and 12 of the third edition, this chapter also has entirely new sections on the techniques that may be used to (*a*) organize programmers and (*b*) establish a structured programming environment. Examples of programs coded in FORTRAN, COBOL, PL/I,

BASIC, and RPG are presented, and the general characteristics of each language are discussed.

**12.**  *System/Program Implementation.* This *new chapter* deals with the final steps required to complete a system development project.

### PART IV: COMPUTER IMPLICATIONS FOR MANAGEMENT

The chapters included in Part IV (which is aimed at the third objective) are

**13.**  *The Computer's Impact on Planning and Organizational Structure.* Although it combines, condenses, and updates materials found in two chapters of the previous edition, this chapter also has a new section that deals with the question of where data should be stored in an organization.

**14.**  *The Computer's Impact on Staffing and Management Control.* Here is another chapter that condenses, combines, and updates topics found in two chapters of the previous edition.

**15.**  *Social Implications of the Business Use of Computers.* Some of the beneficial and negative effects of business computer usage on society as a whole are treated in this *new chapter.* It is thus more sharply focused than the "computers in society" chapter found in the third edition.

**16.**  *The Management of Computing Resources.* The factors, considerations, and procedures that may be relevant in planning, organizing, staffing, and controlling activities in a computer department are the subjects of this *new chapter.*

### PART V: EPILOGUE

The chapter included in this part (which is also related to the third objective) is

**17.**  *Computers and the Future. New* for this edition, this chapter is a brief essay on the future outlook for computer technology, for business information systems, and for society.

**USE OF THIS BOOK**  This text is designed for use in an introductory one-semester or one-quarter course in computer data processing offered at an early stage in a college program. No mathematical or data processing background is required or assumed; no specific computer make or model is featured. The book may be used without access to a machine.

Two issues dealing with program preparation are as unresolved today as they were a decade ago when this book first appeared. The *first* issue is concerned with *how much* should be attempted—i.e., it is concerned with the *depth* of instruction on program preparation that students should receive in an introductory course. Once a decision has been made on this issue of how much should be attempted in a single course (because in many schools future end-users may only take a single course), the *second* issue then involves the selection of the programming language(s) to use.

For many introductory courses, the limited programming language emphasis contained in this book will be sufficient. (Coded examples written in the most popular high-level languages are presented, and the basic language characteristics of each are noted.) However, when emphasis is to be placed on the writing of programs in a specific language for a specific make and model of machine, then the following *two types of instructional materials are generally required:* (1) *a basic text* to provide the necessary breadth to the course and to put program coding in its proper perspective, and (2) *a programming manual* available from a commercial publisher or from the computer manufacturer, and/or notes and materials prepared by the instructor to cope with any idiosyncrasies that may exist at a particular computer installation.

In such situations, this book is well suited for use as the basic text. No attempt has been made in this edition, however, to present the coding rules for any language. In fact, the 57 pages devoted to program coding in Chapter 12 of the third edition have been substantially reduced in this book for economic reasons. Why was this done? Well, on the one hand, there was probably more coding detail presented in the previous edition than was necessary for those courses where only a limited language emphasis is needed. On the other hand, however, much *more* space would be needed to do justice to the syntax of each language presented if the book were used as the *only* text in courses where students are expected to prepare several programs. (But in that case, of course, only one language would probably be selected and students would then be buying many extra pages of material that would not be used.) Given the fact that a wealth of programming language materials now exists in paperback form (there are nearly 200 manuals sold by commercial publishers listed in the January 1978 issue of *Computing Newsletter for Schools of Business;* this listing is certainly not a complete inventory of commercial products; and it does not include any of the dozens of language manuals supplied by computer manufacturers), and given the fact that from these manuals can be selected a relatively inexpensive one that is probably closely targeted to the needs of a particular course, the conclusion reached for this edition was that it was in the best economic interests of the students to leave the coverage of detailed coding topics to the scores of good programming manuals that are available.

The organization of the book into five parts permits some *modular flexibility.* Although the order of presentation is logical and has served the needs of many in the past, there is no necessary reason why all parts must be covered in the sequence in which they appear in the text. For example, if a number of programs are to be written, the first three chapters can be quickly covered, and then the first chapter in Part III can be considered early in the course to provide background for the problem-solving process.

Since this is an introductory text dealing with the general uses, operations, and implications of computers, and since the author has written other volumes that deal with many of the same basic subjects, there are a number of similarities between this book and the other works. In general, however, *when there is an overlap* of the topics presented, *the coverage in this book is likely to be much more thorough* than the coverage given in the others. In addition, extra chapters on hardware/software concepts and on managing computing resources are included here but are missing from *Computer Essentials for Business* (McGraw-Hill Book Company, 1978). Of course, the chapter dealing with the broader social implications of the business use of computers is abridged when compared with similar material presented in the second edition of *Computers in Society* (McGraw-Hill Book Company, 1977).

It is customary at about this point in a preface (although there is always the question of whether anyone is reading a preface at this point) to acknowledge the contributions and suggestions received from numerous sources. A special tribute must go to those equipment manufacturers and magazine publishers who furnished technical materials, cartoons, photographs, and other visual aids. Their individual contributions are often acknowledged in the body of the book.

It is appropriate here, however, to pay special tribute to the publishers of the periodicals from which the cartoons found in this text are taken. More specifically, the cartoon found on page 335 was reprinted with permission of *Creative Computing,* copyright © 1977 by Creative Computing, Morristown, New Jersey 07960. The cartoons found on pages 64, 81, 142, 209, 248, 291, 385, 391, 399, 408, 430, and 437 are reprinted with permission of *Datamation,*® copyright © 1976, 1977, and 1978 by Technical Publishing Company, Greenwich, Connecticut 06830. The cartoons found on pages 79, 85, 87, 157, 235, 293, 324, and 365 are reprinted with permission of *Infosystems,*® copyright © 1976 and 1977 by Hitchcock Publishing Company, Wheaton, Illinois 60187.

Donald H. Sanders

Since computers are used in business (and in other areas of society) because they can produce necessary information, it is appropriate for you to briefly consider the material in Part I before you move on to the discussions of computing devices and their control. More specifically the purpose of the chapters in this first Part is to (1) present some introductory concepts about the subject of information, (2) trace the evolutionary developments in information processing, and (3) place in perspective some of the developments and issues associated with the information revolution that business is currently experiencing. At the conclusion of this Part, you will then have a background for the orientation to computers that is the subject of Part II.

The chapters included in Part I are:

# INFORMATION AND COMPUTERS:
## SOME INTRODUCTORY THOUGHTS

# information and information processing: 1

## concepts and historical developments

LEARNING OBJECTIVES    After studying this chapter and answering the discussion questions, you should be able to: □ Identify the sources of data and the activities associated with data processing □ Discuss the information needs of managers and the properties that management information should possess □ Identify the pressures responsible for the current efforts to improve management information □ Outline some major developments in the evolution of information processing

CHAPTER OUTLINE
Purpose and organization of this book
Information concepts: Information Defined / Sources of Data / Data Processing
Need for management information: What Information Is Needed? / Desired Properties of Management Information

Information improvement and computer processing
Evolution of information processing: The Manual Stage / Machine-assisted Manual Development / Electromechanical Punched Card Development / Computer Development
Summary
Review and discussion questions
Selected references

According to the History of the Royal Astronomical Society, a Captain Smyth of the British Royal Navy was sailing on the Mediterranean Sea in the early 1800s when he encountered a Spanish ship. After entertaining the Spanish captain, Smyth presented him with the *British Nautical Almanac*—a leatherbound set of books containing information to be used in celestial navigation. Since England and Spain had been at war, the Spanish captain may have been surprised by this "generous" gift. Actually, however, Smyth used the information found in French navigational tables to sail his own ship because he knew that the *British Nautical Almanac* contained certain serious errors. The Spaniard left Smyth's ship with the British navigational information under his arm and neither he nor his ship was ever seen again.

**PURPOSE AND ORGANIZATION OF THIS BOOK**

This story teaches us the importance of information in navigation, and it also illustrates the care which should be exercised by those who obtain and use information for decision-making purposes. It is unlikely, of course, that you will spend your future years sailing on the Mediterranean.[1] But it *is* probable that as a future manager and leader in business (or in other fields) you will be greatly affected by the information that you will have to work with. And it is almost certain that much of that information will be produced by computers. Thus, the purpose of this book is to lay a foundation for the *continuing study* that will prepare you for a successful working relationship with, and an understanding of, computerized information processing.

[1] On the other hand, if enough of you buy this book maybe I. . . .

More specifically, the *objectives of this book are* to (1) introduce you to some of the fundamental concepts of (and developments associated with) computerized information processing; (2) provide you with a general orientation to the computer—what it is, what it can and cannot do, how it operates and how it may be instructed to solve problems; and (3) furnish you with some insights into the broad impact that computers have had, are having, and may be expected to have on managers, the environment in which managers work, and the society in which we live.

To achieve these overall objectives, the book is divided into five parts. The first objective is considered in the two chapters of Part I, the chapters in Parts II and III focus attention on the second goal, and the chapters in Parts IV and V deal with the final goal. On a more detailed level, at the beginning of each chapter you will find (1) a summary of what you should learn in that chapter and (2) an outline of the major topics that are presented in the chapter. In total, of course, these chapter learning objectives achieve the overall goals of the book.

In addition to these goals and the approach taken to achieve them, a further purpose of this book is to attempt to reduce the *communications gap* that currently exists between computer specialists and the end-users of (or those who are affected by) the machine's output. Of course, there is nothing new about this problem of lack of communication.[2]

In ancient Babylon a vast public works program was started by the leaders with the objective of building a tower reaching to the heavens. Obviously, a project of such magnitude required a considerable amount of managerial skill as well as the labor of thousands of workers. The book of Genesis tells us that this ambitious project was never completed. The managers had failed to plan for an unusual development. Displeased with the haughty conduct of the people, God confused their language. Supervisors could not communicate with workers; workers could not even understand each other. The project came to a standstill, and the episode has been used for centuries as an example of the consequences of a communications breakdown.

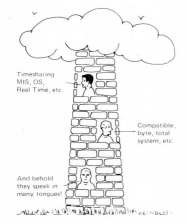

Timesharing
MIS, OS,
Real Time, etc.

Compatible,
byte, total
system, etc.

And behold
they speak in
many tongues!

A whole new language has developed in the past decade in information processing—a language that might be labeled "Computerese" and that must be mastered to some extent by the future manager. New concepts in the design and use of computers are announced with mind-boggling frequency, and these concepts are often described with newly coined words or phrases. Thousands of new computers are installed each

---

[2] Nor is this communications gap unique to the computing field. Representative Ben Grant, in arguing for plain language in a proposed new Texas constitution, pointed out that if one person were to give another an orange, he or she would simply say, "Have an orange." But if a lawyer were the donor, the gift might be accompanied with these words: "I hereby give and convey to you, all and singular, my estate and interests, right, title, claim, and advantages of and in said orange, together with its rind, juice, pulp, and pits, and all rights and advantages therein, with full power to bite, cut, suck, and otherwise eat same. . . ."

year; understanding suffers because it sometimes seems that the number of new terms, "buzz-words," and *acronyms*[3] are increasing at about the same rate.

In the following section and throughout the book, words are defined as they are introduced. *A glossary of commonly used technical terms is included at the back of the book.* You will find that although some Computerese terms sound quite impressive and forbidding—as is often the case with technical jargon—closer inspection will prove them to be relatively simple.

The above remarks have served to introduce you to the objectives of this book. In later chapters we will examine computer systems in some detail. At this point, however, we should place the role of computers in proper perspective. Computers are used *because they produce information;* were this not so, the machines would be merely expensive curiosities. Therefore, in the following pages of this chapter, let us examine the subject of information. After first explaining some *information concepts,* we will then consider the *need for management information,* the *pressures bringing about management information improvement,* and the *evolution of information processing.*

## INFORMATION CONCEPTS

Three elements fundamental to human activities are information, energy, and materials. All these elements are necessary to provide the physical things which humans need—i.e., food, clothing, shelter, and transportation. In addition to supporting physical production, however, information is also the substance of all human intellectual activity; it is basic to education, government, literature, the conduct of business, and the maintenance and expansion of our store of knowledge. The harnessing of energy brought about the industrial revolution, and the attempt to harness and transform information is bringing about another revolution at the present time.[4]

### information defined

The word *data* is the plural of *datum,* which means *fact.* Data, then, are facts, unevaluated messages, or informational raw materials, but they are

---

[3] An acronym is a term formed from the first letters of related words. For example, COBOL is an acronym that stands for COmmon Business-Oriented Language—a language used to instruct computers to take the steps necessary to produce desired information.

[4] This information revolution is the subject of the next chapter. An indication of the scope and importance of information is found in the estimate of the director of the President's Office of Telecommunications Policy that during 1975 "more than 50 percent of the US labor force and more than 50 percent of the gross national product were expected to be devoted to the production, processing, or distribution of information. . . . " See "Washington Info," *Infosystems,* January 1976, p. 14.

not information except in a constricted and detailed sense. Data are independent entities and are unlimited in number. Although often considered to be numerical values, data may also be defined to include nonnumerical perceptions and observations made by human beings and machines.

As used in this text, the term *information* is generally considered to designate data arranged in ordered and useful form. Thus, *information* will usually be thought of as relevant knowledge, produced as output of processing operations, and acquired to provide insight in order to (1) achieve specific purposes or (2) enhance understanding.[5] From this definition, we see that information is the result of a transformation process. Just as raw materials are transformed into finished products by a manufacturing process (Fig. 1-1a), so too are raw data transformed into information by the data processing operation (Fig. 1-1b). The products produced by the manufacturing process have little utility until they are properly applied; similarly, the information produced by data processing is of little value unless it supports meaningful end-user decisions and actions.

The purpose of data processing is to evaluate and bring order to data and place them in proper perspective or context so that meaningful information will be produced. The primary distinction between data and information, therefore, is that while all information consists of data, not all data produce specific and meaningful information that will reduce uncertainty and lead to greater insight (and better decisions).

## ✳ sources of data

The input data used to produce information originate from internal and external sources. *Internal sources* consist of individuals and departments located within an organization. These sources may furnish facts on a

---

[5] The above definition emphasizes management information in what might be termed the "formal" sense. Of course, managers also receive information from overheard conversations, from the actions rather than the words of others, and from other informal sources. In this informal sense, the manager processes the input data mentally and stores in his or her memory the information output for possible future use.

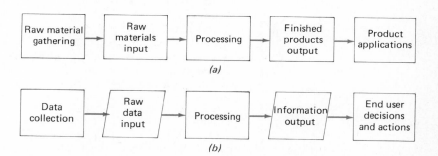

**FIGURE 1-1**

Transformation processes.

regular and planned basis (i.e., on a formal basis) to support decisions if the potential user is aware that the facts are available. Internal data gathered on a formal basis typically relate to events that have already happened; they often represent feedback to managers of the effectiveness and accuracy of earlier plans. Once the need for the data is established (and the value of supplying it is deemed to be worth the cost), a systematic data-gathering procedure is designed to produce the facts.[6] Of course, in addition to these planned data-gathering activities, data may also be received from internal sources on an informal basis through casual contacts and discussions.

*External*, or *environmental*, sources are the generators and distributors of data located outside the organization. These sources include such categories as customers, suppliers, competitors, business publications, industry associations, and government agencies. Such sources provide the organization with environmental and/or competitive data that may give managers important clues on what is likely to happen. Government agencies, for example, furnish businesses with a wealth of environmental statistics—such as per capita income, total consumer expenditures, and population-growth estimates—which are valuable for planning purposes.

### data processing

All data processing, whether it is done by hand or by the latest electronic methods, consists of *input, manipulation,* and *output* operations.

Input activities    Data must be *originated* or captured in some form for processing. Data may be initially recorded on paper *source documents* such as sales tickets or deposit slips, and they then may be converted into a machine-usable form for processing. Alternatively, they may be initially captured directly in a paperless machine-usable form.

Manipulative operations    One or more of the following operations may then need to be performed on the gathered data:

1    *Classifying.* Identifying and arranging items with like characteristics into groups or classes is called *classifying.* Sales data taken from a sales ticket may be classified by product sold, location of sales point, customer, sales clerk, or any other classification that the processing cycle may require. Classifying is usually done by a shortened, predetermined method of abbreviation known as *coding.* The three types of code used are *numeric* (e.g., your social security number), *alphabetic* (grades A, B, and C), and *alphanumeric* (an automobile license plate stamped CSN-1763).

[6] Not infrequently, a procedure for gathering and processing data continues to be followed after the need for the information no longer exists.

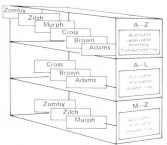

**2** *Sorting.* After the data are classified, it is usually necessary to arrange or rearrange them in a predetermined sequence to facilitate processing. This arranging procedure is called *sorting.* Sorting is done by number as well as by letter. Sales invoices may be sorted by invoice number or by customer name. Numeric sorting usually requires less time than alphabetic sorting in machine-based processing systems and is therefore generally used.

**3** *Calculating.* Arithmetic manipulation of the data is known as *calculating.* In the calculation of an employee's pay, for example, the total of hours worked multiplied by the hourly wage rate would give the taxable gross earnings. Payroll deductions such as taxes and insurance are then computed and subtracted from gross earnings to leave net or take-home earnings.

**4** *Summarizing.* To be of value, data must often be condensed or sifted so that the resulting output reports will be concise and effective. Reducing masses of data to a more usable form is called *summarizing.* Sales managers may be interested only in the total sales of a particular store. Thus, it would be wasteful in time and resources if they were given a report that broke sales down by department, product, and sales clerk.

**Output/records-management activities**   Once the data have been transformed into information, one or more of the following activities may be required:

**1** *Communicating.* The information, in a usable form, must be *communicated* to the user. Output information may be in the form of a vital printed report; but output can also be in the form of a gas bill on a punched card or an updated reel of magnetic tape.

**2** *Storing.* Placing similar data into files for future reference is *storing.* Obviously, facts should be stored only if the value of having them in the future exceeds the storage cost. Storage may take a variety of forms. Storage *media* that are frequently used include paper documents, microfilm, magnetizable media and devices, and punched paper media.

**3** *Retrieving.* Recovering stored data and/or information when needed is the *retrieving* step. Retrieval methods range from searches made by file clerks to the use of quick-responding inquiry terminals that are connected directly (i.e., they are *online*) to a computer. The computer, in turn, is connected directly to a mass-storage device that contains the information.

**4** *Reproducing.* It is sometimes necessary or desirable to copy or duplicate data. This operation is known as data *reproduction* and may be done by hand or by machine.

These, then, are the basic steps in data processing. Figure 1-2 presents these steps and indicates some of the ways in which they are accomplished. The means of performing the steps vary according to whether *manual, electromechanical,* or *electronic* processing methods are used. Many businesses find that the best solution to their processing require-

STEPS IN THE DATA PROCESSING OPERATION

| Processing Methods | Originating-Recording | Classifying | Sorting | Calculating | Summarizing | Communicating | Storing | Retrieving | Reproducing |
|---|---|---|---|---|---|---|---|---|---|
| **Manual Methods** | Human observation; hand-written records; pegboards | Hand posting; pegboards | Hand posting; pegboards; edge-notched cards | Human brain | Pegboards; hand calculations | Written reports; hand-carried messages; telephone | Paper in files, journals, ledgers, etc. | File clerk; bookkeeper | Clerical; carbon paper |
| **Manual with Machine Assistance** | Typewriter; cash register; manual | Cash register; bookkeeping machine | Mechanical collators | Adding machines; calculators; cash registers | Accounting machines; adding machines; cash registers | Documents prepared by machines; message conveyors | Motorized rotary files; microfilm | | Xerox machines; duplicators; addressing machines |
| **Electro-mechanical Punched Card Methods** | Prepunched cards; key-punched cards; mark-sensed cards; manual | Determined by card field design; sorter; collator | Card sorter | Accounting machines (tabulators); calculating punch | | Printed documents; interpreter | Trays of cards | Manual tray movement | Reproducing punch |
| **Electronic Methods** | Magnetic tape encoder; magnetic and optical character readers; card and tape punches; on-line terminals; manual; key-to-disk encoder | Determined by systems design; computer | Computer sorting | Computer | | Online data transmission; printed output; visual display; voice output | Magnetizable media and devices; punched media; computer; microfilm | Online inquiry with direct-access devices; manual movement of storage media to computer | Multiple copies from printers; microfilm copies |

FIGURE 1-2

Tools and techniques for data processing.

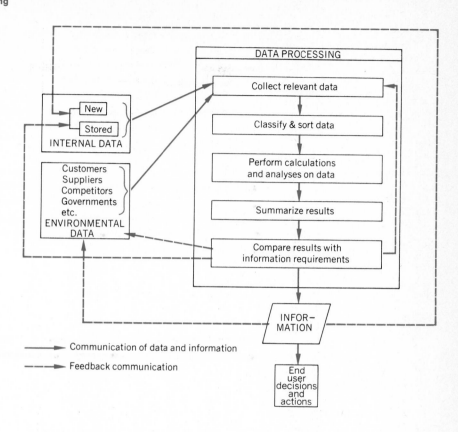

FIGURE 1-3

ments is to use a combination of methods; e.g., manual methods may be used for small-volume jobs while computers may be used for large-volume tasks.

The above brief remarks on the sources of data and the nature of data processing now make it possible to expand Fig. 1-1b. In Fig. 1-3 we see that data input is divided into sources and that data processing is broken down into operational steps. The solid lines represent the possible communication of data and information in a single processing cycle; the dashed lines represent the feedback communication required to obtain additional data and recycle the data base for future processing.

**NEED FOR MANAGEMENT INFORMATION**

Information is needed in virtually every field of human thought and action. At a personal level, if you always had high-quality information you could take better advantage of your future career opportunities and you would be better equipped to make other personal decisions.

But besides being essential to individuals who use it to achieve personal ends, information is also needed by managers in organizations. Managers at all levels must perform such basic management tasks or

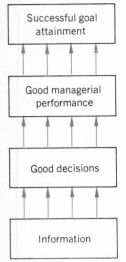

Successful goal attainment

Good managerial performance

Good decisions

Information

FIGURE 1-4

functions as *planning, organizing, staffing,* and *controlling.*[7] The success of any business is determined by how well its executives perform these activities. And how well these functions are carried out is dependent, in part, upon how well the information needs of managers are being met. Why is this? It is because each function involves decision making, and decision making must be supported by quality information. If a manager's information is of poor quality, the decisions that are made will probably suffer and the business (at best) will not achieve the success it might otherwise have had.

In summary, as shown in Fig. 1-4, quality information in the hands of those who can effectively use it will support good decisions; good decisions will lead to effective performance of managerial activities; and effective managerial performance will lead to successful attainment of organizational goals. Thus, information is the bonding agent that holds an organization together.[8]

### what information is needed?

What information does the manager need to manage effectively? A common need basic to all managers is an understanding of the purpose of the organization, i.e., its policies, its programs, its plans, and its goals. But beyond these basic informational requirements, the question of what information is needed can be answered only in broad, general terms because individual managers differ in the ways in which they view information, in their analytical approaches to using it, and in their conceptual organization of relevant facts. An additional factor that complicates the subject of the information needed by managers is the organizational level of the managerial job. Managers at the lower operating levels need information to help them make day-to-day operating decisions. At the top levels, however, information is needed to support long-range planning and policy decisions.

In Fig. 1-5*a* we see that at the lower managerial levels more time is generally spent in performing control activities (e.g., checking to make sure that production schedules are being met), while at the upper levels more time is spent on planning (e.g., determining the location and specifications of a new production plant). Figure 1-5*b* shows that

[7] We will look at some of the implications of computer usage for these functions in Part IV.

[8] Information is also needed to meet demands originating from the environment in which the business operates. Reports of various kinds are required by government bodies. In one extreme example, a farm-products firm handled 173 different federal forms in a single year. Various reports were sent in at different intervals ranging from daily to annually. A final total of 37,683 reports, involving 48,285 labor-hours of work, was submitted! In addition, dues reports are prepared for labor unions, financial reports are expected by creditors and stockholders, and market and product information may be desired by customers and suppliers of raw materials.

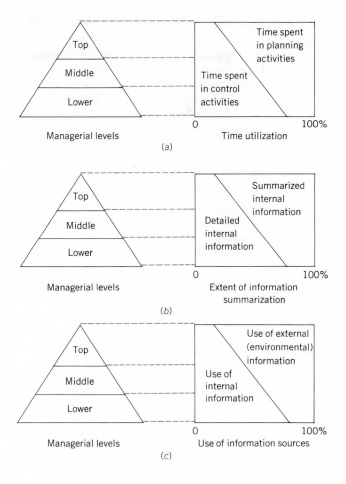

FIGURE 1-5

although lower-level managers need detailed information relating to daily operations of specific departments, top executives are best served with information that summarizes trends and indicates exceptions to what was expected. A final generalization is that the higher one is in the management hierarchy, the more one needs and is likely to use information obtained from external sources (see Fig. 1-5c). A supervisor uses internally generated feedback information to control production processes, but a president studying the feasibility of a new plant needs information about customer product acceptance, pollution control, local tax structures, competitive reactions, availability of labor and suppliers, etc., and this information is environmental in nature.

In summary, the types of decisions made by managers vary, and so information needs also vary. Thus, it is unlikely that we shall soon see (if, indeed, we ever do) an information system that is uniformly suitable and desirable for all managers in an organization.

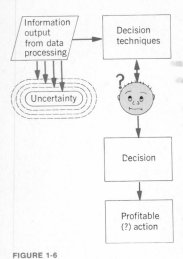

FIGURE 1-6

## desired properties of management information

As a general rule, the more information serves to reduce the element of uncertainty in decision making, the greater is its value (Fig. 1-6). But information is one of the basic resources available to managers, and like other resources it is usually not free. It is therefore necessary that the cost of acquiring the resource be compared with the value to be obtained from its availability. Just as it would be economically foolish for an organization to spend $100 to mine $75 worth of coal, so, too, would it be unsound to produce information costing $100 if this information did not lead to actions that yielded a net return. In other words, information should be prepared if (1) its cost is less than the additional *tangible revenues* produced by its use, (2) it serves to reduce *tangible expenses* by a more than proportionate amount, or (3) it provides such *intangible benefits* as greater insight, faster reaction time, better customer service, etc., which the information *user* considers to be worth the costs involved.

You should keep these brief comments on information economics in mind as we look at the desirability of information that possesses the characteristics of *accuracy, timeliness, completeness, conciseness,* and *relevancy.* Up to a certain point, information that possesses these properties may be expected to be more valuable than information lacking one or more of these characteristics.

Accuracy    Accuracy may be defined as the ratio of correct information to the total amount of information produced over a period of time. If, for example, 1,000 items of information are produced and 950 of these items give a correct report of the actual situation, then the level of accuracy is 0.95. Whether or not this level is high enough depends upon the information being produced. Fifty incorrect bank balances in a mailing of 1,000 bank statements would hardly be acceptable to depositors or to the bank. On the other hand, if physical inventory records kept on large quantities of inexpensive parts achieve an accuracy level of 0.95, this might be acceptable. In the case of bank statements, greater accuracy *must* be obtained; in the case of the parts inventory, greater accuracy *could* be obtained, but the additional value to managers of having more accurate inventory information might be less than the additional costs required. Inaccuracies are the result of *human errors* and/or *machine malfunctions.* Human error (in system design, machine operation, the preparation of input data, and other ways) is the primary cause of inaccuracy.

Timeliness    Timeliness is another important information characteristic. It is of little consolation to a manager to know that information that arrived too late to be of use was accurate. Accuracy alone is not enough. How fast must be the *response time* of the information system? Unfortunately, it is once again impossible to give an answer which will satisfy all situations. In the case of *regular reports,* an immediate response time following each transaction would involve a steady outpouring of documents. The result might well be a costly avalanche of paper that would bury managers. Thus, a compromise is often required. The response time should be short enough so that the information does not lose its freshness and value, but it should be long enough to reduce volume (and costs) and reveal important trends that signal the need for action (see Fig. 1-7). The most appropriate information interval is therefore a matter which must be determined by each organization. However, as we shall see in the next chapter, new quick-response computer-based systems have been developed to give end-users immediate access to the "time-critical" information they need to make operating decisions between regular reporting periods and/or to provide them with prompt answers to nonrecurring questions that are not available from regular reports.

Completeness    Most managers faced with a decision to make have been frustrated at some time by having supporting information that is accurate, timely—and *incomplete*. An example of the consequences of failure to consolidate related pieces of information occurred at Pearl Harbor in 1941. Historians tell us that data available, in bits and pieces and at scattered points, if integrated, would have signaled the danger of a Japanese attack. Better integration of the facts available at scattered points in a business for the purpose of furnishing managers with more complete information is a goal of information systems designers, as we shall see in the next chapter.

Conciseness    Many information systems have been designed on the assumption that lack of completeness is the most critical problem facing managers. This assumption has led designers to employ an ineffective shotgun approach, peppering managers with more information than they can possibly use. Important information, along with relatively useless data, is often buried in stacks of detailed reports. Managers are then faced with the problem of extracting those items of information that they need. Concise information that summarizes (perhaps through the use of tables and charts) the relevant data and that points out areas of exception to normal or planned activities is what is often needed by—but less often supplied to—today's managers.

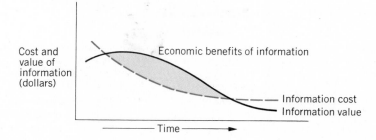

FIGURE 1-7

Relationship between information
cost and value over time.

Relevancy  Relevant information is "need-to-know" information that leads to action or provides new knowledge and understanding. Reports that were once valuable but that are no longer relevant should be discontinued.

**INFORMATION IMPROVEMENT AND COMPUTER PROCESSING**

As long as an important resource is supplied to us when and where we need it, in the right quantity and quality, and at a reasonable cost, we tend to take the resource for granted. It is often only when the supply, quality, and/or cost of the resource deteriorates that we recognize its importance. So it is with management information. Several weaknesses have been encountered with earlier information systems that have often prevented users from receiving information that possessed the desirable properties discussed in the preceding section. And as pressures to improve the quality of management information have built, managers have often turned to computer usage for relief. Included among the weaknesses that have contributed to information improvement efforts are:

1  *Difficulties in handling increased workloads.* Processing capability in many firms has been strained by (1) the growth in the size, complexity, and multinational scope of the firm; (2) the increased requirements for data from external sources such as local, state, and federal governmental agencies; and (3) the demands of managers for more kinds of information.[9] Fortunately, the greater the volume of data that must be processed, the more economical computer processing becomes relative to other processing methods.

2  *Failures to supply accurate information.* If a processing system has gone beyond the capacity for which it was originally planned, inaccuracies will begin to appear and the control of organizational activities will suffer. Computer processing, however, will be quite accurate *if* the tasks to be performed have been properly prepared.

3  *Failures to supply timely information.* Meaningful information is timely information. But with an increase in volume, there is often a reduction in the speed of processing. Managers demand timely information. Unfortunately, although they may receive information about areas of virtual certainty in short order, information that reduces the element of uncertainty is often delayed until such time as it is merely collaborative. Thus, many businesses have turned to the use of computers to speed up their processing.

4  *Increases in costs.* The increasing labor and materials costs associated with a noncomputer processing operation have often caused man-

[9] One drug company recently reported that it was required to furnish the federal government with 200,000 pages of data at a cost of $15 million, and a banking authority reports that if the more than 26 billion checks that were written and processed in the United States in a recent year were placed in a stack, the pile would extend over 1,500 miles into space.

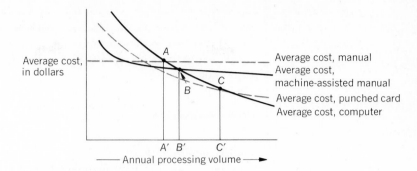

Average cost,
in dollars

Average cost, manual
Average cost,
machine-assisted manual
Average cost, punched card
Average cost, computer

A′ B′ C′
——— Annual processing volume ——→

**FIGURE 1-8**
Average cost relationships.

agers to look to computer usage for economic relief. For example, when compared with other alternatives, the use of computers may make it possible for certain costs to be reduced while the level of processing activity remains stable. Figure 1-8 gives a general idea of the cost relationships between computer processing methods and alternative methods. The curves show the average cost of processing a typical document or record using different processing approaches. Point *A* shows the breakeven cost position between manual and computer processing at a volume of *A′*. When volume is less than *A′*, it would be more economical to use manual methods than a computer. Points *B* and *C* show other breakeven positions. Of course, the cost curves in Fig. 1-8 do not remain constant. Each increase in clerical labor rates and the cost of clerical office supplies, for example, shifts the manual method curves upward, while each new hardware innovation may serve to reduce computer costs and thus shift the computer curve downward. The net result has been to make computer processing methods more attractive at lower processing volumes (see Fig. 1-9).

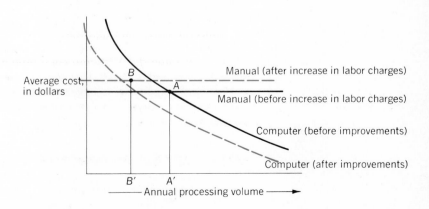

Average cost,
in dollars

Manual (after increase in labor charges)

Manual (before increase in labor charges)

Computer (before improvements)

Computer (after improvements)

B′ A′
——— Annual processing volume ——→

**FIGURE 1-9**

**EVOLUTION OF
INFORMATION
PROCESSING**

Earlier in the chapter (in Fig. 1-2), we classified processing methods into *manual, machine-assisted manual, electromechanical punched card,* and *electronic computer* categories. In the remaining pages of this chapter, let us use these categories to look briefly at the history of information processing.

### the manual stage

For centuries, people lived on earth without keeping records. But as social organizations such as tribes began to form, adjustments became necessary. The complexities of tribal life required that more details be remembered. Methods of counting, based on the biological fact that people have fingers, were thus developed. However, the limited number of digits combined with the need to remember more facts posed problems. For example, if a shepherd were tending a large tribal flock and if he had a short memory, how was he to keep control of his inventory? Problems bring solutions, and the shepherd's solution might have been to let a stone, a stick, a scratch on a rock, or a knot in a string represent each sheep in the flock.

As tribes grew into nations, trade and commerce developed. Stones and sticks, however, were not satisfactory for early traders. In 3500 B.C., the ancient Babylonian merchants were keeping records on clay tablets.

Manual record-keeping techniques continued to develop through the centuries, with such innovations as record audits (the Greeks) and banking systems and budgets (the Romans). In the United States, in the 20 years following the Civil War, the main tools of data processing were pencils, pens, rulers, work sheets (for classifying, calculating, and summarizing), journals (for storing), and ledgers (for storing and communicating).

The volume of business and government processing during this period was expanding rapidly, and, as might be expected, such complete reliance upon manual methods resulted in information that was relatively inaccurate and often late. To the consternation of the Census Bureau, for example, the 1880 census was not finished until it was almost time to begin the 1890 count! In spite of accuracy and timeliness limitations, however, *manual processing methods have the following advantages:* (1) information is in a humanly readable form; (2) changes and corrections are easily accomplished; (3) no minimum economic processing volume is generally required; and (4) manual methods are easily adapted to changing conditions.

### machine-assisted manual development

The evolution of machine-assisted manual processing methods has gone through several phases. In the *first phase,* machines were produced which improved the performance of a *single* processing step. In 1642, for example, the first mechanical calculating machine was developed by Blaise Pascal, a brilliant young Frenchman. And in the 1880s, the typewriter was introduced as a recording aid that improved legibility and doubled writing speeds.

In the *second phase* of machine-assisted methods, equipment was invented which could *combine* certain processing steps in a single operation. Machines that could calculate and print the results were first produced around 1890. They combine calculating, summarizing, and recording steps and produce a printed tape record suitable for storing data. After World War I, accounting machines designed for special purposes (e.g., billing, retail sales, etc.) began to appear. These machines also combine steps and often contain several adding *registers* or *counters* to permit the accumulation of totals (calculation and summarization) for different classifications. For example, the supermarket cash register has separate registers to sort and total the day's sales of health items, hardware, meats, produce, and groceries.

A *third phase* has emerged in recent years. Equipment manufacturers have taken steps to ensure that small calculators and accounting machines are not made obsolete by the computer. Features of these machines are being combined with features taken from computers to create new electronic pocket-sized and desk-sized hardware. Many of these new calculators (computers?) have data-storage capability and can be programmed to perform processing steps in sequence just like computers. However, programmable calculators cannot yet match the speed and versatility of a computer in processing, storing, and retrieving both alphabetic and numeric data.

When compared with the manual processing of the late 1800s, machine-assisted manual methods have the advantages of greater speed and accuracy. However, a higher processing volume is generally required to justify equipment costs, there is some reduction in the flexibility of the processing techniques, and it is relatively more difficult to (1) correct or change data once they have entered the processing system and (2) implement changes in machine-assisted procedures.

**electromechanical punched card development**

Punched card methods have been in *widespread* business use only since the 1930s, but the history of the punched card dates back to about the end of the American Revolution when a French weaver named Jacquard used them to control his looms.

Although punched cards continued to be used in process control, it was not until the use of manual methods resulted in the problem of completing the 1880 census count that they began to be considered as a medium for data processing. The inventor of modern punched card techniques was Dr. Herman Hollerith, a statistician. He was hired by the Census Bureau as a special agent to help find a solution to the census problem. In 1887, Hollerith developed his machine-readable card concept and designed a device known as the "census machine." Tabulating time with Hollerith's methods was only one-eighth of that previously required, and so his techniques were adopted for use in the 1890 count. Although population had increased from 50 to 63 million people in the decade after 1880, the 1890 count was completed in less than 3 years. (Of course, this would be considered intolerably slow by today's standards,[10] but the alternative in 1890 would have been to continue the count beyond 1900 and violate the constitutional provision that congressional seats be reapportioned every 10 years on the basis of census data.)

Following the 1890 census, Hollerith converted his equipment to business use and set up freight statistics systems for two railroads. In 1896 he founded the Tabulating Machine Company to make and sell his invention. Later, this firm merged with others to form what is now known as International Business Machines Corporation (IBM).

Punched card processing is based on a simple idea: Input data are initially recorded in a coded form by punching holes into cards, and these cards are then fed into machines that perform processing steps—e.g., sorting, calculating, and summarizing. The early Hollerith cards measured 3 by 5 inches; different sizes are used today and different coding schemes are employed with modern cards containing either 80 or 96 columns.

The 80-column card    Figure 1-10 shows the typical 80-column punched card. One corner is usually trimmed to help maintain proper positioning during processing. The card is divided into 80 consecutively numbered vertical *columns*. These columns, in turn, have 12 horizontal positions or *rows*. By appropriate coding, each column can record one character of information, i.e., a digit, a letter, or a special character. Columns 5 to 14 in Fig. 1-10 illustrate the numeric punches.

When *letters* of the alphabet are recorded, *two* holes must be punched. Along the top of the card are three *zone* punching positions—the 0 row and the blank area at the top of the card, which is designated as punching positions 11 and 12 (or as areas X and Y). A logical combination of zone and digit punches is required for letters in the Hollerith code. For example, letters A to I are coded by using a 12-zone punch and digit punches 1 to 9. Special characters are coded by using one, two, or three holes.

The 96-column card    The card in Fig. 1-11 is actually only one-third the size of the 80-column card. The 96 columns are separated into three 32-

[10] The 1950 census, using punched card equipment, took about 2 years to produce; the 1970 census yielded figures in a few months.

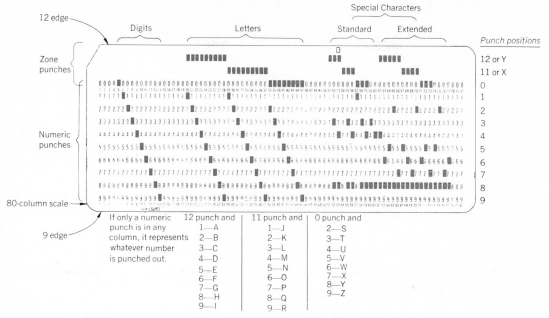

FIGURE 1-10

The punched card and Hollerith
code.

column sections or tiers. The upper third of the card contains positions for
the printing of characters.

In addition to using round rather than rectangular holes, the 96-
column card also differs from the 80-column card in the coding method
employed. The rows of the small card are divided into A and B zone

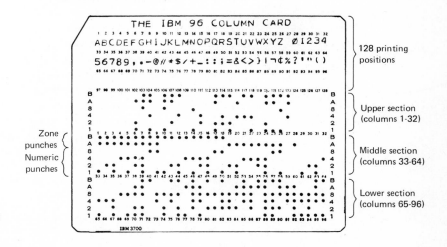

FIGURE 1-11

IBM 96-column card (courtesy IBM
Corporation).

positions and 1, 2, 4, and 8 numeric positions.[11] Columns 60 to 69 in Fig. 1-11 illustrate the coding of digits. The numeral 1 is represented by a single hole punched in the 1 row of column 61. Column 62 codes the numeral 2. But in columns 63, 65, 66, 67, and 69, the numerals are represented by the *sum* of the rows punched; e.g., in column 67 the digit 7 is represented by holes punched in the 4, 2, and 1 rows.

Alphabetic characters are represented by combinations of holes punched in the zone and numeric rows. The nine letters A to I, for example, are coded by holes punched in the A and B rows plus the combination of holes used to represent the numerals 1 to 9. To illustrate, the seventh letter G is coded by holes in the A and B zone positions plus the combination of holes in rows 1, 2, and 4 which add to seven (see column 39 in Fig. 1-11). The special characters represented in columns 70 to 96 are coded by various combinations of holes punched in the six rows.

Fields   How are 80- and 96-column cards used? Thank you for asking. Card columns are laid out in consecutive groups called *fields* for specific purposes. Fields are carefully planned by the application designer and may be of any width from 1 to 80 (or 96) columns.[12] To illustrate, Fig. 1-12 shows the use of a card and fields in a business application.

In this example, a customer invoice (the detailed description of what has been shipped) serves as the source document for the sales accounting card. The card is divided into 11 fields, which contain *reference* data (customer name and number, and invoice date and number), *classification* data (location of sale, trade classification, sales branch, and salesman number), and *quantitative* data used in calculations (quantity sold of a particular item and the item amount). The card contains (1) the descriptive data at the top of the invoice and (2) the data on the first line of the body of the invoice. The *item amount* field is seven columns wide, which means that the maximum amount that can be recorded is $99,999.99 (columns are not used to punch the dollar sign, comma, and decimal point). The card in Fig. 1-12 is often classified as a *detail* card. In preparing the five *additional* detail cards that would be required to capture the invoice data, columns 18 to 56 would be automatically duplicated and columns 74 to 80 would perhaps be punched in the last card. In subsequent processing of the detail cards, *summary* cards may be automatically produced, which will contain such information as total sales made to the particular customer and total sales credited to the salesman and sales branch during a specified time period.

---

[11] We shall have more to say in Chapter 6 about this *binary coded decimal* (BCD) method of data representation.

[12] It should be emphasized that judgment and compromises are required in determining field width. For example, a 15-column employee name field would be satisfactory in most cases—until the personnel department hires Agamemnon Southwesterfield.

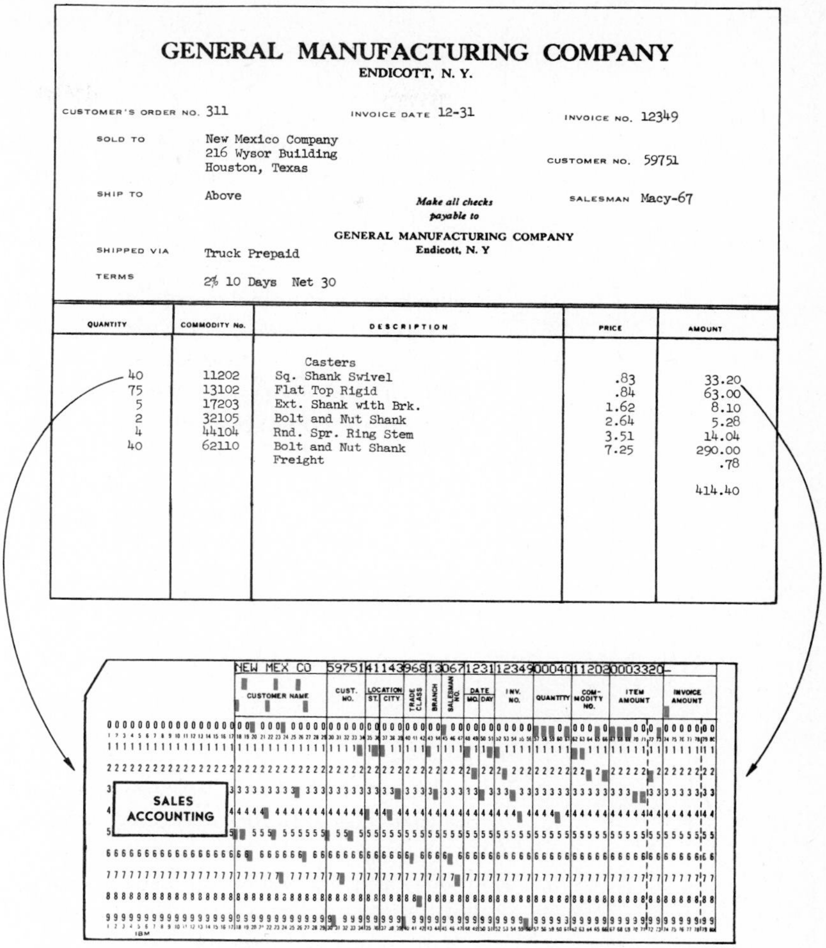

FIGURE 1-12

Data fields (courtesy IBM
Corporation).

**Punched card equipment**    Several punched card machines are needed
to perform the typical processing steps shown in Fig. 1-13.[13] The most
common way of *recording* data in cards is through the use of a keypunch
or *card punch* machine. When a key is depressed, the correct combination of holes is produced in the card. (Should you need to punch some
computer program and/or data cards, the operation of a card punch
machine is discussed in Appendix A at the back of the book.) To check
keypunching accuracy, *verifiers* are used. The verifier is similar to the
keypunch, but instead of punching holes, it merely senses whether or not

[13] A punched card is often referred to as a *unit record* because data recorded in most cards
deal with only one transaction. And electromechanical punched card machines that
perform the steps shown in Fig. 1-13 are sometimes referred to as *unit record equipment*.

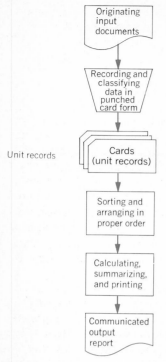

Originating input documents

Recording and classifying data in punched card form

Cards (unit records)

Unit records

Sorting and arranging in proper order

Calculating, summarizing, and printing

Communicated output report

FIGURE 1-13

the holes in the card being tested correspond with the key being depressed. In some machines keypunching and verifying are combined.

*Sorters* and *collators,* as you might expect, are devices for *sorting and arranging* cards. Putting the cards in some desired order or sequence is the job of the sorter. There are as many pockets in the sorter as there are rows in the card being processed; there may also be a reject pocket for cards that do not belong in any other pocket. Sorting (which generally moves from the right column to the left column of the data field) is done *one* column at a time in each sorting *pass.* Thus, the sorting procedure in a data field of five digits would take five passes before the cards would be in the proper numerical *sequence.*

The collator is a machine that can combine two decks of sequenced cards into a single sequenced deck *(merging).* It can also compare agreement between two sets of cards without combining them (*matching*). Other manipulations are possible with two decks of sequenced cards. The collator can check a tray of cards to determine correct ascending or descending order. After the arrangement of the cards in the proper order, they are usually then taken to a machine that can perform calculations on the data.

The *calculator* is directed in its operation by an externally wired control panel. It reads data from input cards, performs (according to the wiring arrangements in the control panel) the arithmetic operations of addition, subtraction, multiplication, and division, and punches the results into (1) the input card that supplied the data or (2) a following card.

The *accounting machine* or *tabulator* is used to *summarize* data from input cards and print the desired reports. It can add and subtract during summarization and has several registers or counters for this purpose. Finally, the *reproducer* is used to duplicate the data found in a large number of cards; it is also used for gangpunching, i.e., copying data from a master card into any number of blank cards, and for punching the holes in mark-sensed cards.

From this very brief survey of punched card data processing, it is obvious that significant improvement was possible over manual methods previously used. Gains in speed and accuracy were made. Punched card equipment proved effective in performing many of the individual steps necessary, e.g., sorting, calculating, and summarizing. But, as the level of equipment sophistication increased, processing procedures tended to become more rigorously defined and standardized. And it was still necessary to have people handle trays of cards between each step. Separate machines must be fed, started, and stopped. *This limited intercommunication between processing stages requiring manual intervention is a major disadvantage.* With the computer this disadvantage is eliminated; no manual interference between data input and information output is required. What sets the computer apart from any other type of data processing machine is the concept of storing, within the machine itself, alterable instructions that will direct the machine to perform automatically the necessary processing steps. Let us now, in the remainder of this chapter, look at the history and development of the computer.

## computer development

In 1833, Charles Babbage, Lucasian Professor of Mathematics at Cambridge University in England, proposed a machine, which he named the *analytical engine*. Babbage was an eccentric and colorful individual[14] who spent much of his life working in vain to build his machine. Babbage's dream—to many of his contemporaries it was "Babbage's folly"—would have incorporated a punched card input; a memory unit, or *store*; an arithmetic unit, or *mill*; automatic printout; sequential program control; and 20-place accuracy. In short, Babbage had designed a machine that was a prototype computer and that was a hundred years ahead of its time. Following Babbage's death in 1871, little progress was made until 1937.

Beginning in 1937, Harvard professor Howard Aiken set out to build an automatic calculating machine that would combine established technology with the punched cards of Hollerith. With the help of graduate students and IBM engineers, the project was completed in 1944. The completed device was known as the Mark I digital computer. (A *digital* computer is one that essentially does counting operations.) Internal operations were controlled automatically with electromagnetic relays; arithmetic counters were mechanical. The Mark I was thus not an *electronic* computer but was rather an *electromechanical* one. In many respects the Mark I was the realization of Babbage's dream. Appropriately, this "medieval" machine is now on display at Harvard University.

The first *electronic* digital computer to be put into full operation was built as a secret wartime project between 1939 and 1946 at the University of Pennsylvania's Moore School of Electrical Engineering. The team of J. Presper Eckert, Jr., and John W. Mauchly was responsible for its construction. However, as was later determined by a federal judge in an important patent suit, "Eckert and Mauchly did not themselves first invent the automatic electronic digital computer, but instead derived that subject matter from one Dr. John Vincent Atanasoff." (Atanasoff was a professor of physics and mathematics at Iowa State College, and did his most important computer work between 1935 and 1942, at which time he stopped work on his prototype and left Iowa State to work at the Naval Ordnance Laboratory.)

[14] He was also something of a literary critic. In "The Vision of Sin," Tennyson wrote: "Every moment dies a man/Every moment one is born." Babbage wrote Tennyson and pointed out to the poet that since the population of the world was increasing, it would be more accurate to have the verse read: "Every moment dies a man, Every moment one and one-sixteenth is born." What he lacked in aesthetic taste he compensated for with mathematical precision!

Vacuum tubes (19,000 of them!) were used in place of relays in the Eckert-Mauchly machine. This computer was called "ENIAC" and could do 300 multiplications per second (making it 300 times faster than any other device of the day).[15] Operating instructions for ENIAC were not stored internally; rather, they were fed through externally located plug-boards and switches. In 1959, ENIAC was placed in the Smithsonian Institution.

In 1946, in collaboration with H. H. Goldstine and A. W. Burks, John von Neumann, a mathematical genius and member of the Institute for Advanced Study in Princeton, New Jersey, suggested in a paper that (1) *binary* numbering systems be used in building computers and (2) computer *instructions* as well as the *data* being manipulated could be stored internally in the machine. These suggestions became a basic part of the philosophy of computer design. The binary numbering system is represented by only two digits (0 and 1) rather than the 10 digits (0 to 9) of the familiar decimal system. Since electronic components are typically in one of two conditions (on or off, conducting or not conducting, magnetized or not magnetized), the binary concept facilitated equipment design.

Although these design concepts came too late to be incorporated in ENIAC, Mauchly, Eckert, and others at the University of Pennsylvania set out to build a machine with stored program capability. This machine— the EDVAC—was not completed until several years later. To the EDSAC, finished in 1949 at Cambridge University, must go the distinction of being the first *stored program electronic* computer.

One reason for the delay in EDVAC was that Eckert and Mauchly founded their own company in 1946 and began to work on the UNIVAC. In 1949, Remington Rand acquired the Eckert-Mauchly Computer Corporation, and in early 1951, the first UNIVAC-1 became operational at the Census Bureau. In 1963, it too was retired to the Smithsonian Institution—a historical relic after just 12 years! The first computer acquired for data processing and record keeping by a *business organization* was another UNIVAC-1, which was installed in 1954 at General Electric's Appliance Park in Louisville, Kentucky.[16]

In the period from 1954 to 1959, many businesses acquired computers for data processing purposes even though these *first-generation* machines had been designed for scientific uses. Managers generally considered the computer to be an accounting tool, and the first applications were designed to process routine tasks such as payrolls and customer billing.

---

[15] William Shanks, an Englishman, spent 20 years of his life computing $\pi$ to 707 decimal places. In 1949, ENIAC computed $\pi$ to 2,000 places in just over 70 hours and showed that Shanks had made an error in the 528th decimal place. Fortunately, Shanks was spared the knowledge that he had been both slow and inaccurate, for he preceded ENIAC by 100 years.

[16] The IBM 650 first saw service in Boston in December 1954. It was an all-purpose machine, comparatively inexpensive, and it was widely accepted. It gave IBM the leadership in computer production in 1955.

Unfortunately, in most cases little or no attempt was made to modify and redesign existing accounting procedures in order to produce more effective managerial information. The potential of the computer was consistently underestimated; more than a few were acquired for no other reason than prestige.

But we should not judge the early users of electronic data processing too harshly. They were pioneering in the use of a new tool not designed specifically for their needs; they had to staff their computer installations with a new breed of workers; and they initially had to cope with the necessity of preparing programs in a tedious machine language. In spite of these obstacles, the computer was found to be a fast, accurate, and untiring processor of mountains of paper.

The computers of the *second generation* were introduced around 1959 to 1960 and were made smaller, faster, and with greater computing capacity. The vacuum tube, with its relatively short life, gave way to compact *solid state* components such as diodes and transistors. Unlike earlier computers, some second-generation machines were designed from the beginning with business processing requirements in mind.

In 1964, IBM ushered in the *third generation* of computing hardware when it announced its System/360 family of computers. And during the early 1970s, several manufacturers introduced new equipment lines. For example, IBM announced the first models of its System/370 line of computers. These machines continued the trend toward miniaturization of circuit components. Further improvements in speed, cost, and storage capacity were realized. In the next chapter we shall look in more detail at some of the recent developments in computer technology.

The computer industry    In 1950, the developers of the first computers agreed that eight or ten of these machines would satisfy the entire demand for such devices for years to come. Of course, we now know that this was a monumental forecasting blunder; in fact, it must go down in history as one of the worst market estimates of all time! By 1956, over 600 general-purpose computer systems (worth about $350 million) had been installed by organizations in the United States; today, such general-purpose installations are numbered in the hundreds of thousands,[17] and this does not count the tens of thousands of very small computers that individuals have recently installed in their homes. Thus, the theme of a recent computer conference—"Computers . . . by the millions, for the

---

[17] Nobody knows the exact number or present value of these computer systems because many computer manufacturers do not officially release installation data. And since there are disagreements in present estimates, it is not surprising that there are large variances in future expectations. For example, the president of one of the large computer industry firms puts the estimate of the installed value of general-purpose systems in 1980 at more than *$90 billion*. But an expert at a leading consulting firm places the figure in 1981 at "only" $70 billion to $75 billion. In either case, the numbers are huge and there are no immediate signs of market saturation in the computer industry.

millions"—now characterizes the size and scope of the computer industry.

There are several dozen *computer manufacturers,* many of whom specialize in scientific, process control, and/or very small general-purpose machines. In terms of the estimated revenues received in 1976 from data processing products and services, the seven largest firms are listed in Fig. 1-14.[18] Of these largest companies, most were initially business machine manufacturers (IBM, Burroughs Corporation, Sperry UNIVAC, and NCR Corporation), or they manufactured electronic controls (Honeywell). Exceptions are Control Data Corporation and Digital Equipment Corporation which were founded to produce computers. As you can see in Fig. 1-14, the industry leader is IBM, with at least 50 percent of the entire industry market. In spite of the economic health of the computer industry as a whole, however, more than a few firms were unable to compete profitably in certain segments of the market in the 1970s. Some of the more notable "dropouts" were General Electric, Xerox, and RCA. There have also been numerous antitrust suits and countersuits involving various manufacturers, IBM, and the federal government in the 1970s.

Computer size categories    Although the first computers were all large enough to store grain in, today's machines vary in size from the large to those that are smaller than this book. Thus, in terms of relative computing power and cost, today's systems may be classified as *micro-sized, mini-sized, small, medium,* or *large.*

A *microprocessor* is assembled from tens of thousands of tiny transis-

[18] Revenue is heavily concentrated in only a few firms in the computer industry. The seven firms in Fig. 1-14 probably account for nearly 80 percent of the data processing revenues received by all United States companies. For more information on the top 50 companies, see Oscar H. Rothenbuecher, "The Top 50 U. S. Companies in the Data Processing Industry," *Datamation,* June 1977, pp. 61–74.

| Company | 1975 Revenue ($, billions) | 1976 Revenue ($, billions) | Percentage Increase |
|---|---|---|---|
| IBM | $11.12 | $12.72 | 14% |
| Burroughs Corporation | 1.45 | 1.63 | 13 |
| Honeywell | 1.32 | 1.43 | 8 |
| Sperry UNIVAC | 1.30 | 1.43 | 11 |
| Control Data Corporation | 1.22 | 1.33 | 9 |
| NCR Corporation | .96 | 1.10 | 15 |
| Digital Equipment Corp. | .53 | .74 | 38 |
| *Totals* | $17.90 | $20.38 | 14% |

FIGURE 1-14

Estimated revenues from data processing products and services.

Source: Adapted from Oscar H. Rothenbuecher, "The Top 50 U.S. Companies in the Data Processing Industry," *Datamation,* June 1977, pp. 61–74.

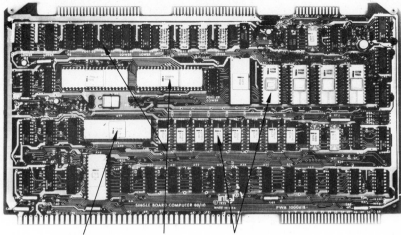

FIGURE 1-15

Complete microcomputer on a single
board (courtesy of Intel Corporation).

Microprocessing element
(see Figure 2-4 for a
magnified view of the
circuitry)

Input/output
connections
and components

Computer storage
elements

tors, resistors, and other electronic components to perform the arithmetic
and logic functions of a computer. The typical microprocessor is fabricated on a single tiny chip of silicon and is combined with other elements
that provide input/output connections, storage, and control to form a
complete *microcomputer* on a board that may be smaller than this page
(see Fig. 1-15). Microcomputers are general-purpose processors that may
perform the same operations and use the same program instructions as
much larger computers. They began to appear in quantity in 1973.
Although they are relatively slow in operation and have relatively limited
data-handling capabilities, these computers are being used in a rapidly
expanding number of applications. Perhaps their most common use at
this writing is to provide control and intelligence functions for some of the
peripheral devices used with larger computer systems. They are also very
popular with hobbyists; as noted earlier, tens of thousands of them have
been purchased by individuals for their personal use and entertainment.
Microcomputers range in price from a few hundred to a few thousand
dollars, depending on the type and number of input/output devices used
and on the amount of storage capacity obtained.

*Minicomputers* (see Fig. 1-16) are small machines, but there is no
clear-cut distinction between the largest microcomputers and the smallest minis on the one hand or between the larger minis and small-scale
business systems on the other. As a rough guide, however, minicomputers typically cost between $2,500 and $25,000, usually weigh less than
50 pounds, and may be plugged into any standard electrical outlet.
Minicomputers perform the same arithmetic-logic functions, use several

FIGURE 1-16

Minicomputer (courtesy Digital
Equipment Corporation).

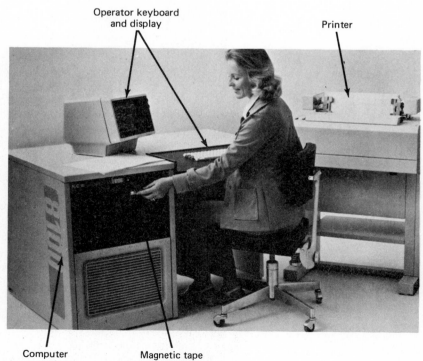

FIGURE 1-17

Small business computer (courtesy
NCR Corporation).

of the same programming languages, and have many of the same circuitry features of larger computers. Although they are general-purpose devices, some are used for special or dedicated purposes such as controlling a machine tool or a process. Others are (1) used for business data processing purposes, (2) connected to larger computers to act as input/output (I/O) and message-switching devices, (3) used in school systems for educational purposes, and (4) used in laboratories for scientific computation purposes. The versatility of minicomputers, combined with their low cost, accounts for their rapid acceptance.

*Small business computers* come in a bewildering range of models and capabilities. Some are desk-sized, are designed specifically to meet the data processing requirements of small businesses, and are similar in basic capabilities to minicomputers (see Fig. 1-17); some are the punched-card-oriented successors to electromechanical punched card installations; and some (see Fig. 1-18) are the smallest models of a line of computers that includes a number of medium-sized and very large processors. These small members of a "family" of computers typically use magnetic tapes (resembling large sound recorder tapes) and magnetic

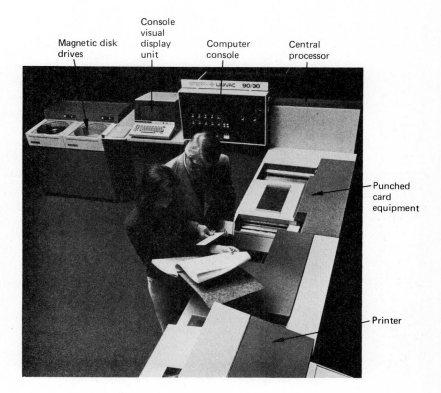

**FIGURE 1-18**

Small-scale business computer (courtesy Sperry UNIVAC Division, Sperry Rand Corporation).

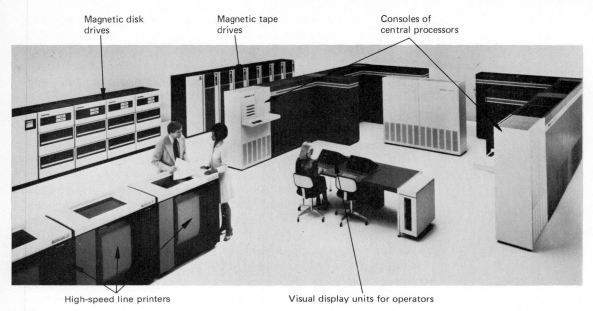

Magnetic disk drives

Magnetic tape drives

Consoles of central processors

High-speed line printers

Visual display units for operators

FIGURE 1-19

Large-scale computer installation (courtesy Burroughs Corporation).

disks (resembling large phonograph records) as data-storage media. They are generally faster than desk-sized models and card processors, have greater internal data-storage capacity, and are thus more expensive. (Desk-sized processors and card-oriented systems typically sell for $20,-000 to $80,000; the smallest models of computer families typically sell for $70,000 to $200,000.)

Medium-sized computers may sell for $200,000 to $1 million, and *larger systems* (see Fig. 1-19) exceed this price range. In return for higher prices, users receive faster processing speeds, greater storage capacity, wider selection of optional equipment, and a lower cost-per-calculation figure.[19]

**SUMMARY** Data are the input from which information is produced, and they are obtained in an organization from internal and external sources. The data

[19] This assumes that the volume of work is sufficient to keep a large machine occupied. If a person can compute the answer to a multiplication problem in 1 minute, and there are 125 million such problems to be solved, the total cost to do the calculations manually would exceed $10 million. The UNIVAC 1 (which in terms of computing power is a very small machine by today's standards) could have done the job for $4,300. However, a large machine today that rents for over $100,000 per month could do the job for less than $4.

processing operation, in its entirety, consists of nine steps; however, some steps may be omitted in specific situations. Manual, machine-assisted manual, electromechanical punched card, and computer methods may be used to perform these steps.

Although information is needed for decision making, it is usually impossible to state specifically what information a manager will need. Regardless of the information needed, however, it should possess the characteristics of accuracy, timeliness, completeness, conciseness, and relevancy. In recent years, the receipt of information lacking one or more of these characteristics has motivated managers to look at the possible use of computerized information systems.

Data processing techniques have been undergoing evolutionary change since the beginning of the human race. This evolution has advanced through four stages, from manual methods to the development of the computer. However, none of these stages should be considered obsolete, for each has its place.

There can be little doubt that the computer is responsible in large measure, for the significant and sweeping change that is now taking place in the field of information processing. The next chapter examines some of the causes and effects of this revolution.

**REVIEW AND DISCUSSION
QUESTIONS**

1    (a) What is management information? (b) What is the difference between data and information? (c) Compare the manufacturing process with the information-producing process.

2    Identify and explain the sources of business data.

3    (a) Identify and explain the basic data processing steps. (b) What processing methods may be used to perform these steps?

4    "Beyond certain basic informational requirements, the question of what information is needed by managers can only be answered in broad, general terms." Discuss this statement.

5    (a) Why does the organizational level of the managerial job affect the information needed? (b) How do informational needs differ?

6    Identify and discuss the desired properties of management information.

7    What factors have focused attention on the need for management information improvement in recent years?

8    The figure below shows the typical total-cost relationships between computer processing methods and alternative methods. (a) Discuss the meanings of points A, B, and C in the figure. (b) "The total cost for computer processing may exceed that for other methods when the processing volume is small." Discuss this statement. (c) Discuss the meanings of A', B', and C' in the figure.

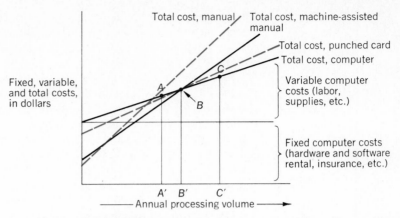

9  What are the advantages and limitations of manual data processing methods?

10  Describe the 80-column punched card and the Hollerith code.

11  Describe the 96-column punched card and the coding employed.

12  What is a field?

13  (**a**) What was the Analytical Engine? (**b**) What features would it have had in common with modern computers?

14  After a survey of a computer center available to you, identify: (**a**) The hardware generation of the equipment. (**b**) The approximate value of the center equipment. (**c**) The names of firms supplying equipment, programs, and supplies to the center. (**d**) The size category of the center's computer (or computers). (**e**) The services offered by the center to its customers.

**SELECTED REFERENCES**    Ackoff, Russell L.: "Management Misinformation Systems," *Management Science* (Application Ser.), December 1967, pp. B147–B156.

Eckert, J. Presper: "Thoughts on the History of Computing," *Computer,* December 1976, pp. 58–65.

Pullen, Edward W., and Robert G. Simko: "Our Changing Industry," *Datamation,* January 1977, pp. 49–55.

Rothenbuecher, Oscar H.: "The Top 50 U. S. Companies in the Data Processing Industry." *Datamation,* June 1977, pp. 61–73.

# the information revolution in perspective

# 2

LEARNING OBJECTIVES   After studying this chapter and answering the discussion questions, you should be able to: □ Explain why technological changes may simultaneously create new opportunities and problems □ Discuss the revolutionary changes that have recently occurred in the development of computer hardware □ Identify three categories of computer software and discuss the developments that have occurred in each □ Describe the characteristics (both positive and negative) of information systems that utilize quick-response and data-base concepts to produce management information □ Identify some of the problems of adjustment affecting organizations and individuals that are accompanying the information revolution

**H**istory records, in a relatively unfavorable light, periods such as the Dark Ages following the fall of the Roman Empire when European political and religious leaders reduced the tempo of change. But it can hardly be said today that the tempo of of change has diminished. Rather, we are now living in a time when revolutionary technological, social, and economic changes are taking place more quickly than ever before in history. Not surprisingly, these changes are threatening to sweep aside many of the current (and sometimes comfortable) practices followed by business organizations. Thus, the managerial techniques that were adequate in the past may not continue to be effective in our rapidly changing environment. For managers working in such an environment, the risks of failure and the rewards of success are probably higher than they have ever been. In fact, a basic challenge to managers in the next few years will be to foresee and manage (and not be swept along by) the changes facing their organizations.

Of course, if rapidly changing conditions are to be controlled, leaders must have high-quality information for decision making. Thus, in the following pages of this chapter we will first briefly consider the *revolutionary environmental changes* with which decision makers must contend. We will then examine the *revolutionary developments in computer technology* and in *management information systems* that can produce the better information that managers must now have. Finally, we will conclude with a brief summary of some of the unresolved *problems of adjustment* that are accompanying the information revolution. In short, the theme of the following pages is presented in Fig. 2-1.

## REVOLUTIONARY ENVIRONMENTAL CHANGES

We are witnessing today rapid *technological* changes taking place on a broad front. These changes, in turn, are often accompanied by pervasive *social* and *economic* changes—and problems. Let us now look more closely at some of these changes that will affect your future.

### scientific and technological changes

The ancient Greeks were obsessed with several dreams. One of these was the Promethean dream of stealing fire from the gods; another was the dream of soaring away from Earth and beyond the planets. Of course, these ancient dreams remained unrealized for thousands of years. Yet in a span of less than forty years, both dreams have now been achieved. The fires of atomic furnaces have been ignited, humans have moved out into space, and their machines have traveled beyond the planets.[1] In addition, microbiologists have learned how to combine bits of genetic material from one organism onto the genes of another species, and this recombinant DNA research has rekindled the ancient dream of learning the divine secrets of the creation of life itself.

Such scientific breakthroughs have encouraged further acceleration and expansion in the *scope* of scientific inquiry.[2] In addition, there has also been a great acceleration in the *speed* with which new knowledge is put to use. Before World War I, there was an average wait of 33 years between an invention and its application. But microprocessors on single tiny chips were developed in the early 1970s and are now being used in games, household appliances, automobiles, and traffic lights (to name just a few applications).

### social and economic changes

A wave of social and economic changes often follows in the wake of new technological developments. For example, a new technological development may create the opportunity in business to improve on a production

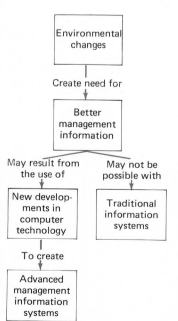

**FIGURE 2-1**

[1] Without computers (and without the microelectronic circuits made possible by the research conducted by military and space agencies and by computer manufacturers) much, if not most, of the technological progress of the past decade would not have been possible. Certainly, without the nearly 200 computers of the NASA Apollo System, men could not have journeyed to the moon.

[2] Although they may seem unbelievable, consider the following facts: Half the total scientific research ever conducted in the United States has been done in the past 10 years; about 90 percent of all the scientists and engineers ever formally trained are alive today; and the output of scientific information is doubling about every 8 to 10 years.

process or to do something that was previously not possible. When such a development occurs, there will usually be those who will seek to take advantage of the new opportunity, even though changes in the ways individuals and groups are organized may then be necessary. And these newly organized groups may then compete for economic resources with established units. Thus, gains achieved by new groups in utilizing the new technology may create problems and economic losses for those that are using older tools and techniques. The development of the automobile, for example, created a new industry and millions of new jobs, but buggy manufacturing organizations were virtually eliminated and their employees were displaced; automobiles have increased individual mobility and suburbs have sprung up, but many older central cities are in decay and their public transportation facilities have deteriorated; and automobiles have been responsible for the construction of convenient new shopping centers, but urban streets are congested, the air is polluted, and the world's oil reserves are being depleted at a rapid rate. In short, as the development of the automobile has illustrated, both positive and negative social and economic effects may be expected when significant technological changes occur.

**managerial implications of these changes**

The managerial implications of rapid scientific, social, and economic changes are clear—managers must be prepared to make continuous readjustments in their business plans. Managers must make more and better decisions about new products and existing products because of their shorter profitable lifespan; they must make decisions about product prices, new markets, and channels of distribution to use; they must be prepared to make decisions in the face of increasingly aggressive foreign and domestic competition; and they must decide on how to finance the necessary resources. Furthermore, these decisions may often involve greater risk and be valid only within a time span that is constantly shrinking. Thus, as reaction time diminishes, opportunities for profitable action are lost because preoccupied managers fail to reach out and grasp them (Fig. 2-2).

In addition to facing pressures of a competitive nature, however, managers must also recognize the social effects of their decisions—e.g., they cannot take actions to utilize the latest technology without at the same time considering the possible effects of such actions on social organizations, existing production systems, and human skills and feelings. To compete profitably in the future, and to take a responsible role in seeking solutions to the social ills which exist in the environment in which they live and work, managers will require information of the highest possible quality. The computer, which is undergoing rapid tech-

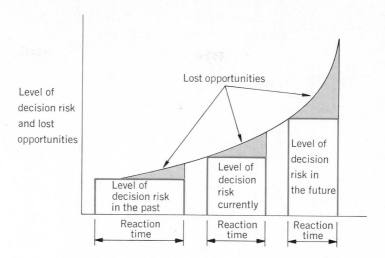

**FIGURE 2-2**

nological improvement, is a tool that can provide the needed information.

## REVOLUTION IN COMPUTER TECHNOLOGY

The computer is a tool that is *contributing* to advances in virtually all fields. Computer-hardware technology is also benefiting from new discoveries in the fields of electronics and physics. Computer *hardware* consists of all the machines that make up a functioning computer system. Basically, these machines accept data input, store data, perform calculations and other processing steps, and prepare information output.

Hardware alone, however, is merely one or more boxes of electronic parts that represent an expense; an equally important (perhaps more important) consideration in the effective use of computers is the *software*. Software is the name given to the multitude of instructions, i.e., the name given to *programs* and *routines* that have been written to cause the hardware to function in a desired way. Let us now briefly look at the technological advances in computer hardware and software.

### hardware developments

Hardware technological development has been incredibly rapid, as may be seen by an examination of the factors of (1) *size,* (2) *speed,* (3) *cost,* (4) *information storage capacity,* and (5) *reliability.* And as Fig. 2-3 shows, the past trends in these factors are likely to continue through the 1980s.

Size    Second-generation computers were much smaller than their predecessors because transistors and other smaller components were substi-

| Hardware Development Factors | 1950 | 1960 | 1970 | 1975 | 1980s |
|---|---|---|---|---|---|
| *Size Factor:* | | | | | |
| Number of circuits per cubic foot | 1,000 | 100,000 | 10 million | 1 billion | Many billions |
| *Speed Factor:* | | | | | |
| Time to execute an instruction in the central processor | 300 microseconds | 5 microseconds | 80 nanoseconds | 25 nanoseconds | 5 nanoseconds or less |
| *Cost Factors:* | | | | | |
| Cost (in dollars) to process 1 million basic computer instructions | 28 | 1 | 0.02 | 0.001 | Less than 0.001 |
| Cost (in cents) to provide storage for one binary number in the central processor | 261. | 85. | 5. | .1 | Less than .05 |
| *Storage Capacity Factors:* | | | | | |
| Primary storage capacity (in characters) of the central processor | 20,000 | 120,000 | 1 million | 10 million | Much greater than 10 million |
| Characters of secondary online storage | — | 20 million | Over 100 billion | Virtually unlimited | Virtually unlimited |
| *Reliability Factor:* | | | | | |
| Mean (average) time between failures of some central processors | Hours | Tens of hours | Hundreds of hours | Thousands of hours | Tens of thousands of hours (years) |

FIGURE 2-3

Summary of hardware developments.

tuted for tubes. And as you can see in Fig. 2-3, this size reduction continues today. It is now possible, through *large-scale integration* (LSI) of electronic circuits (see Fig. 2-4), to pack billions of *circuits* in a cubic foot of space. Furthermore, each circuit contains a number of separate components. Since 1965, in fact, the average number of components per advanced integrated circuit has doubled each year. Thus, by the time you read this sentence, LSI chips may contain the equivalent of 1 million components.[3] These LSI chips may then be arranged and sealed on compact boards, as we saw earlier in Fig. 1-15, page 29.

[3] As the president of the company that produces the chip shown in Fig. 2-4 has noted, "An individual integrated circuit on a chip perhaps a quarter of an inch square now can embrace more electronic elements than the most complex piece of electronic equipment that could be built in 1950. Today's microcomputer, at a cost of perhaps $300, has more computing capacity than the first large electronic computer, ENIAC. It is 20 times faster, has a larger memory, is thousands of times more reliable, consumes the power of a light bulb rather than that of a locomotive, occupies 1/30,000 the volume and costs 1/10,000 as much." See Robert N. Noyce, "Microelectronics," *Scientific American,* September 1977, pp. 63–69.

FIGURE 2-4

A greatly magnified view of the Intel
8080 microprocessor shown as one
element on the board in Figure 1-15
(courtesy of Intel Corporation).

Has the end to the feasible size reduction of computer circuitry been
reached? Hardly. The boards of today will become the tiny chips of
tomorrow. One scientist has speculated that by about the early 1980s it
may be possible to achieve the packing density currently obtained on a
square inch *throughout a cubic inch* of material. The density of electronic
components would then be "about a fourth the density of nerve cells in
the human brain."[4] Thus, it is expected that in the 1980s central processors with the power of today's large computers will occupy the space of a
shoebox!

Speed   Circuit miniaturization has brought increased speed of operation
to the latest computers. Why is this? It is because size reduction means
shorter distances for electric pulses to travel, and thus processor speed
has increased.

Early computer speed was expressed in *milliseconds* (thousandths of a
second); second-generation speed was measured in *microseconds* (mil-
lionths of a second); third- and fourth-generation hardware has internal
operating speeds measured in *nanoseconds* (billionths of a second).
Since circuit speeds are likely to increase by 5 times between 1975 and

[4] F. G. Heath, "Large-Scale Integration in Electronics," *Scientific American,* February 1970,
p. 22.

1985, future machines may have speeds measured in *picoseconds* (trillionths of a second).[5]

Cost   A significant cause of the growth in the number of computer installations is the dramatic reduction in the cost of performing a specific number of operations (see Fig. 2-3). If automobile costs and technological improvements had changed at a rate comparable with computer hardware over the last 15 years, you would now be able to buy a self-steering car for $20 that could attain speeds up to 500 mph and could travel the entire length of California on 1 gallon of gas. Nor does it appear that the end is in sight in computational cost reduction. The cost of certain basic components will continue to decline while their speed and performance increases.

Information storage capacity   Information may be stored for use by a computer in a number of ways. The central processing unit (CPU) of the computer holds data and the instructions needed to manipulate the data internally in its *primary storage,* or *main memory,* section. Figure 2-3 summarizes the trend in primary storage capacity. Perhaps even more impressive has been the improvement in mass *external online* (or *secondary*) storage devices (see Fig. 2-3). These devices are connected directly to, i.e., they are *online* to, the CPU, and they serve as *reference libraries* by accepting data directly from and returning data directly to the CPU without human intervention. Of course, data which the computer may use are also stored outside the CPU in the form of punched cards and magnetic tape, but these facts are *offline* since the CPU does not have direct and unassisted access to them (see Fig. 2-5).

Reliability   The reliability of hardware has improved substantially with the substitution of long-life solid state components for the early vacuum

[5] Such speeds are difficult to comprehend. A space ship traveling toward the moon at 100,000 miles per hour would move less than 2 *inches* in 1 microsecond; it would move only the length of 10 fat germs in a nanosecond. More antiseptically speaking, there are as many nanoseconds in one second as there are seconds in 30 years, or as many nanoseconds in a minute as there are minutes in 1,100 *centuries*. Electricity travels about 1 foot per nanosecond, and this fact imposes an ultimate limit to internal computer speed.

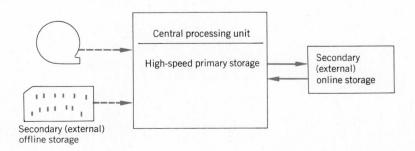

FIGURE 2-5
Computer information storage.

tubes. Much of the research effort directed toward achieving greater reliability has been sponsored by the United States government for space and missile programs. For example, scientists have been working on self-repairing computers that would remain in operation during unmanned space missions lasting many years. The self-repairing concept essentially involves partitioning the computer into functional blocks and building identical components into each block. Some of the parts are used for processing immediately; others serve as standby spares. A failure occurring in one component or subsystem would be detected by a status-sensing device, and the faulty part would be electronically and automatically replaced with a spare.

The down-to-earth benefits of increased reliability are great; for example, self-repairing computers could be incorporated into the intensive-care monitoring and control systems of hospitals where a failure could result in a death. And they would be especially beneficial in those computerized navigational systems that are used to safely bring in aircraft in zero-visibility conditions. If those sections of future earthbound computers with a reduced number of standby spares were replaced during periodic preventive maintenance, the mean (average) time between failures would probably be measured in years rather than in weeks or months. Although completely self-repairing *commercial* computers are still on the drawing boards because of the additional cost of redundant spare parts, this obstacle will likely be overcome in the not-too-distant future as LSI circuit technology produces lower costs.[6]

At the present time, better accessibility of the circuitry enables technicians to get to the problem and quickly effect a repair. Computer circuit boards can be promptly replaced, and equipment *downtime* can be kept to a minimum. It is possible for a malfunctioning computer to be linked to another "diagnostic" computer in order to determine the cause of the problem. For example, NCR Corporation's V-8560 processor has a remote diagnostic capability that permits engineers at an NCR division in San Diego to check out any such processor installed anywhere in the United States. Also, *self-diagnostic* or fault-location features are being built into equipment to help on-site technicians minimize downtime.

### software developments

*Software* is the general name given to all the programs and routines associated with the use of computer hardware. Unfortunately, when compared with the tremendous hardware advances, the developments in the software area seem less impressive. Furthermore, as anticipated

---

[6] One current example of this trend toward much greater reliability is found in the primary storage section of Digital Equipment Corporation's PDP 11/60 minicomputer. This semiconductor memory has an error correction code feature that produces a calculated mean-time-between-failure in excess of 20,000 hours.

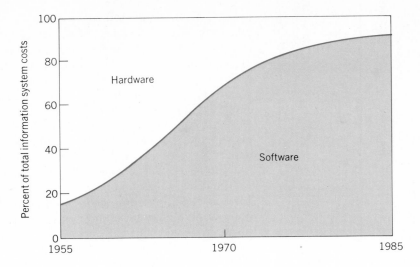

**FIGURE 2-6**

Total cost trends for information systems.

hardware improvements are realized, an overwhelming proportion of the problems experienced in utilizing the computer to produce managerial information will be traceable to software difficulties. Today, in fact, the production of good software is a costly and time-consuming process that generally determines the speed with which computer-based projects are completed. As a result, the investment in programming and systems personnel and in the software they create now far exceeds the investment in hardware in most installations. And as Fig. 2-6 shows, this trend will undoubtedly continue because hardware production is automated while increasingly complex software is still generally written on an artisan basis.[7]

Yet there have been significant gains in the development of software. The three basic software categories are (1) *translation programs,* (2) *applications programs,* and (3) *operating-system programs.* Let us look at the developments in each of these categories.

Translation programs   In the early 1950s, users had to translate problem-solving instructions into special machine codes for each computer. Such instructions typically consisted of strings of numbers (sometimes in a binary form), which were quite tedious to prepare. In addition to remembering dozens of operation code numbers (21 might mean add), the employee performing the task of instructing the computer (a *programmer*)

---

[7] It has been estimated that the human cost to write and check a line of coded instructions in a computer program is over 100 million times as much as the machine cost to execute the line. It is obvious then that human costs should be minimized whenever possible, even if this could lead to somewhat less efficiency in the use of the hardware.

was also required to keep track of the locations in the central processor where the instructions and data items were stored. Initial program coding often took many months; checking instructions to locate errors was about as difficult as writing the instructions in the first place; and modifying programs was often a nightmare.

To ease the programmer's burden, a compromise approach between people and machine was developed which resulted in the introduction of special coding *languages* that save time and are more convenient to use. In using these languages, the programmer writes instructions in a form that is easier to understand—e.g., the programmer may print the word ADD or use the plus symbol rather that use the number 21. Unfortunately, this code is not in the machine's language, and so it does not directly understand the orders. How, then, can the machine execute instructions if they are in a language that it cannot understand? Just as an American and a German can communicate if one of them uses a translating dictionary, so, too, can the programmer and computer communicate if a separate translation program is employed. Briefly, this translating program is loaded into the computer where it controls the translation procedure. The instructions written by the programmer (called the *source program*) are then fed into the computer where they are translated. The result of this operation is a set of machine instructions (called the *object program*) that may then be used to control the processing of problem data.[8]

Almost all problem-solving programs prepared today are first written in languages preferred by programmers and are then translated by special software into the equivalent machine language codes. Continuing efforts are being made to produce software that will permit easier human/machine communication. For example, efforts are being made to develop software that will give the ultimate users of the processed information the ability to prepare programs in languages that are more familiar to them.

Application programs    The programs written for the purpose of solving particular processing jobs also come under the heading of software. These programs are commonly prepared by each using organization to process such applications as payroll, inventory control, and other tasks. Many applications programs must, of course, be prepared by users to process tasks that are unique to their particular needs. In the past, however, much programmer time has been spent in duplicating programs prepared in other companies. Recognizing the wastefulness of such duplication, equipment manufacturers and independent software companies have prepared generalized *applications packages* (or *packaged*

---

[8] Further details on this translation procedure and on several programming languages are presented in Chapter 11.

*programs*) for widely used applications.[9] Retail stores, for example, sell on credit and thus maintain credit records and perform billing operations. Since many retail firms employ essentially the same accounting procedures in such cases, a billing and accounts-receivable application package may often be purchased by a retailer from an outside source and used with good results. But although a packaged program prepared by an excellent programmer specialist may be implemented quicker and may be more efficient and less expensive than a run-of-the-mill program prepared by the user, there is also the possibility that an available package may not fit the needs of the user without extensive modification—a potentially difficult task for user programmers who may be unfamiliar with the package.

Operating-system programs    As the name implies, the *operating system*(OS) was initially a set of programs prepared by equipment manufacturers and users to assist the computer operator. It is the function of the operator to load data input devices with cards and tapes, to set switches on the computer console, to start the processing run, and to prepare and unload output devices. It should not be the operator's job, however, to waste time (both human and machine) doing things that the computer could do more quickly and reliably. Housekeeping duties such as loading and unloading input and output equipment, clearing central processor storage locations between jobs, and loading into storage the next job program and data from the jobs stacked up in a waiting queue are now controlled by the software. Shifting control to specially prepared operating programs thus reduced the operator's work, cut down on the programmer's drudgery (by eliminating the need to rewrite certain input and output instructions for each program), provided relatively nonstop operation, and therefore speeded up the amount of processing that could be accomplished. The name given to the software that aids in performing the housekeeping duties just described is the input/output control system (IOCS)—an important segment of a modern operating system.

The objective of current operating systems is still to operate the computer with a minimum of idle time and in the most efficient and economical way during the execution of application and translation programs. But the operating software is now vastly more complex. More sophisticated software has been required to keep faster and more powerful hardware occupied. An example is the development of *multiprogram-*

---

[9] For example, the users of the small business computer shown in Fig. 1-17 have access to a comprehensive library of industry-oriented programs developed by NCR Corporation. Included among these applications packages are general accounting programs (e.g., payroll, general ledger, and accounts receivable and payable); order processing, inventory, and sales analysis programs; budgetary control programs for government and educational institutions; and programs specifically designed for medical group practices, restaurants, retail stores, and auto dealers. Other manufacturers offer similar packages with their equipment.

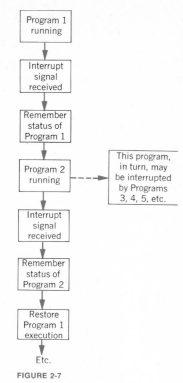

FIGURE 2-7

*ming,* the name given to the *interleaved* execution of two or more different and independent programs by the same computer.[10]

Multiprogramming *is not* generally defined to mean that the computer is executing instructions from several programs at the *same instant* in time;[11] instead, it *does* mean that there are a number of programs stored in primary and/or online storage and that a portion of one is executed, then a segment of another, etc. The processor switches from one program to another almost instantaneously. Since internal operating speeds of CPUs are much faster than are the means of getting data into and out of the processor, the CPU can allocate time to several programs instead of remaining idle while one is bringing in data or printing out information. With multiprogramming, it is thus possible for several user stations to share the time of the CPU (see Fig. 2-7). This *timesharing* feature may permit more efficient use of the capacity of the processor.

In recent years, operating-system development (and specialized hardware) has also made possible the widespread[12] introduction of computers with *virtual storage* capability. Prior to this development, the size of an application program was effectively limited by the size of the computer's primary storage section. This was because the complete program was typically held in primary storage during its entire execution. If the program size did not exceed the limited primary storage capacity, then there was no problem; if, on the other hand, the task required several thousand instructions, then the programmer might be forced to write two or more programs to complete the job. With virtual storage capability, however, the computer can divide total programs into small sequences of instructions called *pages.* Then, only those program pages that are actually required at a particular time in the processing need be in primary storage. The remaining segments may be kept temporarily in online storage, from which they can be rapidly retrieved as needed (see Fig. 2-8). Thus, from the programmer's point of view, the effective (or "virtual") size of the available primary storage may appear to be unlimited.

The incorporation of multiprogramming and virtual storage capabilities into the OS has, of course, complicated matters. For example,

---

[10] If you are mechanically inclined, you may know that the automobile distributor head rotates, makes electrical contact with, and zaps a pulse of electricity to each spark plug in one revolution. Similarly, the computer may allocate a small amount or *slice,* of time—say, 150 milliseconds per second—to each program being executed. Fifteen-hundredths of a second may not seem like much time to you, but that is enough to calculate the amounts owed to hundreds of employees for a given pay period. The result of such speed is that each user has the illusion that he or she has the undivided attention of the computer.

[11] The term *multiprocessing* is used to describe interconnected computer configurations or computers with multiple arithmetic-logic units that have the ability to *simultaneously* execute several programs.

[12] The virtual storage concept was being used in the 1950s in Europe, and Burroughs Corporation introduced the concept in the United States in 1962. But *widespread* acceptance of virtual storage did not occur until IBM announced its intention to employ the technique 10 years later.

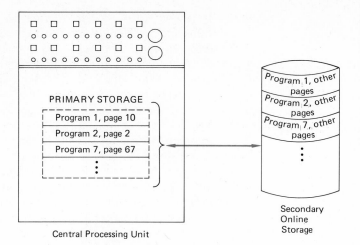

**FIGURE 2-8**

Virtual storage capability.

Central Processing Unit

software must keep track of the locations in primary and secondary storage of each of the several programs and program segments, must remember at what point it should return to an interrupted program, and must, perhaps, assign job priorities to the several tasks waiting to be completed. The operating systems of many of today's computers are, in short, integrated collections of processing programs and a master control program that are expected to perform the *scheduling, control, loading,* and *program call-up* functions described below:

**1** The *scheduling* function involves the selection of jobs to be run on a priority basis from a table or list of jobs to be processed. Available storage space and the most suitable peripheral hardware to use is allocated to the job or jobs being processed. Whenever possible, jobs are selected to balance input/output and processing requirements. They are added to and deleted from the job table as required.

**2** The *control* function consists of a number of activities including *(a)* the control of input and output housekeeping operations; *(b)* the proper handling, shifting, and protection of data, instructions, and intermediate processing results when a high-priority program interrupts the processing of a lower-priority program; *(c)* the timing of each job processed and the allocation of processor time to user stations; and *(d)* the communication of error and control messages to human operators.

**3** The *loading* function includes reading in and assigning storage locations to object programs and data. Checks are also made to prevent the loading and processing of incorrect files.

**4** The *program call-up* function emphasizes the overall control of the OS master program (referred to by such names as *monitor, executive routine,* and *supervisor*) over other software elements, including *translating programs, service programs,* or *utility routines* (for loading programs, clearing storage, sorting and merging data, diagnostic testing of new programs, etc.), and the installation's stored file of *applications programs*. The monitor integrates this assorted software into a single consistent system. The system monitor generally remains in primary storage where it may occupy 25 to 60 percent of the available space; in installations with online storage capability, many of the other programs and routines are kept online and are called up and temporarily stored in the CPU as needed.

Figure 2-9 summarizes the relationship existing between the hardware and software categories discussed in the above pages.

Technological advances in computer hardware and software have both contributed to and been stimulated by a dynamic environment. And as we will see in the next section, managers have sought to implement computer-oriented management information systems that will enable them to cope with rapidly changing conditions.

## DEVELOPMENTS IN MANAGEMENT INFORMATION SYSTEMS

Traditional information systems have often been found wanting because they do not provide information with the desired properties mentioned in Chapter 1—that is, the information they produce may be too costly and is not (1) timely, (2) properly integrated, (3) concise, (4) available in the proper format, or (5) relevant. To reduce the difficulties experienced with traditional approaches, new computer-oriented management information system concepts have been developed (and are now emerging).

### an MIS orientation

What is a management information system (MIS)? Strangely enough, it is not easy to pin down these innocent-looking words, for they are defined in dozens of different ways, and the definitions vary in scope and breadth.[13] At one extreme, a particular MIS could be defined as an all-encompassing system that immediately provides all managers in an organization with any and all needed information. Obviously, this definition would make it impossible for such a system to ever be realized. And at the other extreme, an MIS could be defined as any system that provides information to a manager—without specifying the nature or quality of the information. Of course, this latter system would be easy to attain; in fact, every firm or organization has one. Not surprisingly, the definitions used by most authorities to describe the MIS concept fall somewhere between these extremes.

---

[13] Systems specialists even have difficulty agreeing on the definition of the word *systems*. At one meeting of these specialists, definitions offered ranged from "helping administrators ease decision-making when faced with multidirectional functional alternatives" to "presenting a synthesis of a very diverse network of homogeneous complexities." As *The New York Times* dryly reported: "Jargon came into its own that day.".

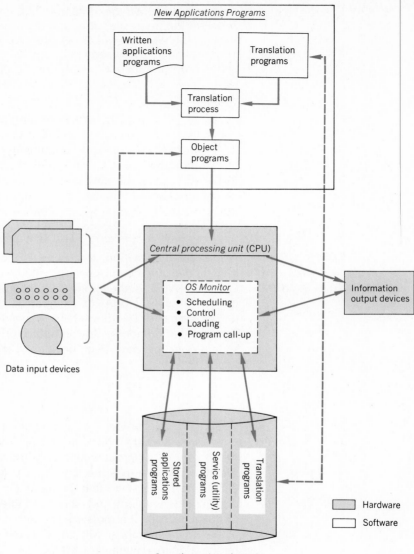

FIGURE 2-9

Operating system elements

For our purposes, a *management information system* may be defined as a network of computer-based data processing procedures developed in an organization and *integrated as necessary* with other manual, mechanical, and/or electronic procedures for the purpose of providing timely and effective information to support decision making and other necessary management functions. The words *computer-based* used in this definition might not be an absolute necessity in an MIS of a very small concern. But since an MIS is expected to produce information that is more timely and more complete than that produced by a traditional information system, a system possessing these capabilities is generally not feasible in larger organizations unless a computer is employed. Also, the phrase *data processing procedure* refers to a related group of data processing steps, or *methods* (usually involving a number of people in one or more departments), which have been established to perform a recurring processing operation. Figure 2-10 illustrates these definitions in the narrow context of information needed by personnel managers. Each line represents a procedure (consisting of a series of steps, or methods, indicated by the squares) that is directed toward achieving the objective of more effective personnel management. Each procedure produces needed information, and several procedures cut across departmental lines. This personnel information system is, of course, only one of several information-producing activities in a business.[14]

Running a business is a complicated process which, in larger organizations, takes place on at least three levels. As we saw in Fig. 1-5, page 13, top executives plan and make policy decisions of *strategic* importance.

[14] Some writers treat the entire business as a single *system* and the component parts of the business as *subsystems*. In this case our personnel system would be labeled a subsystem within the overall business system. We have no quarrel with this treatment since the difference is primarily one of semantics. Some also treat the entire business as a single information system. If total integration were possible, a single system would result from our definition. It should be pointed out, however, that the degree to which information systems (or subsystems) can and should be integrated is rather controversial at this time.

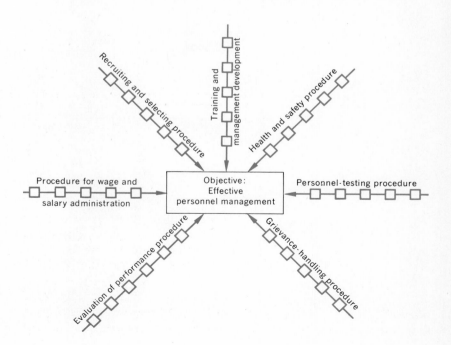

FIGURE 2-10

Personnel information system.

These strategic decisions are then used by middle-level managers who devise the *tactics* to allocate resources and establish controls to implement the top-level plans. And finally, lower-level *operating* managers make the necessary day-to-day scheduling and control decisions to accomplish specific tasks. Figure 2-11 shows some of the representative tasks performed and the information flows needed to support decision making. Generally speaking, the information needed by managers who occupy different levels and who have different responsibilities is obtained from a collection of management information systems (or subsystems). These systems may be tied together very closely; more often, however, they are more loosely coupled.

Although the development of new information systems is a challenging assignment, many organizations have now adopted an MIS orientation

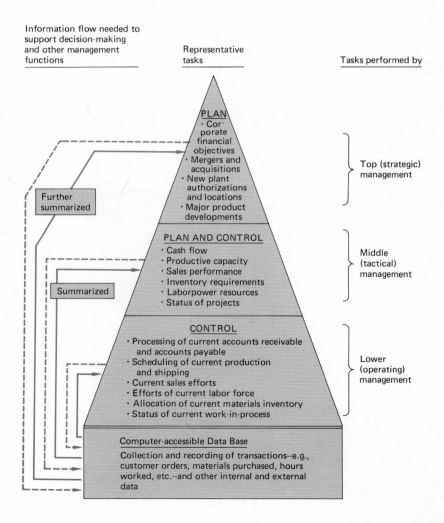

FIGURE 2-11

An MIS orientation.

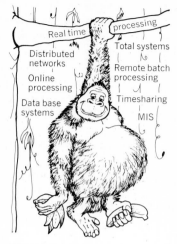

Real time processing

Total systems

Distributed networks

Remote batch processing

Online processing

Timesharing

Data base systems

MIS

**FIGURE 2-12**

and are moving toward the implementation of new systems utilizing concepts that are *quicker responding* and *broader in scope* than those employed with traditional systems. Let us now look at systems possessing these characteristics.

### quick-response systems

*Quick-response systems,* as the name implies, have been developed to increase the timeliness, effectiveness, and availability of information. They may allow users to react more rapidly to changing conditions, reduce waste in the use of time and other resources, and permit quick follow-up on creative ideas. They may also be described by a bewildering variety of Computerese terms. A glance through a few current data processing periodicals shows the subject to be a veritable semantic jungle with many "experts" swinging from different definition vines (Fig. 2-12). We will try to cut through this foliage by examining the concepts of (1) *online processing;* (2) *real time processing,* (3) *timesharing* and *remote computing services,* and (4) *distributed processing networks.*

Online processing    The term *online* is used in different ways. We have seen that a peripheral machine connected directly to and capable of unassisted communication with the central processor is said to be an online device. *Online* also describes the status of a person who is communicating directly with (i.e., has *direct access* to) the central processor without the use of media such as punched cards or magnetic tape. Finally, *online* refers to a *method of processing data.* However, before looking at the concept of *online processing,* we should pause to describe the characteristics of the *batch processing* approach.

Perhaps an illustration will best explain batch processing (it is also called *serial* or *sequential* processing). Let us trace the activities that follow Zelda Zilch's credit purchase of a zither in a department store. The sales slip for this *transaction* is routed to the accounting office where it and others are collected for several days until a large batch accumulates. The data on the slips may be recorded on a machine input medium such as punched cards. The cards are then sorted by customer name or charge-account number into the proper sequence for processing. Processing consists of adding the item description and price of all the recent transactions to the customer's other purchases for the month. Thus, a customer's accounts-receivable master file, perhaps in the form of magnetic tape, must be updated to reflect the additional charges. The sequence in which the new transactions are sorted is an ordered one and corresponds to the sequence on the master file. Figure 2-13 illustrates this batch processing procedure. At the end of the accounting period, the master file is used to prepare the customer statements.

Other files are periodically updated in similar fashion. A *file,* then, is a

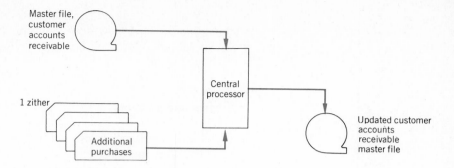

**FIGURE 2-13**
Batch processing.

collection of related records and items treated as a unit. In our example, the zither purchase was one *item* on Zelda's bill; Zelda's bill would represent one charge-account *record;* and the purchase records of all credit customers would make up the accounts-receivable *file.* Furthermore, a set of integrated files may be organized into a data base (see Fig. 2-14).

Batches may be collected at a central computer site or at other locations. One *other* location might be a small business that is a client of a computer service center; another might be a branch office of a large firm. In either case, batches may be collected and converted into the appropriate input medium. These ordered transactions may then be sent to the computer center through the mail, by messenger, or by the use of *remote batch processing stations,* which often employ telephone circuits to transmit data directly into the central computer system. Depending on the type of user and the nature of the input data, the central computer may (1) update online files, (2) process the data and transmit the output information back by mail or messenger, or (3) process the data and transmit the output information back to a printer at the remote station.[15]

The *advantages of batch processing* are that it is (1) economical when a large volume of data must be processed and (2) the most appropriate method for those applications (e.g., payroll) where the delay caused by accumulating data into batches does not reduce the value of the information. However, the *limitations of batch processing* are that it (1) requires sorting prior to processing, (2) reduces timeliness in some cases, and (3) requires sequential file organization—and this may prove to be a handicap if the current status of a record near the end of a file needs to be determined.

Online processing has been developed for certain uses as an answer to the batch processing deficiencies noted above. In contrast to batching,

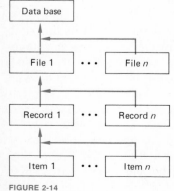

**FIGURE 2-14**
Data hierarchy.

[15] The time lapse here is typically greater than is the case with the methods of online processing we will consider. It may be minutes, hours, or days before the output information is received back at the station. Although priorities may be established, the remote batch job is stored in a queue of jobs waiting to be processed, and when its turn comes, it is executed consecutively to completion.

online (or *direct access* or *random*) processing permits transaction data to be fed under CPU control directly into secondary online storage devices from the point of origin without first being sorted. These data may be keyed in by the use of a terminal, or they may be produced by a variety of other data-collection and transaction-recording devices. Information contained in any record is accessible to the user without the necessity of a sequential search of the file and within a fraction of a second after the inquiry message has been transmitted. Thus, online processing systems may feature *random* and rapid input of transactions and immediate and *direct access* to record contents as needed (see Fig. 2-15).

Online processing and direct access to records *require unique hardware and software.* For example, the capacity of the primary storage unit of the CPU must be adequate to (1) handle the complex online operating-system control program and (2) serve a variety of other storage uses. Also, since many online users may have access to stored records, software security provisions are necessary to (1) prevent confidential information from falling into unauthorized hands and (2) prevent deliberate or accidental tampering with data and program files. Finally, data transmission facilities must be provided to communicate with online terminals located in the next room, on the next block, or thousands of miles away.

The speed of processing *needed* by a business varies with the particular application. As we have seen, batch processing is appropriate for many jobs. Online processing, although quicker responding than traditional methods, may involve different degrees of quickness in the needed response. For example, a system may combine immediate online access to records for inquiry purposes with *periodic* (perhaps daily) transaction input and batch updating of records from a central collecting source. Such a system would meet many needs and would be simpler and less expensive than a real time system (described below) that requires all input, output, and record updating to be done immediately through online terminals.

Real time processing    The words *real time* represent a semantic bucket of worms—you can choose from dozens of definitions that have surfaced. The consensus of opinion is, however, that a real time processing operation is (1) in a parallel time relationship with an ongoing activity and (2) producing information quickly enough to be useful in controlling this current live and dynamic activity. Thus, we shall use the words *real time* to describe an online processing system with severe time limitations.

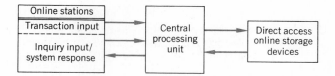

FIGURE 2-15

Online processing.

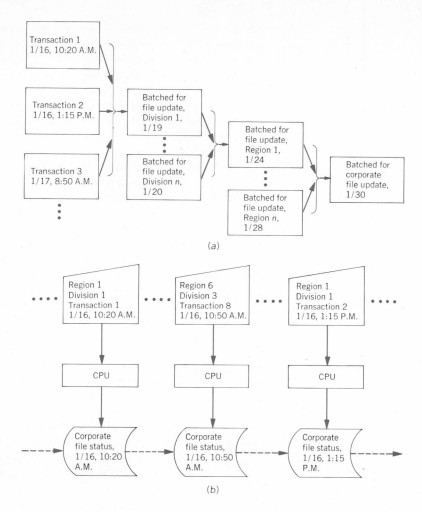

FIGURE 2-16

Possible timing associated with (a) batch processing, and (b) real time processing.

(Figure 2-16 illustrates the difference in timing between batch and real time processing.) A real time system, as defined here, uses online processing; however, as noted above, not all online processing systems need operate in real time.

Since real time processing requires immediate rather than periodic transaction input from all input-originating terminals, many remote stations may be tied directly by high-speed communications equipment into one or more central processors. Several stations may be operating simultaneously, files may be updated each minute, and inquiries may be answered by instant access to up-to-the-minute records.

Among the examples of real time processing are the systems designed to keep track of the availability of motel and hotel rooms, the systems that provide for immediate updating of customer records in savings banks, and the reservation systems used by airlines to control the inventory of available seats. In the airline systems, central computers receive transaction data and inquiries from remote terminals located at hundreds of reservation and ticket sales desks across the nation. In seconds, a customer may request and receive information about flights and available seats. If a reservation is made, the transaction is fed into the computer immediately and the inventory of available seats is reduced. The reverse, of course, occurs in the event of a cancellation. What if a flight is fully booked? If the customer desires to be placed on a waiting list, data such as customer name and telephone number are maintained by the computer. If cancellations occur, waiting-list customers are notified by agents. In addition, the reservation systems of competing airlines are tied together to provide an exchange of information on seat availability. Thus, an agent for any of the participating companies may sell space on *any* of the airlines if the system shows it is available.

Real time processing is required and cooperation is necessary among airlines because of the perishability of the service sold—when an airplane takes off, vacant seats have no value until the next landing. It would be a mistake, however, to assume that real time processing should be universally applied to all data processing applications. A quick-response system can be designed to fit the needs of the business. As you have seen earlier, some applications should be processed on a lower-priority or "background" basis using batch methods; some can be online with only periodic updating of files; and some can utilize real time methods.

Timesharing and remote computing services   *Timesharing* is a term used to describe a processing system with a number of independent, relatively low-speed, online, *simultaneously usable* stations (see Fig. 2-17). Each station provides direct access to the central processor. The speed of the system and the use of miltiprogramming allow the central processor to switch from one using station to another and to do a part of each job in the allocated "time slice" until the work is completed. The speed is frequently such that the user has the illusion that no one else is using the computer.

There are various types of timesharing systems. One type is the in-house installation that is designed for, owned by, and used exclusively in a *single organization*. The number of such dedicated systems is growing rapidly. For example, timesharing systems utilizing minicomputers are popular with managers and engineers who must solve problems that are too large for calculators, but may not be large enough to receive a high priority at the organization's large computer center.

Another type of timesharing system was established a number of years ago by commercial *remote computing services* (RCS) to provide computer resources to *many different client organizations* seeking to process a broad range of business and scientific jobs. Many RCS firms (sometimes referred to as *service bureaus*) will do custom batch processing and will

FIGURE 2-17

Timesharing terminal (courtesy Digital Equipment Corporation).

assume the responsibility for (1) analyzing the client's needs (2) preparing computer programs to perform the needed processing, and (3) converting the client's input data into machine-acceptable form.[16] However, when the timesharing facilities of RCS firms are used, the control of the processing generally remains with the using business. Transactions are initiated from, and output is delivered to, the premises of the user at electronic speeds. The subscriber pays for the processing service in much the same way he or she pays for telephone service: There is an initial installation charge; there are certain basic monthly charges; and, perhaps largest of all, there are transaction charges (like long-distance calls), which vary according to usage. These variable charges are generally based on the time the terminal is connected to the central processing system and/or on the seconds of CPU time used.

In addition to providing raw computing power to timesharing clients—a service that may be vulnerable to the purchase and use by clients of the new, low-cost processors discussed in Chapter 1—many RCS organizations also offer a library of specialized applications programs that are designed to meet the needs of a particular industry. Customers then need only supply the input data and access these online programs to obtain the needed output information. (Some of these RCS firms are now branching into a new service area by selling these specialized programs to clients who have decided to acquire their own small computers.)

[16] For example, Automatic Data Processing, Inc., with revenues of about $200 million per year, does the payrolls for about 400 banks and 30,000 other firms.

Distributed processing networks    In earlier paragraphs we have used the word *timesharing* because it is commonly applied to the interleaved use of the time of a computer. When *one* or *two* processors handle the workload of several outlying terminals, then the term *timesharing* is probably still appropriately descriptive. But when *many* dispersed or *distributed* independent computer systems are connected by a communications network, and when messages, processing tasks, programs, data, and other information-processing resources are transmitted between processors and terminals, then the term *timesharing* may no longer be adequate. Such a distributed computer-communications network is similar in some respects to public utilities such as telephone and electric companies—e.g., electric power plants are geographically dispersed and the energy resources generated are transmitted through a coordinating regional network or grid to the places where the energy resources are needed. (In the past, in fact, timeshared networks were called *information utilities* and *computing utilities*.)

The term *distributed processing network* is now frequently used to describe this extension of timesharing, which may result in a large number of computers and significant software resources being shared among a large number of users. Figure 2-18 shows some of the possible network configurations. Distributed processing networks, like smaller timesharing systems, may be for the use of a *single* organization or for *many* organizations. Figure 2-19, for example, shows the worldwide distributed network that Hewlett-Packard Company has developed for its own internal use. This network, with more than 130 computers located at 94 sites, links manufacturing facilities and sales offices with the company's central computer center in California. Although overall control of the network is maintained by the California center, division computers operate autonomously to process local jobs. And Fig. 2-20 shows a commercial multisubscriber distributed network that offers computing resources to customers in business, government, and education. This network connects over 70 cities on two continents with 40 large-scale computers.[17]

As you might expect, there are both advantages and disadvantages at present to the sharing of computing resources.[18] Some of the *advantages of resource sharing* using timesharing and distributed processing systems are that (1) central processor idle time may be reduced, (2) sophisticated

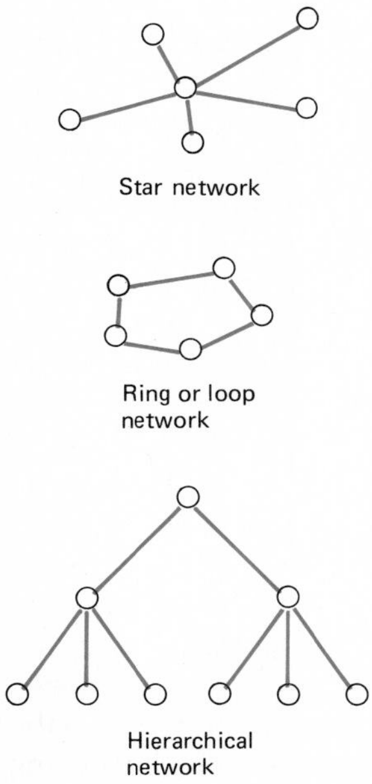

Star network

Ring or loop network

Hierarchical network

FIGURE 2-18

Possible network configurations.

[17] Other examples of single-organization distributed processing networks are the *OCTOPUS* system that connects 1,000 researchers at the University of California with five very large computers, and *Eastern Airlines' network* that links nine large computers in Miami and Charlotte, North Carolina, with over 2,700 ticket agent, flight operations, and internal business operations terminals. And other networks used by multiple organizations are the *ARPA net* that connects over 30 universities and research institutions throughout the United States and Europe with 50 processors ranging in size from minicomputers to giant number crunchers, and the *General Electric network* that uses over 100 computers to serve over 100,000 users in more than 20 countries.

[18] Further discussions of this topic will be presented in later chapters.

FIGURE 2-19

Hewlett-Packard Company
Distributed Processing network.

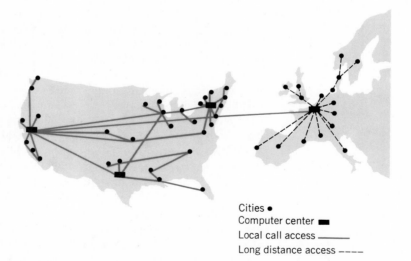

Cities ●
Computer center ■
Local call access ————
Long distance access −−−−

FIGURE 2-20

TYMNET network of Tymshare, Inc.

computers and a growing library of applications programs may be immediately available to end-users whenever needed, (3) skilled professionals
(either in-house or in the employ of RCS firms) may be available to help
users develop their own specialized applications, (4) the possible availability of multiple processors in the system permits peak-load sharing and
provides backup facilities in the event of equipment failure, and (5)
managers may be able to react more rapidly to new developments, and

they may be able to *interact* with the system in order to seek solutions to unusual problems.

Unfortunately, however, some of the *possible disadvantages of resource sharing* at present are that (1) the reliability and cost of the data communications facilities used, and the cost and quality of the computing service received, may be disappointing in some cases, (2) input/output terminals are often rather slow and inefficient when compared with the equipment used with batch processing; and (3) provisions for protecting the confidentiality and integrity of user programs and data files maintained in online storage are generally ineffective against a skilled penetrator.

The quick-response-system concepts that we have now considered are improving the timeliness, effectiveness, and availability of information. In addition, many of these emerging quick-response systems are taking a *broader data-base approach* to the needs of organizations by attempting to provide better integration of information-producing activities. In the following section we shall briefly examine this trend.

**data-base systems**

Better integration of information-producing activities can lead to information that is more complete and relevant. Traditionally, data processing activities have been organized by departments and by applications. Many computers were originally installed to process a large-volume job. Other applications, treated independently, followed, but it soon became clear that this approach was unsatisfactory. Each application program typically operated on data files that had been created specifically for it, but since basic data were often defined and organized in different ways for each application, these facts could not be easily integrated with the data used in other programs run by the organization. Thus, data were often expensively duplicated (with an increase in the possibility of error) because it was impossible to combine these facts in meaningful ways. For example, a great deal of redundant data on a bank customer (e.g., home address, age, credit rating, etc.) might be contained in separate checking account, savings account, automobile loan, and home mortgage files. And integrating file data would be difficult because Charlie Brown, account number 1234, in one file became Charles M. Brown, account number 5678, in another.[19]

Dissatisfied with such conditions, some organizations began looking for ways to consolidate activities using a data-base approach. Although there are some differences of opinion about what constitutes a data-base

[19] A brief survey at one university showed that the data element "student name" was stored in 13 different files and in 5 different formats.

system, the most prevalent view is that such systems are designed around a centralized and integrated shared data file (or *data base*) that emphasizes the *independence* of programs and data. This data base is located in directly accessible online storage. Data transactions are introduced into the system only once. These data are now a neutral resource with respect to any particular program, and specific data elements are readily available as needed to all authorized applications and users of the data base. All data-base records that transactions affect may be updated at the time of input. Of course, the data-base concept requires that input data be commonly defined and consistently organized and presented throughout the business. And this requirement, in turn, calls for rigid input discipline; it also means that someone in the organization must be given the overall authority to standardize (and approve any necessary changes to) data with companywide usefulness.[20]

Why the interest in data-base systems? One reason is that a data-base system, combined with *data-base management software* that will organize, process, and present the necessary data elements, will enable managers to search, probe, and query file contents in order to extract answers to nonrecurring and unplanned questions that are not available in regular reports. These questions migh initially be vague and/or poorly defined, but managers can "browse" through the data base until they have the needed information. In short, the data-base management software will "manage" the stored data items and assemble the needed items from a common data base in response to the queries of managers who are not programming specialists. In the past, if managers wished to have a special report prepared using information stored in the data base, they would probably communicate their needs to a programmer, who, when time permitted, would write one or more programs to prepare the report. The availability of data-base management software,[21] however, offers the user a much faster alternative communications path (see Fig. 2-21).

Perhaps an illustration of the possible use of a data-base system is in order here. Suppose, for example, a personnel manager of a large multinational corporation has just received an urgent request to send an employee to a foreign country to effect an emergency repair of a hydraulic pump that the company stopped making 6 years ago. The employee needed must be a mechanical engineer, must have knowledge of the particular pump (and therefore, let us assume, must have been with

[20] Several authorities believe that although a closely integrated system might not now be planned, it is important for firms to begin now to achieve this standardization so that at a later time they will have the *option* of introducing broader systems.

[21] Data-base management software can be purchased or rented from a computer vendor or a software house. Among the most popular of the over 2,000 software packages now in use are IBM's "Information Management System," Informatics' "Mark IV," Honeywell's "Integrated Data Store," and CinCom Systems' "Total."

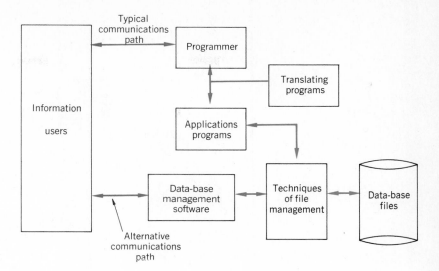

FIGURE 2-21

the corporation for at least 8 years), must be able to speak French, and must be willing to accept an overseas assignment. Obviously, there is not likely to be a report available that will have the names of engineers with just these characteristics. However, the records on each employee in the corporate personnel file stored in the data base do contain information on educational background, date of employment, work experience, and language capability. Although in the past it might have been necessary for the manager to request that a time-consuming program be prepared that would locate employees who match the requirements, with data-base management software it is now possible for the manager to use an online terminal to search through the personnel file and sort out the records of French-speaking mechanical engineers with 8 or more years of company experience. Armed with such information, obtained in a few minutes, the manager can then contact the employees named to fill the overseas assignment.

In addition to having direct access to data generated *within* the organization, a decision maker may also have *externally produced* data readily available for use. Data suppliers may make external data available to users in several ways. In the least-restrictive form, data may be *sold outright* by vendors on some medium such as magnetic tape, and buyers may then incorporate these facts in their data bases in almost any way they choose. Economic statistics and United States census data, for example, may be purchased on tapes from government agencies for use in this way. Some remote computing services offer financial and market-ing data on a *rental basis* to subscribers; users then access these facts from online terminals and pay for the resources used according to the

pricing scheme employed by the supplier.[22] Finally, a user may buy special reports prepared from a data base owned by an outside supplier.

In summary, as you have probably anticipated, *there are both benefits and limitations* at present *to the use of data-base systems.* Among the *possible benefits* are (1) fewer applications programs and lengthy regular reports containing reference data may be needed when managers can directly access the data base, (2) better integration (and less duplication) of data originating at different points is feasible, (3) faster preparation of information to support nonrecurring tasks and changing conditions is feasible, (4) savings in the cost of developing new applications, and in data entry and data storage costs, may be possible, and (5) fewer errors (and thus an increase in data integrity) may result when several records may be updated simultaneously.

[22] Several RCS suppliers, for example, offer a COMPUSTAT data bank that contains annual and quarterly sales and earnings figures on about 2,700 companies; and Data Resources, Inc., offers online data banks dealing with thousands of different economic variables from regional, national, and international sources. For further information on other data vendors, see Joel W. Darrow, "Financial Data Banks: A Guide for the Perplexed," *Computer Decisions,* January 1975, pp. 47–48ff.

But some of the *possible limitations* are (1) more complex and expensive hardware and software are needed; (2) a lengthy conversion period may be needed, higher personnel training costs may be incurred, and more sophisticated skills are needed by those responsible for the data-base system; (3) people may be reluctant to adapt to significant changes in established data processing procedures, and (4) sensitive data in online storage might find its way into unauthorized hands, and hardware or software failures might result in the destruction of vital data-base contents.

In this chapter we have now seen some of the revolutionary changes taking place in technology and in the uses of this technology for information processing purposes. As might be expected, however, rapid change is often accompanied by problems of adjustment.

**ADAPTING TO THE INFORMATION REVOLUTION**

The growth in the development and use of computers in the last decade has made it possible for computer-users to obtain more timely and more complete information. But this growth has brought adjustment problems which affect *organizations* and *individuals* and which must be dealt with in the future. Some of these issues are briefly outlined in the following sections; in later chapters several of them are considered in more detail.

### organizational issues

Computer usage may enhance the efficiency of an organization by providing information that can lead to better planning, decision making, and control of organizational activities. But, as we have seen, technological change may also be harmful as well as helpful in some cases. The following listing focuses on challenges and issues that are currently the subject of concerned study and debate:

1   *The challenges in information systems design.* As implied in earlier pages (and in Fig. 2-11), systems design is a complex and challenging task that has often produced disappointing internal results, a bad public image, and/or economic losses. Designers are currently grappling with the following questions: (*a*) Can a single data base be created to satisfy the differing information needs of administrators at different organizational levels? (*b*) Can decision makers with different job specialities share the same data base? (*c*) How can externally produced data be most effectively incorporated into the data base? (*d*) How can suitable flexibility and adaptability to human needs be built into the system? and (*e*) How can system design and implementation techniques be improved to curb the mounting dissatisfaction of users with time delays, cost overruns, and system inaccuracies?

2   *The systems security issue.* Lack of computer control and problems with the security of information systems have threatened the very exis-

tence of some organizations. Assets have been stolen through computer manipulation; trade secrets have been copied and sold to competitors; systems penetrators have repeatedly broken through the security controls and gained access to sensitive information; and fire, flood, accidents, and sabotage have destroyed irreplaceable computer files. And with many firms moving toward a distributed processing network environment, the number of potentially vulnerable locations in an organization may increase.

**3**  *Computer industry issues.* Some organizations that have tried to compete in the computer industry have gone bankrupt; other giant corporations have suffered large losses trying to compete with IBM (at this writing, several antitrust suits by private firms and the Antitrust Division of the Department of Justice are pending against this industry leader). And although there are many other large and successful competitors in the computer industry—e.g., the firms listed in Fig. 1-14—there are also some smaller organizations that produce equipment that can be used to replace IBM products without any necessary changes to the remaining IBM-supplied software or hardware in the installation. A possible competitive problem facing these "plug-compatible" manufacturers, however, is that future IBM equipment designs could convert some of the present IBM software into proprietary hardware devices that could be distributed throughout the system. Such a move could build a formidable roadblock for the plug-compatible supplier. The issue of computer industry competition is not likely to be resolved in the near future.[23] And another industry issue that has not been completely resolved is the problem of providing adequate protection for the programs supplied by software-producing organizations. Creating the software initially may have been very expensive, but once created it may be duplicated in a few minutes at very little cost. The legal means available to protect the interests of the software developer have not always been satisfactory (an attempt to patent software was killed by the Supreme Court in 1972).

**4**  *Data communications uncertainties.* What has been termed the "regulatory fight of the century" is brewing in Washington at this writing between the computer and telecommunications industries. This fight has developed as data processing and communications technologies have merged in the creation of distributed processing networks. Thus, there is now considerable uncertainty about the governmental regulatory status of organizations that offer *both* computing and communications services. An *unregulated* legal status currently applies to organizations whose communications services are only incidental to their computing services (e.g., an RCS supplier), and a *regulated* legal status currently applies to organizations whose data processing services are only incidental to the furnishing of communications (e.g., the Bell Telephone System of American Telephone and Telegraph Company or AT&T). But between these defined areas are a growing number of hybrid organizations that offer significant services in both communications and data processing. It is in

[23] For further information on this topic, see "More Tumult for the Computer Industry," *Business Week,* May 30, 1977, pp. 58–66.

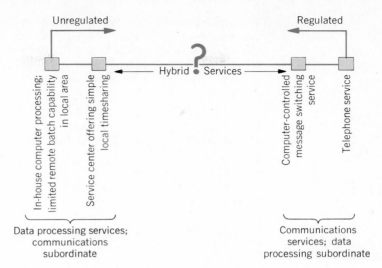

Unregulated                               Regulated

**?**

Hybrid ● Services

In-house computer processing;
limited remote batch capability
in local area

Service center offering simple
local timesharing

Computer-controlled
message switching
service

Telephone service

FIGURE 2-22

The uncertainty of governmental
regulation.

Data processing services;
communications
subordinate

Communications
services; data
processing subordinate

this middle area that the regulatory status is unclear (see Fig. 2-22). However, with the help of past rulings of the Federal Communications Commission (FCC), these hybrid organizations and specialized carriers have been creating communications networks and have been chipping away at the regulated monopoly AT&T has enjoyed in this area for decades. In one case, for example, the FCC decided to give a head start to qualified organizations that wished to establish domestic communications satellite systems that are well-suited for the transmission of high-speed computer data by ruling that AT&T could not directly compete in this field for a period of 3 years. One entry with enormous financial resources that will enter this satellite field to compete with AT&T is Satellite Business Systems (SBS), the property of IBM, Aetna Life and Casualty Company, and Communications Satellite Corporation. And with the SBS approach, customers can avoid the use of local telephone lines because they will have their own earth stations on rooftops that will be capable of two-way communication, via a satellite, with other earth stations in the system. Unwilling to accept adverse FCC decisions and the encroachment on its markets made possible by new technology, AT&T (which is also defending itself against antitrust charges made by the Department of Justice) has taken its case for limiting the amount of competition permitted to Congress. And Congress is considering redrafting the Federal Communications Act of 1934 in an attempt to bring it up to date with technological advances. In summary, then, the distinctions between data processing and data communications have become blurred, hundreds of billions of dollars are involved in the ultimate regulatory decisions, and two of the richest and most powerful organizations in the nation—AT&T and IBM—are squaring off for what may be the most significant industrial confrontation of this century. Virtually every business in the country will ultimately be affected.

5    *Organizational structure questions.* Will the structure of a particular organization be drastically altered in the future as a result of the introduction and use of advanced computer systems? Will the use of distributed processing networks create a need to realign work groups? Will existing departments need to be added to or eliminated? These are just a few of the organizational questions that many firms will face.

6    *Concentration of power issue.* Organizations with limited computing resources may have difficulty competing against those with much greater sophistication in the use of computers for planning and decision making.

7    *The electronic funds transfer systems (EFTS) issue.* The EFTS concept may reduce the need for cash and checks and may permit the future widespread nationwide transfer of "electronic money" between organizations and individuals. Although legal and regulatory confusion currently exists, large commercial banks anticipate using EFTS to improve efficiency and preserve their dominant position in the nation's payments system; some small banks fear that the widespread use of EFTS terminals by the large money-center banks to branch out into new markets will result in their being crowded out of their territories; other savings institutions see the use of EFTS both as a commercial bank competitive threat and as an opportunity to play a larger role in the funds transfer system; small retailers see EFTS as a means of reducing bad check losses; and large retailers may view the concept as a threat to their own credit-card business. In short, powerful organizations have a vital stake in the ways that computers are permitted to influence how "money" is transmitted and accounted for.

8    *The electronic mail issue.* One result of the anticipated development of new and improved data communications resources will likely be that sending mail electronically will not only be much faster, but it may also be much less expensive than using currently available U.S. Postal Service facilities. Communications satellites, for example, will provide users with facilities that will permit the transmission of messages and facsimile images to other users in a few seconds. The speed, flexibility, and cost of sending mail in the future is likely to create further regulatory problems. Will private data communications carriers be permitted to take over much of the mail activity in the nation at the expense of the Postal Service? Or will the Postal Service enter into, and be given some jurisdiction over, the delivery of electronic messages? Many observers believe that as EFTS begins to cut into the number of bills sent (and payment checks returned) by mail, and as the largest companies use satellites to connect major operating centers, the volume of mail delivered by, and the importance of, the Postal Service will decline significantly.

### individual issues

The computer has perhaps the greatest potential to improve the quality of life and well-being of individuals of any tool ever invented. Certainly, there are examples all around us of the many positive benefits that individuals have received from computer usage. Thus, it is probably unfortunate that most of the adjustment issues affecting people that are prominently discussed focus attention on the possible negative aspects of computer use. But there *are* some possible dangers, as the following listing briefly outlines:

1    *Employment concerns.* The greater efficiency made possible by computer usage in an organization may result in job obsolescence and displacement for some employees and disruptive changes in the compatible work groups in which others work.

2    *Systems-design issues.* Faulty systems design has sometimes led to an out-of-control situation in the *originating* and *recording* of input data. That is, data may be gathered about individuals when there is no real need to know; errors of omission and commission may distort the records kept on an individual, and these errors are difficult to correct; and documents and procedures designed for processing convenience may lead to individual confusion and bewilderment. Also, data must be in a standardized form for computer system *classification* and *sorting,* and faulty systems design has often led to a depersonalized treatment of individuals—i.e., the individual has been made to feel like an insignificant number rather than like a human being. Finally, computer system *miscalculations* have resulted in individuals being harassed and inconvenienced.

3    *Data security distress.* The lack of control over data security in a computer system has resulted in the destruction of an individual's records, and in both the accidental and intentional disclosure to unauthorized persons of confidential information of a very personal nature.

4    *Privacy peril.* Lack of control over data storage, retrieval, and communication has led to abuses of an individual's legitimate right to privacy—i.e., the right to keep private (or have kept on a confidential basis) those facts, beliefs, thoughts, and feelings that one does not wish to divulge publicly.

5    *Human self-understanding questions.* As developmental work continues, and as computer programs become better able to solve relatively ill-structured problems and perform tasks that have heretofore been assumed to require human intelligence, will we as individuals alter the way we look at ourselves? Will we think less highly of ourselves if we see computers "outthinking" us?

**SUMMARY**    Technological changes are occurring rapidly today and are creating new opportunities and problems. Rapid reductions in size and cost (and significant increases in speed and storage capacity) of computer hardware, combined with advances in computer software, are contributing to the development of quicker-responding and more integrated MIS concepts to meet the informational need of decision makers.

Quick-response systems utilizing online processing techniques enable managers to react more rapidly and to reduce waste in the use of economic resources. In some cases immediate updating of records from all online transaction-originating terminals is required, and so a real time system must be installed. *Timesharing* is a term that describes a quick-response system with a number of online, simultaneously usable terminals that are connected to the central processor. A *distributed processing network* is an extension of the original timesharing concept that may result in a large number of computers and significant software resources being shared among a large group of users.

Many quick-response systems are taking a broader approach to the needs of organizations by attempting to provide better integration of information-producing activities. *Data-base systems,* utilizing data-base management software, are being designed to help managers find answers to nonrecurring questions.

Difficult problems and challenges face individuals and organizations as they attempt to adapt to changes brought about by the information revolution. A few of these issues have been introduced in this chapter.

**REVIEW AND DISCUSSION QUESTIONS**

1    Discuss this statement: "The basic challenge to the leaders of today is to foresee and manage (and not be swept along by) the flood of changes facing their organizations, and to do this within a democratic framework, for the benefit of society."

2    Why does a technological change simultaneously create new opportunities and problems?

3    (**a**) What changes have taken place in computer hardware? (**b**) In computer software?

4    (**a**) What are the three basic software categories? (**b**) Discuss the developments in each of these categories.

5    What functions are performed by operating systems?

6    What is the purpose and orientation of an MIS? (Hint: see Fig. 2-11.)

7    (**a**) Why have quick-response systems been developed? (**b**) What are the advantages of such systems? (**c**) What is the distinction between online processing and real time processing?

8    (**a**) What is batch processing? (**b**) How does it differ from online processing? (**c**) What are the advantages and disadvantages of batch processing?

9    "Online processing and direct access to records require unique hardware and software." Discuss this statement.

10    (**a**) What is meant by *timesharing?* (**b**) What is a *distributed processing network?* (**c**) What do you think the long-term implications of distributed computer networks will be? (**d**) What are the advantages and limitations of resource sharing?

11    Identify and discuss the data-base approach to information systems design.

**12** (**a**) Will data-base management software have any effect on applications programmers? (**b**) Defend your answer to 12(**a**).

**13** "Difficult problems and challenges face individuals and organizations as they attempt to adapt to changes brought about by the information revolution." Discuss this statement from the viewpoint of (**a**) a systems designer, (**b**) a law enforcement officer, (**c**) a civil liberties advocate, (**d**) a spy or saboteur, (**e**) a junior business executive, (**f**) a college student, (**g**) a competitor of IBM, (**h**) a telephone company executive, (**i**) a bookkeeping machine operator, (**j**) an individual with social security number 350-26-5840, (**k**) a politician, and (**l**) a postal worker.

## SELECTED REFERENCES

In addition to the sources cited in the chapter footnotes, the following references may also be of interest:

Benton, John B.: "Electronic Funds Transfer: Pitfalls and Payoffs," *Harvard Business Review,* July-August 1977, pp. 16–17ff.

Canning, Richard G.: "Making Use of Remote Computing Services," *EDP Analyzer,* September 1977, pp. 1–11.

"Communications Dog Fight," *Dun's Review,* June 1977, pp. 48ff.

Kelley, Neil D.: "Timesharing: A Business of Specialities," *Infosystems,* October 1977, pp. 58ff.

Miller, Frederick W.: " Electronic Mail Comes of Age," *Infosystems,* November 1977, pp. 56ff.

Myers, Ware: "Key Developments in Computer Technology: A Survey," *Computer,* November 1976, pp. 48–75.

"New Trends in Data Processing," *Dun's Review,* July 1977, pp. 93ff.

Nolan, Richard L.: "Computer Data Bases: The Future Is Now," *Harvard Business Review,* September-October 1973, pp. 98–114.

The chapters in Part I have now given you a background for the study of computer concepts. One of the objectives of this book is to give you an orientation to computers (what they are, what they can and cannot do, and how they operate). The chapters in Parts II and III are aimed at this objective. Computer capabilities and limitations are examined and basic *hardware* topics are presented in the chapters of this Part; the process involved in developing *software and information systems* to solve business problems is considered in the chapters of Part III.

The chapters included in Part II are:

# BASIC COMPUTER CONCEPTS

# introduction to computers 3

LEARNING OBJECTIVES   After studying this chapter and considering the discussion questions, you should be able to: ☐ Explain the various ways in which computers may be classified ☐ Identify and discuss some of the important capabilities of computers ☐ Identify and discuss some of the important limitations of computers ☐ Outline the five basic functions performed by computers

CHAPTER OUTLINE

Computer classifications: Analog and Digital Computers / Special-purpose and General-purpose Computers / Scientific and Business Applications

Computer capabilities

Computer limitations

Experiments in artificial intelligence

Functional organization of computers: Input / Storage / Arithmetic-Logic / Control / Output / Extensive Variations Possible

Summary

Review and discussion questions

Selected references

**D**ictionaries assign to the word *awful* such meanings as "monstrous, filling with awe, inspiring dread, and commanding solemn wonder or reverential fear." In recent years you may have found support for each of these meanings—i.e., you may have concluded that "computers are awful"—from computer-related articles and television shows that you have read and watched. Perhaps in one article the computer was pictured as having *human* characteristics, e.g., as being a device that can play checkers and form verbal answers to inquiries. Or perhaps in another account the computer was presented as *subhuman;* stupid errors in billing, for example, could have been cited, such as the case of the woman who was charged for the purchase of 4,000 new tires instead of 4. And at the opposite extreme, the computer may have been placed in a *superhuman* role. In an article in *Smithsonian,* for example, it is estimated that in about the year 1986 a self-programming machine will be developed that will usher in a "new form of intelligent life" on this planet—a form of intelligence similar to HAL, the superhuman computer which was featured in the science fiction film *2001: A Space Odyssey.*[1] Finally, you may have watched a television program that depicted the computer as an *inhuman* instrument that could be used to invade your privacy or to make heartless decisions affecting you without regard for your feelings.

Such contradictory characterizations of computers and their uses may have left you with feelings of excitement, frustration, amazement, awe, or even fear. Although there may be elements of truth in each of these characterizations, they seldom lead to the understanding of computer capabilities and limitations that you will need in the future. Thus, in the pages of this chapter we shall consider (1) the *classes* of computers, (2) their *capabilities,* (3) their *limitations,* (4) their *learning* ability, and (5) their *functional organization.*

## COMPUTER CLASSIFICATIONS

Organizations sometimes offer tours of their facilities to interested parties. Let us assume that you are in a group visiting an insurance company. In the course of your visit, the tour guide asks you to identify the equipment located in a large room. Because you are an intelligent person, you respond that this is the firm's computer. The guide replies, "Yes, this is our medium-sized, fourth-generation, electronic, stored program, digital (a gasp for breath), general-purpose computer used for business purposes."

You recognize what the guide meant by the terms *medium-sized, fourth generation, electronic,* and *stored program.* Computers are some-

[1] See Gregory Benford and David Book, "Promise-Child in the Land of the Humans," *Smithsonian,* April 1971, pp. 58–65.

times classified by size into large, medium, small, mini, and micro categories on the basis of computing power and cost. The fourth-generation age classification is arbitrary and may refer to equipment produced in the 1970s. The stored program concept refers to the ability of the machine to store internally a list of sequenced instructions that will guide it automatically through a series of operations leading to a completion of the task. We will come back to this concept in later chapters.

But what about the other classifying terms used by the guide—what do *digital, general-purpose,* and *business purposes* mean? Let us look at each of these items.

### analog and digital computers

There are two broad classes of computing devices—the analog and the digital. The *analog* machine does not compute directly with numbers; rather, it measures continuous physical magnitudes (e.g., pressure, temperature, voltage, current, shaft rotations, length), which represent, or are *analogous* to, the numbers under consideration. The service station gasoline pump, for example, may contain an analog computer that converts the flow of pumped fuel into two measurements—the price of the delivered gas to the nearest penny and the quantity of pumped fuel to the nearest tenth or hundredth of a gallon. Another example of an analog device is the automobile speedometer which converts drive-shaft rotational motion into a numerical indication by the speedometer pointer.

Analog computers are used for scientific, engineering, and process-control purposes. Because they deal with quantities that are continuously variable, they give only approximate results. The speedometer pointer, for example, might give a reading of 45 miles per hour. But if the pointer were lengthened and sharpened, if the speedometer were calibrated more precisely, and if the cable were given closer attention, the reading might then be 44 miles per hour. Further refinements might give a reading of 44.5 miles per hour. A well-known soap product has claimed for years to be "99 and 44/100 percent pure." Under the best circumstances, an analog computer can achieve a somewhat higher degree of precision than this figure. But in a problem involving $1 million, an analog device might give answers only to the nearest hundred or thousand dollars.

The *digital* computer operates by *counting* numbers. It operates directly on numbers expressed as digits in the familiar decimal system or some other numbering system. The ancient shepherd, it will be recalled, used stones to represent sheep, and these were counted one by one to determine the total number of sheep in the flock. Nothing was measured as an analogous representation of the number of sheep; they were counted directly, and their total was exact. Stones have been replaced by adding machines, desk calculators, and digital computers, but all employ the same counting rules we learned in grade school.

Digital computation results in greater accuracy. While analog computers may, under ideal conditions, be accurate to within 0.1 percent of the correct value, digital computers can obtain whatever degree of accuracy is required simply by adding *places* to the right of the reference or decimal point. Every youngster who has worked arithmetic problems dealing with circles knows that pi ($\pi$) has a value of 3.1416. Actually, however, the value is 3.14159. . . . In 1959, a digital computer worked the value of $\pi$ out to 10,000 decimal places in a short period of time![2]

Digital computers, unlike analog machines, are used for both business data processing and scientific purposes. In special situations (e.g., to simulate a guided missile system or a new aircraft design), desirable features of analog and digital machines have been combined to create a *hybrid* computer. There are also digital computer systems which accept and convert analog data from numerous scientific instruments into digital form for processing (see Fig. 3-1).

### special-purpose and general-purpose computers

Digital computers may be produced for either special or general uses. A *special-purpose* computer, as the name implies, is designed to perform

[2] Alas, later more accurate work showed that this computer had made an error in the 7,480th decimal place.

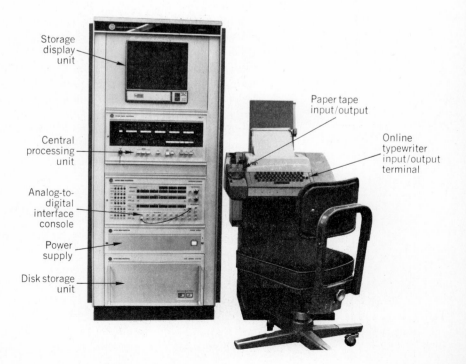

Storage
display
unit

Paper tape
input/output

Online
typewriter
input/output
terminal

Central
processing
unit

Analog-to-
digital
interface
console

Power
supply

Disk storage
unit

FIGURE 3-1

(Courtesy Varian Data Machines).

one specific task. The program of instructions is built into, or permanently stored in, the machine. Specialization results in the given task being performed very quickly and efficiently. A disadvantage, however, is that the machine lacks versatility; it is inflexible and cannot be easily used to perform other operations. Special-purpose computers designed for the sole purpose of solving complex navigational problems are installed aboard our atomic submarines, but they could not be used for other purposes unless their circuits were redesigned. In the past, the cost of hardware made it relatively expensive to dedicate a computer to a single application; in the future, millions of inexpensive microcomputers will be routinely dedicated to processing specialized applications—e.g., there will likely be one in every car to monitor and control fuel, ignition, and other systems; and special-purpose microcomputers will replace electro-mechanical timing and control devices in most large household appliances.

A *general-purpose* computer is one that has the ability to store *different* programs of instructions and thus to perform a variety of operations. In short, the stored program concept makes the machine a general-purpose device—one that has the versatility to make possible the processing of a payroll one minute and an inventory control application the next. New programs can be prepared, and old programs can be changed or dropped. Because it is designed to do a wide variety of jobs rather than perform a specific activity, the general-purpose machine typically compromises certain aspects of speed and efficiency—a small enough price to pay in many cases for the advantage of flexibility.

© INFOSYSTEMS

"This is really a general purpose computer. Features memory allocation, correction, arithmetic processor, bottle-opener..."

## scientific and business applications

A general-purpose central processor is used for both scientific and business applications. What is the difference between these types of applications? What a coincidence that you should ask. . . .

*Scientific processing applications*   A research laboratory may wish to analyze and evaluate a product formula involving 3 variables and 15 terms (which results in 45 different values for each variable). The computer *input* would be the 15-term formula, the 135 values for the 3 variables, and the set of instructions to be followed in processing. The input is thus quite small. The *processing* involved, however, may well consist of hundreds of thousands of different computations—computations that might represent many months of labor if performed by other methods. The *output* necessary for a problem of this type may consist of a few typed lines giving a single evaluation or a few alternatives.

In short, the volume of input/output in scientific data processing is relatively small, and the speed with which these operations are performed is usually not too important. Computational speed, on the other

| Processing Characteristics | Scientific Applications | Business Applications |
|---|---|---|
| Input/output volume | Low | Very high |
| Input/output speed | Relatively unimportant | Very important |
| Ratio of computations to input | Very high | Low |
| Computation speed | Very important | Relatively unimportant |
| Storage requirements | Modest | High |

FIGURE 3-2

hand, is a critical consideration since the bulk of the total processing job involves complex calculation. Storage capacity need only be sufficient to hold instructions, input data, and intermediate and final computational results.

Business processing applications    In contrast to scientifically oriented applications, business tasks generally require faster input and output of data and larger storage capacity. An examination of a typical business application will usually show that the volume of data input and information output is quite large. For example, the billing operation associated with the credit card purchases of an oil company's products involves thousands of customers and hundreds of thousands of sales transactions each month. Each transaction represents input data, while each customer represents an output statement. The running time required by the computer to complete such a business application is usually determined by tbe input/output speeds obtainable.

Computational speed is less critical in business applications because (1) arithmetic operations performed on each input record represent a relatively small proportion of the total job and (2) the internal arithmetic speed of the slowest computer is frequently much greater than the speed of input/output devices.

To summarize (see Fig. 3-2), scientific and business applications typically differ with respect to (1) input/output volume, (2) input/output speed needed, (3) amount of computation, (4) importance of computational speed, and (5) storage requirements. Certain software and hardware control features, together with a wide range of available peripheral input/output and storage devices, permit most modern central processors to flexibly and efficiently serve both types of applications.

The stored program, digital, general-purpose computer used for business purposes (henceforth called *computer* for apparent reasons) possesses certain capabilities, which are summarized in the next section.

## COMPUTER CAPABILITIES

A computer designed to compute
a couple's rapport or dispute,
typed "Yes!" unashamed

when the young lady named
it in her paternity suit.

Gloria Maxson

Although many writers (and cartoonists) have pictured computer systems as having human or superhuman traits, such views tend to exaggerate certain computer capabilities. Yet it is clear that the computer is a powerful *tool* for extending people's brainpower. Peter Drucker has pointed out that human beings have developed two types of tools: (1) those that add to their capabilities and enable them to do something that they otherwise could *not* do (e.g., the airplane) and (2) those that multiply their capacity to do that which they are *already capable* of doing (e.g., the hammer).

The computer falls into the latter category. It is an intelligence amplifier. Carl Hammer, Director of Computer Sciences for UNIVAC, notes that today's computers have built into our society a mind-amplifying factor of over 2,000 to 1; i.e., behind every man, woman, and child in the United States there stands the power of over 2,000 human data processors. Computers can enlarge brainpower because of the properties presented below. These properties have led to the human or superhuman images.

1    *The ability to provide new time dimensions.* The machine works one step at a time; it adds and subtracts numbers; it multiplies and divides

". . . and if any of you have a problem, please remember that my input keyboard is always open."

© DATAMATION ®

numbers (in most cases merely a repetitive process of addition and subtraction); and it can be designed or programmed to perform other mathematical operations such as finding a square root. There is nothing profound in these operations—even the author can perform them! What is significant, as we know, is the speed with which the machine functions. Thus, people are freed from calculations to use their time more creatively. Their time dimension has been broadened; they can obtain now information that could not have been produced at all a few years ago or that could not have been produced in time to be of any value. Karl Gauss, a German mathematician, at a young age had ideas that might have reshaped the study of mathematics in his time. Twenty years of his life were spent, however, in calculating the orbits of various heavenly objects. Were Gauss alive today, he could duplicate his calculations on a computer in a few hours and then be free to follow more creative pursuits. Similarly, the 2 years spent by John Adams in the 1840s in laboriously calculating the position of the planet Neptune could now be duplicated (with greater accuracy) by a computer in a little over a minute. Finally, a more recent illustration will serve to conclude this discussion of computer speed. John Kemeny of Dartmouth College has estimated that the calculations it took a year to complete working around the clock at the atomic laboratories at Los Alamos in 1945 could be done in one afternoon by an undergraduate student while sharing the computer's time with 30 others.

2    *The ability to perform certain logic operations.* Computers are *symbol manipulators*—i.e., they can manipulate in logical ways letters, numbers, words, sentences, mathematical expressions and other symbols to which people have given meaning. For example, when two values represented by the symbols $A$ and $B$ are compared, there are only three possible outcomes: (1) $A$ is *equal to B* $(A = B)$; (2) $A$ is *greater than B* $(A > B)$; or (3) $A$ is *less than B* $(A < B)$.[3] The computer is able to perform a simple comparison and then, depending on the result, follow one of three *predetermined branches,* or courses of action, in the completion of that portion of its work (see Fig. 3-3). Thus, the computer has made a "decision" by choosing between alternative possible courses of action. Actually, however, it might be more appropriate to say that the computer has *followed* decisions made earlier by the programmer. But this simple ability to compare is an important computer property because more sophisticated questions can be answered by using combinations of comparison decisions. For example, if the data in a large listing such as a directory or a table have been organized in some logical order (alphabetically or in numerical sequence), the computer can be programmed to search for a specific data item by looking first at the middle item in the listing. If, as a result of a comparison, the desired item is alphabetically or numerically less than this middle item, the last half of the listing can be quickly eliminated. Thus, this one comparison has cut the search problem in half. An additional comparison using the middle item of the

FIGURE 3-3

[3] The possible outcomes form what logicians forbiddingly call the *law of trichotomy.* Computers also compare numbers to see whether they are positive, negative, or equal to zero.

remaining half of the listing can now be made, and this *binary search* procedure can be continued until the desired item is either located or shown to be missing from the listing. Another illustration of the computer's ability to perform logic operations concerns the "four-color conjecture" problem. For more than a century, mathematicians had been trying to prove that no more than four colors are needed to shade any map so that no adjoining nations are represented by the same color. Finally, two University of Illinois mathematicians examined, in mathematical terms, every imaginable map that could possibly be drawn. They then fed these possible map configurations into a computer to determine if all maps could indeed be drawn with only four colors. The computer "wrestled with the question for some 1,200 hours, during which it made some 10 billion separately logical decisions. Finally, the machine replied yes, and the four-color conjecture turned from theory into fact."[4]

**3**    *The ability to store and retrieve information.* We know that the computer places in internal storage both facts and instructions. The ease with which instruction programs can be changed gives the computer great flexibility. The *access time* required for information to be recalled from internal storage and be available for use is measured in microseconds or more precise units. Few machines that we use have this stored program ability—the instructions generally reside in the human mind and thus are outside the machine. Instructions and data are in a coded form that the machine has been designed to accept. The machine is also designed to perform automatically and in sequence certain operations on the data (add, write, move, store, halt) called for by the instructions. The number of operations that can be performed varies among computer models. The stored program may, as we have just seen, allow the computer to select a branch of instructions to follow from several alternative sequences. The program may also allow the computer to *repeat* or *modify* instructions as required. Computers communicate with human operators by using input and output devices, and they communicate with other machines.

**4**    *The ability to control error.* It is estimated that you or I would make one error in every 500 to 1,000 operations with a desk calculator. A computer, on the other hand, can perform hundreds of thousands of arithmetic operations every second and can run errorless for hours and days at a time. Computers also have the ability to check their own work. By a method known as *parity checking,* computers check on data when they enter storage, when they are moved internally, and when they leave in the form of output. Each character (e.g., number or letter) fed into the computer is represented in a coded form by several binary digits (0s and 1s) called *bits,* just as each number or letter in a punched card is represented by a code. The parity check performed by the computer involves the examination of each character's code to determine whether bits have been added or lost by mistake. More will be said about parity checking in a later chapter.

[4] "Eureka!" *Time,* Sept. 20, 1976, p. 88. This example illustrates computer capabilities both in providing new time dimensions and in performing logic operations. It also shows some of the characteristics of scientific processing applications.

It should not be assumed, however, that computers have unlimited capabilities or that they are free of error. They do have their limitations, and they have been involved in some classic mistakes.

## COMPUTER LIMITATIONS

"I am very annoyed to find out that you have branded my son illiterate. This is a dirty lie as I was married a week before he was born."

"I am forwarding my marriage certificate and 5 children, one of which is a mistake as you can see."

"You have changed my little boy to a girl. Will this make a difference?"

"My husband got his project cut off and I haven't had any relief since. . . ."

From letters to a computer-using Welfare Department

A publishing company customer received a computer-produced invoice requesting that he pay his bill in the amount of "W-2.C." The customer promptly forwarded his check for W-2.C as directed with a note saying, "Out here in the sticks, we dig this crazy new currency you folks have invented." Billing operations have produced other computer goofs. For example, an insurance company kept sending a policy holder a bill for $0.00 and demanding payment, and in Fort Worth, Texas, a man was surprised some months ago to receive a brief, rather cool, letter from an oil company saying that his account was past due by $34.32. The man can be excused his surprise because he had never received a credit card from any oil company. Six weeks passed before the error was discovered, during which time the man kept protesting and the form letters (getting less and less cordial) kept coming in. Of course, it is not always the individual who is victimized. In another case, an aircraft manufacturer sent a supplier a computer-prepared check for $3,000,000 to settle a $3,000 bill. (The supplier could not resist then going to the sales office of the manufacturer and offering to buy an expensive airplane for cash!)

Or consider the case of the genteel New York City man who one month received an unsolicited Playboy Club key and who for months thereafter received bills for $7.50 from Playboy's computer. An attorney's letter was required to get the rabbit off his back. These victims, along with the Phoenix man who was treated for pneumonia and charged for the use of the nursery and the delivery room, perhaps felt as did another victim who said: "The computer is a complete revolution in the ways of doing business, . . . and as in any revolution some innocent people always get slaughtered."

That such stories are carried in newspapers is indication enough that they occur only infrequently. Perhaps in most cases the errors may be traced to humans who failed to give proper attention to the following limitations:

**1**    *Application programs must always be prepared.* The machine does what it is programmed to do and *nothing else.* It can only operate on data; i.e., it can accept data, process it, and communicate results, but it cannot directly perform physical activities such as bending metal. (The processed information may be used, however, to control metal-bending machines.) Furthermore, a program may *seem* to be flawless and operate satisfactorily for some months and then produce nonsense (a bill for $0.00, for instance) because some rare combination of events has presented the computer with a situation (a) for which there is no programmed course of action or (b) where the course of action provided by the programmer contains an error that is just being discovered. Of course, a truly flawless program, supplied with incorrect data, may also produce nonsense. And once incorrect facts are entered into a computer system they are usually not as easy to purge as is the case when manual methods are used.

**2**    *Applications must be able to be quantified and dealt with logically.* The computer will not be of much help to people in areas where *qualitative* considerations are important. It will not, for example, tell you how to "get rich quick" in the stock market; it will not improve much on random selection in arranging a date between two customers of a computer dating service (both may have outrageous personalities, and both may have been less than candid in filling out computer input forms); and it may not signal a change in an economic trend until after the fact. Thus, it will not tell a manager whether or not a new product will be successful if marketed. The ultimate market decision is of a qualitative nature

TO ERR IS HUMAN.
TO REALLY GOOF –
USE A COMPUTER.

©INFOSYSTEMS

because it is involved with future social, political, technological, and economic events; and sales volume levels are thus impossible to predict with certainty. However, the computer will *by simulation* let a manager know how a new product will fare under *assumed* price, cost, and sales volume conditions. The computer, in short, is limited to those applications that may be expressed in the form of an *algorithm;* i.e., the application must consist of a finite number of steps leading to a precisely defined goal, and each step must be specifically and *clearly defined.* Thus, we might say that an algorithm operates on data to produce information. If the steps in the solution of the problem cannot be precisely written down, the application cannot be performed on today's commercial computers. And even if the steps can be defined by a finite set of rules that a computer could follow, there are still some tasks whose execution might take millions or even billions of years on a giant computer. As Joseph Weizenbaum has observed, a program could be written "to try every legal move in a certain chess situation; for each move try every possible response; for each response try its response; and so on until the computer has found a move which, if suitably pursued, would guarantee it a win. Such a program would surely be finite, but the length of time required by a computer to execute it would be unimaginably large. In principle, then, a computer could carry out such behavior; in fact, it cannot."[5]

**3**  *Applications must weigh resources.* Merely because a computer can be programmed to do a job does not always mean that it *should.* Writing programs, although less tedious than in the past because of developments in software, is still a time-consuming and expensive human operation. Thus, nonrecurring tasks or jobs that are seldom processed are often not efficient areas for computer application at the present time. In business data processing, it is usually most economical to prepare programs for large-volume, repetitive operations that will be used many times and that promise fast returns on the time invested in program preparations.[6]

**EXPERIMENTS IN ARTIFICIAL INTELLIGENCE**

Although the superhuman computers found in science fiction do not exist, science fiction has a way of becoming science fact. Research efforts and experiments are currently being conducted in the use of computers to solve relatively ill-structured problems. These research efforts, which are sometimes classified under the heading of *artificial intelligence,* and which are combining concepts found in disciplines such as psychology, linguistics, and computer science, are aimed at learning how to prepare programs (or construct systems) that can do tasks that have never been

---

[5] Joseph Weizenbaum, "The Last Dream," *Across the Board,* July 1977, p. 39. The term *combinatorial explosion* is given to this type of problem where a finite number of instructions generates an impossibly large number of computer operations.

[6] In engineering and scientific computing, the importance of a nonrecurring task often warrants the necessary investment in programming time. An example might be the engineering planning and construction scheduling, by computer, of a single multimillion-dollar office building.

done automatically before and that have usually been assumed to require human intelligence. For example, computers have been programmed to play checkers and chess and to modify their programs on the basis of success and failure with moves used in the past against human opponents. In one checkers-playing program, the computer has continually improved its game to the point where it regularly defeats the author of the program. Thus, the machine has "learned" what not to do through trial and error.

Computers have also been programmed to prove mathematical theorems and compose music, but thus far such research activities are limited and involve "thinking" on the part of the machine in a most limited sense.

Much has been written in the past few years pro and con about the question of whether computers can be programmed to "think" and "learn." Most of the controversy probably stems from (1) a lack of understanding about the processes involved in human thinking and learning and (2) the absence of acceptable definitions of such words as *think* and *learn*.

One test—a game—to determine whether a computer might be considered to possess intelligence and the ability to think was proposed by Alan Turing, a British mathematician. Participants in the game would be two respondents—a machine and a human—and a human interrogator who tries to determine which of the unseen respondents is the human. In answering questions posed by the interrogator (communications terminals are used), the machine tries to deceive while the human respondent tries to convince the interrogator of his or her true identity. Intelligence and the ability to think would, according to "Turing's Test," be demonstrated by the machine's success in fooling the interrogator. Using this test, Turing anticipated that machines with thinking ability would exist by the year 2000.[7]

*Heuristic*[8] is a word that means *serving to discover*. It is used to describe the judgmental, or *common sense*, part of problem solving. That is, it describes that part of problem solving which deals with the definition of the problem, the selection of reasonable strategies to be followed (which may or may not lead to optimum solutions), and the formulation of hypotheses and hunches. Human beings are *far superior* to the computer in the heuristic area of intellectual work. As people's thinking and learning processes become better understood, however, it may be possible to develop new programs and machines with improved heuristic abilities. Certainly, some very able researchers are working toward this

"I appreciate its almost-human thinking capabilities. But I do wish it would stop saying, 'Play it again, Sam.'"

---

[7] Of course, many do not agree with this concept of thinking. As computer scientist Paul Armer has facetiously observed, computers cannot think because people keep redefining thinking to be a process that is just beyond whatever the current ability of the computer happens to be.

[8] Pronounced *hew-ris'tik*.

end. The role of the computer will continue to be that of an intelligence amplifier in an alliance with humanity. The potential of such an alliance, although not unlimited, cannot be restricted in any way that we can now anticipate.[9]

**FUNCTIONAL ORGANIZATION OF COMPUTERS**

The computer solves problems and produces information in much the same way that you do. Let us illustrate this fact by first making a most disagreeable assumption: that in the near future you will have to take a written examination on the material covered in the first few chapters of an accounting book. For the past few days you have been reading the text, trying to catch up on your homework problems, and listening to your professor's lectures. You have written several pages of notes and have memorized various facts, concepts, and procedures. Finally, the examination period arrives, and you begin to work the test problems. Transactions are noted, and proper (?) accounts receive debits and credits. Procedures are followed, you hope, in the correct order. As time runs out, you turn your paper in to the professor and leave, resolving to pay somewhat closer attention to what he or she has to say in the future.

Five functions were performed in the above illustration (see Fig. 3-4). These functions are:

1 *Input*. The input function involves the receipt of facts that can be used. You received data from your accounting textbook and from your professor.

2 *Storage*. Facts received must be stored until they are needed. Your notebook (offline storage) and your brain (online storage) were used to store accounting information and the procedures to use for solving problems.

3 *Calculation*. On your test you performed the arithmetic operations of addition, subtraction, multiplication, and division, either manually or with the help of a calculator.

4 *Control*. On the exam it was necessary to follow certain procedures in the proper order, or sequence; i.e., you could not total an account until all transactions had been recorded, and you did not record the last transaction of the month first because it might have been based on transactions occurring earlier in the month. Control, then, simply means doing things in the correct sequence.

5 *Output*. Your finished test was the output—the result of your data processing operations. It will provide your professor with part of the information needed to arrive at a decision about your final grade.

All computer installations perform these five functions. Figure 3-5 illustrates the *functional* organization of a computer. Let us briefly examine each part of this diagram.

[9] For more information on the fascinating subject of artificial intelligence, see the March-April 1976 issue of *Creative Computing*.

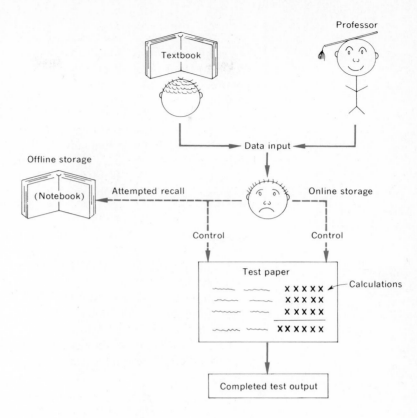

FIGURE 3-4

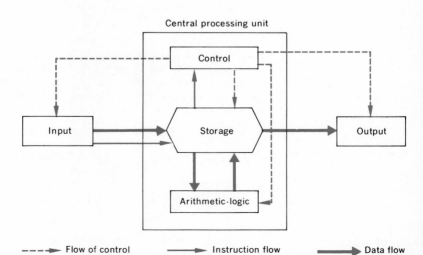

FIGURE 3-5

Computer functional organization.          - - - - ► Flow of control          —————► Instruction flow          ══════► Data flow

### input

Computers, obviously, must also receive facts to solve problems. Data and instructions must be put into the computer system in a form that it can use. There are a number of devices that will perform this input function, as we shall see in the following chapter. They may allow direct human/machine communication without the necessity of an input medium (e.g., the keyboard of a timesharing remote station), or they may present information that typically has been produced offline in batches on an input medium (e.g., punched cards). Regardless of the type of device used, they are all instruments of interpretation and communication between people and the machine.

### storage

The heart of any computer installation is the central processing unit (CPU). Within CPUs of all sizes are generally located storage, control, and arithmetic-logic units (see Fig. 3-6). It is this central processor that makes comparisons, performs calculations, and selects, interprets, and controls the execution of instructions.

The storage section of the central processor is used for *four purposes,* three of which relate to the data being processed. First, data are fed into

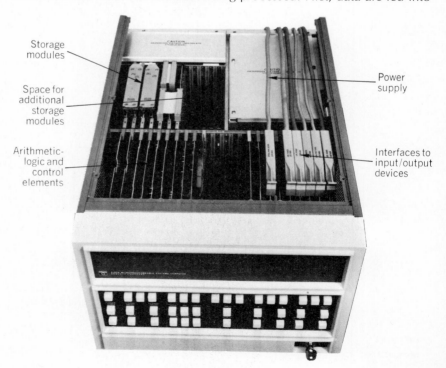

Storage modules

Space for additional storage modules

Arithmetic-logic and control elements

Power supply

Interfaces to input/output devices

FIGURE 3-6

Minisized CPU (courtesy Hewlett-Packard Company).

the storage area where they are held until ready to be processed. Second, additional storage space is used to hold data being processed and the intermediate results of such processing. Third, the storage unit holds the finished product of the processing operations until it can be released in the form of output information. Fourth, in addition to these data-related purposes, the storage unit also holds the program instructions until they are needed.

### arithmetic-logic

All calculations are performed and all comparisons (decisions) are made in the arithmetic-logic section of the central processor. Data flow between this section and the storage unit during processing operations; i.e., data are received from storage, manipulated, and returned to storage. No processing is performed in the storage section. The number of arithmetic and logic operations that can be performed is determined by the engineering design of the machine.

To briefly summarize, data are fed into the storage unit from the input devices. Once in storage, they are held and transferred as needed to the arithmetic-logic unit, where processing takes place. Data may move from storage to the arithmetic-logic unit and back again to storage many times before the processing is finished. Once completed, the information is released from the central processor to the output device.

### control

How does the input unit know when to feed data into storage? How does the arithmetic-logic unit obtain the needed data from storage, and how does it know what should be done with them once they are received? And how is the output unit able to obtain finished information instead of raw data from storage? It is by selecting, interpreting, and executing the program instructions that the control unit of the central processor is able to maintain order and direct the operation of the entire installation. It thus acts as a central nervous system for the component parts of the computer. Instructions are *selected* and fed in sequence into the control unit from storage; there they are *interpreted;* and from there signals are sent to *other* machine units to *execute* program steps. The control unit itself does not perform actual processing operations on the data.

### output

Output devices, like input units, are instruments of interpretation and communication between people and machine. They take information in machine-coded form and convert it typically into a form that can be used (1) by humans (e.g., a printed report) or (2) as machine input in another processing operation (e.g., magnetic tape). In the following chapter we shall take a closer look at several output devices.

### extensive variations possible

All computer systems are similar in that they perform the basic functions just described. However, computers vary widely in their external configurations. Some computers are housed in three boxes, as implied in Fig. 3-5; some are in a single cabinet; some have multiple units for the input and output functions; some *distribute* parts of the storage and control functions to equipment peripheral to the CPU; and some use a single cabinet to house both input and output functions. Figure 3-7 illustrates some of the possible machine combinations. (The input/output and other peripheral hardware and media shown will be surveyed in the next two chapters; a closer look at the CPU will be the subject of Chapter 6.) The boxes labeled "channels" in Fig. 3-7 require a brief explanation here.

A *channel* consists of hardware that, along with other associated monitoring and connecting elements, controls and provides the path for the movement of data between relatively slow input/output (I/O) devices, on the one hand, and high-speed central processor primary storage, on the other. Because of the differences in operating speeds, the CPU would be idle much of the time if it had to hold up processing during the periods that input was being received and output was being produced. Fortunately, most computers built since the mid-1960s have features that make it possible to *overlap* input, processing, and output operations in order to make more efficient use of computing resources. Once the channel has received appropriate instruction signals from the central processor, it can operate independently and without supervision while the CPU is engaged in performing computations. For example, at the same time that the CPU is processing one group of records, one channel can be receiving another group for subsequent processing while a second channel can be supplying processed information to the appropriate output device. A channel may be a separate, small, special-purpose control computer located near the CPU, or it may be a physical part of the CPU which is accessible to both I/O devices and other CPU elements.

In addition to channels, high-speed storage elements called *buffers* also play an important role in overlapped processing. As shown in Fig. 3-8a, data from input devices are fed under channel control into input buffer storage (which may be located in peripheral devices or may be a reserved section of the CPU primary storage). This input buffer has an important characteristic: it can accept data at slow input speeds and release them at electronic speeds. (The reverse is true of the output buffer.) The first input record is entered into the buffer and then trans-

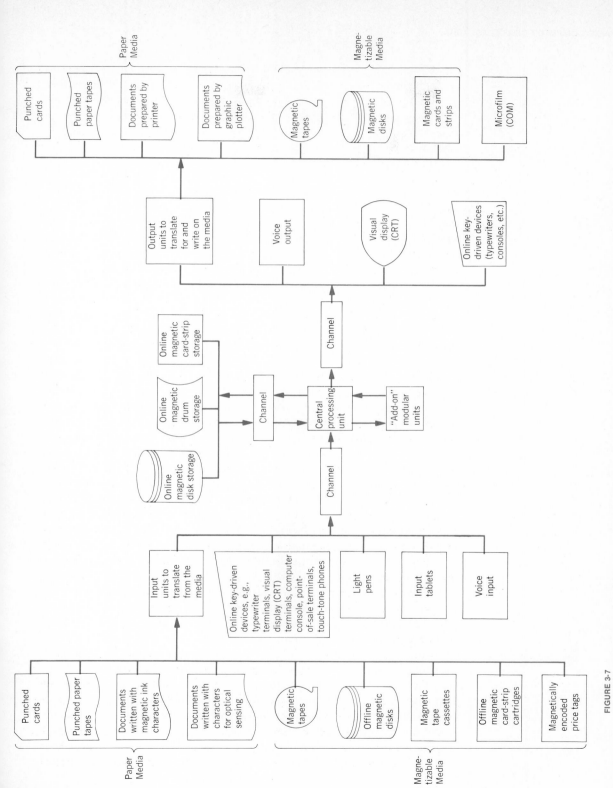

**FIGURE 3-7**

Input-output hardware and media.

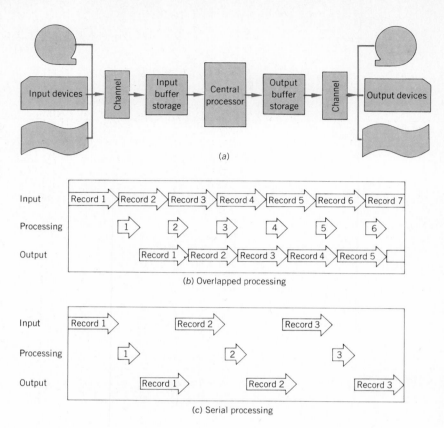

(a)

(b) Overlapped processing

(c) Serial processing

FIGURE 3-8

ferred, under program control, to the main storage unit where processing begins immediately. While the first record is being processed, the input unit is automatically reading a second record into buffer storage (Fig. 3-8b). The processed information for the first record is transferred under program control to the output buffer and then, under channel control, to an output device where the writing operation begins. As soon as the first record is released, the program instructs the buffer to transmit the second record for processing. Thus, at this time in a synchronized system, record 3 is being fed into the input buffer, record 2 is being processed, and record 1 is being written by an output device. The procedure continues until the task is finished. Compared with nonoverlapped or *serial processing* (Fig. 3-8c), overlapped processing is much more efficient.

Other computer system variations (in addition to the physical locations of channels and buffers) exist in the design and construction (or architecture) of the functional elements in the CPU. Figure 3-5 shows the *traditional* design. This design features *single* control, storage, and arithmetic-logic units in the CPU. But there are several ways this traditional design can be modified in order to achieve even greater computing speeds.

Among the possible alternative designs used by some computer systems are the following:

1   *The multiprocessor design.* By adding additional control and arithmetic-logic units (see Fig. 3-9a), several instructions can be processed at the same instant in time. As we saw in the last chapter, multiprogramming involves executing a portion of one program, then a segment of another, etc., in brief *consecutive* time periods. Multiprocessor design, however, makes it possible for the system to *simultaneously* work on several program segments. Thus, this design represents, in effect, a system with two or more central processors.

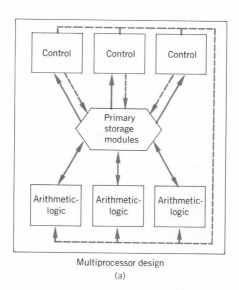

Multiprocessor design
(a)

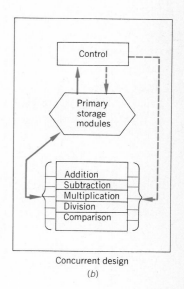

Concurrent design
(b)

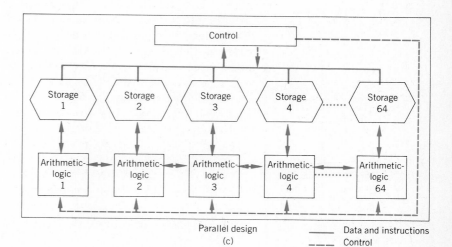

Parallel design
(c)

——— Data and instructions
- - - Control

FIGURE 3-9

**2** *The concurrent (or pipeline) design.* Computing speed can also be increased by separating the arithmetic-logic unit into functional subunits, each of which can operate independently under the direction of the control unit (see Fig. 3-9*b*). When, for example, consecutive and independent program instructions call for the use of separate subunits (e.g., addition, multiplication, and division), the control unit will signal the proper elements to proceed *concurrently* to process all these instructions. Lacking functionally independent subunits, a traditionally designed arithmetic-logic unit will take the first instruction in the sequence and execute it before moving to the next instruction.

**3** *The parallel design.* The ILLIAC IV is a massive "number cruncher" with a control unit that directs the operation of 64 arithmetic-logic units. Each arithmetic-logic unit has its own storage unit (see Fig. 3-9*c*).

These variations from traditional design result in faster computation speed and will be used in many future computer systems.

**SUMMARY**   Electronic computers may be classified in a number of ways. In this book we are interested in digital machines that count sequentially and very accurately, and we are interested in general-purpose equipment that can do a variety of jobs.

Computers extend human brainpower; they are intelligence amplifiers that provide new dimensions in the time available for creative work. They are able to perform certain logic operations. Sophisticated questions can be answered by the combination of many simple machine "decisions." Computers can store and retrieve information rapidly and accurately.

But machines, like humans (especially like humans), are not infallible. They make errors, and they must be told exactly and precisely what to do. Although experiments are being conducted by extremely able researchers in the attempt to improve the machine's heuristic capabilities, they are restricted in practical use to applications that can be quantified and structured into a finite number of steps to achieve a specific goal.

Computers are organized to perform the functional activities of input, storage, arithmetic-logic, control, and output. A multitude of machine configurations and media are used in the performance of these functions. The composition of the CPU is subject to design variation; the most powerful computers generally depart in some way from the traditional design, which features single control, storage, and arithmetic-logic units in the CPU.

**REVIEW AND DISCUSSION QUESTIONS**

**1**   Discuss the various ways in which computers may be classified.

**2**   (**a**) What is an analog computer? (**b**) How does it differ from a digital computer?

**3**   How does a special-purpose computer differ from a general-purpose machine?

**4**   Compare and contrast the processing characteristics typically found in business and scientific applications.

**5**   Why is it possible to say that the computer is an intelligence amplifier?

**6**   Identify and discuss the limitations of computer usage.

**7**   Why does controversy surround the question of whether or not computers can be programmed to "think"?

**8**   Identify and discuss the five functions which are performed by computers.

**9**   "The storage section of the central processor is used for four purposes." What are these four purposes?

**10**   (**a**) What functions are performed in the arithmetic-logic section of the central processor? (**b**) In the control section?

**11**   (**a**) What is the role of a data channel? (**b**) Of high-speed buffers?

**12**   Differentiate between traditional CPU design and (**a**) multiprocessor design, (**b**) concurrent design, and (**c**) parallel design.

**13**   Define the following terms: (**a**) Hybrid computer (**b**) Law of trichotomy (**c**) Binary search procedure (**d**) Combinatorial explosion (**e**) Turing's Test (**f**) Artificial intelligence (**g**) Algorithm (**h**) Heuristic (**i**) Overlapped processing.

**SELECTED REFERENCES**   Articles on "Artificial Intelligence," *Creative Computing,* March-April 1976, pp. 16–26.

Bartee, Thomas C., *Digital Computer Fundamentals,* 4th ed., McGraw-Hill Book Company, New York, 1977, chap. 1.

Weizenbaum, Joseph, "The Last Dream," *Across the Board,* July 1977, pp. 34–46.

# input and output: I

# 4

LEARNING OBJECTIVES   After studying this chapter and answering the discussion questions, you should be able to: ☐ Explain how data may be organized and logically structured, and how files may be organized for storage, retrieval, and processing ☐ Discuss the advantages and limitations of punched cards and punched paper tapes and explain the purposes these media serve ☐ Explain the ways in which data are entered and coded on magnetic tape, and the advantages and limitations of this medium ☐ Summarize the uses, advantages, and limitations of direct input devices utilizing MICR and OCR character-reading techniques ☐ Discuss the approaches used to produce printed and microfilmed output from computers

CHAPTER OUTLINE
**Data organization concepts:** Organizing the Data / Structuring the Data / Organizing and Processing Files
**Punched cards**
**Punched paper tape**
**Magnetic tape:** Direct Data Entry on Magnetic Tape / Magnetic Tape Coding / Magnetic Tape Equipment / Advantages and Limitations of Magnetic Tape
**Magnetic ink character recognition**
**Optical character recognition**

Printed and microfilmed output: Printed Output /
Microfilmed Output
Summary
Review and discussion questions
Selected references


**A**s you know, the CPU in a computer system receives program
instructions and input data from input devices, performs the necessary
data processing steps, and communicates the processed information to
humans through the use of output devices. Later in this chapter (and in
the next chapter) we will study the I/O media and devices that make this
human/machine communication possible. But before we move on to
these topics, it is important for you to understand that before input,
processing, and output can be accomplished in an efficient and economical way, the *data must first be organized* or grouped in some logical
arrangement.

**DATA ORGANIZATION**
**CONCEPTS**
In business information systems, data are generally organized into different levels ranging upward from data items to files and data bases (remember Fig. 2-14?). Let us briefly examine these levels or groupings of data in
the context of an accounts-receivable (A/R) application.


### organizing the data

The object of A/R processing is to (1) keep track of all credit purchases
made by customers during a period, (2) bill customers for all purchases
made during the period, and (3) stay abreast of credit purchase trends,
delinquent accounts, and other relevant information. Sales transaction
tickets may contain several *data items* or *fields*[1]—e.g., customer name,
customer address, date of purchase, item(s) purchased, and customer
account number. Of course, data items may be either *fixed* or *variable* in
length—sales departments may all be coded with a fixed number of

---

[1] Some make the distinction that a field is the designated physical location for a data item on
an I/O or storage medium (such as several columns on a punched card) while the data item
itself represents whatever might be stored or punched in a field. This is probably a valid
distinction, but the terms tend to be used interchangeably.

digits, but customer names and addresses will differ significantly in length.

Related data items are grouped to form a logical *record*. This record contains all the necessary data about some object or entity. In our A/R example, the record would pertain to a credit customer and would include such data as the customer's name, account number, address, and credit limit.

A *file* is a collection of related records. Each record in a file is identified by a *key* or *identifier*. A record key is some data item of interest. In a simple, manually processed A/R file, for example, the primary key could be the last name of customers, and record folders could be organized and filed in alphabetical sequence in a file cabinet. Between billing dates, customer purchases can be used to update record folders in a *transaction file* drawer as shown in Fig. 4-1. When bills are prepared, the records are removed from the transaction file drawer, calculations are made to determine purchase amounts, the transaction file is emptied and the data are transferred to the *master file* in the bottom drawers of the cabinet, and bills are sent to customers. In a computer-

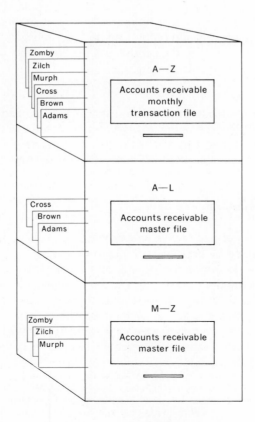

FIGURE 4-1

processed A/R application, on the other hand, the primary key[2] used to organize records in the file is likely to be the customer account number, and these records will be processed in a numerical sequence for billing purposes.

Finally, a *data base* is a collection of logically related files that are organized in various ways to reduce duplication of data items and to provide improved access to, and better integration of, the needed facts. Records in an A/R file, for example, could be linked with sales orders, shipping and routing, contract pricing, and payment records that might be located in other files.

### structuring the data

Logical Relationships    Data must be structured in ways that are logical and meaningful for those in the organization who will use these facts. Of course, different users often need to get at the data in different ways, and this often leads to the development of very sophisticated and complex data structures to support these differing information needs. Although it is beyond the scope of this book to treat in any great detail the almost limitless number of logical data structures that could be designed for computer systems, most of these structures would follow one of the following approaches:

1    *Simple linear structures.* If all data elements are independent and of equal significance, they may be put into some order to form a simple linear structure. Unfortunately, such a structure is often inadequate for business data processing purposes.

2    *List structures.* In this approach, logical records are linked together by the use of pointers. A *pointer* is a data item in one record that identifies the storage location of another logically related record. Records in a customer master file, for example, would contain the name and address of each customer, and each record in this file might be identified by an account number. During an accounting period, a customer may buy a number of items on different days. Thus, the company may maintain a shipping invoice file to reflect these transactions. A list structure could be used in this situation to show the unpaid invoices at any given time. Each record in the customer file would contain a field that would point to the record location of the first invoice for that customer in the invoice file (Fig. 4-2). This invoice record, in turn, would be linked to later invoices for the customer. The last invoice in the chain would be identified by the use of a special character as a pointer.

---

[2] There may also be "secondary" keys used in retrieving and processing records in a file. The customer account number primary key used to sequence records in an A/R file for billing purposes might be replaced by a customer name key when the file is used by employees responding to customer complaints and inquiries.

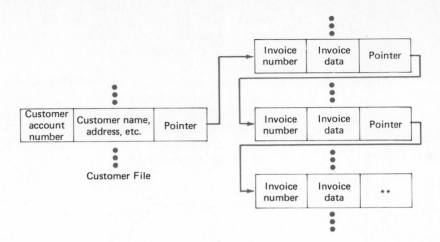

FIGURE 4-2

List structure.

**3**  *Tree structures.* In this hierarchical approach, data units are structured in multiple levels that graphically resemble an "upside down" tree with the root at the top and the branches formed below. There is a superior-subordinate relationship in this type of structure. Below the single-root data component are subordinate elements or *nodes,* each of which, in turn, "own" one or more other elements (or none). Each element or branch in this structure below the root has only a single owner. Thus, as we see in Fig. 4-3, a customer owns an invoice, and the invoice has subordinate items. The branches in a tree structure are not connected.

**4**  *Network structures.* Unlike the tree approach, which does not permit the connection of branches, the network concept permits the connection of the nodes in a multidirectional manner (Fig. 4-4). Thus, each node may have several owners and may, in turn, own any number of other data

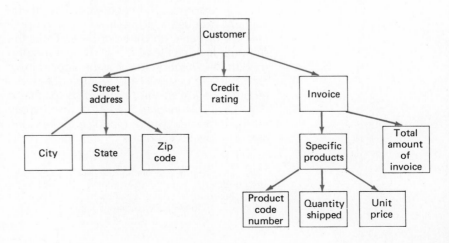

FIGURE 4-3

Tree structure.

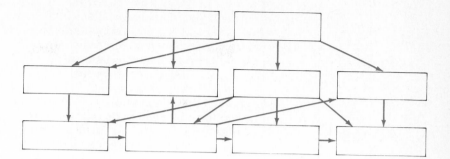

FIGURE 4-4

Network structure.

units. Data management software permits the extraction of the needed information from such a structure by beginning with any record in a file.

Physical structure    Humans visualize or structure data in *logical* ways for their own purposes. Thus, records $R_1$ and $R_2$ may always be logically linked and processed in sequence in *one* particular application. However, in a computer system it is quite possible that these records that are logically contiguous in one application are *not physically stored together*. Rather, the physical location of the records in media and hardware may depend not only on the I/O and storage devices and techniques used, but also on the different logical relationships that users may assign to the data found in $R_1$ and $R_2$. For example, $R_1$ and $R_2$ may be records of credit customers who have shipments sent to the same block in the same city every 2 weeks. From the shipping department manager's perspective, then, $R_1$ and $R_2$ are sequential entries on a geographically organized shipping report. But in the A/R application, the customers represented by $R_1$ and $R_2$ may be identified, and their accounts may be processed, according to their account numbers which are widely separated. In short, then, the physical location of the stored records in many computer-based information systems is invisible to users.[3]

## organizing and processing files

Provisions must be made in a computer-based system to store and retrieve data from appropriate media and devices for subsequent retirement or modification. Several arrangements are used to organize files for storage, retrieval, and processing. The following approaches are among the most important:

[3] Of course, the extent to which the logical structure of the most frequently processed applications corresponds to the physical storage techniques used may determine the amount of processing the system software must perform to reassemble the data to meet user requests. As you might expect, trying to design systems to efficiently serve many users while minimizing the use of computing resources is a difficult task that involves complex tradeoffs.

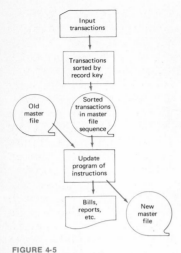

**FIGURE 4-5**

Sequential file processing.

**1**  *Sequential file organization.* In this approach, records in a given file are physically stored in some order according to a record key (e.g., the customer account number). When files are stored offline from the CPU on media such as magnetic tape or punched cards, they are *sequentially organized.* And when the records in such files are updated, *sequential* (or serial or batch) *processing* is used. Figure 4-5 shows the sequential approach to updating files. However, as we saw in Chapter 2, the entire master file may need to be processed just to retrieve and/or update a few records, and this can be inefficient and expensive. Of course, records may also be organized sequentially in an online storage device.

**2**  *Random (direct) file organization.* This approach requires that records in a file be kept in an online storage device. Data thus stored can be directly obtained without searching the whole file, and the time required for online inquiry and updating of a few records is much faster than when batch techniques are used. Obviously, when the computer is given the identifier of the record to be retrieved for processing, it must be able to generate the record's storage location. It might be possible for a record key and an online storage location to have the same identifying number. Unfortunately, such is seldom the case. Instead, an algorithm or *transform* that takes all or part of the record identification number is used to produce a random storage location number. Given a record key at a later time, the algorithm can then locate and retrieve the stored record. Thus, as Fig. 4-6 indicates, it is possible to have random processing with random file organization. But if a large number of records in sequence need to be processed, the computer would have to repeatedly use the transform algorithm to directly retrieve, one by one, each of the needed records, and this would be relatively inefficient and expensive.

**3**  *Indexed sequential file organization.* As you have undoubtedly noticed, there are some processing situations that lend themselves to the sequential organization approach, and there are others that need the benefits to be obtained from a random file organization. Another file

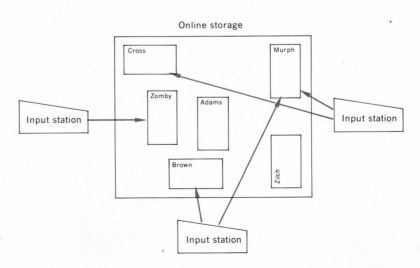

**FIGURE 4-6**

Random processing with random file organization.

| Account Number Key | Storage Area for Customer Data |
|---|---|
| 1492 | 10 |
| 1776 | 11 |
| 1945 | 12 |
| 2232 | 13 |
| 2565 | 14 |
| . | . |
| . | . |
| . | . |

FIGURE 4-7

organization using the *indexed sequential access method* (ISAM) is a compromise approach that combines some of the advantages (and avoids some of the limitations) of both the sequential and random methods. That is, it provides efficient sequential access when large batch processing jobs are to be run, and it also gives direct access to a few records in a much shorter period of time than would be possible if an entire sequential file had to be searched. When ISAM is used, records are stored sequentially by a record key in an online storage device. Sequential processing is thus possible. In addition, however, *indexes* are maintained to permit direct access to selected records without searching the *entire* file. The use of an index is already familiar to you. If you wanted to find information on one or a few topics in this book, you would not begin on page 1 and read every page until you came across the topic(s) of interest. Rather, you would find the subject by turning to the index at the back of the book to locate the page number, and by then turning directly to that page to begin reading. In the same way, a computer can locate a record by using an index rather than by starting every search at the beginning of the file. In an A/R file, for example, customer records may be sequentially organized by account number, and one or more indexes of these account numbers are stored in the online device as shown in Fig. 4-7. (The account number key represents the highest customer account number in the storage location.) Thus, to locate customer number 1932, the computer would be instructed to access storage area 12. (Another index for storage area 12 would probably then be used to further pinpoint the location of the record.) A sequential search, involving only a fraction of the entire file, would then be made to retrieve the desired record. In summary, then, as Fig. 4-8 conceptually shows, ISAM permits records to be processed sequentially or through direct-access processing.

Which of the above file organization approaches is best? There is, of course, no single answer to this question because the best approach is the one that happens to meet the user's needs in the most efficient and economical manner. Each file organization method has distinct strengths and weaknesses which are summarized in Fig. 4-9.

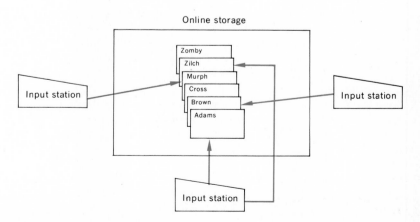

FIGURE 4-8

Direct-access processing with sequential file organization.

## SEQUENTIAL FILE ORGANIZATION

**Advantages**

- Simple-to-understand approach
- Locating a record requires only the record key
- Efficient and economical if the *activity rate*—i.e., the proportion of file records to be processed—is high
- Relatively inexpensive I/O media and devices may be used
- Files may be relatively easy to reconstruct since a good measure of built-in backup is usually available

**Disadvantages**

- Entire file must be processed even when the activity rate is very low
- Transactions must be sorted and placed in sequence prior to processing
- Timeliness of data in the file deteriorates while batches are being accumulated
- Data redundancy is typically high since the same data may be stored in several files sequenced on different keys

## RANDOM FILE ORGANIZATION

**Advantages**

- Immediate access to records for inquiry and updating purposes is possible
- Immediate updating of several files as a result of a single transaction is possible
- Transactions need not be sorted

**Disadvantages**

- Records in the online file may be exposed to the risks of a loss of accuracy and a breach of security; special backup and reconstruction procedures must be established
- May be less efficient in the use of storage space than sequentially organized files
- More difficult to add and delete records than with sequential files
- Relatively expensive hardware and software resources are required

## INDEXED SEQUENTIAL FILE ORGANIZATION

**Advantages**

- Permits the efficient and economical use of sequential processing techniques when the activity rate is high
- Permits quick access to records in a relatively efficient way when this activity is a small fraction of the total workload

**Disadvantages**

- Less efficient in the use of storage space than some other alternatives
- Access to records may be slower using indexes than when transform algorithms are used
- Relatively expensive hardware and software resources are required

FIGURE 4-9

Comparison of file organization approaches.

| Medium | Input Device Used | Output Device Used | Typical I/O Speed Ranges (Characters per Second) | | Typical Storage Capacity |
|---|---|---|---|---|---|
| | | | Input | Output | |
| Punched card | Card reader | Card punch | 150–2,667 | 80–650 | Virtually unlimited (but bulky) |
| Paper tape | Tape reader | Tape punch | 50–1,800 | 10–300 | Virtually unlimited (but bulky and fragile) |
| Magnetic tape | Tape drive | Tape drive | 15,000–1,250,000 | 15,000–1,250,000 | Virtually unlimited (compact, with up to 150 million characters per tape) |
| Magnetic ink | MICR reader | — | 700–3,200 | — | — |
| Paper documents | OCR reader | — | 100–3,600 | — | — |
| | — | Character printer | — | 5–250 | — |
| | — | Line printer | — | 440–39,000 | — |
| Microfilm | — | Recorder | — | 25,000–300,000 | Compact and virtually unlimited |

FIGURE 4-10

Summary of I/O media and devices—
Chapter 4.

Because files vary in character, size, and location (online or offline), a number of I/O media and devices have been developed. In choosing from among the possible alternatives, managers must consider such factors as (1) the nature and volume of the data input, (2) the accessibility of stored data and the speed with which files must be updated, and (3) the costs of I/O alternatives. Not surprisingly, a compromise choice is often necessary.

In the remainder of this chapter, we shall examine paper and magnetizable media and related equipment employed primarily to process high-volume sequentially organized files. The media preserve the files for an indefinite period, and the file storage is *offline* relative to the CPU. Figure 4-10 summarizes some of the characteristics of the media and devices introduced in this chapter. (In the next chapter we will consider I/O and online storage devices that are used in random or direct file processing.)

PUNCHED CARDS   The punched card is a very familiar I/O medium. It serves a *threefold purpose*: it is used to (1) provide data *input* into the CPU, (2) receive information *output* from the CPU, and (3) provide secondary offline

FIGURE 4-11

Card reader (courtesy IBM
Corporation).

*storage* of data and information. Details were presented in Chapter 1 on some card processing concepts and on card coding.

Although it is called a *unit record,* the card does not necessarily contain all the data of a particular file record. It may merely contain data about one record item, and the complete record may thus consist of several cards. Files are organized sequentially in card trays, and batch processing methods are employed.

Manually operated keypunch machines are the primary means of preparing punched cards. Although this is a tedious and expensive operation, the use of keypunch equipment has through the years remained a popular data entry method.

Once the data are punched into the cards, they are fed into the central processor by means of a *card reader* (Fig. 4-11). Cards are placed into a read hopper from where, on command from the program in the central processor, they are moved through the card feed unit past either brush-type or photoelectric-cell reading stations. These stations sense the presence or absence of holes in each card column and convert this information into electric pulses that the computer can accept. The speed with which a card reader can supply input data to a CPU is relatively slow when compared with most other methods (see Fig. 4-10).

Cards may also serve as an output medium through the use of a card punch machine. Blank cards are placed in a punch hopper (Fig. 4-12). Upon command from the program, they are moved, one at a time, to a punch station where processed information is received. After being punched, the holes in the card are compared at a second station with the punching instructions. If no error is detected, the card is then moved to a stacker. When errors are sensed in either reading or punching operations, the device will stop until the error is corrected. In small, card-oriented computer systems, a single *multifunction card machine* is used to perform input, output, sorting, and collating functions. Output speeds are slower than reading speeds when punch card equipment is used because of the slow electromechanical movement of the die punches.

Card punches have proven to be very useful, however, in producing documents that are later reentered into processing operations. An example of such a *turnaround* application is the billing approach used by

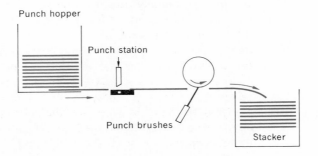

FIGURE 4-12

many public utilities. Bills sent to customers are in the form of cards prepared as computer output. Appropriate data are punched into this card. When a part or all of the card is returned by the customer with his or her payment, it may then be used as an input that requires no keypunching.

Many businesses use punched cards as an I/O medium because they were used with the firm's unit record equipment prior to the introduction of the computer. But *cards possess advantages* other than merely being an old, reliable, and available medium. For one thing, they are complete records of transactions and are thus easily understood. Particular records can be sorted, deleted, and replaced without disturbing other cards. It may be possible to add more data to the cards if necessary. Magnetic and paper tapes lack these advantages. Also, as we have just seen, a card can be used as a humanly readable turnaround document as well as a processing medium. Tape media also lack this feature. Finally, cards are useful as an external storage medium for permanent records.

But *cards have certain inherent disadvantages* that may limit their use in or exclude them from use in a particular application. For example, the number of data characters that can be punched per card is quite low— much less than the number of characters that can be typed on the card with a typewriter. *Data density* is low even when all columns are punched. But in most applications *not* all the columns will be punched, and data density is thus further reduced. For example, if the dollar amount of credit sales transactions in an exclusive retail store may reach or exceed $10,000.00 then the purchase amount field on each card must provide seven columns of space even though most purchases will be for much less (e.g., three columns would be unused if a purchase were made for $75.00).

Cards are fixed in length. If 100 characters are required, an additional card must be used. The size of the card deck is increased, as is the time required to process it. Because tapes are continuous in length, they do not have this drawback. In short, cards are bulky and slow to process.

Finally, cards may be misplaced or separated from their proper file deck. Also, as everyone knows, they cannot be folded, stapled, or mutilated. A bent corner or a warped card can jam equipment and further slow the processing. And obviously, the data in a card cannot be erased so that the card may be used again.

**PUNCHED PAPER TAPE**

Punched paper tape, like cards, is a triple-purpose medium that is suitable for input, output, and secondary offline storage. Perhaps its most popular business use is to capture data as byproducts of some other processing activity. Time and labor are thus saved. For example, paper tape attachments on many timesharing terminals permanently capture input data and output information on tape (Fig. 3-1, page 78, shows such an attachment).

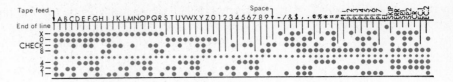

FIGURE 4-13

Eight-channel paper tape code.

Data are recorded on the tape by punching round holes into it. Tape, like the punched card, is laid out in rows *(channels)* and columns *(frames)*. A character of information is represented by a punch or combination of punches in a vertical column. Since there are 10 frames in each inch of tape, it is possible to record 10 characters in that space.

Figure 4-13 illustrates the method of representing data employed with the popular eight-channel tape. The bottom four channels are labeled to the left of the tape with the numerical values 1,2,4, and 8. (The holes between channels 4 and 8 are sprocket holes used to feed the tape through the machines and are not considered in the code.) Decimal digits 1 to 9 can be represented by a hole or a combination of holes in these bottom channels. For example, a single hole punched in channel 2 has a decimal value of 2, while holes punched in channels 4,2, and 1 denote a decimal 7. The X and O channels serve the same purpose as zone punches in cards; i.e., they are used in combination with numerical punches to form alphabetic and special characters. Channel O used alone is the code for zero. The letter A is represented by zone punches in X and O plus numerical 1 hole. The letter B has the same zone punches plus numerical 2, etc. You can examine the remainder of the letters to see the code pattern.

The data coded on punched tape are fed into the CPU by means of a *paper tape reader.* Tape readers, like card readers, sense the presence or absence of holes and deliver this information to the processor. *Paper tape punches* record information received from the CPU by punching holes in blank tape. As you can see in Fig. 4-10, the speed of paper tape input and output is very slow.

*Punched paper tape provides certain advantages* over punched cards. First, because it is a continuous-length medium, there is no upper-limit restriction on the length of records and no wasted space when records are short. Tape thus provides greater data density, which makes for easier handling and storage. Also, it is more economical than cards. The tape required to store 120,000 characters would cost only about one-third of the card figure if *all* columns were punched in the cards—an unlikely assumption in most cases. The equipment required for paper tape punching and reading is small, light, relatively simple in design (thus reducing maintenance costs), and less expensive than comparable card machines.

But *punched tapes have their faults.* It is more difficult to verify the accuracy of tape output than is the case with cards. Errors that are discovered cannot be corrected as easily as in the case of cards. And changes such as the addition to or deletion of records are more difficult with tape than with cards. These problems, of course, result from the continuous length of tape—a feature that may be an asset for some applications and a liability for others. Like cards, tape is easily torn and mutilated.

**MAGNETIC TAPE**    Because of its relatively fast *transfer rate*[4] (the speed at which data can be transferred from the input medium to CPU storage), magnetic tape is the most popular I/O medium being used today for high-speed, large-volume applications. In addition to providing rapid input and output, it is the most widely used secondary offline computer storage medium.

The tape itself may be in a large *reel* or a small *cartridge* or *cassette* (see Fig. 4-14); it is quite similar to the kind used in a sound tape recorder. It is a plastic ribbon coated on one side with an iron-oxide material that can be magnetized. By electromagnetic pulses, data are recorded in the form of tiny invisible spots on the iron-oxide side of the tape, just as sound waves form magnetic patterns on the tape of a sound recorder. Both the data and the sound can be played back as many times as desired. And like the tape used on a recorder, computer tape can be erased and reused indefinitely. Data contained in a tape are automatically erased as new data are being recorded. Thus, careful control and identification procedures are required to prevent important file tapes from being mistakenly used to accept computer output.

---

[4] The transfer rate for magnetic tape depends on such factors as (1) the data density of the magnetized characters on the tape surface (which varies from 200 to 6,250 characters per inch), and (2) the speed with which the tape moves (from 75 to 200 inches per second).

FIGURE 4-14

Magnetic tape cartridge (courtesy IBM Corporation).

### direct data entry on magnetic tape

How is information recorded on magnetic tape? In some cases new input data are initially captured in punched card or paper tape form and are then transcribed on magnetic tape by a special offline *data converter*. In addition to this *indirect* approach to entering data on magnetic tape, however, there are several alternative data entry approaches in which the data are keyed from source documents *directly* into a magnetizable form. Among the popular direct data entry alternatives being used are:

1   *Single-station key-to-tape units.* In this approach the single (or *stand-alone*) tape encoder system includes all components required to produce a prepared tape by keying the data found in a source document. The keyed data may be recorded on standard-sized magnetic tape, or they may be recorded on the smaller-sized tape found in special *cartridges* or *cassettes.* Data recorded on the smaller tape may need to be converted to standard-sized tape prior to computer entry.

2   *Multistation key-to-tape configurations.* In this approach there are several keyboard consoles connected to one or more magnetic tape units by a central controlling device. The controller consolidates the data from the keyboards on the appropriate tape units.

3   *Single-station key-to-diskette units.* Data are recorded on a small, flexible, magnetizable diskette—a *floppy disk* that looks like a thin 45 rpm sound record. Recorded data may then be transferred to magnetic tape for processing.

4   *Multistation key-to-disk configurations.* In this type of data entry system, a minicomputer controls the input from a number of key stations. Data keyed in by a station operator are displayed, edited, and checked for errors, then stored on a magnetic disk resembling a large LP sound record. Periodically, the data stored on the disk are transferred to magnetic tape (Fig. 4-15).

### magnetic tape coding

The approach used to represent data on magnetic tape is similar to that used with punched paper tape. Magnetic tape is divided horizontally into rows (called *channels,* or *tracks*) and vertically into columns or frames. The most commonly used tape codes employ seven and nine channels. Figure 4-16 illustrates the older *seven-channel* tape format. You will note that channel designations are quite similar to those used in punched tape. Data are represented in a coded form.[5] Each vertical frame represents one data character, and the tape-recording density may be from 200 to 6,250 frames per inch depending on the computer system used.

---

[5] The code used here is called binary coded decimal (BCD). In Chapter 6 we will become better acquainted with BCD. We will also examine an extended version of BCD at that time.

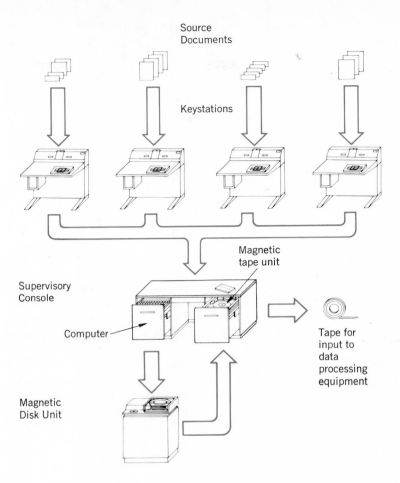

**FIGURE 4-15**

Key-to-disk data entry.

The numerical values are determined by one or a combination of the bottom four channels, while the A and B zone tracks are used in conjunction with the numeric channels to represent letters and special characters. For example, the decimal 7 is represented by an "on" condition in channels 4, 2, and 1. You can test your understanding by observing the coding pattern used for the other alphanumeric characters.

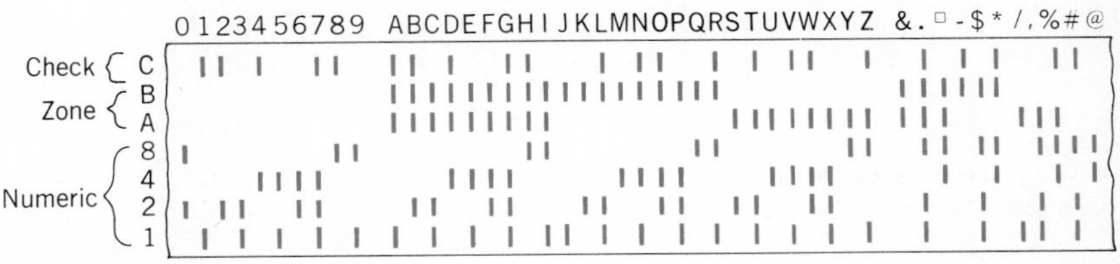

**FIGURE 4-16**

Seven-channel magnetic tape code.

You may have noticed that there are "check" channels in both Fig. 4-13 and 4-16. These channels perform a special *parity checking* function. In Fig. 4-16, for example, you will notice that there are an even number of marks in each frame. When the basic code—e.g., for the digit 1—requires an odd number of marks, there is an additional mark in the check channel. Thus, all valid characters are formed with an even number of marks, and this becomes the basis for a system check of the accuracy of the tape. Both even-and odd-parity codes are used in computer systems.

An *extended* version of the seven-channel tape format is now used in most computer systems. As with the older seven-track tape, this *nine-channel* format employs four numeric tracks and a parity check channel. However, *four* (rather than two) zone positions are available. The additional zone tracks make it possible to extend the code to include lower-case alphabetical and other special characters. Figure 4-17 shows a few characters coded in the nine-channel format. The most frequently used tracks are grouped near the center of the tape so as to reduce the chances of losing data owing to the physical deterioration of the outer edges of the tape. This arrangement gives the code format a peculiar appearance. The equivalent seven-channel tape code positions are shown in Fig. 4-17 to aid in interpretation. For example, the numeral 7 is represented here by an "on" condition in the four zone positions and in the channels equivalent to 4,2, and 1.

Magnetic tape, like paper tape, is a continuous-length, sequential file medium. How then can the computer distinguish between different records on the tape? The answer is that the records are separated by blank spaces in the tape called *interrecord gaps.* Figure 4-18 shows an accounts-receivable file organized on magnetic tape. Customer records may be of varying lengths. They may also be combined into tape *blocks*

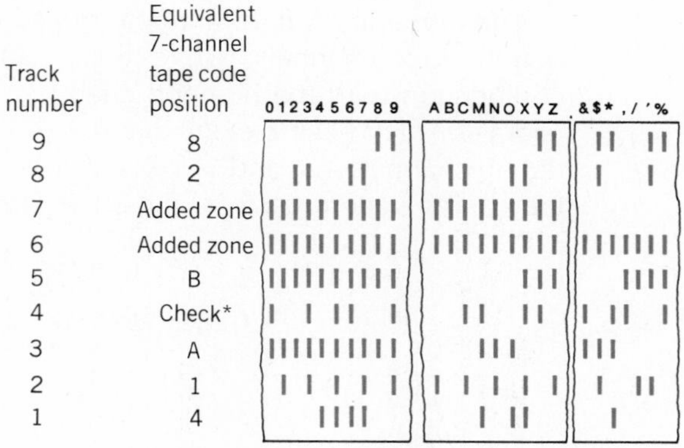

| Track number | Equivalent 7-channel tape code position | | | |
|---|---|---|---|---|
| | | 0 1 2 3 4 5 6 7 8 9 | A B C M N O X Y Z | & $ * , / ' % |
| 9 | 8 | | | |
| 8 | 2 | | | |
| 7 | Added zone | | | |
| 6 | Added zone | | | |
| 5 | B | | | |
| 4 | Check* | | | |
| 3 | A | | | |
| 2 | 1 | | | |
| 1 | 4 | | | |

FIGURE 4-17

Nine-channel extended magnetic tape code.

*The check position here produces odd parity.

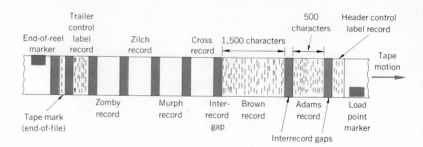

**FIGURE 4-18**

of several records (Fig. 4-19). Interrecord gaps are automatically created by the computer system after the last character in a record (or block of records) has been recorded.

The first several feet of tape are unrecorded to allow for threading on the equipment. A reflective marker known as the *load point* indicates to the equipment the beginning of usable tape, while a similar *end-of-reel* marker signals the end of usable tape. The markers are placed on opposite edges of the tape for machine identification purposes. Between the load-point marker and the first data record is a *header control label,* which identifies the tape contents, gives the number of the program to be used when the tape is processed, and supplies other control information that helps to prevent an important tape from accidently being erased. Following the last data record in a file is a *trailer control label,* which contains a count of the number of blocks in a file. A comparison between the number of blocks processed and the number in the file may be made to determine that all have been accounted for. The end of a file may be signaled by a special one-character record. This special character is called a *tape mark.*

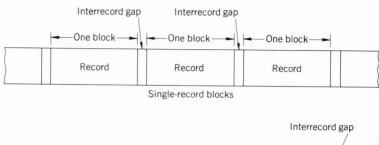

**FIGURE 4-19**

Fewer interrecord gaps save tape and speed data input. This is important when record lengths are short. The program of instructions separates the records within a block for processing.

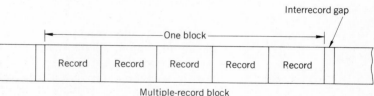

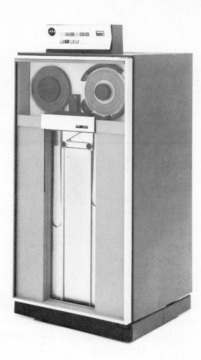

**FIGURE 4-20**

Magnetic tape unit (courtesy IBM
Corporation).

## magnetic tape equipment

The magnetic tape unit shown in Fig. 4-20 is used for both data input
(recording or *writing*) and output *(reading)*. Called by such names as *tape
drives* and *tape transports,* these machines read and write data on the
tape by the use of *read-write heads* (Fig. 4-21). There is one read-write
head for each tape channel. Each head is a small electromagnet with
minute gaps between the poles. In the writing operation, the tape moves
over the gaps while electric pulses from the CPU flow through the write
coils of the appropriate heads causing the iron-oxide coating of the tape
to be magnetized in the proper pattern. When the tape is being read, the
magnetized patterns induce pulses of current in the read coils that feed
the data into the CPU.

The tape is loaded onto the tape drive in much the same way that a
movie projector is threaded (Fig. 4-22). The tape movement during
processing is from the supply reel past the read-write heads to the take-up
reel.

There are usually several tape drives used in an installation. In most
applications, a tape is either read or written in a single pass. Therefore, if
we wish to update our master accounts-receivable file, we may have one
unit reading in the old master file, another feeding in recent transactions,
a third introducing the processing instructions, and a fourth writing the
updated master file.

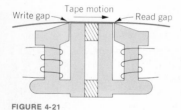

**FIGURE 4-21**

Two-gap read-write head.

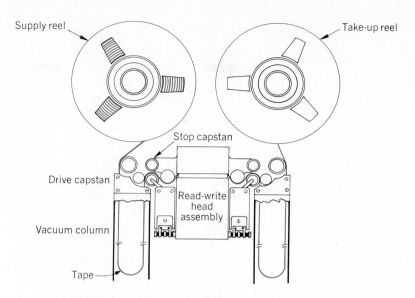

Supply reel

Take-up reel

Stop capstan

Drive capstan

Read-write head assembly

Vacuum column

Tape

FIGURE 4-22

### advantages and limitations of magnetic tape

The *advantages* of magnetic tape can be summarized as follows:

**1** *Unlimited length of records.* Unlike cards, any number of characters can be placed in a record. Files can be as long as necessary.

**2** *Compact storage.* The data density, as we have seen, is far greater than that of cards and paper tape. Data handling is facilitated.

**3** *Reduced cost.* A tape costs much less than the hundreds of thousands of cards that it can replace. Storage space is reduced, and the tape can be reused many times.

**4** *Rapid transfer rate.* Neither cards nor punched tape can compare with magnetic tape in input/output speed (see Fig. 4-10).

**5** *Protection against record loss.* In card systems, there is always the danger of losing or misplacing one or more cards from a file. The use of magnetic tape is a protection against this danger.

Magnetic tape, however, has several *disadvantages.* Included among these are:

**1** *Need for machine interpretation.* Since the magnetized spots are invisible, they cannot, of course, be read by humans. A printing operation must be performed if it is necessary to check or verify tape data.

**2** *Lack of random accessibility.* Because of the sequential nature of tape file processing, it is not generally suitable for jobs that require rapid and random access to particular records. Tape file processing is also not efficient when the job being processed calls for the use of only a small proportion of the total tape records. In either situation, too much time is wasted in reading records that will not be used.

**3**  *Environmental problems.* Specks of dust on a tape can be read as data characters or can cause an improper reading. Special dust-resistant cases must be used to store the tapes. The humidity of the storage area must be controlled. Careful control procedures must be followed to prevent an important file from being erased by mistake. (Instead of losing a card or two, the entire file might be lost—a revolting development!) Stray magnetic fields in close proximity to stored tapes can alter the tape contents. Precautions must be taken to avoid this calamity.

Most of the data that are recorded on the punched cards or tapes that we have now studied have been taken from written documents and transferred to the cards or tapes by a manual keying operation. Several devices, however, have been designed to eliminate manual keying by reading the characters printed on the source documents and converting the data *directly* into computer-usable *input*. In the remainder of this chapter we will look at (1) these *character readers* which are generally used in high-volume sequential processing applications and (2) the *printing* and *microfilming* devices that are used for high-volume *output*.

## MAGNETIC INK CHARACTER RECOGNITION

The magnetic ink character recognition (MICR) concept is widely used by banking and financial institutions as a means of processing the tremendous volume of checks being written. Figure 4-23 shows a sample check coded with a special ink which contains tiny iron-oxide magnetizable particles. The code number of the bank to which the check will be written and the depositor's account number are precoded on the checks. The first bank to receive the check after it has been written encodes the amount in the lower right corner. The check at this point is a unit record and, like punched cards, may then be handled automatically through regular bank collection channels—e.g., from (1) the initial bank receiving the check

| Combined | | | Check | Amount of item |
|---|---|---|---|---|
| Routing | Transit | Account | digit | |
| symbol | number | number | | |

FIGURE 4-23

(Courtesy NCR).

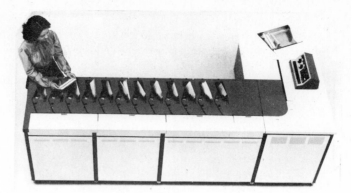

FIGURE 4-24

MICR reader-sorter (courtesy Burroughs Corporation).

to, perhaps, (2) the Federal Reserve bank to (3) the depositor's bank to (4) the depositor's account.

Magnetic ink character *reader-sorter* units (Fig. 4-24) interpret the encoded checks and make the resulting data available to the CPU. They also sort the checks by account number, bank number, etc., into pockets at a rate of about 180 to 2,000 paper documents each minute. As checks enter the reading unit, and immediately prior to the reading operation, they pass through a strong magnetic field which causes the iron-oxide particles in the ink to become magnetized. The read heads are then able to produce recognizable electric signals as the magnetized characters pass beneath them. Each character pattern is divided into many segments and analyzed by built-in recognition circuits to determine which of the 14 characters has been sensed. Valid characters may then be fed directly into a general-purpose computer, or they may be transferred to magnetic tape for later processing.

There are several *advantages* associated with the use of MICR. First, checks may be roughly handed, folded, smeared, and stamped. Yet, this does not prevent recognition with a high degree of accuracy. Second, processing is speeded because checks can be fed directly into the input device. And third, the type font used is easily recognized and read, if necessary, by clerical personnel. The primary *limitation* of MICR is that only a *small number of characters* are used. Since it was designed by and for the banking industry, MICR uses only the 14 characters needed for bank processing. No alphabetic characters are available.

**OPTICAL CHARACTER RECOGNITION**

Unlike MICR, optical character recognition (OCR) techniques make possible the reading of *any* printed character (not just 14), and no special ink is required. Thus, the flexibility of OCR may make it possible for organizations to eliminate or reduce the input keying bottleneck.

Although machines are available that will read hand-printed characters, the automatic reading of handwritten script is still some years in the future. (While your penmanship is undoubtedly beautiful, the author's presents a formidable challenge to the equipment designers.) Most OCR devices being used in business are designed to read *machine-printed* characters, bar codes, and simple handmade marks.

One popular use of OCR is in credit card billing. When a credit sale is made at a gasoline station, for example, the attendant uses an inexpensive imprinter to record the data from the customer's credit card and the amount of the transaction onto a form that is then forwarded to a central processing point. There the document is read automatically by an optical instrument prior to computer processing. Public utilities also use OCR in their billing activities; and registration forms, attendance rosters, and grade reports are optically scanned to maintain student records in some large metropolitan school systems.

Although several types of *optical readers* are available (some have limited flexibility while others are capable of reading entire pages of hand- or machine-printed alphanumeric characters), most of these readers scan the printed matter with a photoelectric device that recognizes characters by the absorption or reflectance of light on the document (characters to be read are nonreflective). Reflected light patterns are converted into electric impulses, which are transmitted to recognition logic circuits. There they are compared with the characters that the machine has been programmed to recognize and, if valid, are then recorded for input into the CPU. If no suitable comparison is possible, the document may be rejected. Figure 4-25 traces pictorially the OCR approach followed by one manufacturer. Up to 3,600 machine-printed characters (or up to 1,200 hand-printed characters) can be read each second by the equipment shown in Fig. 4-25.

In addition to alphanumeric characters, optical scanning equipment can also recognize other forms of coded data. Light and dark bars, for example, are used to code products sold in retail stores. This Universal Product Code (UPC) is printed on the product by the manufacturer. The next time you spring (?) out of bed at 6 a.m. to have a hearty breakfast before your 8 o'clock class, you might find (champion that you are) that your cereal box has a code similar to the one shown in Fig. 4-26. When UPC-marked items are received at a merchant's automated checkout stand (Fig. 4-27), they are pulled across a scanning window and placed in bags. As items are scanned, the UPC symbol is decoded and the data are transmitted to a computer that looks up the price, possibly updates inventory and sales records, and forwards price and description information back to the check stand.

The primary *advantage* of OCR is that it eliminates some of the duplication of human effort required to get data into the computer. This reduction in human effort (1) can *improve the quality (accuracy)* of input data and (2) can *improve the timeliness of information processed*. However, *difficulties* in using OCR equipment may be encountered when documents to be read are poorly typed or have strikeovers, erasures, etc.

Pages containing many
possible character
patterns are placed in the
input hopper

O P Q R S T U V
M N V 4 5 6 7 8
t u v 4 5 6 7 8
9 a A 4 5 6 7 8
K W A 4 5 6 7 8
M C B 4 5 6 7 8
1 2 3 4 5 6 7 8
N O P 4 5 6 7 8

Programmed controller
directs input operation

Pages are automatically fed
from the input hopper

Then moved beneath the
reading system

Character data are transmitted to
integrated circuits for recognition

Data are then recorded on magnetic tape and/or line printer

And pages are directed to
one of three output pockets

**FIGURE 4-25**

(Courtesy Recognition Equipment,
Inc.)

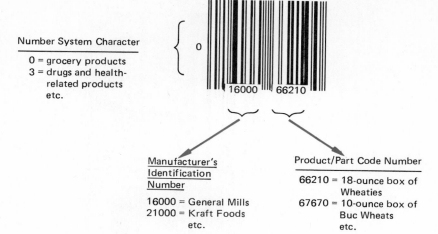

Number System Character

0 = grocery products
3 = drugs and health-
related products
etc.

Manufacturer's
Identification
Number

16000 = General Mills
21000 = Kraft Foods
etc.

Product/Part Code Number

66210 = 18-ounce box of
Wheaties
67670 = 10-ounce box of
Buc Wheats
etc.

FIGURE 4-26

Universal Product Code for box of
Wheaties.

Also, form design and ink specifications become more critical and must
be more standardized than is the case when keypunch source documents
are prepared. Finally, many optical readers are not economically feasible
unless the daily volume of transactions is relatively high.

## PRINTED AND MICROFILMED OUTPUT

### printed output

*Printers* provide information *output* from the CPU in the form of permanently printed characters which have meaning to humans. They are the

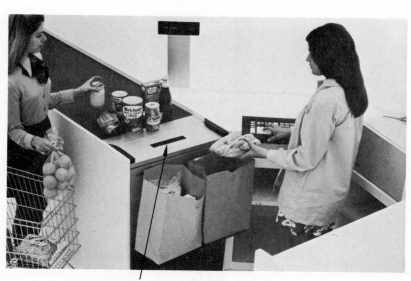

FIGURE 4-27

Optical scanning check-out (courtesy
IBM Corporation).

Optical scanning window

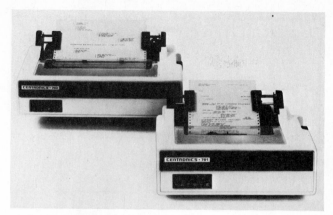

FIGURE 4-28

Serial printers (courtesy Centronics Data Computer Corp.).

primary output device when the information is to be used by people rather than by machine. The printers being produced today fall into the following categories:

**1**  *Serial or character printers.* These devices (Fig. 4-28) may be considered somewhat analogous to souped-up, *one-character-at-a-time* versions of electric typewriters. However, the newer models may be more reliable than typewriters because of their substitution of electronic components for electromechanical elements. The techniques employed to print characters vary widely from *impact methods* that use the familiar approach of pressing a typeface against paper and inked ribbon, to *nonimpact methods* that use thermal, electrical, and chemical technologies. Serial printers are for low-volume printing jobs and are used (1) with minicomputer and microcomputer systems and (2) by the smaller users of timesharing systems and distributed processing networks.

**2**  *High-speed impact line printers.* These printers (Fig. 4-29) use impact methods to produce *line-at-a-time* printed output. The vast majority of high-speed printers in use today are of this type. Impact line printers typically use rapidly moving chains (or trains) of printing slugs or some

FIGURE 4-29

High-speed impact line printer (courtesy Sperry UNIVAC Division, Sperry Rand Corporation).

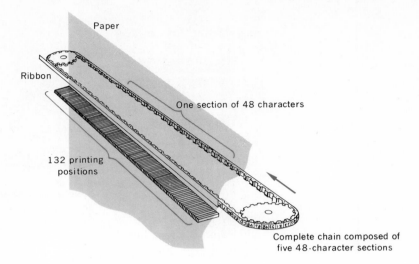

**FIGURE 4-30**

A print chain.

form of a print *cylinder* to print lines of information on paper moving past the printing station. Figure 4-30 illustrates the *print chain* concept. The links in the chain are engraved character-printing slugs. The chain is capable of producing a number of different characters (in Fig. 4-30, there are 48), and there are several sections of the character set in the length of the chain. The chain moves at a constant and rapid speed past the printing positions. Magnetically controlled hammers behind the paper are timed to force the paper against the proper print slugs. The ribbon between the paper and the character leaves an imprint on the paper as a result of the impact. The *drum printer* uses a solid cylinder. Raised characters extend the length of the drum (Fig. 4-31). There are as many circular *bands* of type as there are printing positions. Each band contains all the possible characters. The drum turns at a constant speed, with one revolution being required to print each line. A fast-acting hammer opposite each band picks out the proper character and strikes the paper against

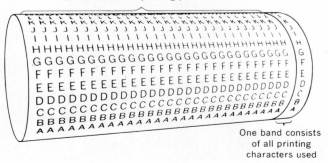

The number of bands corresponds
to the number of printing positions

One band consists
of all printing
characters used

**FIGURE 4-31**

A print drum.

that character. Thus, in one rotation, hammers of *several* printing positions may "fire" when the A row appears; several others may strike to imprint D's, etc. At the end of the rotation, all necessary positions on the paper are printed. The paper then moves to the next line.

**3**    *High-speed nonimpact line printers.* In contrast to impact line printers that can print up to two thousand 132-character lines per minute, these devices (Fig. 4-32) can produce reports at speeds of up to 21,000 lines per minute. Electronics, xerography, lasers, and other newer technologies have made these high-volume systems possible.[6] Each page produced on these printers is an original since there are no carbon copies. Although their cost may exceed the cost of many computer installations, these printers have been found to be economical and reliable when hundreds of thousands of pages must be printed each month. A much wider choice of type faces is possible with these machines than with impact printers, and future advances in these nonimpact machines are likely.

[6] For more information on these technologies, see Frederick W. Miller, "The Non-Diminishing Printer," *Infosystems,* October 1977, pp. 70–72ff.

FIGURE 4-32

High-speed nonimpact printing system (courtesy IBM Corporation).

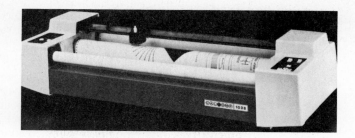

In addition to printing computer output in the form of characters, some devices are also capable of producing graphical output under computer control. For example, a computer-controlled *plotter* can produce engineering drawings, maps, and other pictorial output in a very short time (Fig. 4-33).

### microfilmed output

In spite of the thousands of lines of output that some printers can produce each minute, there is still a substantial mismatch between output by printing and output by the use of other media such as magnetic tape[7] Even when multiple printers are used (see Fig. 1-19, page 32), only a small portion of the time of the CPU may be needed to drive these units. Thus, in some cases it is more efficient and economical to reduce the role of the printer by replacing paper output documents with *microfilm*.

The computer-output-to-microfilm (COM) approach is shown in Fig. 4-34. Output information may be read onto magnetic tape and then, in an offline operation, recorded on microfilm. Or, the *microfilm recorder* may

[7] Magnetic tape devices, you may recall, can write characters at the rate of over a million characters per *second;* the fastest impact printer needs about 4 *minutes* to write that many characters.

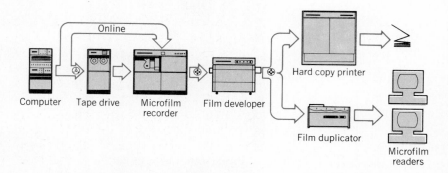

receive the information directly from the CPU. Most microfilm recorders project the characters of output information onto the screen of a _cathode ray tube_ (CRT), which is similar to a television picture tube. A high-speed microfilm camera then films the displayed information at speeds much faster than are possible with printers. After being developed, the film can be viewed directly through special readers by the users of the information; when necessary, paper documents can be produced from the film by a special printer.

**SUMMARY**     Data items are organized into files of related records by record keys, and records and files are fed into computers for processing. The information needed by managers is the output obtained by processing these records and files. Data may be logically structured for users by using list, tree, and network approaches; however, records that are logically grouped for one application may not be physically located together in storage. Files may be organized in at least three ways—sequentially, randomly, or by an indexed sequential approach. Each of these approaches has strengths and weaknesses. In this chapter, we have concentrated on I/O media and devices that are used primarily for high-volume processing of sequentially organized files.

Punched cards are a familiar medium. They are easily understood, and they possess advantages because of their fixed length and unit record nature. However, their data density is low, they are bulky, and they represent a slow means of input and output. Punched paper tape provides greater data density than cards, but, like cards, paper tape is a relatively slow I/O medium.

Magnetic tape is much faster. Its transfer rate is significantly improved by its high data density. It can be erased and reused many times and is thus very economical. Data may be recorded on some other medium and then transferred to magnetic tape by a conversion process, or several alternative data entry approaches may be used to key data from source documents directly onto magnetic tape. Data are usually represented by either a seven- or nine-channel code, and parity checking is used to reduce the chance of error. However, the coded magnetized spots are invisible, and thus a printing operation is required to check or verify tape data. Tape records lack random accessibility.

Character readers reduce the manual effort involved in data input operations. Financial institutions have supported the development of MICR as a means of handling billions of transactions each year. Unfortunately for organizations outside the banking community, there are no alphabetic characters available in MICR. Optical character readers, however, have alphabetic as well as numeric capability and perform efficiently in a number of applications.

Printers are the primary output device when the information is to be used by people rather than by machine. Available printers may be character-at-a-time devices for low-volume applications, or they may be impact or nonimpact machines that can produce thousands of lines per minute. When compared with magnetic tape output, however, printers are still very slow. In some cases, printed output has been replaced by microfilm output.

**REVIEW AND DISCUSSION QUESTIONS**

**1** (**a**) How are data organized in business information systems? (**b**) What role does a record key play in file creation?

**2** Discuss several ways in which data may be logically structured to meet user needs.

**3** "Logical records may not be physically located together in storage." Discuss why this statement is true.

**4** "Several arrangements are used to organize files for storage, retrieval, and processing." (**a**) What are these arrangements? (**b**) What are the advantages and disadvantages of each of these arrangements?

**5** A punched card is a triple-purpose medium. (**a**) What is the meaning of triple purpose? (**b**) What other media are triple purpose?

**6** Define the following terms: (**a**) Data item (**b**) Field (**c**) Record key (**d**) Transaction file (**e**) Master file (**f**) Data base (**g**) Pointer (**h**) List structure (**i**) Tree structure (**j**) Network structure (**k**) Logical record (**l**) Transform algorithm (**m**) ISAM (**n**) Turnaround document (**o**) Data density (**p**) Channels (**q**) Frame (**r**) Transfer rate (**s**) Interrecord gap (**t**) Load-point marker (**u**) Header label (**v**) Print chain (**w**) Parity checking.

**7** (**a**) Discuss the advantages and limitations of punched cards. (**b**) Discuss the advantages and limitations of punched paper tape.

**8** Explain how data are read from and written on magnetic tape.

**9** Discuss the advantages and limitations of magnetic tape.

**10** Explain the approaches used to provide direct data entry on magnetic tape.

**11** Obtain a cancelled check and explain the magnetic ink coding along the bottom of the check.

**12** (**a**) Discuss the advantages and limitations of MICR. (**b**) Discuss the advantages and limitations of OCR.

**13** Identify and discuss three types of printers.

**14** Why would an organization wish to use microfilm output?

**SELECTED REFERENCES**

Baty, Gordon B.: "OCR—Where It's Going," *Journal of Systems Management,* February 1976, pp. 10–15.

Burch, John G., Jr., and Felix R. Strater, Jr.: *Information Systems: Theory and Practice,* Hamilton Publishing Company, Santa Barbara, Calif., 1974, chaps. 8 and 9.

Davis, Gordon B.: *Introduction to Computers,* 3d ed., McGraw-Hill Book Company, New York, 1977, chap. 9.

Martin, James: *Principles of Data-Base Management,* Prentice-Hall, Inc., Englewood Cliffs, N.J., 1976. (For further information on data organization concepts.)

Miller, Frederick W.: "The Non-Diminishing Printer," *Infosystems,* October 1977, pp. 70–72ff.

# input and output: II

# 5

LEARNING OBJECTIVES   After studying this chapter and answering the discussion questions, you should be able to: ☐ Describe some of the characteristics of direct-access devices that use magnetic drums, magentic disks, magnetic cards and strips, and magnetic bubble chips for I/O and online storage ☐ Discuss the uses of online terminals in multiunit data stations, visual display applications, and distributed processing systems ☐ Identify and discuss the most commonly used services for transmitting data from one location to another ☐ Explain how communications processors are used to coordinate data communications activities in computing/communications networks

**M**any organizations find that most, if not all, of their data processing needs are being met quite satisfactorily through the use of the I/O media and devices described in the last chapter. This is true because (1) sequential processing is acceptable—perhaps even preferable—for the type of high-volume applications they process, (2) an unlimited amount of data may be safely and inexpensively retained in offline secondary storage, and (3) the cost of using these media and devices to process sequentially organized files is usually less than the cost of using direct-access devices.

But as we saw in the last chapter, there are also many processing situations where direct access to records organized in a random or indexed-sequential fashion is needed. Thus, in this chapter we shall *first* look at the different types of popular *direct-access devices used for I/O and online secondary storage.* We shall then consider a number of *online terminal devices* that have the ability to (1) produce direct I/O of information without data-recording media being *required,* (2) create a direct online relationship between user and computer, and (3) handle economically a lower and/or more irregular volume of input data. Finally, we shall examine *data communications concepts and techniques* that facilitate direct access to computing resources from remote terminals.

**DIRECT-ACCESS STORAGE DEVICES**

Some of the devices considered in this section are *flexible* in the sense that the storage they provide may be either online or offline. For example, magnetic disk packs can be used indefinitely for online storage. But the disks (and the data they contain) can be removed and stored offline just like tape and cards. It is also worth noting here that the selection of the "best" direct-access storage device to use *involves compromise.* As Fig. 5-1 shows, there is frequently an *inverse relationship* between I/O speed on the one hand and storage capacity on the other. That is, as online storage capacity increases, the speed with which data can be entered and retrieved often declines. Also, as online storage capacity increases, the cost per character stored tends to decrease.

### magnetic drums

Magnetic drums were an early means of primary storage. Now, however, they are sometimes used as online secondary storage when fast response is of greater importance than large capacity. For example, they may be used to store mathematical tables, data, or program modifications that are frequently referred to during processing operations.

A magnetic drum is a cylinder that has an outer surface plated with a metallic magnetizable film. A motor rotates the drum on its axis at a

| Medium | Input Device Used | Output Device Used | Typical I/O Speed Ranges (Characters per Second) | | Typical Storage Uses | | Typical Storage Capacity |
|---|---|---|---|---|---|---|---|
| | | | Input | Output | Online Secondary | Offline Secondary | |
| Magnetic drum | Drum storage unit | Drum storage unit | 230,000–1,500,000 | 230,000–1,500,000 | × | | From 1 to 4 million characters with high-speed drums; up to 200 million characters on slower drum units |
| Magnetic disk | Disk drive | Disk drive | 100,000–1,000,000 | 100,000–1,000,000 | × | × | Virtually unlimited offline storage; from 2 to 200 million characters per online disk pack |
| Magnetic cards/strips | Card/strip storage unit | Card/strip storage unit | 25,000–50,000 | 25,000–50,000 | × | × | Virtually unlimited offline storage; from 25 to 150 million characters per online card/strip cartridge |
| Paper | Typewriter terminal keyboard | Serial printer | 5–120 | 5–250 | — | — | |
| None | Keyboard | CRT visual display | 5–120 | 250–50,000 | — | — | |

**FIGURE 5-1**
Summary of I/O and storage devices—Chapter 5.

constant and rapid rate. Data are *recorded on* the rotating drum and *read from* the drum by *read-write heads,* which are positioned a fraction of an inch from the drum surface. The recording and reading operations are similar to those used with magnetic tape. The writing of new data on the drum erases data previously stored at the location. The magnetic spots written on the drum surface remain indefinitely until they, too, are erased at a future time. Reading of data recorded on the drum is accomplished as the magnetized spots pass under the read heads and induce electric pulses in the read coils.

The stored data are arranged in *bands* or *tracks* around the circumference of the drum. A *fixed* read-write head may be employed for *each* band, or horizontally movable heads (each of which serve a *number* of adjacent bands) may be used.

The computer is able to access stored records directly because each drum has a specific number of addressable locations. A band may be divided into sections, and each section may be given an identifying number. The *direct-access time*—i.e., the elapsed time between the instant when a data transfer from (or to) a storage device is called for and the instant when the transfer is completed—is basically determined by the delay time required for an addressed location to be positioned under a read-write head.[1] If there is a read-write head for each band on the drum, then the speed of rotation will determine the *rotational delay* and thus the access time; if there is only one read-write head for a number of bands, then there will be a further *positional delay* while the head is moved and positioned over the proper band.

### magnetic disks

Magnetic disks are by far the most popular direct-access storage medium. They are typically made of thin metal plates coated on both sides with a magnetizeable recording material. These disks may remain *permanently* in their cabinets (Fig. 5-2), or they may be packaged in portable or replaceable assemblies called *disk packs.* Many installations make economical use of both fixed disk and disk pack units—the fixed disk(s) is used to store system programs and frequently used files, and the disk packs are used for storage of data that may be needed less often. Several disks (the number varies) may be assembled in a disk pack, and each of these packs is capable of storing from 2 to 200 million data characters.[2]

---

[1] Technically speaking, most online devices, including drums, have *direct* but not *random* access to records. *Random access* refers to a storage device in which the access time is independent of the physical location of the data. Since the drum access time varies with the physical location of stored data, it is more technically correct to say that drums provide direct access. The distinction is often not observed, however, and the online units presented here are often described as random-access equipment.

[2] A 200-million-character disk pack could store the contents of about 200 books of this size.

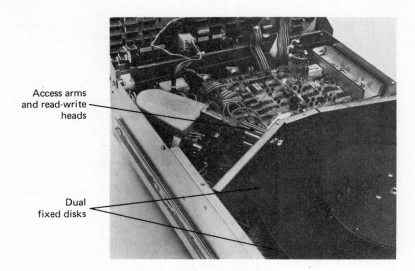

Access arms
and read-write
heads

Dual
fixed disks

**FIGURE 5-2**

Fixed disk drive (courtesy Pertec
Computer Corporation).

Regardless of whether disks are permanently mounted or portable, they are placed on a vertical shaft which rotates at a high, constant speed. A space is left between the spinning disks to allow access arms with small read-write heads to move to any storage location. Data are organized into a number of concentric circles or *tracks,* each of which has a designated location number. There are typically 200 to 800 tracks on the disk surface (Fig. 5-3).

Reading and writing operations are similar to those for drums. Data are recorded in specific locations as magnetized spots. Once recorded, the stored data remain intact even if the power fails in the system. (This *nonvolatile* storage characteristic is, of course, also true of data stored on magnetic tapes and drums.) Figure 5-4 shows one type of read-write head arrangement. Arms move horizontally among the individual disks. The two heads mounted on each arm service *two* surfaces—the top and the

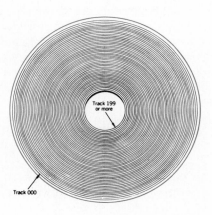

Track 199
or more

Track 000

**FIGURE 5-3**

Tracks on disk surface.

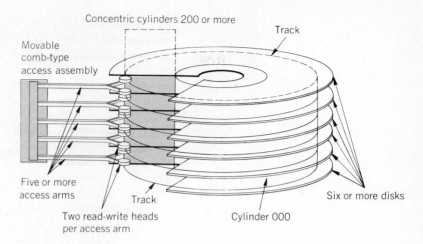

Concentric cylinders 200 or more

Track

Movable
comb-type
access assembly

Five or more
access arms

Track

Two read-write heads
per access arm

Cylinder 000

Six or more disks

FIGURE 5-4

underside of a disk. On command from the CPU, the proper head moves
to the specified disk surface and track, and the desired data are read as
soon as their location spins under the head. Since the heads for *all* disks
move in and out *together,* a number of related records extending vertically through the disks may be quickly accessible. For example, if the
access arm that serves the top recording surface is positioned at the
twentieth track, each of the other access arms would be *similarly positioned.* Thus, *each* of the read-write heads could operate on data in the
twentieth track. All the twentieth tracks together make up the twentieth
*cylinder* of the disks. Just as there are 200 or more tracks on a single
surface, so, too, are there 200 or more cylinders in a multiple stack of
disks (see Fig. 5-4).

When files are organized for direct access by the indexed sequential
method described in the last chapter, a *cylinder index* and a *track index*
may be used to locate a needed record. In Fig. 4-7, page 105, for
example, the "storage areas" in the index might refer to cylinders. If the
computer search program determines that a needed record is located in
cylinder 12, a track index for cylinder 12 would then be accessed and
searched to determine on which track of the cylinder the record is
located.

In addition to devices that use a *single* read-write head per disk
surface—the arrangement shown in Fig. 5-4—there are also other storage
units that employ (1) a *fixed* head for *each* track of a disk surface, or (2)
*multiple heads* on each movable access arm (each head serves a number
of adjacent tracks). In Fig. 5-5, for example, the arm servicing the top disk
surface contains 12 heads. What advantage over the arrangement shown
in Fig. 5-4 do you think there might be to these alternatives?

Interchangeable disk packs come in various sizes and storage capaci-
ties. The pack held by the operator in Fig. 5-6, for example, contains 12
disks and 20 recording surfaces (the top and bottom disks of the pack are

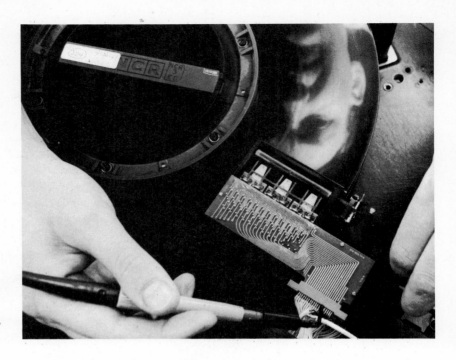

FIGURE 5-5

Multiple read-write heads. (courtesy NCR).

used to protect the data surfaces). Storage capacity of the pack is 100 million characters. It may be housed in the unit shown in Fig. 5-6 with seven others to provide a total of 800 million characters of storage.

Applications of disk technology are not limited to the larger computer installations that would make use of the equipment shown in Fig. 5-6. Interchangeable single "floppy" disks (or diskettes) are also used in minicomputer and microcomputer systems to provide inexpensive, low-capacity online storage. The flexible disk is packaged in a paper or plastic covering, and is not removed from this protective envelope. Rather, the envelope is inserted into the small disk drive (Fig. 5-7), the disk rotates inside the envelope, and the read-write heads access the disk surfaces (data and programs may be stored on both sides of the diskette) through slots in the covering. Diskette storage capacity typically ranges from 250,000 to about 2 million characters.

The access time–required for data to be transferred from a disk to primary storage (and vice versa) is determined by such factors as: (1) the number of access arms (if only a single arm is used and there is a stack of disks, there is a *vertical* positional delay); (2) the amount of *horizontal movement* (or *seek time*) required for the arm to position a head over the proper track (to answer the question you were asked a few sentences earlier, fixed heads for each track would have *no* horizontal movement, and multiple heads on each movable arm would *reduce* the average

**FIGURE 5-6**

Disk storage facility (courtesy IBM
Corporation).

**FIGURE 5-7**

Floppy disk drive (courtesy California
Computer Products, Inc.).

length of movement and thus decrease the access time, but these alternatives are more costly than the single-head-per-access-arm approach); and (3) the *rotational delay* (or *search time*) encountered, i.e., the time required to spin the needed data under a read-write head.

Advantages and limitations of magnetic disks   When compared with magnetic tape, disks have the following *advantages:* (1) random-access processing is possible without first sorting transactions; (2) quick and direct inquiry to records is possible; and (3) a single input transaction may be used to quickly update data-base records in several related files stored on different disks.

Of course, disks also have *limitations* when compared with magnetic tape: (1) disk packs are more expensive than the tape required to provide the same storage capacity; (2) when a tape file is updated, the old master tape remains unchanged and available in case of system malfunctions; when the records in a disk file are updated, however, the old records may be erased when the new records are written on the disk, and this *destructive read-in* characteristic may cause data integrity and/or security problems if a malfunction should occur; and (3) sequential processing using disks may be slower and less efficient than when tapes are used.

### magnetic cards and strips

Wouldn't it be nice to combine the magnetic tape advantages of low cost and high storage capacity with the advantages of rapid and direct record accessibility? This is essentially the objective of devices that utilize magnetic cards and tape strips for mass online storage. A magnetic card may be considered to be a length of flexible plastic material upon which short strips of magnetic tape have been mounted. A number of cards may be placed in a cartridge which, like disk packs, may be removed and stored offline. One device (the IBM Data Cell) uses a card cartridge that resembles a snare drum, and another (the IBM 3850 Mass Storage System or MSS) arranges tube-shaped cartridges in honeycomb storage compartments (Fig. 5-8).

Card and strip equipment has high storage capacity (the MSS, for example, can store online the contents of over 100,000 books of the size you are reading), and the cost per character stored is very low. Data are erasable, but access speed is slow when compared with drums and disks.

### magnetic bubbles and other possibilities

Although magnetic bubble direct-access storage technology is, at this writing, still in its infancy, there are some researchers who believe that magnetic disks will ultimately be replaced by the magnetic bubble

FIGURE 5-8

(Courtesy IBM Corporation).

devices of the future.[3] One reason for this optimism is that since bubble units are made with solid-state electronic chips and have no moving parts, they should be much more reliable than units with spinning disks that use mechanical components.

For our purpose, a magnetic bubble can be thought of as a positively charged island in a sea of negatively charged magnetic film. The presence of a bubble is analogous to the presence of a hole in a punched paper tape column or an "on" condition in a magnetic tape frame. (The absence of a bubble, of course, is analogous to the absence of a punched hole or an "off" condition.) Data may then be represented in bubble storage by the presence or absence of bubbles just as they were in punched tape form by the presence or absence of holes.

Figure 5-9 shows how thousands of coded characters may be stored in a single square-inch package. When data are *placed into* storage, bubbles from the minor loops are transferred to the major loop, carried past a *write* (generate) station, and then returned to the minor loops; when data are *retrieved from* storage, the correct bubbles are transferred, at a signal, from the minor loops into the major loop which carries them past the

---

[3] Bubble storage may have its greatest impact in the next few years on the smaller disk devices. But you should realize that as far as larger disk drives are concerned this prediction will probably *not* come true in the next several years, and, of course, it may never happen. Long-time observers of the computer hardware scene know that at any given time research-ers are working on several new approaches that could eventually replace the technology that currently occupies the dominant position. But these researchers are not shooting at a stationary target; advances are usually also being made in the dominant technology. Furthermore, before the potential of the new approach can be realized, it is possible that some other alternative will achieve a breakthrough that will make both the new approach (and the dominant technology) obsolete.

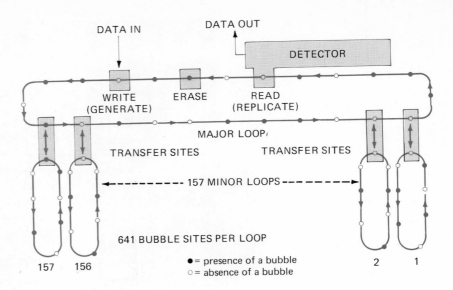

FIGURE 5-9

Magnetic bubble storage (courtesy Texas Instruments Incorporated).

read (replicate) station. The access time, of course, varies with the location of the needed bubbles in the minor loop "pipelines." Magnetic bubble storage is nonvolatile.

Two other direct-access storage approaches that are receiving the careful attention of researchers are:

**1** *Charge coupled device (CCD) systems.* Like a bubble storage device, a CCD circulates the stored data in closed pipelines and uses the charges in a storage crystal to represent data. A CCD is a form of semiconductor that is fabricated on a chip; thus, it is completely electronic, is somewhat faster than bubbles, is very compact, and may be inexpensive to produce in the future. Unfortunately, however, CCD storage is *volatile*—i.e., the stored data are lost when the power is shut off.

**2** *Optical direct-access systems.* Information may be stored on a special light-sensitive plate by modulating electric pulses onto a *laser* light beam that is directed to a given area on the plate surface. A negative image of the varying light pattern—called a *hologram*—is etched on the plate surface and storage is thus accomplished. To retrieve information (without erasing it) a less-intense laser beam is directed to the appropriate hologram to project the image onto sensors that will convert the light into electrical representations of the stored information. A single beam of light can cause the immediate transfer of a "page" of data. Theoretically, storage density and I/O speed is very high. Also, reliability is enhanced because of the absence of moving parts.

**ONLINE TERMINALS**    The *console control panel* of a computer (Fig. 5-10) appears to most observers as a confusing array of lights, switches, and buttons; it is used to load programs, display the contents of a number of special CPU storage

Console typewriter

Console
control
panel

FIGURE 5-10

Computer console (courtesy Sperry
UNIVAC Division, Sperry Rand
Corporation).

locations during program execution, determine the causes of certain
equipment malfunctions, and reset the computer after malfunctions have
been corrected. Often associated with the control panel is a *console
typewriter* (Fig. 5-10), or a keyboard for input and a visual display tube for
output. These typewriter and visual display devices are online terminals
that enable the computer operator to enter data directly into and receive
information directly from the storage unit of the central processor. When
the keys are depressed, the code designation of the keyed characters is
entered into storage. A visual record is also typed or displayed. In
addition, the console keyboard may be used to (1) modify a portion of the
program instructions, (2) test the program of instructions, (3) inquire
about the contents of certain storage areas, (4) alter the data content of
specific storage locations, (5) determine intermediate computing results,
and (6) receive output information in response to inquiries.

Online terminals may be classified as (1) *typewriterlike machines,* (2)
*multiunit data stations,* (3) *visual display units,* or (4) *intelligent devices.*

### typewriter terminals

Typewriter terminals (see Fig. 2-17, page 58) may be quite similar to
console typewriters, but they are located away from the computer room.

© DATAMATION ®

They may be in the next office, in a nearby building, or in the next state. And they may be connected to the CPU by a short cable or by a complex data communications system. Users transmit input data via the keyboard and receive output information from the character-at-a-time printer. Hundreds of thousands of these terminals are now in service.

### multiunit data stations

The term *multiunit data stations* may be used in several ways to describe the equipment used in particular types of applications. Let us look at some of the possibilities.

**1**  *Remote job-entry stations.* Data may be read into a distant CPU by multiple station units. Card and tape readers and/or a manual keyboard may be used for *input,* and *output* information may be either visually displayed or printed at the station (see Fig. 5-11). A wide variety of I/O options is available.

**2**  *Data collection stations.* These stations (and the transaction recording stations discussed below) typically perform limited operations. They have been developed to get data from remote points into the computer as quickly as possible. For example, data collection stations are often used in factories to control the inventory of parts and materials used in

Printed
output

Tape card, and keyboard
input

Displayed
output

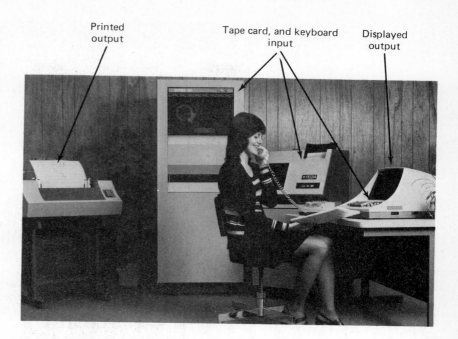

**FIGURE 5-11**

Remote job entry station (courtesy
Entrex, Inc.).

production (Fig. 5-12). Let us assume that an employee needs a dozen hinges to complete a job. The hinges may be obtained from a supply point. A data collection terminal may then be used to transmit the type and number of hinges taken along with the job number to the computer. After an accuracy check is made, the data are accepted and used to update inventory and job cost records.

**FIGURE 5-12**

Data collection station (courtesy IBM
Corporation).

FIGURE 5-13

(Courtesy Burroughs Corporation.)

**3**   *Transaction recording stations.* Savings institutions are among the leading users of online transaction recording devices (Fig. 5-13). Let us assume that a deposit is to be made by a customer. The customer presents his or her bankbook and the amount of the deposit to the teller, who inserts the book into a recorder and keys in the transaction data. The data are then sent to the computer, which adjusts the customer's savings balance. The updated information is relayed back to the remote station where it is entered in the customer's bankbook. The entire transaction is accounted for in a matter of seconds.

**4**   *Point-of-sale stations.* As you saw in Fig. 4-27, page 122, point-of-sale (POS) terminals with automated scanning features that permit the reading of UPC bars are replacing cash registers in *supermarkets* because they can do everything a cash register does plus many other things. And other POS terminals in *department stores* can be used to (a) make direct inquiry about the credit status of the customer, (b) improve inventory control, and (c) produce faster and more accurate sales information. Such a POS terminal may be equipped with a handheld "wand" that can be used to speed up the sales transaction. By passing the wand across a special tag attached to the merchandise, the clerk reads the item description and price into the terminal. (Credit card numbers can also be read in this way.) The terminal may then automatically display the price, compute the total amount of the purchase including taxes, and print a sales receipt.

**5**   *Electronic funds transfer system stations.* Some electronic funds transfer system (EFTS) stations are much like the transaction recording stations referred to above, but they may be *unattended* devices such as *automated teller machines* (Fig. 5-14) that are located on or off the financial institution's premises to receive and dispense cash and to handle routine financial transactions 24 hours a day. For example, you might use a plastic "currency" or "debit" card (which incorporates, perhaps, a magnetically encoded strip of material to supply the computer with your

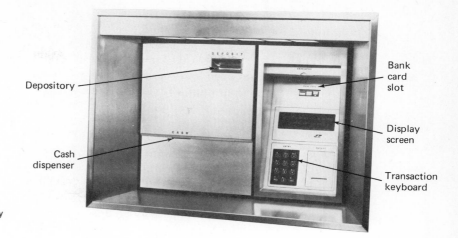

Depository

Cash dispenser

Bank card slot

Display screen

Transaction keyboard

**FIGURE 5-14**

Automated teller machine (courtesy INCOTERM Corporation).

account number and credit limit) to (a) make a deposit to your account, (b) withdraw cash, (c) electronically transfer funds from your account to the account of one of your creditors, or (d) make inquiries about the balance(s) in your account(s). Instructions displayed on a screen guide you through these transactions. And other EFTS terminals owned by, and connected to, the computers of financial institutions may be located at the checkout counters of retail outlets and used in conjunction with store-owned POS stations. These EFTS stations (which may also be located at hotels, hospitals, etc.) are used to (a) transfer funds between accounts— e.g., from the shopper's to the merchant's account; (b) identify customers, authorize credit, and/or authorize debit or credit card cash advances; and (c) guarantee the availability of funds to cover customer checks (Fig. 5-15).

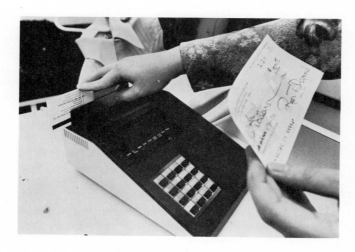

**FIGURE 5-15**

EFTS station at retail outlet (courtesy IBM Corporation).

### visual display terminals

Considerable emphasis is now being placed on visual display terminals, which look like small television sets equipped with a manual keyboard. Although input by means of the keyboard may be no faster than with typing, output is silent and very fast—the screen of the terminal's CRT can be instantly covered with hundreds of characters of displayed information.

There are two basic classes of CRT display terminals. In the *first* category are lower-cost units, which display *only alphanumeric* information. In the *second* class are more expensive units, which are capable of projecting graphs, charts, and designs as well as alphanumeric characters. The first category might be considered a clever "paperless electronic typewriter"; the second class of display units possesses graphic art capabilities not available with the less-expensive devices. Let us briefly look at some of the ways in which these display units are currently being used.

Alphanumeric display applications    Terminals that display only alphanumeric information are well suited for the following purposes:

1    *Obtaining quick response to inquiries.* The visual display unit provides a window into the computer's data base. Status of a customer's credit, prices quoted on stock exchanges, current inventory levels, availability of airline seats, locations of truck shipments and railroad freight cars, locations of unsold seats in a theater or stadium, location and telephone number of students and employees of a university—information such as this is being kept current by various organizations in online files so that it is instantly available for display upon inquiry. The keyboard can be used to update files in order to reflect any transaction that may be made at a display station, e.g., when airplane and theater tickets are sold, when credit purchases are authorized, when an order for additional inventory is placed, etc.

2    *Providing convenient human/machine interaction.* We saw in Chapter 2 that data management software would enable a manager to probe and query files in order to obtain information relevant to some unique problem. The combination of an easy-to-use inquiry language and a visual display unit facilitates this process. The manager, in effect, carries on a "conversation" with the computer system by supplying data and key phrases, while the system responds with displayed end results, intermediate results, or questions. The questions may be in a multiple-choice format so that the manager need only key in the response number. Alternatively, the manager can, with a touch of an electronic *light pen* (Fig. 5-16), call for a more detailed breakdown of an item in a displayed report. The light pen is a photocell placed in a small tube. When the pen is moved by the user over the screen, it is able to detect the light coming from a limited field of view. The light from the CRT causes the photocell to respond when the pen is pointed directly at a lighted area. These electric responses are transmitted to the computer, which is able to

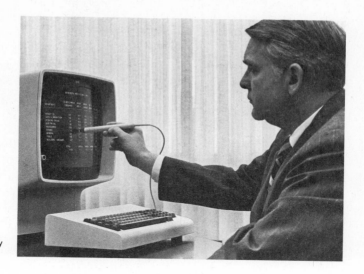

**FIGURE 5-16**

Human/machine interaction (courtesy
IBM Corporation).

determine that part of the displayed item that is triggering the photocell
response.

Graphical display applications   When a designer first gets a new-prod-
uct thought, he or she may make some preliminary sketches to get the
idea down on paper so that it may be more thoroughly analyzed. As the
design is modified, additional drawings may be required; when the idea
is approved, further detailed production drawings are prepared. Thus, the
preparation of drawings may occupy a substantial portion of the
designer's time.

Instruments such as *input tablets* have now been developed which
make it possible for the computer to receive human sketching directly. An
input tablet may be made of glass or plastic and may come in different
sizes as shown in Fig. 5-17. The tablet typically contains hundreds of
copper lines, which form a fine grid that is connected with the computer.
Each copper line receives electric impulses. A special pen or stylus
attached to the tablet is sensitive to these impulses and is used to form the
sketches. However, the pen does not mark directly on the tablet. To
communicate with the machine, the designer merely draws on a piece of
paper placed on the glass or plastic. The tablet grid then senses the exact
position of the stylus as it is moved and transmits this information to the
computer.

As the designer draws, the computer may display the developing
sketch on the CRT. However, there is a difference between the drawing
and the display. Poorly sketched lines are displayed as straight; poor
lettering is replaced by neat printing; and poorly formed corners become
mathematically precise. Changes and modifications in the drawing can
be quickly made; e.g., a line can be "erased" from (or shifted on) the
display unit with a movement of the stylus. Once the initial sketching is

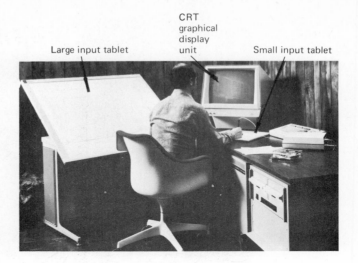

Large input tablet    CRT graphical display unit    Small input tablet

**FIGURE 5-17**

Interactive graphic design (courtesy Tektronix, Inc.).

finished and displayed on the CRT to the satisfaction of the designer, he or she may then instruct the computer to analyze the design and report on certain characteristics. For example, the computer might be asked to work out the acoustical characteristics of a theater that the designer has sketched. The sketch may then be modified by the designer on the basis of the computer analysis, or the machine may be instructed to display a theater with more desirable acoustics. Such direct human machine graphical communication enables the designer to (1) learn what effect certain changes have on the project and (2) save valuable time for more creative work. Graphical display techniques are currently being used in the design of ships, highways, aircraft, electronic circuits (Fig. 5-18), and buildings.

### intelligent terminals

By combining programmable microcomputers or minicomputers with terminal hardware, designers have built terminal systems (Fig. 5-19) that are similar to some smaller computer installations. In fact, the distinction between the small stand-alone computers in a computing network and these *intelligent terminals* is becoming blurred.

A growing number of organizations are using intelligent terminals as an integral part of a *distributed processing system*. On the local level, small jobs are processed using the terminal's user-programmable microcomputer or minicomputer and assorted peripheral and secondary storage devices without any interaction with a higher-level computer. Also, adequate local storage capacity may be available (e.g., on tape cassettes,

FIGURE 5-18

(Courtesy California Computer
Products, Inc.)

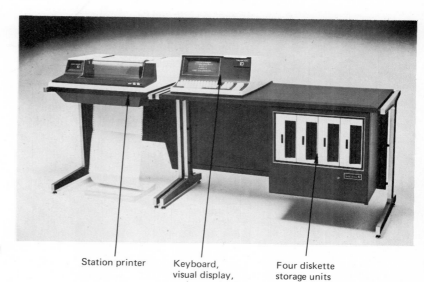

FIGURE 5-19

Intelligent terminal with self-standing
computing capability using COBOL,
RPG, and BASIC high-level
programming languages (courtesy
Datapoint Corporation).

Station printer

Keyboard,
visual display,
and central
processor

Four diskette
storage units

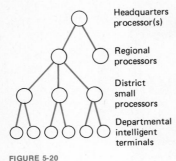

Headquarters
processor(s)

Regional
processors

District
small
processors

Departmental
intelligent
terminals

**FIGURE 5-20**

Hierarchical distributed processing
system.

diskettes, or magnetic bubble chips) to permit local users to store frequently needed data and to thus avoid the expense of making constant inquiries of a larger computer system in the organization. But the terminals are also used to make programmed error-detection checks to determine the validity of locally produced data and to classify and order these facts in a specified way prior to forwarding them to the computer(s) at a higher level in the organization for storage or further processing. The higher-level computer(s) in the organization may be used to manage large data bases and to serve the lower-level processors by executing jobs that require extensive computations. In short, intelligent terminals may be low-level satellite processors in a distributed processing *hierarchy* that may have several levels (see Fig. 5-20).[4]

## VOICE COMMUNICATION

Input units, basically, do nothing more than convert human language into machine language. Why, then, doesn't someone invent a machine that will enable a person to talk to the computer in English? As a matter of fact, a few manufacturers have done just that. Although the vocabulary is quite small, sound waves have been converted into machine language. Speech recognition, however, is not a widely used input technique at this time.[5]

When we look at the *output* side of verbal communication, however, we find that computers are now being used to give English responses in reply to human inquiries transmitted to a central computer over regular telephone lines. All the spoken words needed to process the possible inquiries are generally prerecorded on a magnetic or photographic film drum. Each word is given a code. When inquiries are received, the processor composes a reply message in a coded form. This coded message is then transmitted to an *audio-response* device, which assembles the words in the proper sequence and transmits the audio message back to the station requesting the information.

Audio-response techniques, combined with briefcase-sized keyboard devices, turn every standard telephone into a potential computer terminal. An equipment sales representative, for example, can use any available phone to check on product availability prior to contacting an important customer. An inquiry may be keyed directly into the home-office

[4] Of course, as we saw in Chapter 2 (and in Fig. 2-18), other distributed processing configurations using star or ring structures are also possible.

[5] One application that is receiving attention is the use of speech recognition techniques to determine the identity of a person seeking entry to a secure area (voice patterns are as unique as fingerprints). A phrase consisting of several words is spoken and the equipment then digitally compares this sound with the stored sounds made earlier when authorized persons uttered the same phrase. For more information on voice communication applications, see John R. Hausen, "The Computer Gets a Voice," *Infosystems*, August 1977, pp. 50ff.

computer system. A computer-compiled audio response could then give the sales representative the necessary inventory information. If the sales efforts lead to success, another phone may later be used to enter an order directly into the information system.

**DATA COMMUNICATIONS**   Numerous references have been made in earlier pages about remote I/O stations and terminals that are connected online to a computer. The number of these installed terminals has grown very rapidly in the United States in recent years (Fig. 5-21). But this growth would not have been possible without the availability of data communications techniques that facilitate I/O operations, and so we need to take a closer look at these techniques. *Data communication,* of course, simply refers to the means and methods whereby data are transferred between processing locations.

There is, certainly, nothing new about data communications. Human runners and messengers have been used since the beginning of recorded history. The Greek runner carrying the message of victory on the plains of Marathon has inspired a present-day athletic event. And the Pony Express won the admiration of a nation in the brief period of time before it was replaced by telegraph service.

### data transmission services

Data transmission services are available from domestic *common* or "public" *carriers* such as *telephone companies* (e.g., AT&T, General Telephone & Electronics or GT&E, and others), and *telegraph companies* (Western Union). In addition to these better-known carriers, there are also smaller *specialized common carriers* that may concentrate most of their attention on offering services of a particular type (e.g., the primary focus

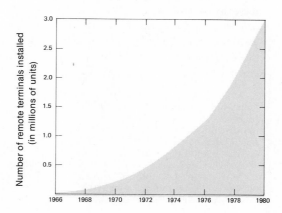

FIGURE 5-21

Terminal installations using data communications (United States, 1966–1980). Source: Stanford Research Institute.

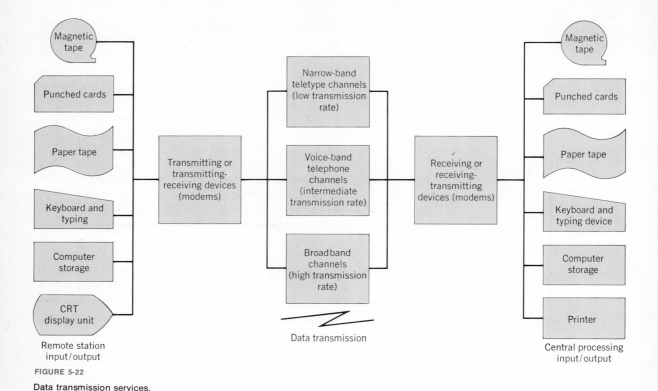

FIGURE 5-22

**Data transmission services.**

of attention may be on the transmission of data or pictures rather than on voice transmission). Generally speaking, these specialized carriers only transmit data between a limited number of the larger cities.[6]

Figure 5-22 shows the types of transmission *channels* or highways used to carry data from one location to another. These channels employ wire lines, cables, and/or microwave radio circuits which, like I/O devices, vary in data-handling speed.

Since many of the data transmission channels now in use are telephone facilities that were designed primarily for voice communications, you will notice in Fig. 5-22 that between the computing equipment and

---

[6] Since much of the data traffic in the nation is between these densely populated areas, however, and since they have no expensive facilities to maintain in smaller cities and towns, the specialized carriers were initially able to underprice their larger competitors who had traditionally based their charges on the average cost of transmission throughout their entire networks. The larger carriers protested vigorously to the FCC and to Congress that the specialized carriers were trying to "skim the cream" off the revenue from the low-cost markets—an act that would force them to raise the price of service to the higher-cost small markets. This controversy has not yet been resolved, but, of course, the larger carriers have now lowered their rates on competitive routes.

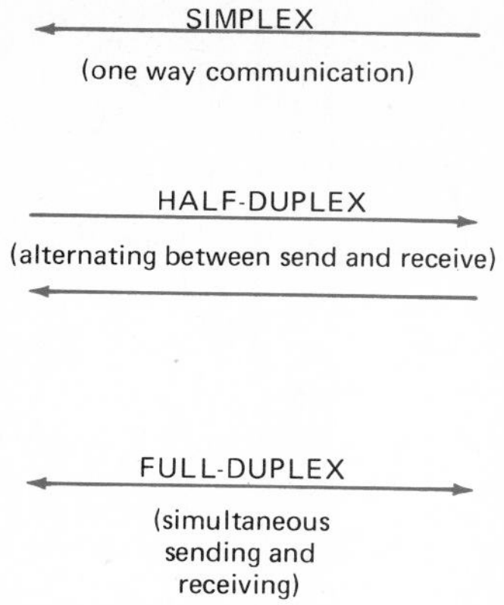

SIMPLEX

(one way communication)

HALF-DUPLEX

(alternating between send and receive)

FULL-DUPLEX

(simultaneous
sending and
receiving)

**FIGURE 5-23**

Data transmission circuits.

the transmission channels are located devices called *modems* which convert the computing equipment digital signals into signals that can be used by voice-oriented transmission systems.[7] You will also notice in Fig. 5-23 that three types of circuits are used for data transmission purposes. The *simplex circuit* permits data to flow in *only* one direction. A terminal connected to such a circuit would be either a *send-only* or a *receive-only* device. But a terminal connected to a *half-duplex* line could *alternately* send data to and then receive information from a CPU. Half-duplex circuits are widely used. When two-way *simultaneous* transmission is needed between a terminal and a CPU, a *full-duplex* connection must be used.

*Teletype* channels transmit data at slow speeds (from about 5 to 30 characters per second), but this is quite adequate for input by means of manual keying. Standard voice-grade *telephone* channels permit more rapid transmission. Speeds of well over 300 characters per second are possible. Telephone circuits are used to communicate large amounts of data stored in cards and tapes. A telephone channel is connected to I/O equipment at the sending and receiving points and may be used for both voice and data transmission. Let us assume, to use a simple example, that a branch sales office is ready to transmit sales orders to the main plant. A clerk at the branch office dials the proper number at the main plant to notify it of a transmission. When the employee at the receiving station is ready to accept the message, both parties push a data button, at which point the voice communication cuts off and the data transmission begins.

If the data volume between locations is sufficient, it may be economical for the company to acquire a *dedicated* or *leased* line(s) which can be used for both voice and data purposes. A dedicated line permanently (or semipermanently) connects communicating locations directly. No dialing is required to make connections. If data volume is not sufficient to justify the higher cost of a private line, however, or if the higher speeds available from private lines are not needed, then the regular *dial-up telephone switching network* should be used. In this case, the cost of data messages, like that of long-distance calls, is determined by time use. Of course, the user of the dial-up network has no control over the message-switching circuits that will handle the data transmission. Thus, during one hookup, satisfactory circuits may be received, and in the next older switching mechanisms may be encountered that allow line "noise," fading, and "crosstalk" to interfere with the accurate transmission of the data.

Some users of telephone channels have found it to be more economical and reliable to deal directly with a specialized common carrier rather

---

[7] Modem stands for modulator-demodulator. Modems are not necessary when newer transmission facilities designed specifically to transmit digital data signals are used.

than directly with a telephone company. Telenet Communications Corporation, for example, has a network of computers that receives customer data coming in over telephone lines. These data are temporarily stored and organized in "packets" of up to 128 characters in the Telenet system. The packets are then computer-routed and transmitted at high speed over dedicated AT&T telephone lines to a Telenet office near the final data destination. At this office, data in the packets are reassembled into the complete message for transmission to the final destination. For the user of the Telenet service, the transmission cost is frequently less than if the user had relied on less-efficient means of directly utilizing telephone channels. Thus, specialized carriers such as Telenet are often referred to as *value-added packet switching* services.

---

**International**
- *INTELSAT system.* This *In*ternational *Tele*communications *Sate*llite Consortium includes about 100 member nations on six continents. INTELSAT is headquartered in Washington D.C., which is also the home of the *Com*munications *Sate*llite Corporation (COMSAT), an organization that was chartered by Congress in 1962 to be the United States representative to INTELSAT. COMSAT performs a management function for INTELSAT. Beginning with Early Bird in 1965, several generations of satellites have now been launched by INTELSAT, and these now form a global communications system that accounts for a major proportion of all long-distance international communications.

**Domestic**
- *AT&T system.* Although AT&T currently has several satellites aloft, it is banned by the FTC from offering, via satellite, private line service to customers until 1979. At that time a partnership of AT&T and GT&E plans to enter the domestic leased-line business.
- *RCA Communications system.* The first to offer domestic satellite service, RCA at this writing has two SATCOM satellites in orbit. Major transmitting/receiving stations are located in six large cities from New York to California.
- *SBS system.* As we saw in Chapter 2, *S*atellite *B*usiness *S*ystems is likely to be a major force in future data communications. An affiliate of IBM, Aetna Life and Casualty Insurance Company, and COMSAT, SBS is expected to be in operation by 1981.
- *Western Union System.* With two WESTAR satellites in orbit at this writing, Western Union has major ground stations in five cities and, of course, a nationwide network of telegraph lines. In addition to moving data for its own customers, Western Union also leases satellite channels to American Satellite Corporation—a specialized carrier that concentrates on the high-speed transmission of data.

FIGURE 5-24

Satellite data transmission systems.

*Broadband* channels use very high frequency electric signals to carry the data message at maximum speeds of around 100,000 characters per second. These broadband circuits may be groups of voice-grade wire channels, or they may be microwave radio circuits. Such transmission facilities are expensive and are now required by only the large companies. Broadband facilities are used for transmitting data between magnetic tape units or from one computer storage unit to another.

When microwave radio facilities are used, the message may be transmitted along a terrestrial route by repeater stations that are located, on the average, about 25 miles apart. Alternatively, the message may be beamed to a *satellite* that acts as a reflector by accepting signals transmitted from one point on Earth and returning the same signals to some other point on Earth. The satellite appears from Earth to be a stationary target for the microwave signals because it is precisely positioned 22,300 miles above the equator with an orbit speed that matches the Earth's rotation. Dozens of satellites are now in orbit to handle international and domestic data, voice, and video communications. Figure 5-24 gives a brief summary of some of these satellite systems.

### coordination of data communications

The data communications environment has changed rapidly in just a few years. A typical online system of the mid-1960s is shown in Fig. 5-25a. Terminals were linked by transmission facilities directly to a central computer. Such a system is still quite appropriate for many organizations. But some of today's large distributed computing/communications networks are quite different, and the coordination required for efficient network use is quite complex. These systems must link together hundreds of terminals at dozens of dispersed locations (Fig. 5-25b).

Figure 5-25b shows some possible ways in which *communications processors* (typically minicomputers or microcomputers) may be used for the following purposes:

1   *Remote concentration of messages.*[8] The *remote concentrator* (Fig. 5-26) reduces transmission costs by receiving terminal input from many low-speed lines and then concentrating and transmitting a compressed and smooth stream of data on a higher-speed and more efficient facility. (Although faster communications channels are more expensive, they can do more work, and thus the cost per character transmitted may well be reduced.)

---

[8] A hard-wired *multiplexor* is also used to perform this concentration function. Although the multiplexor is less expensive than the concentrator, it is not programmable and thus does not have the flexibility of the concentrator.

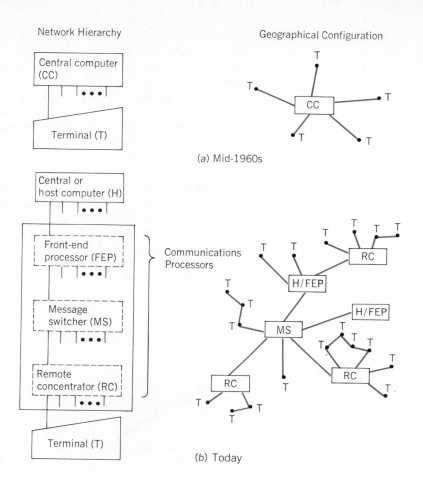

**FIGURE 5-25**

Data communications environments.

**2**   *Message switching.* The *message switcher* receives and analyzes data messages from points in the network, determines the destination and the proper routing, and then forwards the messages to other network locations. If necessary, a message may be stored until an appropriate outgoing line is available.

**3**   *Front-end processing.* The *front-end processor* is located at a central computer site. Its purpose is to relieve the main computer—i.e., the *host computer*—of a number of the functions required to interact with and control the communications network.

The functions of communications processors differ from one network to another, and there may be an overlapping of functions. A message-switching processor, for example, may also function as a remote concentrator; a front-end processor may perform message-switching functions; and, in less complete networks, the host computer may perform most or all of the functions of the front-end processor.

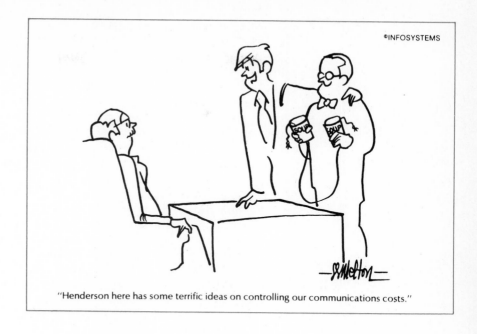

©INFOSYSTEMS

"Henderson here has some terrific ideas on controlling our communications costs."

Communications system console

Communications processor

Disk storage for collection and concentration of data

**FIGURE 5-26**

Equipment for remote concentration, message switching, and data collection (courtesy Burroughs Corporation).

SUMMARY
When direct access to records is required, several types of devices may be used for I/O and online secondary storage. Selection from among these devices typically involves compromise: There is frequently an inverse relationship between the speed of data transfer on the one hand and storage capacity on the other. Also, as online storage capacity increases, the cost per character stored tends to decrease. Thus, magnetic disk units tend to be slower than drum devices, but they also usually provide greater storage capacity and a lower cost per character stored. Disks are currently the most popular direct-access medium, but magnetic bubble technology or some other approach may in time change this situation.

Console keyboards, remote job-entry stations, data collection and transaction recording stations, point-of-sale and EFTS terminals, visual display stations, input tablets and light pens, intelligent terminals—all these online instruments enable people to communicate directly with any record stored in the direct-access devices. Audio communication from computers to humans has proved to be practical.

Data communications facilities relay information between remote points. A wide range of data transmission services is available. These services vary in data-handling speed and cost. The manager must plan carefully in choosing among the alternatives. Advanced communications networks using programmable processors for such functions as remote concentration of messages, message switching, and front-end processing have been developed in recent years.

REVIEW AND DISCUSSION QUESTIONS

1  "With direct-access devices there is frequently an inverse relationship between speed and cost per character stored, on the one hand, and storage capacity on the other." Explain and give examples.

2  (a) What factors determine the direct-access time of magnetic drums? (b) What factors determine the direct-access time of magnetic disks?

3  A manufacturer makes a disk drive that has permanently mounted disks, and each disk has a read-write head for each track. What might be the advantages and limitations of this approach?

4  When compared with magnetic tape, what are the advantages and limitations of magnetic disks?

5  Explain how a cylinder index and a track index may be used to locate a needed record stored in a magnetic disk device.

6  Explain the difference between the seek time and the search time in retrieving data from a disk drive.

7  (a) How are data represented in magnetic bubble storage? (b) Why does the access time vary with the magnetic bubble storage approach?

8  How may the console typewriter be used?

9  (a) What is the purpose of a data collection station? (b) Of transaction recording stations? (c) Of POS stations? (d) Of EFTS stations?

**10**   (**a**) What two basic classes of CRT display terminals are available? (**b**) How may each category be used? (**c**) What is an intelligent terminal?

**11**   How may audio-response units be used? Give examples.

**12**   Identify and discuss the most commonly used transmission channels for carrying data from one location to another.

**13**   Assume that you are a manager faced with deciding what type of data communications service to use. Discuss how you would evaluate the alternatives in light of such factors as (**a**) the number and location of I/O stations, (**b**) the volume of data to be communicated, (**c**) the timing of messages, and (**d**) the speed requirements.

**14**   What possible applications are there for the simplex, half-duplex, and full-duplex modes of data communication?

**15**   Define the following terms: (**a**) Disk pack (**b**) Nonvolatile storage (**c**) Rotational delay (**d**) Destructive read-in (**e**) Charge-coupled device (**f**) Hologram (**g**) Automated teller machines (**h**) Light pen (**i**) Input tablet (**j**) Common carrier (**k**) Transmission channels (**l**) Leased line (**m**) Modem (**n**) Dial-up switching network (**o**) Value-added packet switching service (**p**) INTELSAT system.

**SELECTED REFERENCES**    Canning, Richard G.: "Developments in Data Transmission," *EDP Analyzer,* March 1973, pp. 1–14.

Feidelman, Lawrence: "The New Look of Data Entry," *Infosystems,* December 1977, pp. 46–47ff.

Hansen, John R.: "Terminals Get Smarter; So Do Users," *Infosystems,* March 1977, pp. 56ff.

Kramarsky, David: "Business Satellites in Management's Orbit," *Administrative Management,* January 1977, pp. 28–29ff.

Louderback, Peter D.: "A Community's First Reaction to EFT: Mostly Favorable," *Management Controls,* January-February 1977, pp. 4–9.

Menkus, Belden: "The Enigmatic Intelligent Terminal Expands Capabilities," *Administrative Management,* March 1977, pp. 82–84ff.

Myers, Ware: "Key Developments in Computer Technology: A Survey," *Computer,* November 1976, pp. 48–75.

————: "Current Developments in Magnetic Bubble Technology," *Computer,* August 1977, pp. 73–81.

Newton, Harry: "What's the Word on Data Communications?" *Computer Decisions,* December 1976, pp. 19–22.

Smith, Lee: "The Domsat War Gets Tougher and Costlier," *Dun's Review,* May 1977, pp. 72ff.

# the cpu: 6

## concepts and codes

LEARNING OBJECTIVES  After studying this chapter and answering the discussion questions, you should be able to: □ Outline the conceptual storage areas found in the CPU and explain how storage locations are identified and used for data processing □ Discuss the capacity of each storage address and the various approaches that are used to organize the storage unit □ Explain the binary numbering system and how it compares with the familiar decimal numbering system □ Describe how computers represent data in codes that are related to a binary numbering system

It is now time to take a closer look at the central processor. As you will remember, the typical CPU contains the storage unit, the arithmetic-logic unit, and the control unit. In this chapter we shall be concerned primarily with *storage concepts and related topics*. More specifically, we shall examine (1) the *conceptual areas* of the storage unit, (2) the *locations* in the storage unit, (3) the *capacity* of storage locations, (4) the *numbering systems* associated with computers, and (5) the *codes used to represent data* in computer systems. In the first part of the next chapter, we shall look at primary storage components and the operation of the arithmetic-logic and control units; in the latter part we shall briefly compare some of the characteristics of microcomputers and minicomputers with the CPU features found in larger systems.

## CONCEPTUAL STORAGE AREAS

We know that the storage unit contains the data to be processed and the program of instructions. As a general rule, any storage location in the central processor has the ability to store *either* data or instructions; i.e., a specific physical space may be used to store data for one operation and instructions for another. The programmer (or the "housekeeping" software prepared by programmers) determines how the location will be used for each application.[1]

For each program, there will be, typically, four areas assigned to group related types of information. These conceptual areas are shown in Fig. 6-1. They are referred to as *conceptual areas* because it is important to remember that they are *not fixed* by built-in physical boundaries in storage. Rather, they vary (thus the broken lines in Fig. 6-1) at the discretion of the programmer. Three of the four areas (input, working, and output) are used for *data-storage* purposes. The *input storage* area, as the name indicates, receives the data coming from the input media and devices. The *working storage* space corresponds to a blackboard or a sheet of scratch paper; it is space used by the program to hold data being processed as well as the intermediate results of such processing. The *output storage* section contains processed information that is awaiting a *read-out* operation. The *program storage* area, of course, contains the processing instructions.

A typical *data-flow* pattern is indicated in Fig. 6-1. Data remain in the input area until needed. Since the actual processing occurs in the arithmetic-logic unit, data are delivered to this unit from input storage and processed, and the final results move through the output storage area to the user. Intermediate figures, generated in the arithmetic-logic unit, are

---

[1] As we will see in the next chapter, there may be exceptions to this statement. Some CPUs, for example, have "read-only" storage elements that have predetermined functions and are not available to the applications programmer.

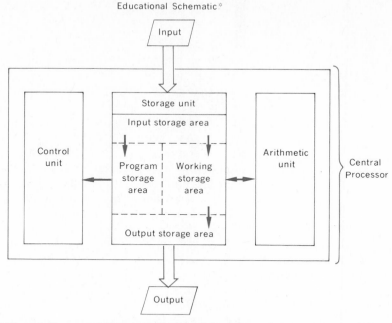

Educational Schematic*

FIGURE 6-1

Conceptual storage areas (courtesy Sperry UNIVAC Division, Sperry Rand Corporation).

* The specific areas of storage used for a particular purpose (input storage, program storage, etc.) *are not fixed but rather vary from program to program.* The programmer defines the limits of these reserved areas for each program. Therefore, broken lines (rather than solid ones) are used in the diagram to indicate this flexibility of area boundaries.

temporarily placed in a designated working storage area until needed at a later time. Data may move back and forth between working storage and the arithmetic-logic unit a number of times before the processing is completed.

*Instructions* move from the program storage area to the control unit. The first program instruction is sent to the control unit to begin the step-by-step processing procedure. Other instructions move into the control unit at the proper time until the job is completed.

## ✓ STORAGE LOCATIONS AND THEIR USE

A post office box is a storage location that is identified by a specific number and is capable of holding many different items. For example, a letter placed in a box yesterday may contain instructions on how to build a birdhouse; the card placed in the same box today may be an electric bill for $22.12. Instructions are stored one day and numerical quantities the next; contents change, but the box and the box number remain the same. Many such boxes may differ only in their identification numbers.

In a computer there are also numbered storage locations for holding both data and instructions. These "boxes," or "cells," are referred to as *addresses.* Like a post office box number, the address number remains the same and is independent of the contents. But unlike a post office box, which can hold several different messages at the same time, an address stores only one unit of data at a time. The addresses in a storage unit containing 4,096 locations would be numbered from 0000 to 4095. Thus, one unique address will be designated 1776. It is necessary to emphasize that *there is an important distinction between the address number and the contents of the address.* Why is this distinction important? It is important because one of the principles of programming is that basic machine language instructions deal directly with address numbers rather than with the contents of the address. For example, suppose that $315 is stored in address 1776. If the programmer wants that amount printed, she will not instruct the computer to print $315. Rather, she will order the machine to print 1776, and the computer will interpret this instruction to mean that it should *print the contents of address 1776.* Just as you can locate friends in a strange city if you know that their home address is 4009 Sarita Drive, so, too, can the computer locate the desired information if it knows the location number.

Perhaps an example illustrating some of the concepts that have been introduced would be appropriate at this time. In our example let us consider "a atlas aardvark." What is "a atlas aardvark"? Well, A. Atlas Aardvark is not a "what," he is a "who"—he is the Zoology Editor for Imprint Publishing Company. He is also the first person paid each week (Atlas has gone through life being first in line). Let's look at how his paycheck might be processed by Imprint's PAC (Peculiar Automatic Computer).

The payroll *data* are prepared on punched cards each week for each employee. Last week the following data were punched into Atlas's card: (1) he worked 40 hours; (2) he receives $10 an hour; (3) he has 20 percent of his total income taken out for taxes; and (4) he has hospitalization insurance, which costs him $5 each week.

Instructions have been prepared by Imprint's programmer to direct the computer in the payroll operation. The following steps must be performed:

1   The machine must be started.

2   An employee's payroll data must be read into storage for processing.

3   Hours worked must be multiplied by the hourly rate to find the *total earnings.*

4   Total earnings must be multiplied by the withholding percentage figure to find the amount of tax deduction.

5   To the tax withheld must be added the hospitalization insurance deduction to arrive at the *total deduction* figure.

6   The total deduction must be subtracted from the total earnings to find the take-home earnings.

**7**   A check must be printed for the amount of the take-home earnings, and it must be payable to the correct employee.

**8**   The machine must be stopped at the end of the processing operation.

Program instructions are also presented to the PAC in the form of punched cards.

Figure 6-2 shows the PAC storage locations. Although the programmer may assign the instructions to *any section* of the storage unit, she has chosen to read them into addresses 06 to 18. These locations thus become the *program storage* area. The first instruction (in address 06) identifies the locations for the payroll data (00, 01, 02, 03, and 04). The data could just as well have been placed in addresses 19 to 23, and so this is also an arbitrary decision.[2]

Let us use Fig. 6-3 to follow through the process that is required to prepare Atlas's paycheck. (The circled address numbers represent each step in the process.) After the computer operator has loaded the instructions into storage, the payroll data cards are placed into the card reader, the PAC controls are set at address 06, and the processing begins. This initial control setting feeds the first instruction into the control unit where it is interpreted. Signals are sent to the card reader, which carries out the command. Atlas's card is read, and the data are transferred to *input storage*. The control unit will execute the instructions automatically *in sequence* after the initial control setting until it is directed by a specific instruction to do otherwise. Therefore, as soon as the instruction in address 06 has been complied with, the control unit automatically begins interpreting the contents of address 07.

The next command instructs the control unit to copy the contents of

[2] Obviously, the data could not go into addresses 06 to 18 since these locations are now occupied by instructions. If a payroll item were mistakenly entered into a program section location, it would "erase" the instruction properly located in the address. At some later time the item would enter the control unit where it would be interpreted as an instruction. If such an error should occur, the result would be quite unpredictable but invariably disastrous.

| 00 | 01 | 02 | 03 | 04 | 05 |
|---|---|---|---|---|---|
| | | | | | |
| 06 Read payroll data card into addresses 00, 01, 02, 03, and 04. | 07 Write contents of address 01 into arithmetic unit. | 08 Multiply contents of arithmetic unit by contents of address 02. | 09 Duplicate preceding answer in address 05. | 10 Multiply contents of address 03 by preceding answer in arithmetic unit. | 11 Add contents of address 04 to preceding answer in arithmetic unit. |
| 12 Subtract preceding answer in arithmetic unit from contents of address 05. | 13 Move preceding answer to address 23. | 14 Write check for amount in address 23. | 15 Make check payable to contents of address 00. | 16 If last card, then go to address 18. | 17 Go to address 06. |
| 18 Stop processing. | 19 | 20 | 21 | 22 | 23 |

FIGURE 6-2

PAC storage.

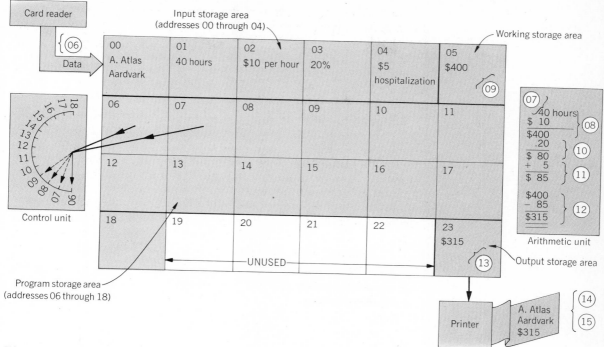

FIGURE 6-3

address 01 into the arithmetic-logic unit. The control unit does not care that the contents of 01 are 40 hours (the next employee's time may differ). It is merely concerned with carrying out orders, and so 40 hours is placed in the arithmetic unit. And, in sequence, the processing continues: The 40-hour figure is multiplied by $10 per hour to find total earnings (instruction in address 08); this total earnings figure is duplicated (instruction, 09) in address 05, which is the *working storage* area; the tax deduction is found to be $80 (instruction, 10); the total deduction figure is $85 (instruction, 11); and Atlas's take-home pay is $315 (instruction, 12). The $315 is transferred to address 23 by the next order in the sequence. (It could just as easily have been placed in any of the unused locations.) From this *output storage* area, the information is sent to the printer, which, under program control, prints the paycheck. If Atlas's card had been the last one in the deck, the instructions in addresses 16 and 18 would have halted the process. Since other cards follow, however, the control unit receives the next order in the sequence. This instruction tells the control unit to reset itself to address 06. And so the process automatically begins again.

To summarize, several important concepts have been demonstrated in this example:

**1**   Input, working, output, and program storage areas are required, but they are not fixed in the PAC. Rather, they are determined by Imprint's programmer.

**2**   The PAC is able to obey several *commands,* e.g., READ, WRITE, ADD, SUBTRACT, MOVE. This ability to execute specific orders is *designed and built into* the machine. Every computer has a particular set, or *repertoire,* of commands that it is able to obey.

**3**   Computers execute one instruction at a time. They follow sequentially the series of directions until explicitly told to do otherwise. Figure 6-4 is a diagram, or *flowchart,* of the payroll procedure. The computer moves through the instructions in sequence until it comes to a *branchpoint* and is required to answer a question: Have data from the last card been fed into storage? The answer to the question determines which path or branch the computer will follow. If the answer is no, then the procedure is automatically repeated by the use of the technique known as *looping;* if the answer is yes, the processing stops. Instructions that result in the transfer of program control to an instruction stored at some arbitrary location rather than to the next location in storage may be *conditional* or *unconditional* transfer commands. If the change in sequence is based on the outcome of some test, then it is a conditional transfer; if not, it is an unconditional branch. Can you identify the conditional and unconditional transfer instructions in Fig. 6-4?

✓ **CAPACITY OF STORAGE LOCATIONS**

Up to this point we have not bothered to define the storage capacity of *each address.* All we have said is that an address holds a specific data or instructional element. Actually, the storage capacity of an address is *built into* the machine. In some computers each address may contain only a *single character* (9, A, $, *). These systems are said to be *character addressable.* Other machines are designed to store a *fixed number of characters* in each address (JONES, XY1234, GO TO 06). These characters are treated as a single entity or unit; i.e., the computer treats them as a single data *word* or instruction *word.* Thus, machines designed to store a specified number of characters in an address are said to be *word addressable.* Figure 6-5 shows character-addressable and word-addressable storage. Character-addressable machines, on the one hand, are said to have *variable word-length storage.* Word-addressable machines, on the other hand, are said to have *fixed word-length storage.*

Perhaps an example will help clarify the differences between fixed and variable word-length storage. Let us assume that we are again going to place payroll data into PAC storage. The following data concern Mr. Cy ("Crab") Grass, the Botany Editor at Imprint Publishing Company:

| Employee | Hours worked | Hourly rate | Tax deduction | Hospitalization |
|----------|--------------|-------------|---------------|-----------------|
| Cy Grass | 40 | $9.50 | 15% | $5 |

Is PAC a fixed or a variable word-length machine? For illustration pur-

Start

A loop

06

07

08

09

10

11

12

13

14

15

16
Last card? — Yes → 18 Stop

No

17
Go to 06

FIGURE 6-4

poses and for reasons to be explained shortly, we will consider it to be both (after all, it is a Peculiar Company product).

## fixed word-length storage

We'll assume that each PAC address will store eight characters.[3] Figure 6-6a shows how the payroll data might be organized into 40 byte-sized cells in storage.[4] Addresses 00 to 04 are used.

Figure 6-6a also shows a disadvantage of fixed word-length storage. Each data word must be eight characters long, and these eight characters must be moved and operated on as a unit. If, as in address 01, only two characters are needed, the other six spaces in the word will be filled with zeros or will be blank.[5]

## variable word-length storage

Most of the earliest computers used a fixed word-length architecture. But variable word-length machines that could make more efficient use of storage space were quickly designed for business purposes. Figure 6-6b shows how the payroll data might be stored if PAC were a variable word-length computer. Space to store 22 additional characters is now available. Each space has an address. The intersections of the numbers at the top and in the column to the left designate the address numbers. The name "Cy," for example, is stored in addresses 00 and 01.

A fixed word-length computer identifies the stored word it is looking

---

[3] The number of characters that various fixed word-length computers can store depends on the machine design. A Control Data Corporation Cyber 170, for example, is a modern design that holds 10 alphanumeric characters in each address. Other machines with fixed word-lengths of two, four, six, and eight alphanumeric characters have been produced. Eight characters has been arbitrarily selected for our example.

[4] No, *byte* is not, in this case, an example of the author's spelling prowess. A byte is a character or unit of information consisting of eight binary digits. We will discuss this matter further later in the chapter.

[5] Although it may be possible for a programmer to *pack* several data items into a single fixed-length word by using proper instructions, extra steps are then required in the processing.

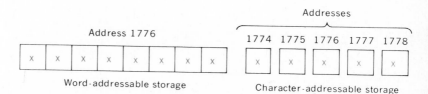

Addresses

Address 1776    1774  1775  1776  1777  1778

| X | X | X | X | X | X | X | X |

| X | X | X | X | X |

Word-addressable storage    Character-addressable storage

FIGURE 6-5

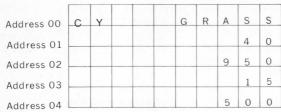

(a) Fixed word-length storage

(b) Variable word-length storage

FIGURE 6-6

for by simply referring to an address number. But how can a variable word-length machine identify the particular word it is seeking when an eight-character word such as "Cy Grass" has eight addresses? There have been two approaches used to resolve this dilemma.

**1** *The wordmark approach.* This approach was used in earlier computers and may be of historical interest. *Wordmarks* were set by programmers to represent the *end* or termination of a word. If the computer *stopped* processing a word when the presence of a wordmark was sensed, what address number was used to identify the beginning of that word? The answer obviously was the highest numbered (or "rightmost") address in the word. Figure 6-7 shows how a data word was retrieved from storage for printing purposes. The command "PRINT 190" caused the machine to automatically move from address 190 serially to the left until a wordmark (shown as the line under the letter H) was encountered. The same command—PRINT 190—in a word-addressable machine would yield the same results if HELP! was located in that address, but the computer would retrieve all the characters as a single unit.

**2** *The length-specification approach.* Modern computers (e.g., the models of the IBM System/370 family) specify a variable-length word with an instruction which (a) identifies the lowest numbered address in the word, and (b) indicates the number of address locations to be included in the word. A wordmark is thus not needed. Figure 6-8 illustrates this approach. Retrieval begins with address 186 and continues for the specified number of locations.

### a comparison

To review our understanding of the above paragraphs, let us compare fixed and variable word-length storage systems:

**1** *Storage efficiency.* Generally speaking, variable word-length equipment makes the most efficient use of available space for business purposes.

**2** *Internal data transfer.* Depending upon the computer, data are transferred or retrieved a character at a time or a word at a time.

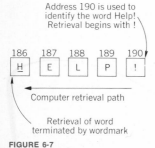

Address 190 is used to identify the word Help! Retrieval begins with !

Computer retrieval path

Retrieval of word terminated by wordmark

FIGURE 6-7

Wordmark retrieval.

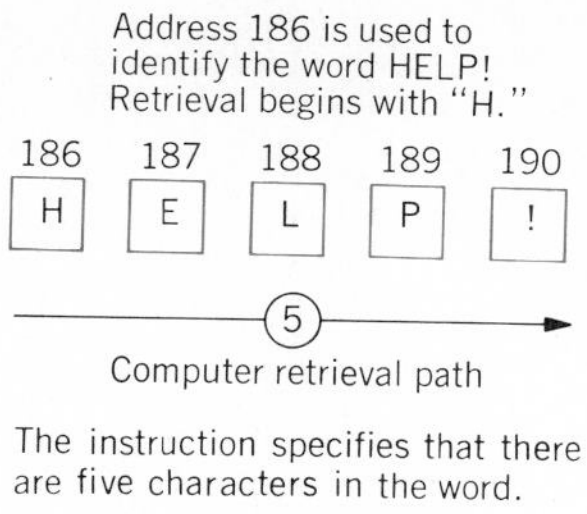

Address 186 is used to identify the word HELP! Retrieval begins with "H."

| 186 | 187 | 188 | 189 | 190 |
|-----|-----|-----|-----|-----|
| H | E | L | P | ! |

⑤ →

Computer retrieval path

The instruction specifies that there are five characters in the word.

**FIGURE 6-8**

Length specification retrieval.

**3** *Arithmetic speed.* Variable word-length machines perform arithmetic operations in a *serial* fashion, i.e., one position at a time. For example, when two 8-digit numbers are added, eight processing cycles are required. Fixed word-length computers, however, are classified as *parallel* calculators; i.e., they can add any two data words in a *single* step without regard to the number of digits in the words (Fig. 6-9). Obviously, then, machines operating with fixed word lengths have faster calculating capability. But this faster speed must be paid for since the necessary circuitry is more complex and thus more expensive.

**4** *Computer usage.* Most popular business computers are variable word-length machines. This is not surprising if you remember that business applications place greater emphasis on I/O speed and storage capacity than on speed of computation. Variable word-length processors give managers what they need at a relatively low cost. In large-scale scientific computing, however, the fixed word-length storage approach is preferred because of the faster calculating and data transfer speeds that can be provided.

### a byte-addressable combination

It is apparent that each method of organizing the storage unit has advantages and drawbacks. Recognizing this fact, the ingenious Peculiar Company designers of the PAC [and, incidentally, the designers of (1) the IBM System/370 series, (2) the Sperry UNIVAC Series 90 computers, and (3) the products of other manufacturers] developed a machine that could be operated as either a variable or a fixed word-length computer. Program control, in effect, organizes the computer for either business (using variable-length words) or scientific (using fixed-length words) applications. How is this possible? Let us look at the storage organizational structure for the answer to this question.

Each alphanumeric character placed in storage is represented by a code consisting of 8 binary digits (bits)[6]; and *each* of these coded

[6] We will discuss bits at some length in the next section.

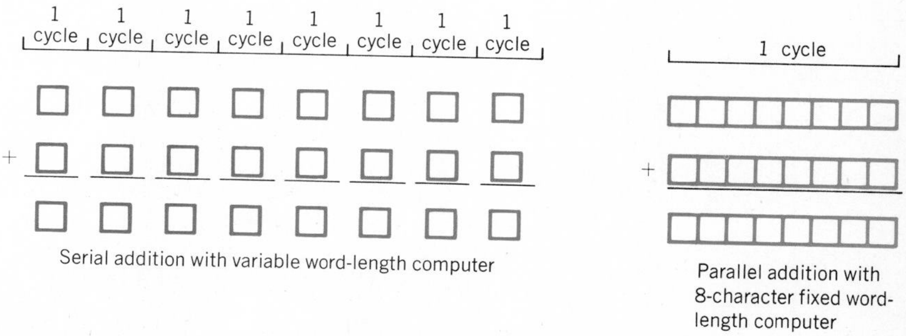

Serial addition with variable word-length computer

Parallel addition with 8-character fixed word-length computer

**FIGURE 6-9**

Arithmetic speed.

*Variable word format*

□    1 byte=1 coded alphanumeric character;
            a variable number of bytes make up a word.

*Fixed word formats permitted*

□□    2 bytes=halfword

□□□□    4 bytes=word

□□□□□□□□    8 bytes=doubleword

**FIGURE 6-10**

Address formats.

characters, or *bytes,* may be identified in storage since single character locations are given *specific address numbers.* Thus, by using an appropriate set of instructions, the programmer can manipulate these characters into words of varying lengths as needed. The *length-specification approach* described above and in Fig. 6-8 is used to identify the variable-length words retained in storage. With each byte or character having an address, it is easy to see how variable-length words can be created.

But bytes can also be *grouped together and operated on as a unit.* Programmers can elect to use, for example, other available instructions that will cause the computer to automatically retrieve, manipulate, and store as a single unit a fixed word of 4 bytes. Or, they may choose to group 8 bytes into a *double word* and have the machine function in this fixed-word format. Figure 6-10 illustrates the word formats possible with many currently used computers.

Without getting bogged down here in the details of computer design, we may summarize the above comments by repeating that many modern computers use (1) a built-in instruction set to operate on variable-length words, with the instruction itself specifying the number of characters in the word, and (2) additional instruction sets that operate automatically on fixed amounts of data—either halfwords (2 bytes), full words (4 bytes), or double words (8 bytes). This ability, through program instructions, to manipulate different groupings gives PAC users with both business and scientific applications a great deal of flexibility. Maybe the PAC isn't so peculiar after all!

Regardless of the capacity of the available storage locations, however, the numbers, letters, and special characters contained in storage must be in a coded form that the computer can use.

## COMPUTER NUMBERING SYSTEMS

Anthropologists have reported on the primitive number systems of some aboriginal tribes. The Yancoes in the Brazilian Amazon stop counting at three. Since their word for "three" is "*poettarrarorincoaroac,*" this is understandable.

Albert Sukoff

Computers represent data in a code that is related to a binary numbering system. It is thus desirable to understand numbering systems.

## decimal numbers

The first numbering systems were of an *additive* nature. That is, they consisted of symbols such as | for one, | | for two, | | | for three, etc. Each symbol represented the *same value* regardless of the position it occupied in the number. Unfortunately, calculations are difficult when such systems are used. In fact, you can calculate answers to problems that would have baffled wise people of earlier centuries. A big reason for your advantage has been the development of *positional* numbering systems. In such systems there are only a limited number of symbols, and the symbols represent different values according to the position they occupy in the number (5 = the Roman numeral V, but 51 does not equal VI because the meaning 5 has changed with the change in its position). The number of symbols used depends on the *base* or *radix* of the particular system. The decimal system, of course, has a base of 10 and has 10 symbols (0 to 9).[7] The *highest* numerical symbol will always have a value of one *less* than the base.

By the arrangement of the numerical symbols[8] in various positions, any number may be represented. We know that in the decimal system the successive positions to the left of the decimal point represent units, tens, hundreds, thousands, ten thousands, etc. We may fail to remember, however, that what this means is that each position represents a particular *power* of the base. The number 15,236 represents the sum of[9]

$$(1 \times 10^4) + (5 \times 10^3) + (2 \times 10^2) + (3 \times 10^1) + (6 \times 10^0)$$

In *any* positional numbering system, the *value of each position represents a specific power of the base.* To test your understanding of the concepts that have now been introduced, let us look at the following problems:

**1**   What is the decimal equivalent of $463_8$? (The subscript 8 following the number 463 indicates that this is an *octal* base number.) Since the *base* is *now eight* rather than 10, the possible symbols are 0 to 7 (the symbols 8 and 9 do not exist in this case). Each position in the number $463_8$ represents a power of its base. Therefore,

---

[7] There is nothing particularly sacred about a base of 10. Probably the only reason it was originally developed and is now in widespread use is that people happen to have 10 fingers. Other systems have been created. For example, the Babylonians had a base of 60 (of course, they also did their writing on mud pies); the Mayas of Yucatán used a base of 20 (a warm climate and a group of barefooted mathematicians?); and a base of five is still used by natives in New Hebrides.

[8] There is also nothing sacred about the shape of the symbols we use to represent quantities. We know that the symbol 2 has a certain meaning, but any number of other marks could be defined to serve the same purpose. A version of the Arabic numerals we use is thought to have originated in India around 200 B.C.

[9] Students occasionally forget their algebra and have to be reminded that $n^0$ is, by definition, 1; i.e., any number raised to the zero power equals 1.

$$(\underline{4} \times 8^2) + (\underline{6} \times 8^1) + (\underline{3} \times 8^0). \leftarrow \text{Octal Point}$$

*or*    $(4 \times 64) + (6 \times 8) + (3 \times 1).$

*or*    $(256) + (48) + (3). = 307_{10}$    The decimal equivalent

**2**    What is the decimal equivalent of $1001_2$? (We are now using a base of two.) With a base of two, the only possible symbols are 0 and 1. Again, each position in the number $1001_2$ represents a power of its base. Therefore,

$$(\underline{1} \times 2^3) + (\underline{0} \times 2^2) + (\underline{0} \times 2^1) + (\underline{1} \times 2^0). \leftarrow \text{Binary point}$$

*or*    $(1 \times 8) + (0 \times 4) + (0 \times 2) + (1 \times 1).$

*or*    $(8) + (0) + (0) + (1). = 9_{10}$    The decimal equivalent

These problems have demonstrated that (1) the lower the numbering base, the fewer the possible symbols that must be remembered, and (2) the smaller the base, the more positions there must be to represent a given quantity. Four digits (1001) are required in base two to equal a single decimal digit (9). You may also have observed that the decimal point becomes the *octal point* in a base-eight system and the *binary point* in base two.[10] It would thus appear that we have sneaked up on the *binary* or *base-two* numbering system used by digital computers.

**binary numbers in computers**

It was pointed out in Chapter 1 that John von Neumann suggested that binary numbering systems be incorporated in computers. Although the suggestion came too late to prevent the very first machines from using the decimal system, von Neumann's suggestions were quickly adopted in subsequent designs.

Why the rush to binary? There are several very good reasons:

**1**    It is necessary that circuitry be designed only to handle 2 binary digits (bits) rather than 10. Design is simplified, cost is reduced, and reliability is improved. less subject to breakdowns

**2**    Electronic components, by their very nature, operate in a binary mode. A switch is either open (0 state) or closed (1 state); and a transistor either is not conducting (0) or is (1).

**3**    Everything that can be done with a base of 10 can be done with the binary system.

Binary counting begins, just as with any number base, with 0 followed by 1. But now we have run out of symbols. How do we represent 2 when there is no such symbol? Just as we represent the next highest value in any base when we have used our highest number in the first position to the

---

[10] The point, of course, merely serves to separate the whole from the fractional part of a number. It may be called the *radix point,* or *real point,* regardless of the numbering system being used.

left of the real point, we use a zero place marker in the first position and put the next lowest symbol in the next position to the left. Thus, 2 in decimal is the same as 10 in binary. The important thing to remember in counting in the binary system is that the place positions, instead of representing units, tens, hundreds, thousands, etc., now represent unit, 2, 4, 8, 16, 32, etc. Thus, the decimal value of $110011_2$ is

| Power of base | $2^7$ | $2^6$ | $2^6$ | $2^4$ | $2^3$ | $2^2$ | $2^1$ | $2^0$ |
|---|---|---|---|---|---|---|---|---|
| Decimal equivalent | 128 | 64 | 32 | 16 | 8 | 4 | 2 | 1 |
| Binary number | | | 1 | 1 | 0 | 0 | 1 | 1 |

*or*   $32 + 16 + 2 + 1 = 51_{10}$

Computers operate on binary digits when making calculations, and we have now seen how it is possible for binary numbers to be converted back into a convenient decimal form. But, of course, decimal numbers must be converted into some binary format prior to computer processing. How might this be done? How thoughtful of you to ask. Decimal numbers may be converted to their binary equivalents by the use of a *remainder method.* For illustration purposes, the number $250_{10}$ is chosen. The conversion procedure simply consists of dividing the original decimal number by 2 and all successive answers by 2 until the process can continue no further. The binary value is read from the successive remainder values. For example,

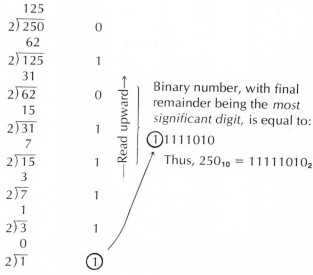

Remainder

$$
\begin{array}{r}
125 \\
2\overline{)250} \\
62 \\
2\overline{)125} \\
31 \\
2\overline{)62} \\
15 \\
2\overline{)31} \\
7 \\
2\overline{)15} \\
3 \\
2\overline{)7} \\
1 \\
2\overline{)3} \\
0 \\
2\overline{)1}
\end{array}
\quad
\begin{array}{l}
0 \\
1 \\
0 \\
1 \\
1 \\
1 \\
1 \\
①
\end{array}
$$

—Read upward→

Binary number, with final remainder being the *most significant digit,* is equal to:

①1111010

Thus, $250_{10} = 11111010_2$

**COMPUTER DATA REPRESENTATION**

Up to this point we have been discussing "pure" binary numbers. Although computers designed strictly for scientific purposes may use only pure binary in their operations, business-oriented machines (or computers which are designed to process both business and scientific applications) may use some *coded,* or *modified,* version of pure binary to represent decimal numbers. Numerous data representation formats have been developed. The most popular for business purposes, however, are the *binary coded decimal* (BCD) codes.[11]

### binary coded decimal system

With BCD it is possible to convert *each* decimal digit into its binary equivalent rather than convert the entire decimal number into a pure binary form. The BCD equivalent of each possible decimal digit is shown in Fig. 6-11. Because the digits 8 and 9 require 4 bits, *all* decimal digits are represented by 4 bits. Converting $405_{10}$ into BCD would yield the following result:

$$405_{10} \text{ in BCD} = \underbrace{0100}_{4}/\underbrace{0000}_{0}/\underbrace{0101}_{5} \text{ or } 010000000101$$

(By using the remainder method, we could convert $405_{10}$ into $110010101_{2}$, but BCD values are much easier for us to determine.)

With 4 bits there are 16 different possible configurations ($2^4$). The first 10 of these configurations are, of course, used to represent decimal digits. The other six arrangements (1010, 1011, 1100, 1101, 1110, and 1111) have decimal values from 10 to 15. These six arrangements are *not used* in BCD coding; i.e., 1111 *does not* represent $15_{10}$ in BCD. Rather, the proper BCD code for $15_{10}$ is 0001/0101. The "extra" six configurations are used by programmers for other purposes, which we need not dwell on here.

We have seen that BCD is a convenient and fast way to convert numbers from decimal to binary. But it is hardly sufficient for business purposes to have only 16 characters available. The following section explains how additional characters are represented in the central processor.

| Decimal Digit | Place Value | | | |
|---|---|---|---|---|
| | 8 | 4 | 2 | 1 |
| 0 | 0 | 0 | 0 | 0 |
| 1 | 0 | 0 | 0 | 1 |
| 2 | 0 | 0 | 1 | 0 |
| 3 | 0 | 0 | 1 | 1 |
| 4 | 0 | 1 | 0 | 0 |
| 5 | 0 | 1 | 0 | 1 |
| 6 | 0 | 1 | 1 | 0 |
| 7 | 0 | 1 | 1 | 1 |
| 8 | 1 | 0 | 0 | 0 |
| 9 | 1 | 0 | 0 | 1 |

FIGURE 6-11

Binary coded decimal numeric bit configurations.

[11] Many modern computers use *both* BCD and pure binary forms of data representation. For example, input data are received and stored in the CPU in a BCD format. Prior to computations, those numbers that are to be used in arithmetic operations *may* be converted to a pure binary form by the computer. Following binary arithmetic operations, the results are converted back to a BCD format before being written out.

### six-bit alphanumeric code

Instead of using 4 bits with only 16 possible characters, equipment designers commonly use 6 or 8 bits to represent characters in *alphanumeric versions* of BCD. Two *zone* positions are added to the four BCD positions in the 6-bit code. With 6 bits it is thus possible to represent 64 different characters ($2^6$). A seventh parity checking position is commonly added (Fig. 6-12). We have already seen examples of 6-bit alphanumeric BCD code being used to represent data in paper tape and seven-channel magnetic tape. Now that the binary numbering system has been introduced, it becomes clearer why the bottom rows of tape are labeled 8, 4, 2, and 1. These values merely represent positions to the left of the binary point. It was pointed out in the discussion of magnetic tape coding that the decimal 7 is represented by an "on" condition in the numeric channels marked 4, 2, and 1. It is now apparent that being "on" means that a 1 bit is represented in these positions, i.e., that 7 = 0111 in BCD.

Data are stored internally in many of the computers in operation today by the use of tiny doughnut-shaped "cores," which may be magnetized in either of two directions.[12] These cores are thus capable of representing a 1 or a 0. Seven cores stacked in a vertical column are used in some computers to represent a number, letter, or special character. Figure 6-13 shows how the decimal 7 is represented. An imaginary line passes through the cores. The shaded cores are magnetized in a direction that corresponds to a 1 bit. Like a switch, they may be considered in an "on" state. The unshaded cores are in an "off" state and represent a 0 bit. The A and B cores are the zone cores. A combination of zone (A and B) and numeric (8, 4, 2, and 1) cores may be used to represent alphabetic and special characters just as they do in tape coding. The parity check core is also shown in the off state, indicating that odd parity is used in this particular code.[13]

The 6 bits permit 64 different coding arrangements. This number is sufficient to code the decimal digits (10), capital letters (26), and a number of punctuation marks and machine control characters. Six bits

---

[12] We shall have more to say about core storage in the next chapter.

[13] The code represented here is called the Standard BCD Interchange code and is used to represent data internally in some computers. Seven-channel tape code differs slightly in that even parity may be used.

FIGURE 6-12

| Check bit | Zone bits | | Numeric bits | | | |
|---|---|---|---|---|---|---|
| C | B | A | 8 | 4 | 2 | 1 |

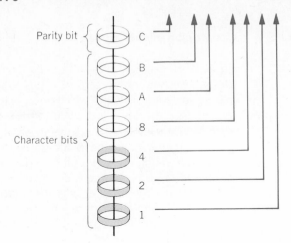

FIGURE 6-13

Six-bit alphanumeric code represented in storage.

are *not sufficient,* however, to provide lowercase letters, capital letters, and a greatly expanded number of special and control characters.

### eight-bit alphanumeric codes

To permit greater flexibility in data representation, equipment designers *extended* the 6-bit alphanumeric BCD code to 8 bits. With 8-bit coding, it is possible to provide 256 different arrangements ($2^8$). Each 8-bit unit of information, you will remember, is called a *byte.* Bytes may be used to represent a single character, or the programmer may use the eight cores to "pack" two decimal digits into one byte.

The nine-channel magnetic tape format discussed in Chapter 4 utilizes an 8-bit extended version of BCD. There are four (rather than two) zone bit positions available in an 8-bit code (Fig. 6-14). In a core storage device, eight data cores plus a check core are again stacked in a column and used internally in many CPUs to represent a coded character (Fig. 6-15).

Selected characters are presented in Fig. 6-16 in the four codes most commonly encountered in data processing. (Parity check bits are excluded.) These codes include the Hollerith punched card code,

| Check bit | Zone bits | | | | Numeric bits | | | |
|---|---|---|---|---|---|---|---|---|
| C | $\bar{Z}$ | $\bar{Z}$ | $\bar{Z}$ | $\bar{Z}$ | 8 | 4 | 2 | 1 |

FIGURE 6-14

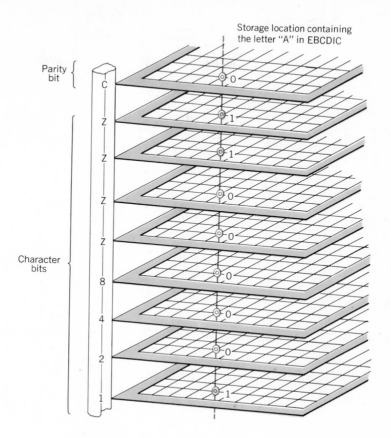

FIGURE 6-15

Eight-bit alphanumeric code
represented in storage.

explained in Chapter 1, and the 6-bit Standard BCD Interchange code, mentioned above. In addition, there are *two* 8-bit codes currently being used in modern computers. One, the Extended Binary Coded Decimal Interchange Code (EBCDIC) developed by IBM, is used in that firm's System/370 series, and in other machines produced by different manufacturers.

Another code, the American Standard Code for Information Interchange (ASCII), is popular in data communications and is used to represent data internally in the NCR Century line of computers.[14] You will note

---

[14] ASCII is also referred to as USASCII and ANSCII. The confusion is caused by changes in the name of the organization that developed the code. The code was developed by the American Standards Association (which later became the United States of America Standards Institute, and is now known as the American National Standards Institute, Inc.) in cooperation with users of communications and data processing equipment. The purpose of the developers of ASCII was to establish a standard interchange code that could be used to provide machine-to-machine and/or system-to-system communication both directly and through the data transmission network. There are both 7- and 8-bit versions of ASCII.

| Character | Hollerith card code | Standard BCD interchange code | Extended BCD interchange code (EBCDIC) | ASCII-8 |
|-----------|---------------------|-------------------------------|----------------------------------------|---------|
| 0 | 0 | 00 1010 | 1111 0000 | 0101 0000 |
| 1 | 1 | 00 0001 | 1111 0001 | 0101 0001 |
| 2 | 2 | 00 0010 | 1111 0010 | 0101 0010 |
| 3 | 3 | 00 0011 | 1111 0011 | 0101 0011 |
| 4 | 4 | 00 0100 | 1111 0100 | 0101 0100 |
| 5 | 5 | 00 0101 | 1111 0101 | 0101 0101 |
| 6 | 6 | 00 0110 | 1111 0110 | 0101 0110 |
| 7 | 7 | 00 0111 | 1111 0111 | 0101 0111 |
| 8 | 8 | 00 1000 | 1111 1000 | 0101 1000 |
| 9 | 9 | 00 1001 | 1111 1001 | 0101 1001 |
| A | 12-1 | 11 0001 | 1100 0001 | 1010 0001 |
| B | 12-2 | 11 0010 | 1100 0010 | 1010 0010 |
| C | 12-3 | 11 0011 | 1100 0011 | 1010 0011 |
| D | 12-4 | 11 0100 | 1100 0100 | 1010 0100 |
| E | 12-5 | 11 0101 | 1100 0101 | 1010 0101 |
| F | 12-6 | 11 0110 | 1100 0110 | 1010 0110 |
| G | 12-7 | 11 0111 | 1100 0111 | 1010 0111 |
| H | 12-8 | 11 1000 | 1100 1000 | 1010 1000 |
| I | 12-9 | 11 1001 | 1100 1001 | 1010 1001 |
| J | 11-1 | 10 0001 | 1101 0001 | 1010 1010 |
| K | 11-2 | 10 0010 | 1101 0010 | 1010 1011 |
| L | 11-3 | 10 0011 | 1101 0011 | 1010 1100 |
| M | 11-4 | 10 0100 | 1101 0100 | 1010 1101 |
| N | 11-5 | 10 0101 | 1101 0101 | 1010 1110 |
| O | 11-6 | 10 0110 | 1101 0110 | 1010 1111 |
| P | 11-7 | 10 0111 | 1101 0111 | 1011 0000 |
| Q | 11-8 | 10 1000 | 1101 1000 | 1011 0001 |
| R | 11-9 | 10 1001 | 1101 1001 | 1011 0010 |
| S | 0-2 | 01 0010 | 1110 0010 | 1011 0011 |
| T | 0-3 | 01 0011 | 1110 0011 | 1011 0100 |
| U | 0-4 | 01 0100 | 1110 0100 | 1011 0101 |
| V | 0-5 | 01 0101 | 1110 0101 | 1011 0110 |
| W | 0-6 | 01 0110 | 1110 0110 | 1011 0111 |
| X | 0-7 | 01 0111 | 1110 0111 | 1011 1000 |
| Y | 0-8 | 01 1000 | 1110 1000 | 1011 1001 |
| Z | 0-9 | 01 1001 | 1110 1001 | 1011 1010 |

FIGURE 6-16

Common methods of representing data.

that the Standard BCD code and EBCDIC differ primarily in the zone bit coding.

From the preceding paragraphs, it is now obvious that several data representation methods may be substituted for pure binary in business computer systems. Fortunately, a single computer system can make use of multiple codes. As we see in Fig. 6-17, for example, a card reader may be accepting Hollerith coded cards, but the code on these cards can be converted into Standard BCD, EBCDIC, or ASCII codes prior to being stored in the CPU. Data recorded on paper and magnetic tape may be in the code format used by the CPU, and thus no conversion may be required during input or output. Output to a card punch is generally converted from the CPU format to the Hollerith code prior to punching. Also, the internal CPU code is matched to the printer character set prior to printing.

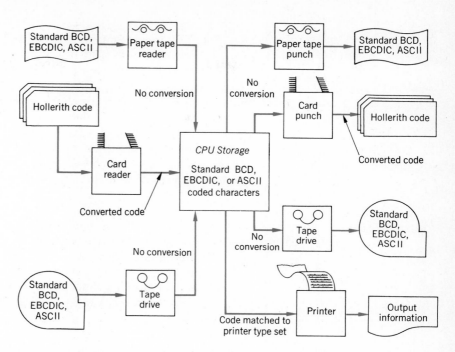

FIGURE 6-17

Multiple code usage.

**SUMMARY**  Storage locations may contain either data or instructions. For each program, data are typically stored in three conceptual areas—the input storage area, the working storage area, and the output storage area. Instructions are held in a program storage area. These areas vary in size and location depending upon the particular job being processed.

Locations in storage are identified by address numbers. Programmers (or software prepared by programmers) keep track of address contents because when instructions are written to manipulate these contents, they must indicate in some way the address locations. Programmers have a fixed number of instruction commands at their disposal. These commands are built into the particular machine being used. When a program is run, the machine is set at the first instruction and it then follows sequentially the series of directions until told to do otherwise.

Each address may contain either a single character or a word consisting of a fixed number of characters. Character-addressable machines also store words (fields), but instead of being fixed in length, these words are of variable length. Fixed word-length computers perform computations faster than variable word-length equipment and are therefore preferred in scientific installations. Most large-scale computers are organized with fixed word-length capability. Since calculations represent a lesser part of the business processing job, most small- and medium-sized business computers have been built with variable word-length capability for more efficient storage utilization. Modern computers may often be operated as either variable or fixed word-length machines.

Binary numbers are used to simplify computer design and take advantage of the two states that electronic components may be in. Scientific computers may use a straight binary means of representing data. Computers designed to process business applications, on the other hand, may use a binary-related code to designate numbers, letters, and special characters. Six- and eight-bit character codes are a popular means of representing alphanumeric data. Such codes are often alphanumeric versions of the 4-bit numeric binary coded decimal system.

Although 64 characters are represented with 6 bits, it may be desirable to have a larger number of bit configurations. Most computers built today use 8-bit bytes to code up to 256 different bit combinations.

**REVIEW AND DISCUSSION QUESTIONS**

1   (**a**) Identify and discuss the four conceptual storage areas. (**b**) What is the typical data-flow pattern in the storage unit?

2   Define the following terms: (**a**) Address (**b**) Command repertoire (**c**) Branchpoint (**d**) Looping (**e**) Wordmark (**f**) Data word (**g**) Instruction word (**h**) Conditional transfer (**i**) Unconditional transfer (**j**) Byte.

3   Explain the distinction between the address number and the contents of the address.

4   (**a**) Distinguish between word-addressable and character-addressable computers. (**b**) Compare fixed and variable word-length storage systems.

5   Most current minicomputers are designed with a single fixed word-length storage format of 2 bytes. Discuss the advantages and disadvantages of this design approach. (Hint: Consider the compromise between economy on the one hand and performance on the other.)

6   "Many modern computers can be operated as either variable word-length or fixed word-length machines." Discuss this comment.

7   "The highest numerical symbol will always have a value of one less than the base." Explain and give examples.

8   "In any positional numbering system, the value of each position represents a specific power of the base." Explain and give examples.

9   Why have computers been designed to use the binary numbering system?

10   (**a**) What is the binary equivalent of $85_{10}$? (**b**) What is the decimal equivalent of $1110011_2$?

11   (**a**) What is $150_{10}$ in BCD? (**b**) What is the straight binary equivalent of $150_{10}$? (**c**) Compare BCD and straight binary coding.

12   Why has the 6-bit Standard BCD code been extended to 8 bits?

13   (**a**) What are the two popular 8-bit codes? (**b**) Who developed these codes?

# the cpu:
## components and comparisons

# 7

LEARNING OBJECTIVES   After studying this chapter and answering the discussion questions, you should be able to: ☐ Identify and explain the purpose of smaller storage sections in the CPU that perform special processing and control functions ☐ Discuss the factors that should be considered by managers in selecting storage media and devices ☐ Summarize the main characteristics of the primary storage devices used in modern computers ☐ Explain, in general terms, how the arithmetic-logic and control units function in the CPU to produce output information

**W**e continue our study of the CPU in this chapter by first examining some of the *types of storage elements that may be found in a central processor* so that we will then be in a position to consider the *primary storage components* that are currently being used by computer designers. Following these topics, we shall turn our attention to the CPU's *arithmetic-logic* and *control units*. Finally, we shall briefly *compare some of the characteristics of CPUs of different sizes.*

## TYPES OF CPU STORAGE ELEMENTS

You have already seen in Chapters 4 and 5 how compromises between operating speed, storage capacity, and cost per character stored apply in the use of different types of *secondary* storage media and devices. What you should also realize, however, is that there may also be a *storage hierarchy within the CPU* that involves speed and cost compromises. Every CPU will, of course, have a *primary storage* (or main memory) section that holds the active program(s) and data being processed. But in addition, there may also be several specialized storage elements located in the CPU (Fig. 7-1), and some of these elements are both faster and more expensive per character stored than primary storage. What are some of these possible elements? What a coincidence that you should ask. . . .

### specialized storage elements

As Fig. 7-1 illustrates, small storage sections that perform special *processing* and *control* functions may be found in a CPU. One such section is a

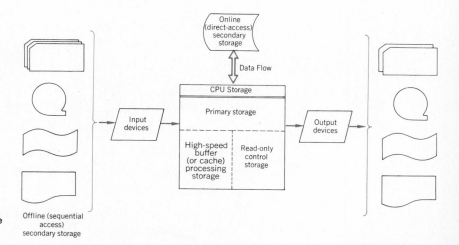

FIGURE 7-1

Components in the computer storage hierarchy.

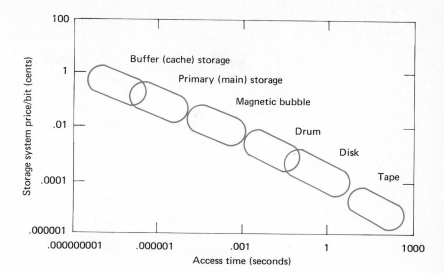

FIGURE 7-2

Cost/speed tradeoffs in storage hierarchy. (Adapted from David A. Hedges, "Microelectronic Memories," *Scientific American*, September 1977, p. 138.)

very *high-speed buffer* (or *cache*) memory that is used as a kind of "scratch pad" to temporarily store very active data and instructions during *processing*[1] operations. Results of computations or intermediate values that will soon be used again by the CPU, for example, may be quickly retrieved from this element. Data may be transferred automatically between the scratch pad and the primary storage, so that the cache memory is usually invisible to the programmer. Although the access time possible with buffer storage is faster than when primary storage is used, the circuitry necessary to achieve this greater speed is relatively expensive. (See Fig. 7-2 for a comparison of storage costs and speeds in a computer storage hierarchy.)

Another special storage section that may be found within the CPU is used for *control* purposes. The most basic operations in a computer are carried out by hardwired circuits consisting of solid-state electronic components. These fundamental tasks may then be combined to produce higher-level operations (e.g., subtract values, move data, make comparisons, etc.) by additional hardwired circuits, or these same operations may be performed with a series of special program instructions. These *micro-programs* (or *firmware*)—so called because they deal with very low-level machine operations—are thus essentially substitutes for additional hardware and are typically held in the CPU in a special control storage device.

In contrast with primary and buffer storage devices which are read/write *random access memory* (RAM) units, this control storage section

---

[1] *Registers* are also small, high-speed storage devices in the CPU that are used for processing. We will discuss several registers later in the chapter when we look at the arithmetic-logic and control units.

generally acts as a _read-only memory_ (ROM) device during the processing of an application. It will usually not accept input data and instructions from applications programmers. In some cases, the microprograms are permanently fused in the storage device and cannot be changed or altered; in other cases, the microprograms _can_ be altered or replaced— i.e., the control storage device may be a reloadable control storage (RCS) unit such as a special floppy disk drive in the CPU,[2] or it may be a programmable read-only memory (PROM) located in one or more integrated circuit chips. The microprograms used in business computer systems are usually furnished by the CPU manufacturer, or they are prepared by programmer specialists rather than by applications programmers.

_One common use_ of the microprograms held in the control storage device is to interpret applications program instructions that are basically foreign to the circuitry of the computer being used and decode them into the fundamental machine steps that the hardwired circuitry can accept.[3] For example, microprograms loaded into the RCS section of IBM System/370 computers will enable those machines to run applications programs prepared for earlier IBM computers. Also, the smaller models in the System/370 line use microprograms to decode and execute programs prepared for the larger models even though the larger models have hardwired functions that are not available in the smaller versions. Finally, microprograms in an ROM device can be used to increase the efficiency of a processor (usually a minicomputer or a microcomputer) by controlling the performance of a few specialized tasks. A generalized CPU can thus be made to operate in different ways for different users merely by changing microprograms.

### storage selection factors

In light of the wide selection of storage media and devices that exist in the computer storage hierarchy, it is not surprising that difficult compromise decisions are often required by managers in choosing the storage elements needed for their information systems. The following questions should be considered in making these decisions:

1    _What processing speeds are required?_ Processing speed is affected by many factors, including _access time._ The fastest access time is available from internal cache and primary storage. If processing speed is the paramount consideration and cost is secondary, then the choice could be

---

[2] The RCS unit in the IBM System/370, models 138 and 148 has a storage capacity of about 131,000 characters. Key operating system functions and other basic operations are stored in this RCS disk device.

[3] This topic will be considered again in Chapter 11.

a CPU with sufficient internal storage to hold most of the necessary data. Only the fastest online secondary devices (e.g., fixed-head-per-track disk units and bubble storage chips) would be appropriate in this situation.

2   *What storage capacity is needed?* The *amount* of data to be stored now and in the future must be considered. Determining the storage capacity of various central processors is not always as easy as it sounds. For example, a manufacturer's literature may advertise a machine with 16,384 addressable storage locations. [This figure is usually rounded back to the nearest thousand—that is, 16,000—and would be abbreviated 16K where K (or kilo) represents thousands.] But is the machine word, character, or byte addressable? If it is word addressable, how many characters are there in the fixed word? And if it is character addressable, what is the number of bits in the character? (An 8-bit byte provides greater storage than a 6-bit character because two decimal digits may be packed in a byte.) A fixed word-length storage of 16K may be considerably larger than a variable word-length storage of 24K.

3   *How safe are the data?* Most organizations consider it highly desirable not to lose data stored internally or in direct-access devices in the event of a power failure in the equipment room. We have seen that most online direct-access storage devices are able to hold data permanently in the absence of power and are therefore said to be *nonvolatile*. However, primary storage in some CPUs is inherently *volatile* and provision must be made to protect storage contents if there is a power interruption.

4   *What type of record accessibility is required?* The processing methods used and the file organization techniques employed are very important in determining storage requirements.

5   *What is the most economical choice?* Compromises between speed, capacity, and record accessibility are generally required in the interest of economy. When direct access is needed, the question of whether slower but less expensive online storage can be substituted for high-speed primary storage must be considered. For business purposes the answer to this question is frequently yes.

## TYPES OF PRIMARY STORAGE COMPONENTS

Data have been stored internally in a CPU in many ways over the years. The ENIAC, for example, used vacuum tube storage, and each tube was able to hold only a single bit. Storage capacity was thus tiny by present standards. The most popular computer in the mid-1950s (the IBM 650) used a magnetic drum as the internal storage instrument.

Magnetic core storage technology was first applied in the mid-1950s, and it was only a short time before these tiny rings became the dominant primary storage medium. Core storage remained the dominant technology for nearly 20 years. In fact, it has only been in the last few years that computer manufacturers have tended to select semiconductor storage chips over core devices for their new hardware designs. Thus, core storage remains a significant technology for primary memory, and tens of thousands of existing computers currently utilize this technology. Let us now, in the next few pages, consider core, semiconductor, and other storage components in more detail.

### magnetic core storage

In the last chapter we saw that magnetic cores are tiny doughnut-shaped rings which can be magnetized in either of two directions. These rings are pressed from a ferromagnetic and ceramic mixture and are then baked in an oven. Early cores were the size of small washers and, by today's standards, were expensive and slow in operation. But pressure to improve speed, capacity, and cost resulted in the development of highly automatic production techniques for pressing, baking, testing, and assembling the cores. Cores have now been reduced to about the size of a pin head; access time has been greatly improved; and the cost per bit of storage has been significantly reduced. (Access speeds now range from less than 300 nanoseconds to 2 microseconds.)

Figure 7-3 shows that if a wire carrying a sufficiently strong electric current passes through a core, the core will be magnetized by the magnetic field created around the wire. Perhaps you have wrapped a wire around a nail and connected the ends of the wire to a battery to make an electromagnet. You might have been surprised when you disconnected the battery to find that the nail still had the ability to act as a magnet. As Fig. 7-3 shows, the core, like the nail, remains magnetized after the current stops.

In Fig. 7-4, the current flow from left to right has magnetized the core in a counterclockwise (0-bit) direction. But when the current flows in the opposite direction, the core becomes magnetized in a clockwise (1-bit) fashion. A core can be quickly changed from an "off" or 0-bit condition to an "on" or 1-bit state simply by reversing the current flow passing through the core.

A large number of cores are strung on a screen of wires to form a *core plane*. These planes, resembling small square tennis rackets, are then arranged vertically to represent data as indicated in Fig. 6-15, page 177. A storage plane might be 128 cores wide and 128 cores long, thus giving a total of 16,384 cores per plane. A stack of seven (6-bit code) or nine (8-bit code) planes would then be needed to store 16,384 alphabetic characters and provide for a parity check.

With hundreds of thousands of cores in a CPU, how is it possible to select and properly magnetize just seven or nine in such a way that the desired character is *written into* storage? Let us use an imaginary plane to see how 1 bit in a character is selected (Fig. 7-5). The other bits making up the character are similarly chosen in the other planes. To make selection possible, two wires must pass through each core at right angles. By sending only *half* the necessary current through each of two wires,

FIGURE 7-3

Magnetizing a core.

Current is applied

Current is removed;
core remains magnetized

FIGURE 7-4

Two-state data representation.

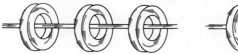

only the core at the intersection of the wires is affected. All other cores in the plane either receive no current at all or receive only half the amount needed to magnetize.

With a character now written into core storage, how does the computer *retrieve* it? For retrieval a third *sense* wire may be threaded diagonally through each core in a plane. The computer tests, or reads out, the magnetic state of a core by again sending electric current pulses through the two wires used in the write operation. The direction of this current is such that it causes a 0 to be written at that core position. If the core is magnetized in an "on" or 1 state, the writing of a 0 will abruptly *flip* the magnetic condition of the core and the changing magnetic field will induce a current into the sense wire. The reaction picked up by the sense wire tells the computer that the core contained a 1 bit. If *no reaction* is sensed, the computer will know that the core is already magnetized in the 0 state. Since only one core is being read at any given instant in a plane, only a *single* sense wire need be threaded through all the cores.

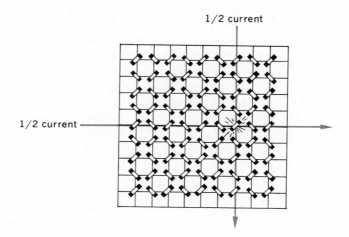

FIGURE 7-5

Core selection.

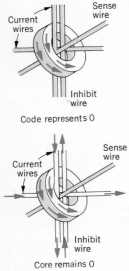

Code represents 0

Core remains 0

FIGURE 7-6

Core inhibit wire.

But wait a minute! If all cores storing a character have been changed from a 1 to a 0 state as a result of the reading, haven't we destroyed the character in its original location? The answer to this is usually yes, but only momentarily. Fortunately, by means of a fourth *inhibit* wire, the cores containing 1 bits are restored to their original state. Simply stated, the processor now tries to write back 1s in every core read an instant earlier. If the core in the plane was originally a 1, it will be restored; if it was originally a 0, it will remain that way, and a pulse of current will be sent through the inhibit wire in the plane to cancel out the attempt to write a 1 (Fig. 7-6).

*Magnetic cores have been popular for internal storage because:* (1) they are durable; (2) they provide safe, nonvolatile storage; (3) they provide access time measured in nanoseconds; (4) they are inexpensive in their operation and erasable; and (5) they provide quick random accessibility to records. However, as we shall see in the next section, there are limitations to core storage devices when compared with semiconductor memory chips.

### semiconductor storage

Semiconductor storage elements are tiny integrated circuits. Both the storage cell circuits and the support circuitry necessary for data writing and reading operations are packaged into tiny chips. There are several semiconductor storage technologies currently in use. Although we certainly need not go into these different storage approaches in any detail, the faster and more expensive *bipolar semiconductor* chips are often used in the arithmetic-logic and high-speed buffer storage sections of the CPU; while the slower and less expensive chips that employ *metal-oxide semiconductor* (MOS) technology are used in the main memory section.

The storage cell circuits in some semiconductor chips contain (1) a transistor that acts in much the same way as a mechanical on-off toggle switch and (2) a capacitor that is capable of storing an electrical charge. Depending on the switching action of the transistor, the capacitor either contains no charge (0 bit) or it does hold a tiny charge (1 bit). Figure 7-7 shows how 64 bits might be arranged in a segment of a chip.[4] To locate a particular cell for writing or reading, row and column addresses (in binary) are needed. The storage location of the shaded cell in Fig. 7-7 is the row numbered 011 (3) and the column numbered 101 (5). Since the charge on the capacitor tends to "leak off," provision is made to periodically "regenerate" or refresh the stored charge. Therefore, a semiconductor device using such an approach provides *volatile* storage; i.e., the data

---

[4] Many chips used at this writing store 4,096 bits; recently announced chips that store 16,384 bits are entering production, and larger capacity (64K bit) chips will soon be available.

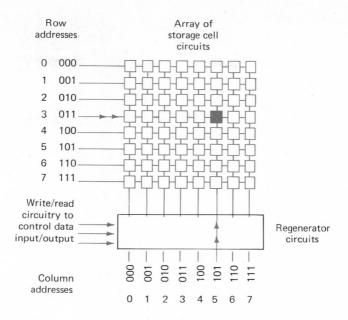

FIGURE 7-7

Semiconductor storage concepts.

stored would be lost in the event of a power failure.[5] A backup *uninterruptible power system* (UPS) is thus desirable in installations with volatile semiconductor storage.

In spite of the volatile storage characteristic, however, semiconductor memory chips have found their way into the newer models of most manufacturers for several very good reasons:

**1** *Economic factors.* The cost per bit of semiconductor storage has declined an average of 35 percent per year since 1970,[6] and there is no end in sight to these cost reductions. Furthermore, with core storage the associated circuitry is complex and expensive, regardless of the storage capacity served. Therefore, because of this high fixed-cost factor, the cost per bit of small core memories is much greater than the cost per bit of storage of a large-capacity core memory. With semiconductor storage, however, the cost is primarily in the chips and their packaging and not in the supporting circuitry. Thus, the fixed cost is low, and the cost per bit of storage in a microcomputer is about the same as the cost per bit of storage in a larger computer. (It is hardly a surprise, then, that chips are now used almost exclusively in microcomputers and in recently designed minicomputers.)

**2** *Compact size.* Semiconductor chips require less than half the space

---

[5] Not all semiconductor devices offer volatile or "dynamic" storage. Some, such as the units that are found in personal microcomputers and pocket calculators, are *static* memories that are nonvolatile. And, as we saw in Chapter 5, magnetic bubble semiconductor chips provide nonvolatile storage.

[6] See Robert N. Noyce, "Microelectronics," *Scientific American,* September 1977, p. 67.

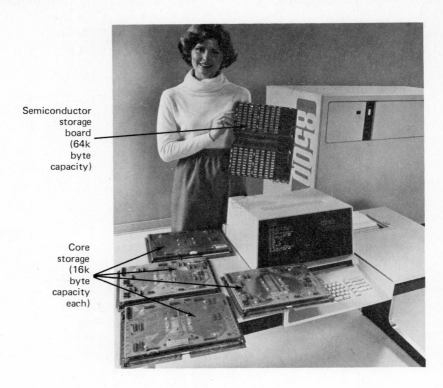

Semiconductor storage board (64k byte capacity)

Core storage (16k byte capacity each)

FIGURE 7-8

(Courtesy NCR Corporation.)

needed by core storage devices of similar capacity. (The 64K-byte semiconductor storage board held by the person in Fig. 7-8 has the same capacity as the four 16K-byte core modules placed beside the console display.)

3  *Faster performance*. Semiconductor devices are capable of faster performance than core storage units. Their more compact size, of course, contributes to this faster speed. (The faster core memories, however, will outperform some slower MOS chips.)

## other storage possibilities

In the early 1950s, it was found that a tiny *film* of magnetic material could be deposited on a flat plane of insulating glass or plastic so that film spots could be magnetized in either of two stable preferred directions. However, the promise offered by *planar technology* was not achieved rapidly enough, and so the emphasis in the development of new storage techniques shifted to other approaches.

Of course, thin-film storage cells do not have to be in the form of flat spots. Instead, they may be in a *plated-wire* form. Manufacturing cost per bit of storage capacity is low because of the automatic production techniques employed. Plated-wire primary storage has been used in some NCR and UNIVAC computers.

In addition to the storage function, every CPU must have components to perform the arithmetic-logic and control functions. Let us now look at these components of the CPU.

## THE ARITHMETIC-LOGIC UNIT

The arithmetic-logic unit is where the actual data processing occurs. All calculations are performed and all logical comparisons are made in this unit. In Chapter 6 we traced through a simplified program to process Editor Aardvark's weekly paycheck. Some of the program instructions used then are reproduced in Fig. 7-9.

The instruction in address 07 calls for the computer to write the contents of address 01 into the arithmetic unit. Implicit in this instruction is the requirement that the arithmetic-logic unit have storage capability. It must be able to store temporarily the data contained in address 01. Such a special-purpose storage location is called a *register*. Several registers will be discussed in the following paragraphs because they are basic to the functioning of the arithmetic-logic and control units. The number of registers varies among computers, as does the data-flow pattern. Before briefly examining some variations, let us trace the instructions in Fig. 7-9 through the PAC computer.

Up to this point we have written the instructions in addresses 07 to 11 so that we would understand them. Figure 7-10 shows how these same instructions may be coded and stored for PAC's convenience. The first processing instruction, CLA 01, tells PAC to *CL*ear the contents of the arithmetic-logic unit of all data and to *A*dd (store) the contents of address 01 to a register known as the *accumulator*. Thus, 40 hours—the contents of address 01—are now held in both address 01 and the accumulator (Fig. 7-11*a*).

The second instruction in address 08 is MUL 02. The computer interprets this instruction to mean that the contents of address 02 ($10) are to be *MUL*tiplied by the contents in the accumulator (40 hours) to get Aardvark's gross pay. Execution of this instruction may take the following form (Fig. 7-11*b*):

1 The contents of address 02 are read into a storage register in the arithmetic-logic unit.

| 07 | 08 | 09 | 10 | 11 |
|---|---|---|---|---|
| Write contents of address 01 into arithmetic unit | Multiply contents of arithmetic unit by contents of address 02 | Duplicate preceding answer in address 05 | Multiply contents of address 03 by preceding answer in arithmetic unit | Add contents of address 04 to preceding answer in arithmetic unit |

FIGURE 7-9

(Source: Figure 6-2)

| 07 | 08 | 09 | 10 | 11 |
|---|---|---|---|---|
| CLA 01 | MUL 02 | STO 05 | MUL 03 | ADD 04 |

FIGURE 7-10

**2** The contents of the accumulator and the contents of the storage register are given to the *adder*. The *adder* (and its associated circuits) is the primary arithmetic element because it also performs subtraction, multiplication, and division on binary digits.

**3** The product of the multiplication *is stored in the accumulator*. The 40 hours previously there has been erased by the arithmetic operation.

The third instruction in the processing sequence is STO 05. The contents in the accumulator are *STO*red in address 05. The read-in to address 05 is destructive to any information that might be there. The read-out from the accumulator is nondestructive (Fig. 7-11c). The fourth instruction, MUL 03, is handled exactly like the second instruction, so we need not repeat the execution.

The fifth instruction in the sequence, ADD 04, simply tells the computer to ADD the contents of address 04 to the contents of the accumulator. The hospitalization insurance deduction of $5 is the contents of 04; the tax deduction of $80 is now the contents of the accumulator. Why? Because when the fourth instruction is carried out, the $400 in the accumulator is multiplied by 20 percent (the contents of 03) to get a product, which is then stored in the accumulator. As Fig. 7-11d shows, the contents of 04 are read into the storage register (thus erasing the previous contents); the adder totals the contents of the accumulator and the storage register; and the sum is stored in the accumulator.

It is apparent that every arithmetic operation requires two numbers and some result. Subtraction, for example, requires a minuend and a subtrahend to find a difference; multiplication uses a multiplicand and a multiplier to find a product. Although obviously two numbers and a result are handled by every computer arithmetic-logic unit, different processing and storage approaches have been developed to manage the two data words and the result.

You may recall from Chapter 6 that computations in variable word-length machines are on two digits at a time (in a serial fashion), while fixed word-length processors operate on two *groups* of digits at a time (in a parallel mode). A variable word-length business computer may perform calculations through a *storage-to-storage* approach; i.e., a digit or byte from each of two variable-length data words A and B may be moved from *primary storage* to the arithmetic-logic unit, operated on, and the result *returned* to the primary storage location originally occupied by data word A (Fig. 7-12). This approach, as we have seen in Chapter 6, is slower, but less expensive circuitry may be used and more flexible use of storage may be possible.

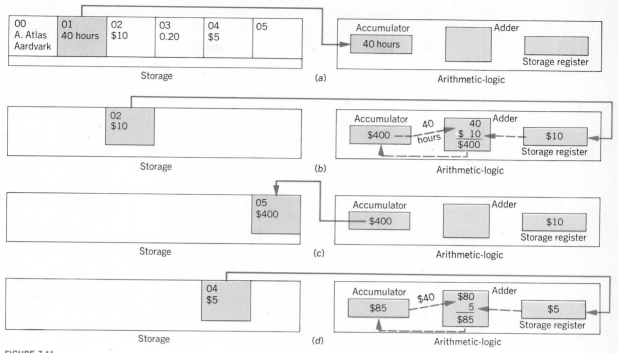

**FIGURE 7-11**

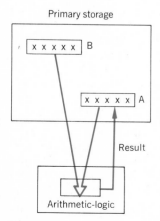

**FIGURE 7-12**

Storage-to-storage approach.

Fixed word-length computers may transfer data words from primary storage to a varying number of registers. Data from two such registers, e.g., the storage register and the accumulator, may be operated on in parallel. The result may be stored in a register or moved back to a primary storage location, as shown in Fig. 7-11. Current processors that use both variable-length words for business applications and fixed-length words for scientific applications must have, of course, arithmetic-logic circuitry and registers that permit the handling of either type of application. The IBM System/370 series, for example, permits the use of the storage-to-storage approach for business processing but also makes 16 general purpose registers available for fixed word-length applications.

Logic operations usually consist of comparisons. The arithmetic-logic unit may compare two numbers by subtracting one from the other. The sign (negative or positive) and the value of the difference tell the processor that the first number is equal to, less than, or greater than the second number. Three branches may be provided in the program for the computer to follow, depending on the result of such a comparison. Many processors are designed with a *comparer* in the arithmetic-logic unit. Data from an accumulator and a storage register may be examined by the comparer to yield the logic decision. Alphabetic data may also be compared according to an order sequence.

**THE CONTROL UNIT**     The control unit of the processor *selects, interprets,* and *executes* the program instructions. The arithmetic-logic unit responds to commands coming from the control unit. There are at least two parts to any instruction: the *operation,* or *command,* that is to be followed (for example, ADD, SUB, MUL, and GO TO) and the *address,* which locates the data or instructions to be manipulated. The basic components contained in the PAC control unit are the *instruction register, sequence register,*[7] *address register,* and *decoder.*

Let us trace an instruction through the PAC control unit to see how it is handled. We shall again use Aardvark's pay data along with the payroll program shown in Fig. 7-13. Let us assume that the instruction in address 07 has just been executed and that forty hours is the contents of the accumulator. The following steps are performed in the next *operating cycle* (the circled numbers in Fig. 7-13 correspond to these steps):

1     The instruction in address 08 (MUL 02) is *selected* by the *sequence register* and read into the *instruction register* in the control unit. (The sequence register does not store the instruction. We shall have more to say about the sequence register in step 5 below.)

2     The operation part of the instruction (MUL) and the address part (02) are *separated.* The operation is sent to the decoder where it is *interpreted.* The computer is built to respond to a limited number of commands, and it now knows that it is to multiply.

3     The address part of the instruction is sent to the *address register.*

4     The signal to move the contents of address 02 into the arithmetic-logic unit is sent; the command to multiply goes to the arithmetic-logic unit where the instruction is *executed.*

5     As the multiplication is being executed, the sequence register in the control unit is increased by one to indicate the location of the next instruction address. When the program was started, the sequence register was set to the address of the first instruction by the programmer. By the time the first program instruction was finished, the contents of the sequence register had automatically been advanced to the next instruction address number. In other words, the first address in the payroll program was 06 (read data in), and the sequence register was set to 06. As that instruction was being executed, the sequence register automatically moved to 07 and then to 08, and now it is again automatically moved to 09. It keeps this up until instructed to do otherwise. From the last chapter you will recall that when the sequence register gets to address 17, it encounters an instruction that reads GO TO 06. This command alters the normal stepping of the sequence register and resets it at address 06.

6     The instruction at address 09 moves into the instruction register, and the above steps are repeated.

[7] The instruction register is also called the *operation register* and the *control register,* while the sequence register is sometimes referred to as the *control counter* or *instruction counter.*

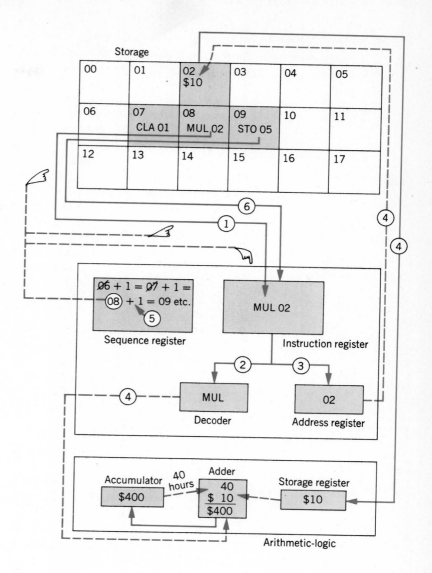

FIGURE 7-13

We may identify separate processor phases, or cycles, in the above procedure. Step 4 is the *execution cycle*. The other steps comprise the *instruction cycle*. Thus, there are two phases in the performance of each instruction. Computers are generally *synchronous;* i.e., the various operations are synchronized by an electronic clock, which emits millions of regularly spaced electronic pulses each second. Commands are interpreted and executed at proper intervals, and the intervals are timed by a specified number of these pulses.

**CPU COMPARISONS—A
BRIEF SURVEY**

In Chapter 1 you saw that CPUs range in size from microcomputers to large-scale systems. Now that you have a better understanding of CPU concepts and components, it is possible to conclude our study of central processors with a brief comparison of a few of the characteristics of representative CPUs ranging in size from the very large to the very small. As you might expect (and as you can see in Fig. 7-14), selected CPUs also vary greatly in operating speed, storage capacity, and cost.

The CRAY-1 is a supercomputer designed to process complex scientific applications. Two 64-bit data words can be added in parallel in one machine cycle to give the CPU an extremely high operating speed. (You will notice that the CRAY-1 *cycle time*—i.e., the time required to execute a basic operation—is much faster than any of the other CPUs listed in Fig. 7-14.) You may think it strange that the CRAY-1 does not have a high-speed buffer storage section. Actually, however, the *entire* primary storage section makes exclusive use of the type of components that are generally reserved only for a buffer section in less powerful machines. This usage, combined with the large number of arithmetic-logic semiconductor chips required to process fixed-length words of large size, makes the CRAY-1 very expensive.

Opposite ends of the IBM System/370 family of mainframe computers are represented in Fig. 7-14 by the large-scale 168 model and the small-scale model 115.[8] Both IBM models have byte-addressable storage, but both also have an instruction set that permits the manipulation of bytes into words of 32 bits, into halfwords, or into doublewords as needed (remember Fig. 6-10?). Both 370 models are thus designed to process both scientific and business applications. Since high-speed buffer storage is used in the 168 but not in the 115, the 168 is much faster. You can examine Fig. 7-14 to see the other significant differences between these processors.

Digital Equipment Corporation's (DEC) line of PDP-11 minicomputers is one of the most popular in the industry. Opposite ends of this computer family are represented in Fig. 7-14 by the model 70 and the model 03.[9] Like the IBM processors, both DEC models are byte-addressable, both have data paths to operate on groups of 16 bits at a time, and both are suitable for scientific and business applications. But unlike the 370 models, the PDP-11s cannot group bytes into larger word lengths. Both

[8] The *largest* 370 computer is the model 3033 which is somewhat faster than the 168 (the cycle time of the 3033 is 58 nanoseconds). Also, the high-speed cache storage capacity of the 3033 is twice that of the 168.

[9] It is rather difficult to classify these models. For example, is the model 70 a large minicomputer or is it a small-scale mainframe CPU? And is the model 03 a small minicomputer or is it one of the larger microcomputers? The development time for minicomputers is typically much shorter than it is for a larger mainframe family. Thus, during the years between announcements of the larger mainframe vendors, minicomputer manufacturers are able to bring out later versions of their products that incorporate the latest technology. As a result, CPUs that may be considered minisized may also possess technical features that are absent from larger (but technologically older) mainframe models.

| Comparative Categories and Features | Representative CPUs | | | | | |
|---|---|---|---|---|---|---|
| | Cray Research, Inc. CRAY-1 | IBM 370/168 | IBM 370/115 | Digital Equipment Corp. PDP-11/70 | Digital Equipment Corp. PDP-11/03 | Intel Corp. SBC 80-10 |
| Relative size | Supercomputer | Large-scale mainframe | Small-scale mainframe | Large minicomputer (small-scale mainframe?) | Small minicomputer (large microcomputer?) | Microcomputer on a board |
| Storage addressing | Fixed word-length (64-bit word) | Combination of byte-addressable and 32-bit word | Combination of byte-addressable and 32-bit word | Combination of byte-addressable and 16-bit word | Combination of byte-addressable and 16-bit word | Single 8-bit bytes only |
| Buffer (cache) storage features: | | | | | | |
| • Technology | — | Bipolar semiconductor | — | Bipolar semiconductor | — | — |
| • Capacity | — | 32K bytes | — | 2K bytes | — | — |
| • Access time | — | 80 nanoseconds | — | 240 nanoseconds | — | — |
| Primary storage features: | | | | | | |
| • Technology | Bipolar semiconductor | MOS chips | MOS chips | Core planes | Core planes or MOS chips | MOS chips |
| • Capacity | Up to 1.048 million 64-bit words | Up to 8.39 million bytes | Up to 393K bytes | Up to 4.96 million bytes | Up to 57K bytes | Up to 4K bytes PROM; 1 K bytes RAM |
| • Access time | 12.5 nanoseconds | 320 nanoseconds | 480 nanoseconds | 1.26 microseconds | Core: 1.15 microseconds MOS: 750 nanoseconds | 1.1 microseconds |
| Arithmetic-logic features: | | | | | | |
| • Number of semiconductor chips | 278,000 | 20,000 | 1,800 | 600 | 4 | 1 Intel 8080A chip |
| • Cycle time | 12.5 nanoseconds | 80 nanoseconds | 480 nanoseconds | 300 nanoseconds | 3.5 microseconds | 2.5 microseconds |
| CPU physical characteristics: | | | | | | |
| • Shape and size | Cylindrical; 9-foot diameter base, 6.5 feet high | Rectangular; 845 cubic feet | Rectangular; 62.5 cubic feet | Rectangular; 27.1 cubic feet | Rectangular; 0.52 cubic feet | Rectangular; 6¾″ × 12″ |
| • Weight | 10,500 pounds | 5,100 pounds | 1,800 pounds | 500 pounds | 35 pounds | ½ pound |
| Basic purchase price | $8 million | $4.5 million | $175,000 | $63,000 | $2,000 | Less than $1,000 |

FIGURE 7-14

Comparative characteristics of representative CPUs.

DEC models make use of both core and semiconductor storage components. A small cache storage section is used in the model 70 to improve performance.

Finally, a representative microcomputer is Intel Corporation's SBC 80-10, the microcomputer on a board shown in Fig. 1-15, page 29. This complete computer is a character-addressable processor that operates only on single 8-bit bytes. Program instructions are held in primary storage in nonvolatile PROM semiconductor chips; a small (1K bytes) RAM section for data storage is also found on the CPU board. Additional boards are available to increase the storage capacity of both the PROM and RAM sections by 16K bytes. A single Intel 8080A chip (see Fig. 2-4, page 41) provides all the arithmetic-logic and control circuitry. The special registers discussed in this chapter—e.g., the accumulator and the instruction register—and six general-purpose registers are found on this chip.

**SUMMARY**    There is a storage hierarchy in a typical data processing system as a result of design compromises. The properties of speed, capacity, safety, and record accessibility and the matter of economics must be considered in selecting the appropriate storage elements. In addition to the primary storage section, a smaller high-speed buffer storage section, which increases processing performance, is often found in CPUs. Read-only memory devices are also incorporated in some CPUs for control purposes.

Primary storage is often provided by the use of planes of magnetic cores. In recent years, however, semiconductor storage chips have found their way into the newer models of most manufacturers because of economic and performance factors.

The arithmetic-logic unit does the actual processing under program control. During the execution cycle, data stored in primary storage or in registers are moved to the arithmetic-logic unit. There they are manipulated by adder circuits to yield a result that may be stored in a register (e.g., the accumulator) or transferred to some other storage location. The control unit selects, interprets, and sees to the execution of instructions in their proper sequence. Several basic registers are required to perform the control function.

In spite of their many similarities, however, computers can differ significantly in a number of characteristics. A brief comparison of representative CPUs has been presented in this chapter.

**REVIEW AND DISCUSSION QUESTIONS**

1    Discuss the storage hierarchy that exists at a computer installation available to you.

2    Define the following terms: (**a**) Access time (**b**) Nonvolatile storage (**c**) Destructive read-in (**d**) Sense wire (**e**) Inhibit wire (**f**) Microprograms (**g**) Cache (**h**) Read-only memory (**i**) Register (**j**) Synchronous computer (**k**) Instruction cycle (**l**) 16K storage capacity (**m**) Execution cycle (**n**) Static memory (**o**) Dynamic storage (**p**) Cycle time.

3    What factors should be considered in determining the data-storage facilities that are needed?

**4**   Discuss some uses of the small specialized processing and control storage sections found in many CPUs.

**5**   (**a**) How is information stored in ferromagnetic cores? (**b**) Once stored, how is it retrieved?

**6**   (**a**) Differentiate between an RAM and a PROM. (**b**) Discuss some uses of microprograms stored in an ROM device.

**7**   (**a**) How is information stored in semiconductor chips in a CPU? (**b**) Compare the advantages of core and semiconductor storage devices.

**8**   (**a**) What is the accumulator? (**b**) What is the adder?

**9**   "Current processors permit the use of the *storage-to-storage approach* for business processing." Explain this sentence.

**10**   Define and explain the function of (**a**) the instruction register, (**b**) the sequence register, (**c**) the address register, and (**d**) the decoder.

**11**   Using Fig. 7-14 as a guide, research a different make of CPU and compare it with one or more of those listed in Fig. 7-14.

**SELECTED REFERENCES**

Gorman, Alyn J., Edmund J. Armon, and Kathleen M. Febrenbach: "Survey of Small Business Computers," *Datamation,* September 1977, pp. 189–191ff.

Hodges, David A.: "Microelectronic Memories," *Scientific American,* September 1977, pp. 130ff.

Lettieri, Larry: "Mostly Mainframes '77," *Computer Decisions,* May 1977, pp. 60ff.

Terman, Lewis M.: "The Role of Microelectronics in Data Processing," *Scientific American,* September 1977, pp. 168–174.

Toong, Hoo-Min D.: "Microprocessors," *Scientific American,* September 1977, pp. 149ff.

You will recall that one of the basic objectives of this book is to provide an orientation to the computer— what it is, what it can and cannot do, and how it operates. Computer capabilities, limitations, and *hardware* operations were presented in the chapters in Part II. Thus, the purpose of the chapters in this Part is to outline and then consider in some detail the steps involved in developing the *software* and *information systems* that make it possible for computer hardware to produce the information needed by decision makers.

The chapters included in Part III are:

# USING COMPUTERS TO SOLVE PROBLEMS

# information system development: 8

## overview and analysis

**LEARNING OBJECTIVES** After studying this chapter and answering the discussion questions, you should be able to: □ Explain why information system changes are necessary, and how computer-based systems can be adapted to changing conditions □ Identify the steps in a system study and explain why system studies are essential □ Outline and discuss the major activities that are performed during system analysis □ Identify a number of tools and techniques that may be used for data gathering and for system analysis □ Describe what the results of the system-analysis stage should be

Summary
Review and discussion questions
Selected references

On Tuesday when it hails and snows
The feeling in me grows and grows
That hardly anybody knows
If those are these and these are those.

Winnie-the-Pooh

**T**his quote could describe the feelings of managers who must make important decisions to deal with the conditions or problems they face. Generally speaking, these conditions or problems result from changes in the *status quo,* and these changes, in turn, will usually provide the impetus for changes in the information systems used by the organization's managers. The changes that may produce problems or modified conditions in one or more areas of an organization (and that may then lead to changes in the organization's information systems) may come from the following sources:[1]

1   *The environment.* Pressures from external sources such as competitors, customers, suppliers, and government agencies can lead to significant changes in a short period of time. For example, new government regulations dealing with the accounting for employee pension plans and with the preparation of employee occupational safety and health reports have presented problems for managers in recent years. Complying with new mandatory regulations obviously requires prompt changes in (or additions to) the organization's information systems.

2   *Top executives of the organization.* Top managers may make decisions to (*a*) acquire or merge with other organizations, (*b*) introduce a new product line, (*c*) reorganize and consolidate or decentralize company operations, (*d*) build a new production or distribution facility, (*e*) implement new budgeting procedures to try to improve managerial planning and control, or (*f*) determine the reasons for operating problems in order to take corrective action. Such decisions will certainly change the status quo; information systems changes are likely to follow.

---

[1] For a detailed discussion of the sources of systems change, see Theodore C. Willoughby, "Origins of Systems Projects," *Journal of Systems Management,* October 1975, pp. 18–26.

**3** *A specific operating department within the organization.* Although changes initiated by the above sources will certainly have an impact on departments in an organization, managers and others in these departments may also initiate changes in their own operations and in the information systems that they use. In fact, the systems changes that are made at the request of the departmental users of the information output often turn out to be much more satisfactory than the systems changes that are forced on these users by other sources. Of course, department managers often initiate operating and systems changes in order to gain recognition and receive tangible and intangible rewards.

**4** *The information processing department within the organization.* The group responsible for developing the information systems in a business is in a position to identify areas of needed systems improvement. During the development of a suggested system change initiated by one of the above sources, for example, the systems specialists may uncover unsuspected weaknesses that should be corrected.

To summarize, then, frequent changes originating from a number of sources create conditions or problems that managers must deal with, and the systems that provide them with needed information must continuously be adapted to changing conditions. In this book, of course, we are primarily concerned with computer-based information systems. But computer hardware, by itself, does not solve a single business problem. As Fig. 8-1 indicates, there are usually many activities that lie between the realization of a need for information and the use of computer hardware to satisfy the need on a regular basis. And these activities or steps are constantly being repeated as new systems are developed (or as old ones are modified) in order to give the computer a detailed set of up-to-date

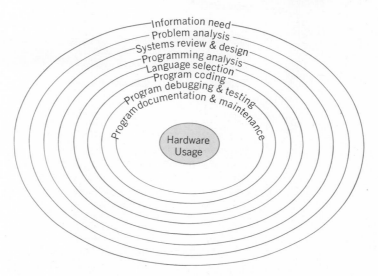

FIGURE 8-1

instructions that will enable it to produce information that is relevant to current conditions and problems.[2]

**SOLVING PROBLEMS USING COMPUTERS: AN OVERVIEW**

The procedure that is generally used to make it possible for computers to supply problem-solving information involves the following steps:

*System Analysis*

1   *Definition of the problem and the objectives.* The particular problem to be solved, or the tasks to be accomplished, must be clearly identified; the objectives of managers in having the tasks performed must be known.

2   *Problem analysis.* Data pertaining to the problem must be gathered, organized, and interpreted. From this analysis may come a recognition of computer potential, i.e., a recognition that the computer could be used to achieve a problem solution.

*System Design*

3   *System review and design.* The present procedures should be reviewed to determine what improvements are possible. These procedures should be redesigned to meet current needs. New system designs should consider the scope of the problem, the form and type of input data to be used, and the form and type of output required.

*Programming*

4   *Programming analysis.* The new system specifications must be broken down into the specific arithmetic and logic operations required to solve the problem.

5   *Program preparation.* The specific steps must next be translated or coded into a language and form acceptable to the processor.[3]

*Implementation*

6   *Program debugging and testing.* The coded program must be checked for errors and tested prior to being used on a routine basis to ensure that the correct problem is being solved and that correct results are being produced.

7   *Program documentation and maintenance.* Conversion to the new approach must be made; the program must be properly stored when not in use; it must be described in writing (and supporting written documents must be developed and kept on file); and it must be revised and maintained as needs change.

The purpose of this chapter and the four that follow is to survey these

---

[2] Without such up-to-date software, the computer itself is merely an expensive and space-consuming curiosity. In fact, as far as most users of information are concerned, the solution of problems is what is important, and the use of computer hardware in the solution process may only be incidental.

[3] As used here, programming is defined as the process of converting broad system specifications into usable machine instructions. It is *not* merely program preparation or *coding;* rather, programming consists of steps 4 through 7 and is a time-consuming and error-prone process that does not begin and end with the writing of lines of code on a sheet of paper. In some organizations the system specifications are prepared by system analysts and the later steps are generally handled by programmers and computer operators. Close cooperation is, of course, required. In other organizations, combination analyst/programmers are used to develop information system projects.

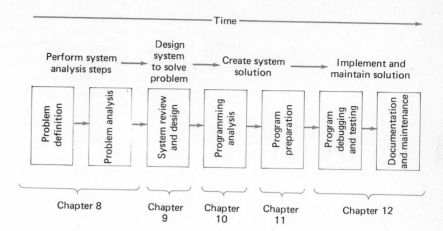

FIGURE 8-2

Procedure for solving problems with
computers.

seven steps that comprise the system development/programming process.
The *first two steps* are included in the *system analysis* stage which is
discussed later in this chapter. The *system design* stage (step 3) is the
subject of the next chapter. The *programming* steps required to create a
system solution (steps 4 and 5) are considered in Chapters 10 and 11, and
the final two programming steps necessary to the *implementation* of the
system solution are studied in Chapter 12. Figure 8-2 summarizes (1) the
steps involved in using computers to solve business problems and (2) the
organizational outline of the book in discussing these steps.

Although we will soon be discussing system analysis topics, it is
probably appropriate to pause here first to briefly consider some important preliminary system development concepts.

**PRELIMINARY SYSTEM
DEVELOPMENT
CONCEPTS**

System development studies are made to improve current operations and/
or to respond to changing conditions. For example, the purpose of a study
in a smaller organization may be to redesign noncomputer systems and
determine the feasibility of installing a first computer. In organizations
with existing computer facilities, the purpose of a system study may be to
(1) revise and update existing procedures using currently available hardware, (2) develop new applications for existing hardware, or (3) determine the feasibility of redesigning and converting existing systems to new
hardware.

### general system development standards

Potential system development projects should be studied and evaluated
on the basis of *technical, economic,* and *operational* criteria. In one

*technical* sense, most contemplated business systems are feasible; the job *can* be done, and *hardware* exists to implement the system. However, preparing the necessary *software* to implement the project may be too formidable a task to undertake with the present number of employees, or it may be beyond the technical capabilities of the current staff.

Whether it would be *economically* feasible to add personnel, acquire new hardware, etc., is, of course, a matter that should be evaluated. In some cases, top executives may specify that unless a new system project can produce a minimum annual rate of return—e.g., 20 percent—on the investment required to implement the project, it will not be approved.

Finally, can we assume that a proposed system that appears to meet technical and economic criteria will be successful if implemented? Not necessarily. If people in the *operational* areas that prepare the data input and use the information output are not sold on the new system and do not want to make it work, it is likely to fail to achieve its goals. A careful system study is thus essential if development standards are to be met.

### essential nature of the system study

A *system study* is the investigation made in an organization to determine and develop needed informational improvements in *specified* areas. In the context of this chapter, the needed improvements will involve using a computer to achieve specific objectives. There are at least three reasons for making a system study:

**1** Substantial investment may be involved in using a computer, and *a proper study reduces the risk of loss.*

**2** Many of the common *pitfalls associated with inadequate planning may be avoided.*

**3** The *study may point the way to substantial benefits.*

Reducing economic risk    Computer usage is justified when one or more of the following conditions is present: (1) greater processing speed is both *desired and necessary.* (2) processing complexities *require* electronic methods, and/or (3) the investment in the computer system is offset by tangible or intangible economic benefits.

But there are numerous examples of businesses that have not achieved economic gains from their computers. In one case, a utility company estimated that a customer information system would cost $2.5 million to develop and would achieve economic benefits sufficient to pay for this investment over a 4-year period. The project was abandoned, however, after $7 million in development costs had been incurred and it was then estimated that an additional $8 million would be required to complete

"Before we have the treasurer's report I'd like to call attention to the little packets of tissue in front of each of you."

© DATAMATION ®

the system.[4] And according to a recent survey conducted by the accounting firm of Peat, Marwick, Mitchell & Co. among 147 financial and data processing executives, only 30 percent of these executives reported that they were satisfied with the economic return on their information system investment.[5]

[4] Dismal examples such as this one are not limited to businesses. The data processing operations of the federal government annually waste millions of tax dollars because properly conducted system studies have not been carried out. For numerous examples, see *Problems Found with Government Acquisition and Use of Computers from November 1965 to December 1976* (Washington: General Accounting Office, Mar. 15, 1977). See also the two-part series by Victor Block, "Computer Wasteland USA," appearing in *Infosystems* in October 1977, pp. 40–41ff., and November 1977, pp. 50–51ff.

[5] Nor is it likely that these disappointing results are all behind us as the following little poem by Jackson Granholm points out:

> For I dipt into the future, far as human eye could see,
> Saw multitudinous computers of generations yet to be;
> Heard the wailing, moaning, muttering of users
>     all nonplussed,
> And the cry of corporate officers faced again
>     with going bust. . . .

1   *Lack of top management support.* Top executives have often failed to provide the needed leadership and have sometimes been antagonistic to system solutions proposed by specialists who speak in terms that they do not understand.

2   *Failure to specify objectives.* A system study should be directed toward achieving *specific* goals. It is a responsibility of users to specify what they want in the way of quality management information—a responsibility that many have been reluctant to assume. Computer usage should be considered *only* when goals can best be reached by electronic means.

3   *Excessive reliance on vendors.* Computer manufacturers can provide many valuable services. But it is unrealistic to expect them to be objective if (as has sometimes been the case in the past) they are given the job of conducting a system study to determine the feasibility of acquiring new hardware or software.

4   *Lack of awareness of past estimation-error patterns.* The following error patterns are among those that have been common in the past: (*a*) initial system development time, the difficulty of training system users, and the problems associated with system implementation have generally been underestimated; (*b*) the degree of employee resistance to change has been "surprisingly" high; (*c*) development and operating costs have often been understated while savings estimates have been too optimistic; and (*d*) the differences between organizations have often been underestimated with the result that hardware/software resources suitable for one firm may be unacceptable for a "similar" firm in the same industry.

5   *The crash-program pitfall.* It typically requires many months to design and implement a complex new information system. Yet it is not uncommon for managers to attempt a crash program in much less time because (*a*) they do not appreciate the magnitude of the task and (*b*) they wish to achieve immediately the benefits that the computer is supposed to provide. The data processing system produced by a crash program generally leaves much to be desired. It often fails to meet needs; it requires that a disproportionate amount of time be taken to correct errors and oversights; and it encounters resistance from personnel who were not properly prepared for it.

6   *The hardware-approach pitfall.* Executives have been known to contract for a new computer first and then decide on how it can be used. The hardware approach typically dispenses with any meaningful system study; an elusive intangible called prestige is its goal; and the effects of change on personnel are given little consideration.

7   *The improper-priority pitfall.* One of the consequences of a lack of top management support and of failure to specify objectives

FIGURE 8-3
Common pitfalls.

clearly has been that critical application areas have been ignored. Processing emphasis is placed on lower-priority tasks. A thorough system study should identify the critical functions.

8    *The inadequate-staffing pitfall.* Members of the study team should have an intimate knowledge of the business, and/or they should be competent in the technical aspects of systems and data processing. Although their talents are often in demand elsewhere in the organization, these people must be released from other duties if a proper study is to be made. Entrusting the study effort to an "average" group yields only average results at best.

9    *The excessive "pioneering" pitfall.* There are many competitive advantages in being the first to develop a new system or application. But in the past some pioneers have found their advantages to be only temporary while their costs were much greater than the costs of their competitors.

10    *The "total system" pitfall.* Attempts have been made in the past to design totally integrated and very complex systems in one major effort rather than to proceed with the less ambitious (but less risky) approach of carefully implementing system modules.

11    *Lack of control pitfall.* New systems have been designed, for example, without the necessary initial attention being given to provisions that would allow for the proper control of data integrity and system security. Such systems have then had to be reworked at considerable expense to incorporate the necessary data and system controls.

FIGURE 8-3    (*continued*)

These gloomy facts support the contention that computer acquisition and use can be risky. The costs associated with acquiring and using a computer can be hard to predict. The difficulty is not caused by hardware rental or purchase costs, for such costs are known. Rather, the difficulty is caused by the unpredictability of software and operating costs (which are likely to be much larger than hardware costs). And, of course, when expenses are hard to pin down, tangible savings resulting from computer usage become equally difficult to predict. A properly conducted system study will not eliminate economic risk, but it can substantially reduce it.

Avoiding common pitfalls    Financial loss may be an end result of failure to conduct an appropriate system study. In the past, numerous mistakes made by business managers have contributed to this undesirable end.[6]

[6] See the sources listed in footnote 4 for numerous examples of the types of mistakes made by administrators in the federal government.

These same snares will undoubtedly serve as the future *means* by which unwary managers (through their failure to conduct a proper study) will bring about economic losses for their firms. Several of the more *common pitfalls* to be avoided are summarized in Fig. 8-3.[7]

Study benefits   An important benefit of the system study is that it enables an organization to steer clear of many pitfalls and thus to reduce the possibility of financial loss. In addition, the *time and money invested in a system study may yield the following benefits:*

**1**   *Current system savings may be achieved by the cleaning up of outdated procedures that have evolved over long periods.* Obsolete reports and duplication can often be eliminated; significant cost reductions may thus be possible regardless of whether or not a computer is used. In fact, it is likely that the cost reductions attributed to many computers are the result of system improvement.

**2**   *A healthy reevaluation of purpose and goals may result.* The major problems and opportunities of an organization may be made explicit, perhaps for the first time. Long-range planning is likely to be encouraged by this definition. Operating personnel may better understand what is expected of them; they may better appreciate the problems of other departments of the organization, and this appreciation can lead to better cooperation and coordination of effort.

The above pages have demonstrated the essential nature of the system study in planning for computer usage. Let us now look at an approach to be followed in conducting such a study.

### steps in the system study approach

A system study is conducted to provide answers to such questions as: (1) What data processing improvements are needed? (2) Should new information systems be designed? and (3) Should a computer be used to achieve data processing objectives? In answering these and other questions, the team[8] making the study should follow a step-by-step system

---

[7] Perhaps after examining Fig. 8-3 you have concluded that potential pitfalls have been grossly exaggerated. In some cases you are correct, and few, if any, problems have occurred. But there have been reasons enough in the past for Ephraim McLean, professor of Information Systems, University of California at Los Angeles, and Lawrence Welke, president of International Computer Programs, Inc., to describe the life cycle of a typical computer data processing system as (1) *wild euphoria* when the new system is announced, (2) *growing concern,* (3) *"near total disillusionment* as the systems people realize almost all the goals set down in stage 1 are unattainable (mainly because management has not set down what it wants),"* (4) *unmitigated disaster,* (5) *search for the guilty,* (6) *punishment of the innocent,* and (7) *promotion of the uninvolved.* (The last three stages occur in quick order, according to Mr. Welke.)

[8] In broader system studies involving extensive redesign of existing procedures, a team approach is generally followed; in less complicated systems projects the "team" may shrink to one analyst.

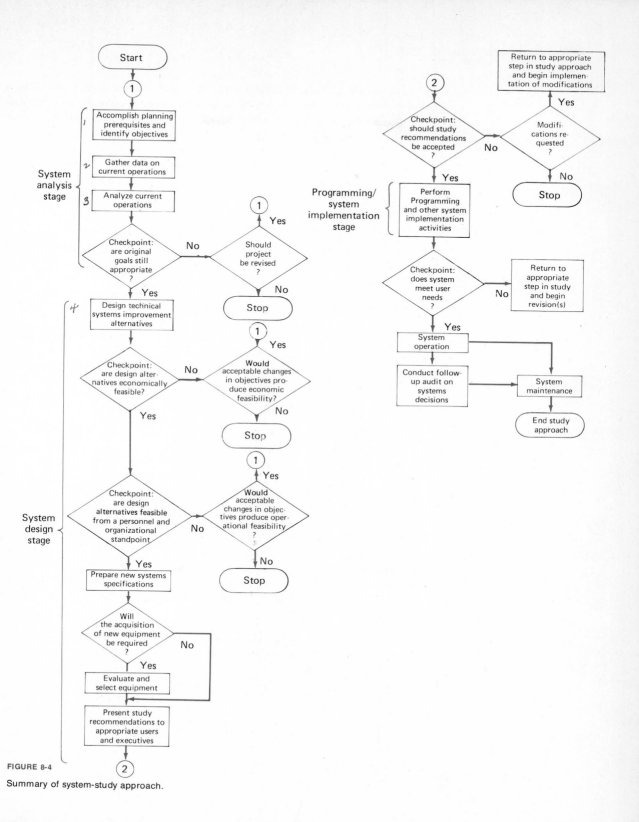

FIGURE 8-4

Summary of system-study approach.

development approach to (1) *accomplish planning prerequisites and identify the objectives,* (2) *gather data on current operations,* (3) *analyze current operations,* (4) *determine feasible solutions,* and (5) *decide on the most appropriate solution.* (In addition to these steps, as we will see in later chapters, it will also be necessary to *program* and then *implement* the solution.) Fig. 8-4 presents a general summary of the system-study approach.

THE SYSTEM-ANALYSIS
STAGE

As you have seen in Figs. 8-2 and 8-4, the system-analysis stage includes the early steps in the system development effort. Let us now take a closer look at these steps.

### planning prerequisites and identification of objectives

The account of an early well-managed survey is found in the Bible in chapter 13 of the Book of Numbers. A team of 12 "analysts" was sent by Moses to spy out the Promised Land and report back their findings. *Three important prerequisite principles* were observed in this survey:

1   *The survey had support at the highest levels.* God told Moses: "Send men to spy out the land of Canaan . . . from each tribe of their fathers shall you send a man, every one a leader among them." Moses certainly had support at the highest level! Of course, we have seen that the impetus for information system changes may originate from a number of sources. But regardless of who is sponsoring the change, top-level management support is a prerequisite to the success of the change effort.

2   *The survey team consisted of highly respected individuals.* Only tribal leaders were sent on the mission. System study members are often selected for the offsetting talents they can bring to the job. It is common to find at least one team member (and very possibly the leader of the study team) who represents the interests of the end-user(s) of the proposed new system and who has a knowledge of the information needs of the business areas affected by the change. Another team member (e.g., a systems analyst or chief programmer) should be familiar with system development and the technical side of data processing. A third member of the team should probably be an internal auditor who can assume the responsibility for building the proper controls into the new system. These controls, for example, should help ensure that adequate (a) input, processing, and output provisions are installed and maintained to provide for *data integrity;* (b) *system security* techniques are incorporated; and (c) *system testing* is accomplished prior to regular use. The team leader should be chosen on the basis of proven managerial ability for he or she must plan, organize, and control the project. It is the leader's job to (a) understand the scope, purpose, and goals of the study; (b) schedule and coordinate the team effort and keep interested parties informed of the team's prog-

ress; (c) secure the cooperation of company employees who can contribute to the study; and (d) achieve the end objectives.

3   *The scope and objectives of the survey were clearly stated.* Moses specifically told the 12 to investigate the richness of the land, the physical and numerical strength of the occupants, and the defensibility of their cities. In a system study, the nature of the operation(s) that is (are) to be investigated, and the objectives that are to be pursued, should also be specifically stated; the relationship of the study to other company projects should be noted; and the organizational units in the company that are to be included and excluded should be identified. After the definition of the study's scope and direction, it is important to specify the objectives that are to be pursued. Figure 8-5 summarizes some goals that are commonly sought.

---

*Expense reduction objectives*
(Benefits of a tangible nature)

1   Reduce clerical labor expense

2   Reduce supervisory and other nonclerical labor expense

3   Reduce equipment expense

4   Reduce space and overhead expense

5   Reduce supplies expense

6   Reduce inventory carrying expense

*Revenue raising objectives*
(Benefits which are usually intangible)

1   Shorten processing time; improve timeliness of information

2   Increase processing capacity to expand marketing efforts, increase production efficiency, etc.

3   Acquire more accurate information

4   Acquire more comprehensive information

5   Improve operating control

6   Improve customer service

7   Acquire new information (sales analyses, cost analyses, etc.)

8   Achieve better planning and control through the use of quantitative decision techniques that were not previously available

*Other objectives*

1   Attain prestige and a progressive image

2   Meet clerical labor shortages

3   Prepare required government reports

---

FIGURE 8-5
Common system study objectives.

The biblical survey team returned to Moses after 40 days. There was agreement on the richness of the land (and this report was "documented" with examples of the fruit that it produced). There was lack of agreement, however, on the strength of the people occupying the Promised Land. Sessions were held during which the differing viewpoints were presented.

It is usually necessary for the team members to hold preliminary sessions with the managers of all departments that the study will affect. Such *requirements sessions* allow these managers to participate in setting or revising specific system goals and should give each manager the opportunity to (1) identify those factors that are critical to the success of his or her contribution to the system's goals, (2) determine how these critical factors can be measured, (3) determine, for each critical factor, what *quantifiable* measurement constitutes success, and (4) acquire information that will be needed to ensure achievement of "success measurements."

This participation of end-users is both necessary and logical; it enables those most familiar with existing methods and procedures to make suggestions for improvement and to personally benefit from the change. Furthermore, these managers are the ones who performance is affected by any changes, and they are the ones whose cooperation is needed if the study is to yield satisfactory results.[9]

Before concluding this discussion of goal definition, it is appropriate to point out that *a repeating or iterative process may be necessary before this first study step is considered complete.* There is no definite procedure to be followed before detailed data gathering can begin. A top executive may believe that a systems study is needed because of informational deficiencies; he or she may prepare a general statement of objectives and then appoint a manager to conduct the study. A number of requirements sessions may be held to translate general desires into more specific goals; the scope of the study may be enlarged or reduced; objectives may be similarly changed as more facts are gathered. When it appears that tentative approval has been reached on objectives, the study leader should put these goals *in writing* and send them to all concerned for approval. If differences remain, they should be resolved in additional requirements sessions.

Some less-experienced team members may become impatient with the "delays" in system development caused by additional sessions. Wiser heads know, however, that the really lengthy and expensive delays occur when users discover very late in the development process that the

---

[9] For a more detailed discussion of the importance of the end-user in system development, see William Ainsworth, "The Primacy of the User," *Infosystems,* April 1977, pp. 46–48, and May 1977, pp. 50–52ff.

designed system is unsatisfactory because of earlier requirements over-sights that result in missing or incomplete information.[10]

Before the more detailed investigation begins, the team leader should prepare a *written charter* for approval by the executive or steering committee in charge of the overall data processing program. This charter, when approved, should include (1) a detailed statement of the study's scope and objectives (2) a grant of authority to permit the team to cross departmental lines and receive top priority on the working time of specified individuals (who should be informed of this authority grant by a high-level executive), and (3) a development schedule giving a target date for the completion of the study recommendations and interim dates for the presentation of progress reports to the executive or steering commit-tee in charge.

This development schedule should be based partly on the rate at which data processing specialists can be expected to complete the project, but it should also take into consideration the rate at which users can participate in, absorb, and utilize the new system. *Checkpoints* should be built into the system development project. Progress reports prepared at these specified times provide facts to enable an executive or steering committee to exercise overall control over the study team and the project. Reviews by users, managers, and auditors are periodically needed to determine the accuracy and completeness of the study effort and to ensure that the system project remains feasible from an economic and operational standpoint. Approval to continue the study should be received by the team at each control point before the effort is continued. Several general checkpoints are illustrated in Fig. 8-4.

**data-gathering operations**

The study-team members must first gather data on current operations before they can design suitable alternatives to achieve specified goals. In short, they must find out *where they are* before they can determine *where they want to go*. In identifying objectives, it is likely that preliminary data were gathered. But more details are now needed to determine the strengths and weaknesses of current procedures. As a result of informa-tion brought to light during this study step, it may be desirable to revise

---

[10] As Richard G. Canning notes, "the relative cost of correcting an error increases exponen-tially with the project phase in which the error is detected. A requirements error that is not found until the testing phase can cost 10 to 100 times as much to fix as it would cost had it been found during the specification phase." See "Getting the Requirements Right," *EDP Analyzer,* July 1977, p. 5. A thorough discussion of the importance of the preliminary steps in the system study approach is presented in this article.

the scope and goals of the investigation. The iterative process may be continued.

The data gathered must be accurate, up to date, and sufficiently complete, for they will become the input to the design stage. On the other hand, however, if the analysts are not careful, they may become so mired down in relatively unimportant details at this stage that time schedules cannot be met.

Questions to be answered    The data to be collected will vary from one study to another, but in most cases the following general questions about the operations being studied should be answered: (1) *What output results* are currently being achieved? (2) *What processing is needed* and *what processing resources are being used* to produce this output? (3) *What input data* are processed to produce output results? You recognize, of course, that these questions refer to the input, processing, and output components found in any data processing system. However, this input-processing-output sequence is often reversed during the steps in a system study because the team must have an early understanding of current output before it can properly identify, separate, and analyze the processing and input activities that are relevant to the current output, and because study goals are commonly expressed in terms of the output information needed. Figure 8-6 provides a list of more specific questions that may be asked in the course of gathering data.

Many well-managed firms base their ultimate decision to install a new system on a *return-on-investment* (ROI) analysis. The profit improvement expected to result from the system is compared with the computer hardware/software investment to see if the investment appears to be justified. Anticipated profit improvement is affected, in part, by the comparison of current processing costs with the similar costs of proposed alternatives. Thus, the team must gather data about the *current* costs to process a given volume of information. Information about processing *volume* is also needed to determine the complexity and cost of proposed alternative methods. The following cost figures related to the operations under study should be collected: (1) charges for payroll and associated fringe benefits; (2) cost of processing equipment (in the form of rental and/or depreciation charges); (3) charges for office materials, supplies, forms, etc.; and (4) overhead charges (office space used, insurance, utilities, etc.).

Data-gathering tools and techniques    The following tools and techniques are among those that may be useful during data-gathering operations:

1    *Organization charts.* These charts indicate, by position titles, the place in the organization of each job, the formal lines of authority and

*System Output Questions*

What output reports are prepared? What other output is received?
What is the purpose of the output information?
Who uses the output information? How is the output information actually being used?
How accurate is the output? Do controls exist to ensure accuracy?
How timely is the output? How is output stored and retrieved?
Have controls been established to maintain the security of output information?

*Processing Questions*

What records and files are being kept to support the operation?
How frequently—daily, weekly, or monthly—is the processing being performed? What is the volume or magnitude of work in each phase of the operation? What volume fluctuations occur in the operation?
What is the cause of these fluctuations?
What is the flow of work; i.e., what sequence of steps is followed to perform the processing?
What controls have been incorporated to maintain data integrity and prevent processing errors? What security controls are there?
Have processing standards been established? Are they followed?
What departments are involved in the processing? What place in the organization do they occupy? What is the primary function of these departments?
How many people are involved in the processing? What are their skill levels?
How much time is required for processing?
What processing and storage equipment is being used? For how long?
What materials and supplies are being used? In what volumes?
How much does it cost to perform the processing?

*System Input Questions*

How are data introduced into the system? What source documents are received? How are they stored and retrieved? What source documents are actually used?
Where does input originate? In what form? Who originates the input?
What is the frequency of input—daily, weekly, or monthly?
What is the maximum volume received? The minimum? The average?
When do the peak periods occur? The slack periods?
Do procedure manuals and standards exist in the input department(s)? How reliable is this documentation?
What controls are there on the accuracy, integrity, and security of input data and source documents?
What is the speed, storage capacity, and cost of input media and devices?
What is the cost of input preparation?

FIGURE 8-6

Data-gathering questions.

reporting relationships among positions, and the assigned role of work units in the total structure. Thus, the availability of up-to-date organization charts can give the members of the study team a better understanding of the general nature of the organization and a greater appreciation of the role of each manager in the decision-making hierarchy. Such knowledge is needed prior to and during the data-gathering operations.

**2** *Organization standards.* System development work is a continual task in most businesses of any size. Of course, the goals of each study differ, and the study-team membership may vary for each project, but the system study approach remains relatively constant. A *standards manual* that spells out the steps to be completed and the procedures to be followed during (and after) data-gathering operations is generally of great value both to the organization and to a particular study team. The organization benefits from methodical studies that tend to be better controlled, more thorough, and more consistent. And the team members benefit because the manual may give them the answers to numerous questions—e.g., What is the next step? How should this step be accomplished? How should this procedure be documented? What documentation standards should be followed? When have we gathered enough data? In short, a standards manual eliminates the need for each study team to "reinvent the wheel." Furthermore, system components produced according to organizational standards are much more easily integrated into broader information systems that are corporatewide in scope.

**3** *Requirements sessions with users and suppliers.* The importance of these sessions was discussed earlier. The early and active participation of those who use the output information and those who prepare the input data and process it will be very helpful during data-gathering operations. Such participation should reduce the team's data-gathering task since these people represent a storehouse of information on current procedures. Also, sessions with these individuals can serve to focus the team's attention on the most important areas.

**4** *System charting.* A *flowchart* is a graphic tool or model that provides a means of recording, analyzing, and communicating information. For example, appropriate symbols may be used by an analyst to *record* quickly the flow of data in a current procedure from the originating source, through a number of processing operations and machines, to the output report. The flowchart *picture,* or schematic, may assist the analyst in acquiring a better understanding of the procedure than would otherwise be possible. It may also aid in procedure *analysis* and then in improvement; e.g., it may point out bottlenecks that may be eliminated in the flow of data. Flowcharts are frequently used to *communicate* the essential facts of a problem to others whose skills are needed in the solution. The *system flowchart* provides a broad overview of the processing operations that are being accomplished (and/or that should be performed). Primary emphasis is placed on data flow between machines and work stations, e.g., on input documents and output reports. The amount of detail furnished about *how* a machine or work station is to convert the data on input documents into the desired output is limited. In the design

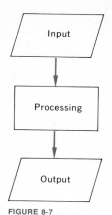

FIGURE 8-7

Basic system charting symbols.

of all flowcharts it is necessary that standard *symbols* be used to record and communicate information clearly.[11] Symbols representing input, output, and general processing (Fig. 8-7) are frequently used in system flowcharts. The same basic I/O symbol may be used to show *any* type of media or data. The arrows connecting the shapes indicate the direction of data flow. The main flow is generally charted from top to bottom and from left to right. The *shape* of the symbol and *not its size* identifies the meaning. For example, the rectangular processing box may vary in size, but the shape still designates that processing is being performed. Notation within the charting symbol further explains what is being done. Frequently, the basic I/O symbol is *replaced* in system flowcharts by other I/O symbols whose shape suggests the type of medium or device being employed (Fig. 8-8). These symbols are familiar to us since they have been used in earlier chapters. Additional commonly used system flowchart symbols are shown and described in Fig. 8-9. Preparing flowcharts is helpful in gathering data on current operations. Data inputs are identified, and each input preparation step is charted using the proper symbols. Files and equipment being used are also identified, the processing sequence is shown, the departments involved are located, and the output results are indicated. Of course, it is often the case that a system is too complex to be adequately described in a single flowchart. In such situations, there is likely to be an overall "macro chart" or "table of contents" that describes the general input-processing-output components of the system. There may then be a hierarchy of more detailed "micro charts," each of which is a module that deals with one segment of a main or higher-level chart. This decomposition of the general concept of the system into a series of more detailed input-processing-output graphic presentations is the technique followed *(a)* in IBM's HIPO (Hierarchy plus Input-Process-Output) approach to system analysis and design, and *(b)* in SofTech's SADT (Structured Analysis and Design Technique) approach.

5   *Questionnaires and special-purpose forms.* A *questionnaire* is a printed form that contains a set of questions. The purpose of such a form, of course, is to give the team the answers to the type of questions raised in Fig. 8-6. Questionnaires and specialized data-gathering forms are often keyed to the activities presented in a flowchart. They give the details of processing frequencies, input and output volumes, workers performing each activity, time required to complete each step, and materials and supplies used. Several system analysis and design approaches that have been built around the use of specialized forms by computer manufacturers and others are now being used by businesses. One such forms-driven approach is IBM's Study Organization Plan (SOP). Five data-gathering forms are used to describe the existing system (Fig. 8-10). When completed, the *message sheets* or forms provide detailed facts on current output and input; the *file forms* show the data stored in the system; and

---

[11] The symbols approved by the American National Standards Insitute (ANSI) are the ones that are used in this text. For more details on flowchart symbols and their use, see Ned Chapin, "Flowcharting with the ANSI Standard; A Tutorial," *Computing Surveys*, June 1970, pp. 119–143.

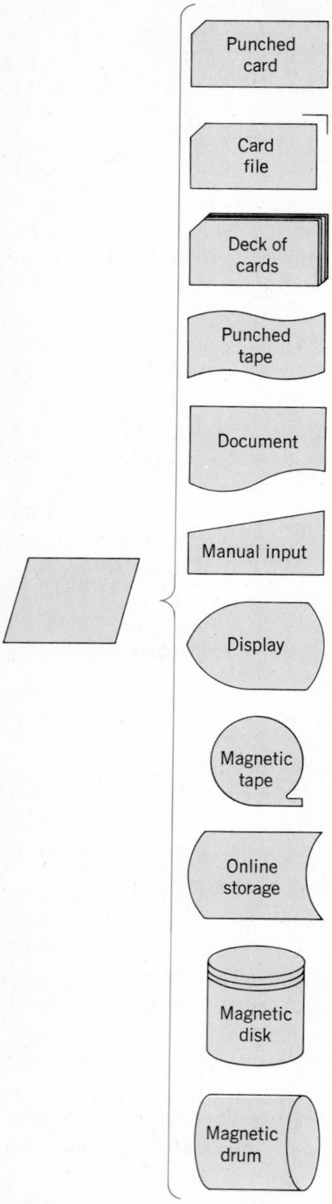

Punched card

Card file

Deck of cards

Punched tape

Document

Manual input

Display

Magnetic tape

Online storage

Magnetic disk

Magnetic drum

FIGURE 8-8

I/O (and storage) specialized symbols.

the *operation forms* present the detailed processing steps performed by the system. A separate operation sheet is typically keyed to each step outlined by the system flowchart on the *activity sheet*. Finally, the organizational environment of the current system and the costs of the system are presented on the *resource usage sheet*.[12] Another forms-driven method of data gathering and analysis is used in NCR's Accurately Defined Systems (ADS) approach. Five interrelated forms are again prepared by analysts. A definition of all system outputs is completed on the first form, and system input data are noted on the second. The remaining forms provide for a description of the historical data stored in the system, together with a listing of the computations and logic needed to use the new and stored data to produce system output.

6   *Interviews and observations*. Interviews are needed to gather the data, prepare charts, and fill in questionnaires and special-purpose forms. Interviews also serve as a check on the reliability of procedures manuals and other existing system documentation. The analyst must conduct the necessary interviews with skill and tact.[13] Another valuable data-gathering technique used by analysts is to personally observe people as they perform the tasks required by the system being studied. One observation approach is for the analyst to take an input document and "walk it through" the processing procedure. A walk-through also presents an opportunity for the analyst to obtain suggestions from employees about ways in which procedures might be improved.

7   *Operational review sessions*. When the study-team members feel that they have gathered all the data that are necessary, they should, as a final check on their accuracy and completeness, present these facts to operating personnel for verification and approval.

**analyzing the current system**

During the data-gathering operations, emphasis was placed on *what* was being done. But it is now time for the team members to analyze their findings.

Purpose of analysis   The purpose of analysis is to learn *why* the system operates as it does and to prepare suggestions on *how* the study goals may best be achieved. More specifically, the team members are now interested in analyzing and documenting their findings in order to (1) identify the decisions that the system must support and the data and procedures in the system that are essential to the decision makers in the

---

[12] The IBM manual, *Documentation Techniques* (IBM Corporation, Manual C20-8075) gives more detailed information on these forms. The SOP approach has been compared with other techniques in J. Daniel Couger, "Evolution of Business System Analysis Techniques," *Computing Surveys*, September 1973, pp. 167–198.

[13] For interviewing tips, see Thomas R. Gildersleeve, "Conducting Better Interviews," *Journal of Systems Management*, February 1976, pp. 24–28.

| Symbols | | Meaning of Symbols |
|---|---|---|
| | Auxiliary operation | An operation which supplements the main processing function but which is performed by a machine that is not directly under the control of the CPU. |
| | Offline storage | A symbol representing data stored in external offline storage. Storage media may be cards, paper tapes, magnetic tapes, paper documents, etc. |
| | Manual operation | Any offline process geared to the speed of a human being is represented by this symbol. |
| | Communications link | Automatic data transmission from one location to another. |
| | Annotation flag | This "flag" is connected by the dashed line to a flow line to provide additional explanatory notes. The dashed line may be drawn on either the left or right. The vertical line may also be drawn on the right or left. This symbol is used for both system and program flowcharts. |
| | Merge | Used to indicate the combining of two or more sets of items into one set. |
| | Extract | Used to indicate the removal of one or more specific sets of items from a file or other set of items. |
| | Collate | Combining merging with extracting. Two or more files or sets of items are combined and then two or more files or sets of items are extracted. |
| | Sort | Used to indicate the arranging of a file or other set of items into a sequence. |

**FIGURE 8-9**

Additional system flowchart symbols.

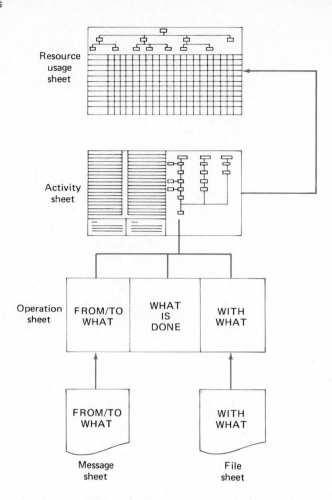

Resource
usage
sheet

Activity
sheet

Operation
sheet

| FROM/TO WHAT | WHAT IS DONE | WITH WHAT |

FROM/TO
WHAT

WITH
WHAT

Message
sheet

File
sheet

FIGURE 8-10

IBM SOP data-gathering forms
(courtesy IBM Corporation).

organization, (2) identify the weaknesses and problems in the present system so that they will not be carried over to a new system, (3) clean up any contradictions or inaccuracies that have developed up to this point in the investigation, (4) reconsider the appropriateness of the original study objectives, and (5) prepare a progress report for user and executive approval.

Tools used in analysis    The following tools may be used in analyzing the current system:

1    *Checklist of questions.* Questions dealing with procedural, personnel, organizational, and economic considerations should be answered. Some representative questions are presented in Fig. 8-11.

2    *Additional review sessions.* Operating managers can explain *why* activities are being performed, and they can answer most of the *procedural* questions presented in Fig. 8-11.

**3** *System flowchart analysis.* The system flowcharts that were prepared during the collection of data can also be used during this analysis period. A hierarchy of system flowcharts that describes the input-processing-output components of a system can be used as analysis documents by the study team to help identify essential data, files, and procedures, and to locate gaps, discrepancies and other problems in the present system. For example, flowchart analysis may disclose bottlenecks; unnecessary files may be discovered (e.g., the charts may show a file where information is stored but from which little or nothing is being removed); and duplications and omissions may be identified.

**4** *Forms analysis.* The input-processing-output forms (such as those used in the SOP and ADS approaches) that describe I/O documents and processing logic are also helpful both in identifying key data items and in uncovering those items that are collected, processed, and stored—but are seldom, if ever, used. Special *input/output tables* may be used to show the relationship that exists between system inputs and outputs. Input source documents are listed in rows on the left of a table (see Fig. 8-12), while the output reports produced by the system are identified in the table columns. An "x" is placed at the intersection of a row and column when a particular source document is used in the preparation of a specific report. For example, in Fig. 8-12 form A is needed in the preparation of reports 1 and 4. The input/output or *grid table* enables the analyst to identify and isolate independent subsystems quickly for further study. This is done by (a) drawing a vertical line down any *single* report column and *then* (b) drawing a horizontal line across any row with a covered x, etc., until further vertical and horizontal lines are impossible. For example, if we draw a line down column 1, we cover only one x—the one indicating that form A is used in preparing report 1. If we then draw a horizontal line along the form A row, we cover the x in column 4. We then draw a vertical line down column 4 and a horizontal line along any row with a covered x. The result of this procedure is that forms A, B, and E and reports 1, 2, and 4 combine to form an independent subsystem.

**The top-down analysis methodology**   If the system being analyzed is relatively large and complex, a "divide and conquer" analysis methodology is often used to break the system down into smaller components. This is essentially the methodology employed when IBM's HIPO and SOP techniques are used. A top-level function or procedure is identified, analyzed, and then broken down (or "decomposed") into a series of second-level components (each of which may also be further reduced into still lower-level components). A hierarchy of understandable subfunctions may be the result of this *top-down analysis* methodology.

**Results of analysis**   Regardless of the tools and techniques used in analyzing the system, the output of the analysis stage should be (1) a *documentation package*—i.e., a complete record of the documents used in the present system along with an account of what the team has learned about the resources and procedures required to operate and maintain the system—and (2) a *progress and recommendations report* that presents

*Procedural considerations*

**1** Are documents being produced relevant to the needs of the business? When were they originated? Who originated them? For what purpose?

**2** Is faster reporting desired? Is faster reporting necessary? Can the processing sequence be improved? What would happen if the document were delayed? If it were eliminated?

**3** Is greater accuracy needed? Could less accuracy be tolerated, i.e., is the expense involved in error checking greater than the cost of committing the error? Is adequate control maintained over document preparation? Does excessive control add to expense?

**4** What monetary value do users place on the document? Are they willing to have their budgets charged with all or part of the cost of preparation?

**5** Is the document in a useful form? Has writing been minimized? When were forms designed? Who designed them? For what purpose?

**6** Does an output document cause action when it is sent to a manager? If not, why is it sent? If it does, what decisions are made?

**7** Is the document filed? If so, for how long? How often is it referred to? Does the filing cost exceed the value of having the document available?

**8** Can documents be combined? Is the same information duplicated on other reports? In other departments? If so, can procedures be integrated?

**9** Is there any part of the document which is ignored? Are unnecessary facts recorded? Are additional facts needed? Are the correct number of copies prepared?

**10** Is exception reporting feasible? Do current reports clearly point out exceptions?

**11** Are additional documents needed? What additional documents? Is computer processing required? Are packaged programs available which will meet the needs of the business?

**12** Is system capacity adequate? Do bottlenecks exist? Is overtime required? What can be done to eliminate peak loads?

**13** Is customer service adequate? What improvements can be made?

*Personnel and organizational considerations*

**14** Are documents being prepared in the proper departments? By the right people? Could departments be combined? Could any work units be eliminated? What effects would organizational change have on personnel?

**FIGURE 8-11**
Questions for analysis.

15    What effect would any procedural changes have on personnel? Would they be agreeable to such changes? What would have to be done to reduce resistance to change? What would be done with those whose jobs would be eliminated or changed? If new jobs were created, what consideration would have to be given to selecting and training workers to staff these vacancies?

*Economic considerations*

16    What is the cost of the present system? What would be the cost of processing with revised current procedures? Approximately what would it cost to satisfy needs using other alternatives? If the cost of achieving study goals is greater than current costs, are possible intangible benefits likely to be worth the extra expense?

FIGURE 8-11    *(continued)*

the team's findings, evaluations, and proposals to those responsible for approving the study.

The minimum *documentation package should probably include:* (1) up-to-date organization charts showing the areas that are affected by the system; (2) a narrative that describes the operations of the present system; (3) complete and accurate system flowcharts; (4) forms and layouts describing all I/O documents, data definitions of required items, and the sequence and logic of processing procedures; (5) samples of all documents currently used; and (6) summaries of interviews, review sessions, personal observations, etc. Such documentation is needed to support the progress and recommendations report and to answer questions about system details that will inevitably occur during the later stages of the system development process. And if new system development is postponed or interrupted, the availability of the documentation package may make it unnecessary to retrace the early system analysis steps when development is resumed.

The *progress and recommendations report should contain:* (1) a restatement of the original scope and objectives of the study along with an

| Input Source Documents | Output Reports | | | | | | | |
|---|---|---|---|---|---|---|---|---|
| | 1 | 2 | 3 | 4 | 5 | 6 | 7 | 8 |
| Form A | x | | | x | | | | |
| Form B | | x | | x | | | | |
| Form C | | | x | | | | | |
| Form D | | | | | | x | | |
| Form E | | x | | x | | | | |
| Form F | | | x | | | | | x |
| Form G | | | | | x | | x | |

FIGURE 8-12

Input/output table.

evaluation of the appropriateness of these goals in light of the facts now available; (2) a brief summary of the operations of the present system, if applicable, along with a detailed statement of present problems or opportunities; (3) a recommended *set of general specifications* for any system additions or modifications that are needed in order to overcome weaknesses and produce accurate, timely, and relevant information; (4) a consideration of the *operational feasibility* of the recommended changes—i.e., a consideration of the personnel and organizational factors that would be affected; and (5) an estimate of the likely *economic consequences* of the recommended system changes.

Upon receipt of this analysis-completion report, those responsible for system development must try to evaluate the *efficiency* and *effectiveness* of present and proposed systems. When a system is described as being *efficient,* it means that the system is "doing things right"—i.e., it is making economic use of such resources as time, money, computer hardware/software, and materials to produce output with a minimum of waste. And when a system is said to be *effective,* it means that it is "doing the right things"—i.e., it is producing relevant information that meets the real needs of the decision makers in the organization. (It is obvious that an ideal system would be both efficient and effective, but it is also clear that there would be no need to conduct a study of such a system.) If the system being studied is effective in producing the right information, but is inefficient and wasteful, then perhaps the first alternative that should be considered is a modified and more efficient version of present methods.[14] On the other hand, if it is efficient but ineffective—i.e., if it economically produces the *wrong* information—then a thorough redesign is needed.

After evaluating the study team's progress and recommendations report, responsible managers may decide to revise the study goals or cancel the project (see Fig. 8-4), postpone system development until a later date, allow the team to proceed to the system design phase with the understanding that economic and operational feasibility tests must be met before a new system design will be given final approval, or give the team full authorization to design and implement the new system. In the next chapter we will look at system design concepts.

**SUMMARY**    Changes in the information systems in an organization may come about as a result of changes initiated by sources outside the business or as a result of decisions made by executives, information users, and data processing specialists within the firm. Several stages are typically fol-

---

[14] There may be at least two reasons for updating current operations. *First,* other possible alternatives should *not* be compared with obsolete and outdated procedures. It is quite possible that an option that is attractive when compared with outdated methods might not be the best choice when compared with redesigned procedures. And *second,* an updating of current operations may prevent useless forms, reports, and records from being preserved in a conversion to an alternative.

lowed when new computer-based information systems must be developed or when old procedures must be adapted to changing conditions. These stages are (1) system analysis, (2) system design, (3) program preparation, and (4) system/program implementation.

However, potential system additions or changes must be considered and evaluated on the basis of technical, economic, and operational criteria. Failure to plan properly for computer usage may subject an organization to financial loss; careful study, on the other hand, may yield positive benefits and may help the firm avoid common pitfalls.

A system study follows a step-by-step development approach. The system-analysis phase includes (1) accomplishing planning prerequisites and identifying system objectives, (2) gathering data on current operations, and (3) analyzing the current situation. Tools, techniques, and suggestions that may be useful in carrying out these steps are discussed in the chapter.

**REVIEW AND DISCUSSION QUESTIONS**

1   (**a**) How may pressures from sources external to a business create the need for changes in the firm's information systems? (**b**) How can decisions made by top executives, department managers, and information system specialists lead to changes in the firm's information systems?

2   Identify and discuss the steps that must be followed to use computers to process business data.

3   "Potential system development projects should be studied and evaluated on the basis of technical, economic, and operational criteria." Discuss this statement.

4   (**a**) What is a system study? **b** Why is it essential?

5   (**a**) What pitfalls may be avoided by conducting a proper system study? (**b**) What benefits may be obtained from a system study?

6   Identify and briefly discuss the steps in the system study approach.

7   What activities are included in the system-analysis stage of a system study?

8   (**a**) What are the prerequisite principles that should be observed in making a system study? (**b**) What are the common objectives of computer usage?

9   Who would you select to be on a team that is expected to study the accounts-payable system in a large firm?

10   (**a**) What is a requirements session? (**b**) An iterative process? (**c**) Why is a written charter needed by the study team?

11   Why should checkpoints be built into a system development schedule?

12   (**a**) What questions should be answered during the data-gathering step of the system analysis process? (**b**) What data-gathering tools and techniques might be used during this step?

13 (**a**) How might a study team benefit from the use of a standards manual? (**b**) How might the organization benefit from such a manual?

14 (**a**) What is a system flowchart? (**b**) How is it used?

15 (**a**) What symbols are used in system flowcharts to represent input and output? (**b**) To represent a manual operation?

16 What is the relationship between HIPO and the top-down analysis methodology?

17 (**a**) Identify and discuss the purpose of the data-gathering forms found in SOP. (**b**) Summarize the ADS approach to data gathering.

18 (**a**) What is the purpose of analyzing the current system? (**b**) Identify and discuss the tools and techniques that might be used in analyzing the current system.

19 (**a**) What is an input/output table? (**b**) How is it used?

20 (**a**) What should be included in the documentation package prepared at the end of the system-analysis stage? (**b**) What should be in the progress and recommendations report?

21 Distinguish between an efficient system and an effective system.

**SELECTED REFERENCES**

Ainsworth, William: "The Primacy of the User," *Infosystems,* April 1977, pp. 46–48; and May 1977, pp. 50–52ff.

Axelson, Charles F.: "How to Avoid the Pitfalls of Information Systems Development," *Financial Executive,* April 1976, pp. 25–31.

Beard, Larry H.: "Planning a Management Information System: Some Caveats and Contemplations." *Financial Executive,* May 1977, pp. 34–39.

Canning, Richard G.: "Getting the Requirements Right," *EDP Analyzer,* July 1977, pp. 1–14.

Couger, J. Daniel, and Robert W. Knapp: *System Analysis Techniques,* John Wiley & Sons, Inc., New York, 1974.

Gildersleeve, Thomas R.: "Conducting Better Interviews," *Journal of Systems Management,* February 1976, pp. 24–28.

Willoughby, Theodore C.: "Origins of Systems Projects," *Journal of Systems Management,* October 1975, pp. 18–26.

# information system system development:

# 9

## the design stage

LEARNING OBJECTIVES   After studying this chapter and answering the discussion questions, you should be able to: ☐ Explain the purpose of, and the steps in, the system design stage of a system development project ☐ Identify a number of basic issues that influence the choice of design alternatives ☐ Discuss several tools and techniques that may be used during the system design stage ☐ Outline the contents of (a) the design specifications report to users and (b) the final system design report to top executives ☐ Discuss some factors to be considered in the selection and acquisition of equipment needed to implement a new system

CHAPTER OUTLINE

**Determination of alternatives: some issues influencing design:** Conceptual Design Issues / The Issue of System Flexibility / The Issue of System Control / The "Make" or "Buy" Issue / Human Factors and Operational Issues / The Issue of Economic Tradeoffs

**W**hen we finished the last chapter, the managers responsible for approving system development projects had just received a progress and recommendations report from the study team. How will the managers react to the recommended set of general specifications for system additions or modifications that they have received? Will they consider recommended changes to be feasible from an operational and economic standpoint? (This reads like the plot of a soap opera, doesn't it?) Well, in this chapter we assume that the team has been given approval to design a new system to meet the informational needs of users in the organization.

During analysis the team learned *what* procedures were currently being followed; an understanding of *what* should be done was also obtained. Now, *the purpose of the design stage is to* (1) determine feasible system alternatives that will achieve the recommended results, (2) settle on a single set of detailed specifications for the system solution, and (3) recommend, if necessary, any changes in hardware/software and other processing resources that may then be required to implement the solution. In short, system designers must decide *how* to produce an efficient (economical) and effective (relevant and useful) system.

*This is not an easy task!* As Fig. 9-1 shows, there are many considerations that have a bearing on the design process. For example, such variables as the personnel, material, and financial resources of the organization; the differing informational needs of users; the different design tools, techniques, and guidelines employed as standards by different

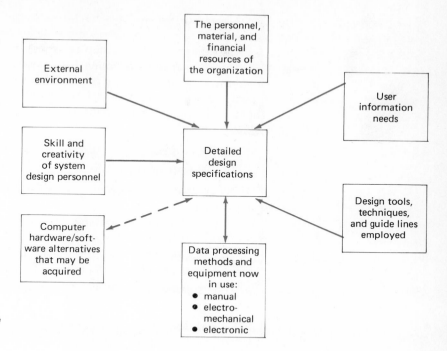

**FIGURE 9-1**

Some considerations bearing on the
design process.

organizations; the different methods of data processing (manual, electro-mechanical, electronic) that may currently be in use; the wide range of computer hardware/software that might be installed in, or may be acquired by, an organization; the speed with which new hardware/software alternatives are introduced; the skill and creativity of the designers; the lack of static testing conditions caused by a rapidly changing environment—all these ingredients have a bearing on the design process, add to the difficulty of the design task, and present practical limits to the number of system alternatives that can actually be evaluated.

Although the above considerations prevent the formulation of *exact* rules to follow in creating a system solution, it is possible to develop a better understanding of several of these design factors, and it is possible to discuss some of the general concepts and guidelines that may govern the design process. Thus, in the following pages of this chapter we will study (1) some basic *issues that influence the determination of design alternatives,* (2) some *tools and techniques used in system design,* (3) the format of the *detailed design specifications* that should be prepared, and (4) some *guidelines for hardware/software evaluation, selection, and acquisition.* We shall also briefly outline the contents of the *system design report* that the team should prepare at the end of the system design phase.

**DETERMINATION OF
ALTERNATIVES: SOME
ISSUES INFLUENCING
DESIGN**

A *preliminary step* that must be taken by the system designers is to make sure that they have a clear understanding of what is expected of the new system.[1] Once this initial step is accomplished, the designers are then ready for the *next step, which is to determine feasible alternatives* that could supply the necessary results. There are usually a number of issues involving methodology and the use of resources that must be resolved before this step can be concluded. *Included in these issues are questions about:*

1   The type of conceptual design model that should be employed

2   The flexibility that should be designed into the system

3   The nature and number of the control provisions that should be included

4   The advisability of "making" the system in-house or of "buying" it from an outside supplier

5   The attention that should be given to human factors and organizational considerations (the operational feasibility issue)

6   The economic tradeoffs that should be made (the economic feasibility issue)

Let us now look at each of these areas of inquiry.

**conceptual design issues**

You may remember from Chapter 2 that obtaining well-designed information systems is a challenge that organizations are now facing as they attempt to adapt to the information revolution. This does *not* mean, of course, that designers have not been successful in producing information systems that are much more responsive and comprehensive than those that existed just a few years ago, for we know that they have. But progress has not yet measured up to the predictions made several years ago by a few zealots who envisioned a completely integrated "total system" built around a single online data base that would instantly give managers and other users in the organization all the information they needed to make their decisions. Perhaps one reason for this "lack of progress" was that the total system model was a fallacious design concept that failed to recognize the complexities of operating a modern business.

Although some authorities equated the total system model with a management information system (MIS) and then concluded that the MIS

---

[1] As you know, a clear set of specifications for the new system should have been prepared at the end of the system-analysis stage. But executives may have changed these specifications. Furthermore, it is possible that some (or all) of the design work will be performed by specialists who did not participate in the analysis phase and who are thus not familiar with the proposed system.

was a mirage,[2] most MIS designers have always followed less ambitious conceptual models or long-range plans that take an evolutionary approach. Usually, these models or plans allow for a gradual integration of information-producing systems and provide overall guidance to designers as they implement a series of shorter projects.[3] Obviously, then, the selection of a conceptual design model is important since it affects the approach that designers will use in the shorter projects. However, there are usually a number of uncertainties associated with the selection of a conceptual design model. Why is this selection a challenge? Let us first develop a few background ideas before we attempt to answer this question that you have so thoughtfully raised.

As noted in Chapter 2, the management of medium-sized and larger organizations is a complicated process which takes place on at least three levels.

Top executives perform vital *strategic* planning and decision-making activities. They are charged with weighing risks and making major policy decisions on such matters as new product development, new plant authorizations and locations, corporate mergers and acquisitions, etc. They must also consider future technological developments in planning long-range strategy. Thus, as we saw in Chapter 1, the key factors that must be considered by top executives as they study a problem often are of an external nature.

The *tactical* management decisions made by middle managers deal with the implementation of strategic decisions. Resources are allocated, authority is delegated, and control is maintained so that the strategic plans will be carried out. Lower-level *operating* managers make the day-to-day scheduling and control decisions that are needed if specific tasks are to be accomplished. Actual results of an operation are carefully checked against planned expectations, and corrective actions are taken as needed. Certain types of internal information resulting from operating decisions are summarized and fed back to upper managerial levels by existing information systems. The information flow to support decision making may be generalized as shown in Fig. 9-2.

&INFOSYSTEMS

"My computer doesn't understand me."

[2] See John Dearden, "MIS Is a Mirage," *Harvard Business Review*, January–February 1972, pp. 90–99. As defined in Chapter 2, MIS refers to a number of systems (or subsystems, if the entire organization is viewed as a single system) that are integrated as necessary to provide timely and effective managerial information. Such a concept of MIS views integration as possibly desirable but not as absolutely essential, and such a concept is not a mirage.

[3] This approach is generally somewhat conservative because (1) broad studies take a long time, are quite complex, require the efforts of highly paid employees who may be in short supply, are likely to be risky, and often do not show any prospect of immediate tangible benefits; (2) substantial gains may be possible sooner if short project applications are placed on the computer; (3) resistance is often encountered from employees who do not want to experiment with the familiar system on a very broad scale; and (4) the planning and coordination of broad studies is complicated since in many cases no single individual can really understand such studies.

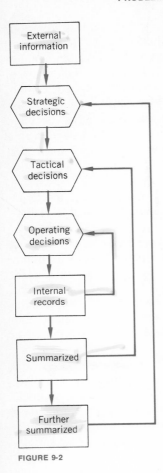

**FIGURE 9-2**

Figure 9-3*a* depicts the three management levels, each with its own information needs. In addition to what might be termed the *horizontal* structure shown in Fig. 9-3*a*, an organization is also divided *vertically* into different business specialties or functions, which generate separate information flows (see Fig. 9-3*b*). Combining the horizontal managerial levels with the vertical business specialties produces the complex organizational structure shown in Fig. 9-3*c*. Underlying this structure in Fig. 9-3*c* is a data base consisting, ideally, of internally and externally produced data relating to past, present, and predicted future events.

With the above concepts in mind, we are now in a position to better appreciate the problems and challenges that designers face. More specifically, system designers must grapple with the following questions:

**1** *Should a "top-down" or "bottom-up" approach to system development be followed?* The *top-down approach* begins with studies of (*a*) broad organizational goals and (*b*) the types of decisions made by organizational executives. From these studies comes a model of the information flow in the organization and the design requirements for the system. The *advantages* of this approach are that it is a logical and sensible way to attack a problem (buildings, airplanes, and computers are essentially designed in this way), and it can make it easier to integrate system elements. The *disadvantages,* however, are that it is very difficult to define the organizational goals and the decision-making activities of executives in the precise terms required for system design, and there is thus the risk of building a large and expensive system that is not effective. The *bottom-up approach,* on the other hand, begins at the operating level with the existing procedures for processing transactions and updating files and then builds the add-on modules to support planning, controlling, and decision-making activities as they are needed. The *advantages* of this approach are that smaller "bites" of work are tackled, and the danger of building a large, complex, and ineffective system is minimized. The disadvantages are that this approach may not lead to the development of high-potential systems above the operating level, but if such higher-level systems *are* attempted, it will then be necessary to redesign (at considerable expense) the existing programs and procedures to provide the integration of information that higher-level managers require. Given these considerations, it is not surprising that system designers often accept the challenge to develop a hybrid design philosophy that attempts to use the best attributes of each of these approaches.[4]

**2** *Can a single data base be created to satisfy the differing information needs of the three managerial levels?* Most information systems today serve the needs of operating managers and, to a lesser extent, middle managers. They provide internally produced data dealing with past and

---

[4] For more information on conceptual design approaches, see Robert L. Paretta, "Designing Management Information Systems: An Overview," *The Journal of Accountancy,* April 1975, pp. 42–47; and John A. Zachman, "Control and Planning of Information Systems," *Journal of Systems Management,* July 1977, pp. 34–41.

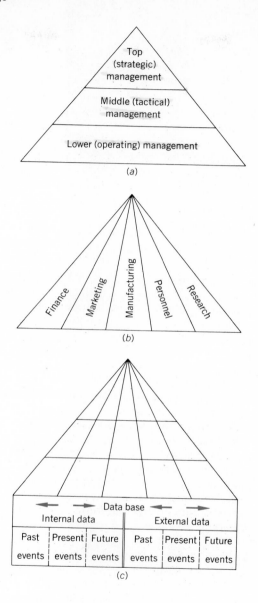

FIGURE 9-3

current activities. Although some firms are using internal data and carefully developed planning models incorporating assumptions about external conditions to *simulate* responses to the "what if?" questions of top
executives,[5] the fact remains that most current systems focus on internal
and historic events and produce output of only limited use in strategic

[5] We will look at simulation in some detail in Chapter 13.

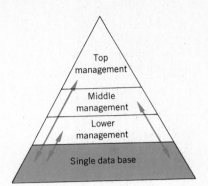

FIGURE 9-4

planning. Whether to attempt to organize and structure a *single* data base
to meet varying needs or to create *different* bases for different horizontal
levels is a problem facing designers. Figure 9-4 depicts the alternatives.

3    *Can different business specialties share the same data base?* Can the
system supply from a single data base the information needed by marketing, production, finance, and personnel managers at different levels, or
must separate vertically oriented data bases be designed for each spe-
cialty? Different business functions have generally had their own information systems. Attempting to integrate these separate systems into one or
more corporate data bases that will serve the broader needs of many
managers is a formidable challenge, but the effort is being made.

4    *Can externally produced data be incorporated into a data base?* To be
of value to managers at the higher echelons, a system must supply
information about the external world, and this information must be
complete, timely, and accurate. But the quality of externally produced
data is more difficult to control than internal data quality, and external
data has been expensive to obtain. The growing availability of external
data in machine-sensible form and/or the use of external data banks will
make more data available to the firm's data bank. It is the designer's
responsibility to see that these new facts are incorporated into an MIS in
meaningful ways.

5    *To what extent should an attempt be made to "solve the triangle"?*
That is, to what extent should the designers attempt to create an overall
system that would simultaneously satisfy the information needs of most or
all of the segments shown in Fig. 9-3c? Although the tendency of some
unwary organizations may be to attempt the triangle solution, the complexity of the problems involved usually dictates that designers take a
more gradual and conservative approach.

From the discussion in this section, it should now be obvious why the
choice of a conceptual plan or model for system design is so important—
and so challenging. Certainly, the issues raised here will have a direct
bearing on the alternatives considered during the design phase of the
system development effort.

## the issue of system flexibility

Another important issue that has a direct bearing on the design alternatives to be considered involves the degree of *flexibility*—i.e., the degree to which a system is able to adapt to a wide variety of circumstances—that needs to be built into the system. Such factors as the type of industry, the stability of the products made or sold, and the nature of the competition all help determine the amount of flexibility that is needed. For example, those managers who work in a stable industry, have only a few staple products or services to sell, and are consistently able to capture a predictable share of their markets would probably not be as interested in information system flexibility as those who must function in a rapidly changing industry and who must attempt to produce, price, and keep track of a large number of complex products that are subject to the pressures of changing demand and competitive reactions.

The likelihood of future system changes obviously affects the need for flexibility. A fact that is sometimes overlooked in the design phase is that most systems are likely to be changed several times during their useful life. And these changes are often unpredictable. Furthermore, the cost of revising and maintaining systems to meet changing conditions is one of the largest cost elements in the use of computer-based information systems. Designers may thus face a dilemma: they can ignore the flexibility issue, produce a system that has (perhaps) lower design and implementation costs, and then incur the high costs required to periodically restructure the system, or they can initially spend the additonal time (and money) to create a flexible design that may require fewer future changes. The *total cost* over the life of the system may well turn out to be less when flexibility is a design goal (see Fig. 9-5). In short, given the unpredictability and "cussedness" of events, designers should perhaps adopt the motto that "if we can't make it right, we had better make it adaptable."[6]

Another factor that affects the need for flexibility is the management style and philosophy of different managers. Two managers—A and B—who occupy the same position over a period of time will probably have different information needs. Manager A, for example, may want highly condensed reports with little detail, but manager B may wish to delve into detailed reports and seek many facts before making a decision. Political analysts tell us that former President Eisenhower was the type of executive who wanted fewer details, while former Secretary of Defense Robert McNamara was an executive B type who sought numerous facts. An issue facing the system designer, then, is how to make it possible for executive B to succeed executive A without requiring that the software be restruc-

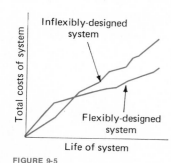

FIGURE 9-5

---

[6] For a number of suggestions on how to do this, see David Frost, "Designing for Generality," *Datamation,* December 1974, pp. 59–61; and Joseph W. Wilkinson, "Designing a Common Data Base," *Cost and Management,* March–April 1976, pp. 25–59.

tured. If staffing changes are possible during the life of a system, then a flexible design approach may be needed.

We have already seen, of course, that different degrees of flexibility *can* be designed into a system. In Chapter 4, for example, it was noted that a system design that (1) uses complex list, tree, or network data structures, (2) incorporates random or indexed-sequential file organizations, and (3) employs the latest and most sophisticated online hardware and data management software to give managers immediate access to records in one or more data bases for inquiry and file updating purposes can be very flexible. But we have also seen that such a design may be much more expensive (at least initially) than some relatively inflexible systems that use sequentially organized files and batch processing hardware and software.[7]

Of course, there are numerous design combinations and possibilities between these two extremes. Some applications can be designed to be processed on a lower-priority or "background" basis using batch techniques, some systems can be online with only periodic updating of files, and some that involve critical areas may utilize real time methods. Many medium-sized and larger businesses that have not yet considered using data-base processing techniques will probably begin to move in this direction in the future. Thus, they should probably take steps now to establish a *data-base administrator function* so that someone in the organization can be given the authority to begin to standardize (and document in a *data dictionary*) tke data definitions, record formats, and file structures that have companywide usefulness so that future data-base system design will be facilitated.

The issues and considerations that have now been outlined in this section should be evaluated by designers as they seek to establish efficient and effective alternatives during the design phase. A summary of questions bearing on flexibility that should be studied includes: (1) What data will be allowed to enter the system and what facts will be excluded? (2) How much detail will be permitted in the accepted data? (3) What approaches will be used to organize data elements and files? (4) To what extent, if any, will there be linkages or integration between data elements and files? (5) What approaches will be used to access data? and (6) What I/O and storage media and/or devices will be most suitable?

**the issue of system control**

An essential requirement of any system alternative considered during the design phase must be that vital and relevant data are not lost or stolen;

---

[7] As you may remember from Chapter 2, such files are often created especially for, and thus are dependent on, a particular application program. The problems associated with this approach are discussed in the section in Chapter 2 entitled "Data-Base Systems."

errors are not introduced into the data before, during, or after processing; and data are not stored, retrieved, modified, or communicated without proper authorization. In other words, designers must make sure that procedures and controls are built into any alternative to ensure that the *integrity* of the data and the *security* of the system are not impaired.

Input and output error-detection procedures, redundant checks on processing accuracy, provisions for system recovery in the event of failure, provisions for testing the logic of the system prior to its implementation—these and other control elements should be built into the system early rather than added on later when the task would be much more difficult and expensive.[8] Since the implemented system will be subject to periodic audit reviews that test the adequacy of these control provisions, one or more auditors should play an active role in this phase of the design process. To check on control procedures, auditors will trace transactions through a system from input to output. Thus, this *audit trail* must also be designed into the system.

A basic issue facing designers in the control area is how to balance the goal of a high degree of data integrity and system security against the possibility of creating a complex and "overcontrolled" system that is expensive to operate and that produces delays in getting the information into the hands of end-users.

### the "make" or "buy" issue

Should a new design be created in-house, or should an existing applications package or custom-built system be bought from one of the more than 800 outside suppliers?[9] Some of the pros and cons of using applications packages were briefly outlined in Chapter 2. Generally speaking, the make-or-buy decision often revolves around the lower cost, faster implementation, and reduced risk (the package is available for testing) advantages that may accrue to packages balanced against the possible in-house or custom-built design advantages of greater operating efficiency and the ability to satisfy unique needs more effectively. (In trying to

---

[8] System control implications and procedures will be discussed in detail in a number of later chapters so we need not go into these topics here. However, some excellent sources of information on control topics and procedures are found in Richard G. Canning, "The Importance of EDP Audit and Control," *EDP Analyzer,* June 1977, pp. 1–13; The "Audit Practices Report" and the "Control Practices Report" of the *System Auditability and Control Study,* The Institute for Internal Auditors, Altamonte Springs, Fla., 1977; and Robert L. Patrick, "Sixty Ingredients for Better Systems," *Datamation,* December 1977, pp. 171ff.

[9] It is estimated that there are more than 3,000 separate and distinct package products now on the market. Frost and Sullivan, a market research firm, further estimates that package sales will amount to nearly $900 million annually by 1984. Also, some vendors contract to supply a "turnkey system" to businesses. These custom-built system houses may sell the customer a computer (typically, it is a minicomputer) and then provide the custom programming, training, and maintenance support needed.

appeal to many potential users, the package product may sacrifice processing efficiency and effectiveness in areas important to a particular organization.) Whenever possible, however, the use of an appropriate application package should always be considered as an alternative in the design phase.

Some of the factors that should be considered in evaluating possible packages include:

1    *Package quality.* A check of current users should be made to evaluate the suitability, ease of use, performance, and reliability of the package.[10]

2    *Vendor reputation.* Is the vendor financially strong? Will adequate technical support be provided to install, maintain, and update the package?

3    *Documentation furnished.* Is documentation adequate to enable company personnel to maintain and modify the system?

### human factors and operational issues

Will the proposed alternatives be easy for people to understand and use? Will decision makers be allowed enough time to learn to work with, and effectively use, the alternatives selected? (As Fig. 9-6 shows, it would be unwise to install a new system without allowing time for managers to move up the learning curve.) Will the selected alternatives give prompt response, relieve people of unnecessary chores, and be pleasant to use? Will they handle exceptions gracefully and give individuals choices on how to deal with them? Will error-correcting procedures be effective and

[10] For an evaluation of 199 popular packages, see Herbert L. Gepner, "User Ratings of Software Packages," *Datamation,* December 1977, pp. 117–121ff. *Datamation* has published user ratings in each December issue for several years.

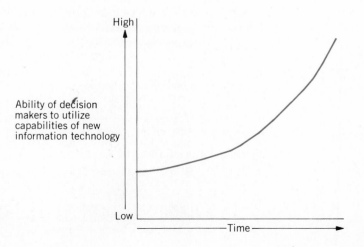

FIGURE 9-6

Management learning curve in using new information technology.

efficient? If the system contains personal data, will the alternatives safe-guard *personal privacy?* These and many other questions bearing on the operational feasibility of a system must be considered when alternatives are determined. If a system is nonresponsive, and if it harasses and wastes the time of users and those it is supposed to serve, then it will be resisted and it will not be trusted. Such a system will probably achieve few of its goals; at best, the results will only be marginal. We will consider human factors and operational issues again in Chapters 14 and 15.

### the issue of economic tradeoffs

The economic issue has been left for last in this section, but *not* because it is less important than the others. Rather, it has been placed here because the question of economic feasibility underlies the whole system design and development effort. The decisions made by designers and other study-team members in considering *all* the above issues (e.g., the conceptual design model to use, the degree of flexibility to design into the system, the decision to make or buy system components) can be reached *only* after careful thought has been given to the economic resources of the organization and to the economic criteria that have been established by those responsible for approving system projects.

A number of economic tradeoffs must typically be made before the final design alternatives can be selected. A very flexible data-base system that can immediately update and retrieve all records in the system might be nice to have, but the team elects to settle for a less expensive online processing approach that gives immediate access to records that are only periodically updated using batch techniques; designers on the study team would like the challenge of creating all components in the new system, but the team decides to give serious attention to a less expensive package from a vendor; auditors on the team would like to see a maze of control procedures built into the system, but others convince them that the additional development and operating costs involved would exceed the somewhat greater risks assumed. And so it goes.

As you saw at the beginning of this chapter, there are so many variables having a bearing on the design process that it is impossible to establish exact rules to follow to create a system solution. The questions and issues that we have now examined may be resolved in different ways by different teams using different resources in different environments. Different design tools and techniques may also be used.

**DESIGN TOOLS AND
TECHNIQUES**          The following tools and techniques are among those that may be useful during the system design stage:

1    *Organizational standards.* Comments were made in the last chapter about the value of having standards that spell out the steps to be com-

pleted and the procedures to be followed during system analysis. These comments apply with equal force to the design stage. A *standards manual* will be a valuable tool if it outlines such things as (a) a consistent design philosophy and approach, (b) the procedures to follow in designing and preparing specifications for output reports and input forms and documents, (c) the methodology to follow in designing records and files and in creating the processing logic that will use new and stored data to produce the specified output, (d) the control and testing criteria that are normally expected to be built into any system, and (e) the documentation criteria that must be met.[11] Another valuable tool would be a corporate *data dictionary* that documents the standardized data definitions, record formats, and file structures that have companywide usefulness.

**2**   *Top-down design methodology.* We have seen in earlier pages that system development efforts may follow a top-down analysis and design approach. Top-down methodology has received a lot of attention in recent years because it appears to be a disciplined approach to organizing complexity. The top-down design technique requires the early identification of the top-level functions or procedures in the proposed system. A breakdown of each top-level function into a hierarchy of understandable lower-level modules or components is then necessary. *Hierarchical function diagrams or charts* such as those used in IBM's HIPO technique are helpful tools in the design process. A top-level chart is typically drawn up to show the total structure and the hierarchical placement of the lower-level modules and components that are needed (Fig. 9-7a). Lower-level module and component diagrams keyed to the top-level chart (Figs. 9-7b and 9-7c) may then be created during the design process to show (a) the output result(s) of the module/component, (b) the necessary input(s), and (c) the particular series of processing steps that are needed to produce the output and support the system. Several iterations will usually take place in this design and charting process. Designers may start with relatively simple charts showing general design solutions and then gradually refine this first effort to produce more complete diagrams containing increasing amounts of detail as the design requirements become clearer. In other words, designers are able to identify and deal with a controllable amount of complexity by proceeding from general concepts of the system to detailed designs in a step-by-step manner.

**3**   *Design reviews and walk throughs.* Although representatives of users should be members of the study team, there should be periodic sessions held so that all interested users can review the design progress. Such sessions enable the team to gain the benefit of the users' knowledge, and they may build user commitment to the project. In one such session, for example, users may be given a graphic description or overview of a proposed system design. Team members may then present sample system outputs and "walk through" the input and processing operations to describe the handling of data and the flow of control. During this walk through, users should be *encouraged* to look for errors and to voice their

[11] For more details on system design standards, see Susan Wooldridge, *Systems and Programming Standards,* Petrocelli/Charter, New York, 1977, pp. 63–80.

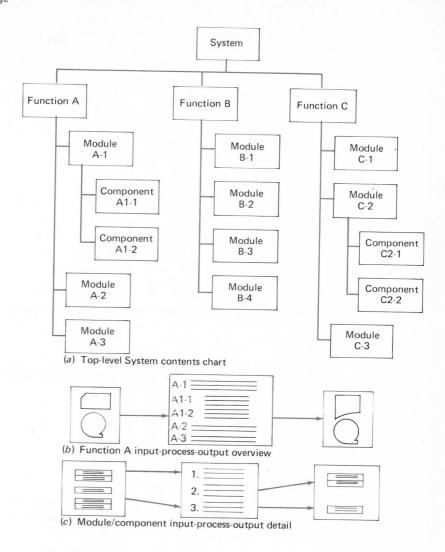

(a) Top-level System contents chart

(b) Function A input-process-output overview

(c) Module/component input-process-output detail

FIGURE 9-7

approval or opposition to various aspects of the design. (Of course, one or more follow-up sessions should be held to make sure that any errors have been corrected.) Such user participation will probably result in a better system product, and it may also reduce later resistance to the final design.

**4**   *Special charts, forms, and tables.*  In the last chapter, you saw how system flowcharts, the special forms used in IBM's SOP and NCR's ADS techniques, and special input/output tables could be used in analyzing an existing system. It should come as no surprise, then, to learn that these same charts, forms, and tables are also very helpful during the design stage. Knowing how input-processing-output is currently being accomplished provides a foundation on which to build. Weaknesses that were spotted during analysis can now be corrected, and the relationships that have been shown to exist between inputs and outputs can now be used to design a broader and more integrated system.

5 *Automated system design approaches.* In addition to manual tools and techniques used during system design, it may also be possible to use the computer itself in the system development process. The ISDOS (Information Systems Design and Optimization System) project at the University of Michigan is pioneering in the automatic design and construction of information systems through the development of (a) a "problem statement language" that enables the problem definer to state his or her needs in complete and unambiguous terms (b) a computer software package that analyzes the problem statement, (c) a software package of algorithms and procedures to design "optimum" systems in accordance with stated criteria, (d) a software package to design and construct data files, and (e) a translating program that uses inputs from various packages to produce system object programs. At this writing, several ISDOS modules are still under development, but ISDOS represents an important effort. (Others are using ISDOS automated system design concepts in their research.[12]) Computers may also be used in the system design process to evaluate various hardware/software alternatives. For example, if a new computer system appears to be needed, a computer can be given the firm's processing requirements and can then *simulate* the performance of these requirements using cost/performance models of selected computer alternatives. In other words, *a computer is used to evaluate other computer hardware and software configurations.*

**DESIGN SPECIFICATIONS REPORT**

It is assumed at this point that the study team has analyzed the current operations and has settled on the most feasible design alternatives to achieve the study goals. Now it is time to prepare a progress report outlining the detailed set of written and documented system specifications that will achieve these goals.

This report should be reviewed and approved by user departments before the system development effort is permitted to continue. *The prepared specifications should include:*

1 *The output requirements.* The output specifications should include the form, content, and frequency of reports. Volume figures are also needed.

2 *The input requirements.* Included in the input specifications should be the source documents to be used, the means of preparing and transmitting those documents, the frequency of preparation, and the volume figures expected. The stored file data that will be required should be identified.

[12] See, for example, J. F. Nunamaker, Jr., Benn R. Konsynski, Jr., Thomas Ho, and Carl Singer, "Computer-aided Analysis and Design of Information Systems," *Communications of the ACM,* December 1976, pp. 674–687.

**3**  *The file and storage requirements.* The size, contents, storage media, record formats, structure, organization, access restrictions, and degree of permanency of any affected files should be spelled out. The amount of usage, the volume figures expected, and the frequency of updating should be specified.

**4**  *The processing specifications.* The new procedures must be defined. How the inputs will be used to prepare the desired outputs should be clearly indicated.

**5**  *Control provisions.* The steps to be taken to provide the necessary system control should be specified. System testing and conversion procedures should also be spelled out in as much detail as is possible at this time.

**6**  *Cost estimates.* Preliminary estimates of (*a*) setup costs and (*b*) annual operating costs using the new system approaches should be made.

**7**  *Manual processing procedures.* All the elements of the system that will be processed manually should be outlined. Particular attention should be given to the manual methods that may be used in input data preparation.

**DECISION MAKING:
STUDY TEAM**

Computer usage is justified when the tangible and intangible economic benefits to be gained are greater than comparable benefits received from other alternatives. The type and number of alternatives to be considered vary, of course, from one system study to another. In some situations, noncomputer options may be preferable; for some organizations the results of a study may indicate that the use of a remote computing service (RCS) or a timesharing service would be a desirable solution; in many cases, the system can be implemented using existing hardware and software; and in some development projects, implementation may call for the acquisition of new hardware/software resources.

*In selecting an RCS,* the study team would consider such factors as: (1) the proximity, reputation, and financial stability of the center; (2) the quality of center personnel and their experience in dealing with similar systems; (3) the care exercised in safeguarding documents and providing backup facilities; and (4) the costs of using the center.

*In choosing a timesharing service,* the study team would be interested in such factors as: (1) the reputation and financial stability of the service; (2) the quality of service personnel and their ability to assist in system implementation; (3) the reliability of the service, e.g., its loading and therefore its response time, and its backup facilities; (4) the controls available to protect the security and integrity of user data and programs maintained in online storage; (5) the availability of programming languages and accurate library programs; and (6) the costs associated with using the service.

Regardless of whether an RCS or a timesharing service is chosen, the team should be required to present its findings and the economic basis for

"We're trading you in for another model, Mighty One."

© DATAMATION ®

its recommendations to a top executive or steering committee for the final decision. For the remainder of this chapter we shall assume that the team believes that new computing hardware is justified. However, portions of the material that follows are appropriate in a study that does not result in the acquisition of new equipment.

Once the decision to obtain new equipment has been made (with the approval of top executives), there are a number of other questions that should be studied by the team members before they present their final recommendations. These questions include:

1    *What equipment should be considered?* What hardware/software package would best meet company needs? Can consultants help in equipment evaluation and selection?

2    Which hardware/software package offers the greatest *return on investment?* Can the company afford the investment at this time?

3    Have all possible *acquisition methods* (rent, lease, or buy) been evaluated?

4    Have *organizational and personnel aspects* received proper consideration? (These topics will not be considered at this time, but will be discussed in later chapters.)

## equipment evaluation and selection

To select is to choose from a number of more or less suitable alternatives. Evaluation should be based on the ability of several computers and/or peripheral devices to process the detailed set of written system specifications that have been prepared.

If the new equipment is to replace or upgrade existing hardware, the team will need to give consideration to the concepts of compatibility and modularity. *Compatibility* is a term that may be associated with the software of a computer. If the programming aids, data, and instructions prepared for one machine can be used by another without conversion or program modification, the machines are said to be *compatible*. Many manufacturers of third- and fourth-generation computers have designed "families" of machines to provide compatibility for the user. The IBM System/360 family of machines, for example, consists of several models differing in size and power. Yet some of these models are both hardware compatible, i.e., the basic machine language instructions of one model will run on others, and software compatible, i.e., the higher-level language programs are interchangeable with little or no modification needed. Furthermore, System/370 models are compatible with each other and will run many existing 360 programs without change. Obviously, the team would place a high priority on selecting equipment that is compatible with, and does not require a costly rewriting of, the programs developed for the existing hardware.

An alternative to replacing existing hardware is to expand its capabilities. The concept of *modularity* (also called *open-ended design* and *upgrading*) allows a computer installation to change and *grow*. To the original CPU can be attached additional units as the need arises, just as additional freight cars can be hooked onto a freight train. Users can begin with small systems and build up the installation gradually; it is not necessary that final capacity be provided at the outset. In addition to *adding on,* true modularity also makes it possible to replace smaller components with larger versions while other hardware remains unchanged.

How does the modularity concept differ, then, from compatibility? *Two or more different* machine systems are compatible if they can accept the same input data and programs and produce the same output. A *single* system has modular capability if it can grow (see Fig. 9-8).

The evaluation and selection of equipment is a complicated task. *The selection approaches that have been widely used are summarized in Fig. 9-9.* Regardless of the approach used, however, the study team should also compare the *quantitative and qualitative factors listed in Fig. 9-10* to further limit the choices.

One final warning may be in order before we conclude this discussion of equipment selection. Figure 9-11 shows the findings of several organi-

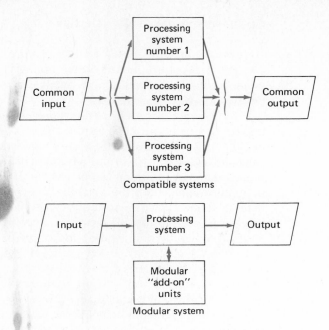

FIGURE 9-8

zations that have studied the relationship between software cost per instruction and hardware capacity. As Fig. 9-11 shows, relative software costs may be expected to increase rapidly as the hardware approaches 100 percent utilization. Yet many hardware procurement decisions have been made on the assumption that average software production costs will remain essentially unchanged regardless of hardware limitations—i.e., that they will follow the dashed "selection myth" line. Such an assumption may, of course, lead to unwise equipment decisions. The study team should be aware that as hardware investment continues to decline as a percentage of total information systems cost, and as software costs continue to grow (refer back to Fig. 2-6), the decision which will minimize the *total cost* of a new system may be to acquire enough hardware capacity to avoid the steep rise in the software production cost curve. (Of course, this does not mean that a giant computer should be initially acquired to handle all foreseeable applications, but it does mean that consideration should be given to selecting equipment with modularity and compatibility in mind.)

At this point (or perhaps at an earlier point), an estimate of the expected return on investment of the surviving choices should be made for economic justification and analysis purposes.

**estimated return on investment**

The costs associated with the options remaining might be compared with the cost of improved current methods of performing the work. Let us assume that, as a result of one cost comparison, it is expected that there will be negative effects on after-tax earnings for the first 2 years, but that after this initial period substantial positive returns are anticipated. It is known that top executives believe that the equipment should yield a satisfactory return over a 5-year period or it should not, at least for the time being, be acquired. Since the organization can earn a 20 percent return on investments made in plant and equipment, it is also the feeling of top managers that the equipment investment should be postponed if it cannot produce a similar return.

Armed with this information, the study team prepares the table shown in Fig. 9-12. Column 1, the effects on cash flow, represents the economic

---

**1** *Single-source approach.* This noncompetitive approach merely consists of choosing the hardware/software package from among those available from a selected vendor. There is a lack of objectivity in this approach; unfortunate results have been produced; but it has often been used in the "selection" of smaller-in-house packages.

**2** *Competitive-bidding approach.* System specifications are submitted to vendors with a request that they prepare bids. Included in the bid request may be a requirement that cost and performance figures be prepared for a specified *benchmark* processing run. The vendors select what they believe to be the most appropriate hardware/software packages from their lines and submit proposals. Sometimes this bidding approach yields excellent results. But frequently vendors do not prepare the proposals they are capable of making. Other possible shortcomings in bidding include the facts that: (a) system specifications may be altered to improve procedures or, perhaps, place the vendor's package in the best possible light (the study team must then compare bids based on different specifications—a most difficult comparison indeed, as the vendors well know); and (b) program running (or throughput) times may be underestimated in the bids because inadequate allowance is made for housekeeping and set-up times.

**3** *Consultant-evaluation approach.* Qualified data processing consultants can assist businesses in selecting the hardware/software package. Consultants can bring specialized knowledge and experience and an objective point of view to bear on the evaluation and selection problem.

**4** *Simulation approach.* As we have already seen, specialized computer programs are available from a number of organizations to simulate the performance of selected hardware/software alternatives. Simulation programs are capable of comparing the input, output, and computing times required to process specific applications on all available commercial computers made in this country. Simulation provides fast, accurate, objective (and relatively expensive) evaluation.

**FIGURE 9-9**

Equipment selection approaches.

**Economic factors**

1. Cost comparisons
2. Return on investment
3. Acquisition methods

**Hardware factors**

1. Hardware performance, reliability, capacity, and price
2. Presence or absence of modularity
3. Number and accessibility of backup facilities
4. Firmness of delivery date
5. Effective remaining life of proposed hardware
6. Compatibility with existing systems

**Software factors**

1. Software performance and price
2. Efficiency and reliability of available software
3. Programming languages available (not promised)
4. Availability of useful and well-documented packaged programs, program libraries, and user groups
5. Firmness of delivery date on promised software
6. Ease of use and modification

**Service factors**

1. Facilities provided by manufacturer for checking new programs
2. Training facilities offered and the quality of training provided
3. Programming assistance and conversion assistance offered
4. Maintenance terms and quality

**Reputation of manufacturer**

1. Financial stability
2. Record of keeping promises

FIGURE 9-10

Equipment selection factors.

effects expected by the team if updated current procedures are replaced by a selected computer system. In other words, this column shows the expected effects of the acquisition on net income plus depreciation. Column 2 shows the *present value* of $1 received in years 1, 2, 3, etc., when the required rate of return is 20 percent. At the end of 1 year, 20 percent interest on $0.8333 is $0.1667. Thus, the present value ($0.8333) plus the interest ($0.1667) gives $1 at the end of a year. Column 3 is the product of column 1 multiplied by column 2. The *time-adjusted* return on investment is exactly 20 percent if the total of column 3 is zero. A negative total means that the 20 percent return cannot be expected. In our example, the estimated return is found to *exceed* 20 percent.

### equipment acquisition methods

It is the job of the study team to evaluate acquisition methods and recommend the one best suited to the company. *Equipment may be acquired in the following ways:*

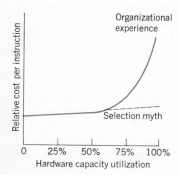

FIGURE 9-11

**1** *Renting.* In a majority of computer installations, hardware is rented from the computer manufacturer.[13] This is a flexible method that does not require a large initial investment. It is also the most expensive method if the equipment meets company needs for 4 or 5 years or longer.

**2** *Purchasing.* Although the rental method is the most popular, there is evidence of a trend toward greater equipment purchasing. Greater interest in purchasing is due to (a) the fact that it is the least expensive method when hardware is kept for several years; (b) the greater reliability, longer physical life, and greater expected residual value of the latest hardware; and (c) the belief of some managers that the risk of becoming "locked-in" to a particular configuration is reduced by their ability to do a better job of long-range systems planning.

**3** *Leasing.* Under one typical leasing arrangement, the user tells the leasing company what equipment is desired. The leasing organization arranges for the purchase of the equipment and then leases it to the user for a long-term period (usually 3 to 5 years). This method combines some of the advantages of both renting and purchasing. Other leasing arrangements are possible. For example, IBM has a 1- or 2-year lease that is less expensive than its rental plan.

Figure 9-13 summarizes the advantages and disadvantages of each acquisition method. The study team should weigh these merits and faults carefully before making its choice.

### presentation of study-team recommendations

> I go . . . the bell invites me,
> . . . for it is a Knell
> That summons thee to Heaven or to Hell.
>
> Shakespeare, *Macbeth,* Act II, Scene 1

[13] According to International Data Corporation, a research firm, 60 percent of all installed computers are rented or short-term-leased from the manufacturer, 28 percent are purchased, and 12 percent are leased from companies that specialize in computer equipment leases. For more information on acquisition methods, see "Should It Be Lease or Buy?" *Dun's Review,* July 1977, pp. 82–83ff.; and Ted Szatrowski, "Rent, Lease, or Buy?" *Datamation,* February 1976, pp. 59–62ff.

| Year | 1 Effects on Cash Flow of Acquisition | 2 20% Discount Factors | 3 Present Value of Cash Flow |
|------|---------------------------------------|------------------------|------------------------------|
| 1 | $-100,000 | 0.8333 | $ -83,333 |
| 2 | -25,000 | 0.6944 | -17,360 |
| 3 | +45,000 | 0.5787 | +26,042 |
| 4 | +75,000 | 0.4823 | +36,172 |
| 5 | +110,000 | 0.4019 | +44,209 |
| | | Total | $ + 5,730 |

FIGURE 9-12

*Rental*

*Advantages*

1. No large purchase price required.
2. Risk of technological obsolescence reduced. *(eliminated)*
3. Maintenance included in rental charges.
4. Agreement may be cancelled without penalty after brief period.
5. Greater flexibility in changing equipment configurations.
6. Possibility of applying some part of rental charges to later purchase.

*Disadvantages*

1. Most expensive if equipment is used for long period of time.
2. Rental charges remain same throughout life of agreement.
3. Rental charges may increase when monthly usage exceeds a specified number of hours.

*Lease*

*Advantages*

1. Less expensive than rental over life of the lease.
2. No large purchase price required.
3. Maintenance is included in the lease charges.
4. No additional charges when equipment is used beyond a specified number of hours monthly.
5. Lease charges decline after specified period.
6. Possibility of applying part of lease charges toward later purchase.

*Disadvantages*

1. User contracts for equipment over long time period.
2. Reduced flexibility—user is obligated to pay a contracted charge if lease is terminated prior to end of lease period.

*Purchase*

*Advantages*

1. Generally least expensive if machine is kept over long time period.
2. No additional charges when equipment is used beyond specified number of hours monthly.
3. Certain tax advantages accrue to the purchaser.

*Disadvantages*

1. Equipment maintenance not included in the purchase price.
2. Risk of technological obsolescence—of being "locked-in" to a system which does not continue to meet changing company needs.
3. A large initial capital outlay is required.

FIGURE 9-13

Factors to consider in equipment acquisition.

Guided by a written charter, which defined the scope and direction of their efforts, the study team has analyzed the relevant facts; from this analysis has come a detailed set of systems specifications designed to achieve the study goals. After careful consideration of alternatives, the team may have concluded that computer usage is justified. A particular hardware/software package may have been chosen, and the best acquisition method for the company may have been agreed upon. The team has made many decisions. But the *final* decisions are made by top-level managers. It is now the job of the team to prepare a *system design report* and to make recommendations; it is the responsibility of top executives to decide.

*The report of the system study team should cover the following points:*

1   A restatement of study scope and objectives

2   The procedures and operations that will be changed

3   The anticipated effects of such changes on organizational structure, physical facilities, and company information

4   The anticipated effects on personnel and the personnel resources available to implement the change

5   The hardware/software package chosen, the reasons for the choice, and the alternatives considered

6   The economic effects of the change, including cost comparisons, adequacy of return on investment, and analysis of acquisition methods

7   A summary of the problems anticipated in the changeover

8   A summary of the benefits to be obtained from the change

## DECISION MAKING: TOP MANAGERS

I have two nights watched with you, but can perceive no truth in your report.

Shakespeare, *Macbeth,* Act V, Scene I

Top executives must evaluate the recommendations made by the team to detect any evidence of bias[14] and decide whether the benefits outweigh the disadvantages. Suspicion of bias or of an inadequate effort may be justified if the points outlined above are not included in the recommendation. For example, suspicion is probably warranted if little or no mention is made of the personnel or organizational aspects of the change, if the alternatives considered are really just "straw men" which are obviously inadequate, or if feasibility depends solely on vaguely defined and suspicious intangible benefits.

If the decision is to accept the recommendations of the team, top executives should then establish subsequent project performance controls. Personnel must be assigned to create the system solution, an implementation schedule should be drawn up, and periodic reports on progress should be required. In the following chapters we shall look at these programming and system implementation steps shown earlier in Fig. 8-2.

---

[14] After all, if the change is made, some members of the study team may expect to move into positions of greater influence.

SUMMARY

The purpose of the design stage of the system development process is to (1) determine feasible system alternatives that will achieve the necessary results, (2) settle on a single set of detailed design specifications for the system solution, and (3) recommend, if necessary, any changes in hardware/software and other processing resources that may then be required to implement the solution.

These are not easy tasks, and a number of iterations may be required before they are accomplished. In determining feasible system alternatives, for example, there are usually a number of issues involving methodology and the use of resources that must be resolved. Several of these issues (e.g., the type of conceptual design model to use, the degree of flexibility needed, the economic tradeoffs that must be made) are discussed in the chapter. Several of the tools and techniques used by system designers have also been presented.

Once feasible design alternatives have been determined, a design specification report should be presented to users for approval. When approval of the specifications has been received, it may then be necessary for the study team to make decisions about changes in computing equipment and in other resources that may be needed. A final system design report that incorporates the findings and recommendations of the team should then be prepared for top managers. If a decision is made to accept the team recommendations, the system development process will then move into the programming and system implementation stages.

REVIEW AND DISCUSSION
QUESTIONS

1   (a) What is the purpose of the design stage of a system development project? (b) Why is system design a difficult task?

2   Identify and discuss five basic issues that influence system design.

3   (a) Discuss the "total system" design concept. (b) Why is the selection of a conceptual design model important?

4   (a) Define and discuss the "top-down" approach to system development. (b) Define and discuss the "bottom-up" approach to system development.

5   Identify and discuss the factors that help determine the amount of flexibility that is needed in an information system design.

6   (a) Describe a system design that would offer a great deal of flexibility. (b) Describe one that would be relatively inflexible in a changing environment. (c) What are the advantages and disadvantages of each of the systems you have described?

7   What questions bearing on design flexibility should be considered?

8   "Designers must make sure that procedures and controls are built into any alternative to ensure that the integrity of the data and the security of the system are not impaired." Discuss this statement.

9   (a) What are the advantages and limitations of purchased software

packages? (**b**) What factors should be considered in evaluating such packages?

**10** What operational feasibility factors should be considered during system design?

**11** "A number of economic tradeoffs must typically be made before a final system design can be selected." Discuss this statement.

**12** Identify and discuss five design tools/techniques that may be used during the system design stage.

**13** How may a top-down methodology be used during system design?

**14** What should be included in a design specification report?

**15** (**a**) What factors should be considered in selecting an RCS? (**b**) In selecting a timesharing service?

**16** (**a**) What is meant by the term *compatibility*? (**b**) Why should these concepts be considered during equipment evaluation and selection?

**17** (**a**) Discuss the equipment-selection approaches that may be employed. (**b**) What factors should be considered in equipment selection?

**18** Assume that the table below shows the economic effects expected by a study team if a selected computer system is acquired to replace a current information system. Assume also that top executives believe that any equipment investment should yield a 10 percent return over a 6-year period or the equipment should not be acquired.

| Year | 1<br>Effects on<br>Cash Flow of<br>Acquisition | 2<br>10%<br>Discount<br>Factors* | 3<br>Present<br>Value of<br>Cash Flow |
|---|---|---|---|
| 1 | $-100,000 | 0.9091 | $-90,910 |
| 2 | -75,000 | 0.8264 | -61,980 |
| 3 | -25,000 | 0.7513 | -18,782 |
| 4 | +50,000 | 0.6830 | +34,150 |
| 5 | +100,000 | 0.6209 | +62,090 |
| 6 | +150,000 | 0.5645 | +85,675 |
| | | | Total $+10,243 |

* Source: Billy E. Goetz. *Quantitative Methods: A Survey and Guide for Managers,* McGraw-Hill Book Company, New York, 1965, p. 526, table 8a.

(**a**) On the basis of the information presented above, should the acquisition be made? (**b**) Why? (**c**) What would a total of zero in column 3 of the table mean?

**19** (**a**) Discuss the possible computer acquisition methods. (**b**) What are the advantages and disadvantages of each method?

**20** Computer hardware may be rented, leased, or purchased, but what about computer software? Contact representatives of several organizations offering programs to learn their acquisition policies.

**21**    What points should be covered by the study team in the final system design report to top managers?

**SELECTED REFERENCES**

Canning, Richard G.: "The Arrival of Common Systems," *EDP Analyzer,* January 1977, pp. 1–13.

————: "The Importance of EDP Audit and Control," *EDP Analyzer,* June 1977, pp. 1–13.

Foss, W. B.: "Guidelines for Computer Selection," *Journal of Systems Management,* March 1976, pp. 36–39.

Frost, David: "Designing for Generality," *Datamation,* December 1974, pp. 59–61.

Gepner, Herbert L.: "User Ratings of Software Packages," *Datamation,* December 1977, pp. 117–121ff.

Keen, Peter G. W., and E. M. Gerson: "The Politics of Software Systems Design," *Datamation,* November 1977, pp. 80–84.

Paretta, Robert L.: "Designing Management Information Systems: An Overview," *The Journal of Accountancy,* April 1975, pp. 42–47.

Peters, Lawrence J., and L. L. Tripp: "Comparing Software Design Methodologies," *Datamation,* November 1977, pp. 89–94.

————: "Is Software Design 'Wicked'?" *Datamation,* May 1976, pp. 127ff.

Richards, A. G.: "Assessment of System Performance in Computer Selection Evaluations," *The Australian Computer Journal,* March 1976, pp. 19–24.

"Should It Be Lease or Buy?" *Dun's Review,* July 1977, pp. 82–83ff.

Sterling, Theodor D., and K. Laudon: "Humanizing Information Systems," *Datamation,* December 1976, pp. 53–56ff.

*System Auditability and Control Study,* The Institute for Internal Auditors, Altamonte Springs, Fla., 1977. Of interest here are the "Audit Practices Report" and the "Control Practices Report."

Szatrowski, Ted: "Rent, Lease, or Buy?" *Datamation,* February 1976, pp. 59–62ff.

Wilkinson, Joseph W.: "Designing a Common Data Base," *Cost and Management,* March–April 1976, pp. 25–29.

Wooldridge, Susan: *Systems and Programming Standards,* Petrocelli/Charter, New York, 1977, pp. 63–80.

Zachman, John A.: "Control and Planning of Information Systems," *Journal of Systems Management,* July 1977, pp. 34–41.

# programming 10
# analysis

LEARNING OBJECTIVES   After studying this chapter and answering the discussion questions, you should be able to: □ Explain the purpose of programming analysis □ Explain the purpose of a program flowchart □ Identify the basic symbols used in program flowcharts and construct a simple chart using those symbols □ Discuss the purpose of, and basic parts of, a decision table □ Outline the benefits and limitations of flowcharts and decision tables

After the system analysis and design stages discussed in the last two chapters have been completed, and after a set of system design specifications to achieve the desired goals has been prepared, the programming process may begin. Breaking down the new system specifications into the very detailed arithmetic and logic operations required to solve the problem is the purpose of programming analysis. Two common tools used for analysis purposes are the *program flowchart* and the *decision table.*

## PROGRAM FLOWCHARTS

Flowcharts have existed for years and have been used for many purposes. As noted earlier, the system flowchart provides a broad overview of the processing operations that are to be accomplished, but it does not go into detail about how input data are to be used to produce output information. A *program flowchart,* on the other hand, does present a detailed graphical representation of how steps are to be performed *within* the machine to produce the needed output. Thus, the program flowchart evolves from the system chart.

### an elementary example[1]

Professor Shirley A. Meany, an accounting professor, wishes to compute an average (arithmetic mean) grade for a beginning accounting student based on the 35 tests she has given during the semester. (Professor Meany teaches a rigorous course!) In Fig. 10-1, we see that the system followed is one in which the grade data for the student are punched into cards that are then fed into a computer for processing. The computed average is printed, and Professor Meany manually updates her grade book and then prepares her final grade report on the student. We shall be concerned with only one student, but, of course, any number of student grade averages could easily be automatically processed by the computer.

In Shirley's grade preparation diagram, a single processing box is labeled "compute grade average." Unfortunately, such an instruction is not sufficient for the computer. Thus, as a part of the programming process, the programmer must specify each step needed to compute the average grade. In short, the *single* processing box labeled "compute grade average" in the system flowchart becomes the basis for a detailed *program* flowchart.

Only a few symbols, when properly arranged, are needed in program charting to define the necessary steps. These symbols are illustrated in Fig. 10-2 and are described below.

Input/output    The basic I/O symbol is also used in program flowcharting to represent any I/O function. The specific symbols designating cards,

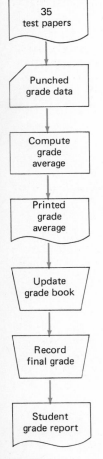

35
test papers

Punched
grade data

Compute
grade
average

Printed
grade
average

Update
grade book

Record
final grade

Student
grade report

FIGURE 10-1

Grade preparation system.

---

[1] Examples of programs to solve this problem are coded in several different programming languages in the next chapter. This simple problem has been deliberately chosen so that problem details will not obscure the basic coding concepts that are presented.

| Symbol | Name |
|---|---|
| 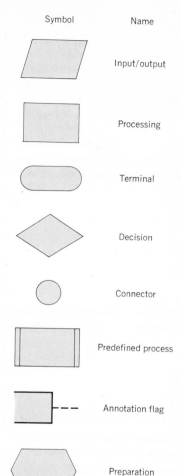 | Input/output |
|  | Processing |
|  | Terminal |
|  | Decision |
|  | Connector |
|  | Predefined process |
|  | Annotation flag |
|  | Preparation |

**FIGURE 10-2**

**Program flowchart symbols.**

tapes, etc., are generally not used with program diagrams. Figure 10-3 presents a portion of a program chart (the total chart shows the steps required to compute the average grade by Professor Meany). The I/O symbol here means that a punched card containing a student grade is to be read into the computer. The same symbol, of course, could be used to represent any output form.

Processing    Again, the rectangle represents processing operations. But now the processing described is a *small segment* of the major processing step called for in the system chart. Arithmetic and data movement instructions are generally placed in these boxes. Two processing symbols are shown in Fig. 10-3. The upper box provides for the accumulation of the total number of points in the CPU arithmetic-logic unit. Thus, when the last grade card has been read, the total of all the test scores will be stored in the accumulator. The lower processing box is a *counter* that is incremented (or stepped up by one) each time the *loop* in Fig. 10-3 is executed. So when the last card has been processed, the counter will indicate the number of tests taken. To get an average grade, as you know, the total number of points must be divided by the number of tests taken. Therefore, the lower processing box gives the denominator, the upper box the numerator.

Termination    The terminal symbol, as the name suggests, represents the beginning and the end of a program. It may also be used to signal a program interruption point when information may enter or leave. For example, to detect certain errors in input data the programmer may provide a special program branch ending in a terminal symbol labeled "HALT."

Decision    The I/O and processing symbols, typically, have two flow lines (one entry and one exit), while the terminal has a single entrance or exit line. The diamond-shaped decision symbol, on the other hand, has one entrance line and *at least* two exit paths or branches.[2] As Figure 10-3 shows, exit paths may be determined by a yes or no answer to some stated condition or *test*—in this case, the condition to be determined is whether or not the last grade card has been processed. If the answer is yes, then the total of all exam scores is contained in the accumulator and the program can branch away from the loop that it has been following by reading cards and totaling scores successively. If the answer to the test is no, the program continues to process the grade cards until they are all

[2] Don R. Cartlidge writes that "to accurately represent all the weird and wonderful choices of data processing, several more arrows are needed. One should exit left and be labeled 'Maybe,' one to the top should say 'Maybe Not,' and one should point into the paper and say 'Who Knows?' Perhaps there should be one more that points out of the paper, aimed right between the reader's eyes, that says 'Who Cares?'" See "Go and Sin No More," *Computer Decisions,* March 1976, p. 41.

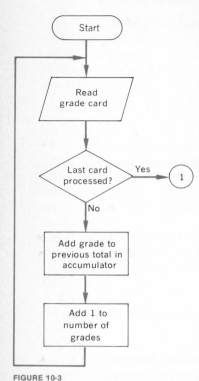

FIGURE 10-3

Partial flowchart of grade-averaging example. (This chart shows a loop with a counter and a test for last record.)

accounted for. Other examples of the use of the decision symbols are shown in Fig. 10-4.

**Connector**    The *circular connector* symbol is used when additional flow lines might cause confusion and reduce understanding. Two connectors with identical labels serve the same function as a long flow line; i.e., they show an entry from another part of the chart, or they indicate an exit to some other chart section. How is it possible to determine if a connector is used as an entry point or an exit point? It is very simple: If an arrow *enters but does not leave a connector,* it is an exit point and program flow is transferred to that identically labeled connector that *does* have an outlet.

Figure 10-5 completes the chart begun in Fig. 10-3 and shows the program steps that must be performed by Professor Meany to compute the average grade. This chart also illustrates the use of connector symbols. As we have seen, when the last card is processed, the computer is ready to figure the average grade. This step is performed by the first processing instruction below the upper connector labeled "1." The remaining steps in the chart are self-explanatory.

**Predefined process**    Programmers frequently find that certain kinds of processing operations are repeated in one or more of the programs used by their organization. For example, a department store programmer may find that the steps needed to compute cash discounts are being repeated several times in some programs and used in a number of different programs. Instead of rewriting this small subordinate routine each time it is needed, the programmer can prepare it once and then integrate it into the program or programs as required. *Libraries* of these predefined processes, or *subroutines,* are often maintained to reduce the cost and time of programming. Thus, a single predefined process symbol replaces a number of operations that are not detailed at that particular point in the chart. In short, the subroutine receives input from the primary program,

The number $X$ is shown being tested to determine whether it is equal to zero, greater than ($>$) zero, or less than ($<$) zero, i.e., a negative value.

In this case, the two variables $Y$ and $Z$ are compared ("$Y:Z$" means to "compare $Y$ to $Z$").

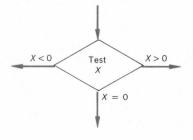

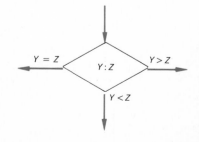

FIGURE 10-4

Decision symbol examples.

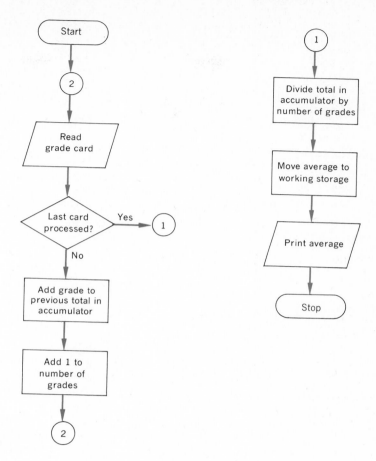

**FIGURE 10-5**

Program flowchart to average grades.

performs its limited task, and then returns the output to the primary program.

Annotation flag   The comments made in Fig. 8-9 also apply to program flowcharts.

Preparation   The preparation symbol indicates a program modification or change. It would be the appropriate symbol to use, for example, to indicate a switch setting.

### a simple business example

The flowchart in Fig. 10-6 shows how an unsympathetic department store might handle the billing of *overdue* accounts. A late payment penalty is

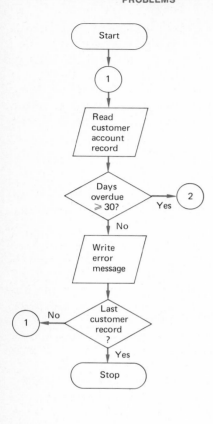

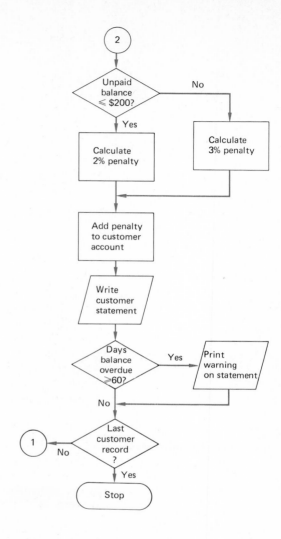

**FIGURE 10-6**

Program flowchart showing an
accounts-receivable penalty
procedure.

charged to accounts 30 or more days overdue.[3] The amount of the
penalty is based on the unpaid balance in the account: If the balance is
over $200, i.e., if the balance is *not* equal to or less than ($\leqslant$) $200, the
penalty is 3 percent; otherwise a 2 percent charge is levied. The amount
of the penalty must be added to the next bill sent to the customer. If the
account is 60 days or more overdue ($\geqslant$), a warning message is printed on
the bill. Accounts which are *less than* 30 days overdue ($<30$) are not

---

[3] In Fig. 10-6, the symbol $\geqslant$ means *equal to or greater than*. Therefore $\geqslant 30$ refers to
accounts equal to or greater than 30 days overdue. Similarly, $\leqslant$ means *equal to or less than*.

included in this procedure. But in the event that such an account is entered by mistake, provision is made to prevent it from being processed (see the left side of Fig. 10-6). The store's credit manager, Fuller ("Hammer") Nastee, handles, on an individual basis, those accounts that remain unpaid after a certain time. To test your understanding of Fig. 10-6, determine what actions would be taken if a particular account with a balance of $300 were 60 days or more overdue. (The answer is given a few pages later in this chapter.)

### benefits and limitations of flowcharts

The following *benefits* may be obtained through the use of flowcharts:

1   *Quicker grasp of relationships.* Before any problem can be solved, it must be understood. The relationships that exist among problem elements must be identified. Current and proposed procedures may be understood more rapidly through the use of charts. It may be quicker and easier for analysts or programmers to chart a lengthy procedure than it is for them to describe it by means of pages of written notes. Thus, more time may be devoted to acquiring understanding.

2   *Effective analysis.* The flowchart becomes a model of a program or system that can be broken down into detailed parts for study. Problems may be identified; new approaches may be suggested.

3   *Effective synthesis.* Synthesis is the opposite of analysis; it is the combination of the various parts into a whole entity. Flowcharts may be used as working models in the design of new programs and systems. Elements of old approaches may be combined with new design ideas to give an effective processing plan.

4   *Communication.* Flowcharts aid in communicating the facts of a business problem to those whose skill are needed in the solution. The adage that "a picture is worth a thousand words" contains an element of truth when the pictures happen to be flowchart symbols.

5   *Proper program documentation.* Program *documentation* involves collecting, organizing, storing, and otherwise maintaining a complete historical record of programs and the other documents associated with the organization's data processing systems. Proper program documentation is needed for the following reasons: *(a)* Documented knowledge belongs to an organization and does not disappear with the departure of a programmer. *(b)* If projects are postponed, proper documentation will indicate the problem definition, task objective, extent of prior work, etc., so that the work done will not have to be duplicated. *(c)* If programs are modified in the future (and modification occurs in many cases), proper documentation will brief the programmer on what was originally done and will thus help her or him to understand the problem better. *(d)* When staff changes occur, good documentation serves a training function by helping new employees understand existing programs. *(e)* Good documentation will aid greatly in future program conversion when new

hardware/software packages are acquired. *(f)* Poor documentation represents a fundamental weakness in internal control and is an indication of poor management. From what we have seen of the nature of flowcharts, it is obvious that they provide valuable documentation support for all but the simplest of programs.

6    *Efficient coding.* The program flowchart acts as a guide or blueprint during the program preparation phase. Instructions coded in a programming language may be checked against the flow chart to make sure that no steps are omitted.

7    *Orderly check-out of programs.* If the program fails to run to completion when submitted to the computer for execution, the flowchart may help in the *debugging* process; i.e., it may help in detecting, locating, and removing mistakes. The programmer can refer to the chart as he or she rechecks the coding steps and logic of the written instructions. If, during a test utilizing data that produce known answers, the program runs but delivers incorrect results, the flowchart may again help to detect errors and oversights.

8    *Efficient program maintenance.* The maintenance (through necessary modification) of operating programs is facilitated by flowcharts. The chart helps the programmer concentrate attention on that part of the information flow which is to be modified.

In spite of their many advantages, flowcharts have a few *limitations*. The *first* is that complex and detailed charts are sometimes laborious to plan and draw, especially when a large number of decision paths are involved.[4] A *second* limitation in such a situation is that although branches from a *single* decision symbol are easy to follow, the actions to be taken given certain specified conditions would be difficult to follow if there were *several* paths. For example, the answer to the question asked earlier about what action should be taken with the $300 account that was 60 days overdue was probably not immediately obvious even though Fig. 10-6 outlines a relatively simple procedure. But with more complex problems, the appropriate actions become much more obscure when flowcharts are used. Under such circumstances, flowcharts may be replaced or supplemented by decision tables.

**DECISION TABLES**    A *decision table* can be a powerful tool for defining complex program logic. Figure 10-7 shows the basic table format. The table is divided by the bottom horizontal heavy line into two main parts: the upper part, which contains the *conditions and questions* that are to be considered in

---

[4] During the program preparation stage, sections of original charts may be added to, deleted, patched, and otherwise marked up to the point where they become nearly illegible. Since considerable time and effort could be required to manually redraw complex charts, special automatic flowcharting programs have been developed, which use a high-speed printer to produce the charts in good form.

| Table Heading | | Decision Rules | | | | | | |
|---|---|---|---|---|---|---|---|---|
| If _____ Condition | | | | | | | | |
| And _____ (question) | | | Condition | | | | | |
| And _____ stub | | | entries | | | | | |
| Then _____ | | | | | | | | |
| And _____ Action | | | Action | | | | | |
| And _____ stub | | | entries | | | | | |

FIGURE 10-7

Decision table format.

reaching a decision; and the lower part, which contains the prescribed *action* to be taken when a given set of conditions is present.

### a simple business example—again

The conditions and questions are written in the *condition stub* to the left of the heavy vertical line. The contents of the condition stub correspond to the statements and questions contained in the *decision symbols* of the flowchart; the *condition entries* to the right of the heavy vertical line in the figure correspond to the branches or *paths* going out from decision symbols in a flowchart. Thus a condition entry may be a simple yes (Y) or no (N); it may be a symbol which shows relationship between variables ($>$, $<$, $=$, $\geq$, etc.); or it may be the outcome of certain tests (code 1, code 2, etc.). The *action statements,* which correspond to the action statements located in nondecision symbols of a flowchart, are written in the *action stub*. The conditions may be listed in any convenient order; the actions are listed in the order in which they are normally executed. To briefly summarize, the upper (condition) parts of a decision table are generally concerned with "IF" statements (which are made or implied) and with the responses to those IF statements, while the lower (action) quadrants deal with "THEN" statements and responses to the specified conditions. In short, IF certain conditions exist, THEN specified actions should be taken.

A maze of possible flow paths may exist between START and STOP in a program. Each of the columns in the table *body* is the equivalent of *one* path through the flowchart and is called a *rule*. When a table is completed, each rule column which is used contains one or more condition entries. An example should help clarify matters.

Figure 10-8 shows the decision table for the accounts-receivable penalty procedure charted in Fig. 10-6. You will notice that the statements in the condition stub correspond to the questions being asked in the flowchart decision symbols. You will also note that the action state-

**Decision Rule Number**

| Accounts-Receivable Penalty Procedure | | 1 | 2 | 3 | 4 | 5 | 6 | 7 |
|---|---|---|---|---|---|---|---|---|
| Condition | Number Days Balance Overdue | <30 | <30 | ≥30 | ≥30 | ≥60 | ≥60 | |
| | Number Days Balance Overdue | | | <60 | <60 | | | |
| | Unpaid Balance ≤ $200? | | | Y | N | Y | N | |
| | Last Customer Account Record? | N | Y | N | N | N | N | Y |
| Action | Calculate 2% Penalty | | | x | | x | | |
| | Calculate 3% Penalty | | | | x | | x | |
| | Add Penalty to Customer Account | | | x | x | x | x | |
| | Write Customer Statement | | | x | x | x | x | |
| | Print Warning on Statement | | | | | x | x | |
| | Write Error | x | x | | | | | |
| | Go to Next Account Record | x | | x | x | x | x | |
| | Stop | | x | | | | | x |

FIGURE 10-8

Decision table for accounts-receivable penalty procedure (*Source:* Fig. 10-6).

ments correspond to the directions given or implied by the other flowchart symbols. A few paragraphs earlier this question was asked: What actions would be taken if an account with a balance of $300 were 60 days or more overdue? Let us now look at column 6 (which follows that particular path through the flowchart) to check the answer. The first entry in the column shows that the account is 60 days or more overdue. The second condition is irrelevant in this case, and so the space in rule 6 is left blank. The second entry tells us that the unpaid balance is not equal to or less than $200, and so therefore it must be greater than that figure. The third entry merely shows that the last record has not yet been processed. Thus, the set of conditions in rule 6 has defined our problem! (The other condition sets have defined all the other feasible paths or situations.)

Now what about the *answer* (finally!) to the problem? An x has been placed in column 6 opposite each appropriate action that helps satisfy the given set of conditions. You can compare your answer with the one indicated in Fig. 10-8. You may also want to trace through the table and the flowchart to see what actions are taken when other possible conditions occur.

In our simple business example we have compared a decision table with the flowchart of the problem. But in actual practice, tables are not necessarily compared with charts. Why? Simply because there may be no flowchart. As noted earlier, tables may be used as chart substitutes. A number of small interconnected tables may be quickly constructed to express the logic required to solve complex problems.

## benefits and limitations of decision tables

The following *benefits* may be obtained from the use of decision tables:

1   *Less danger of omitting a logical possibility.* Tables force the programmer to think the problem through. For example, if there are three conditions to be considered, each of which can be answered yes or no, then there are $2^3$ or 8 possible paths or rules.[5] Some of these conceivable paths may not, of course, be pertinent to the problem. But by knowing the total number of paths, the programmer lessens the danger of forgetting one.

2   *Better communication between interested parties.* Tables can perform a valuable communication function. An analyst may design a new system and present it in the form of a table or tables to other analysts, programmers, and managers and executives. The table format is easily followed by others. Flowchart symbols, on the other hand, are not always standardized, and this factor may hinder their communication value. Tables appear to be easier for many managers to follow than flowcharts. Operating managers can quickly trace and verify those paths in the procedure that are of greatest interest to them.

3   *Easier construction and adaptability.* Tables are easier to draw up than comparable flowcharts. They are also easier to change since it is a relatively simple matter to add conditions, rules, and actions to a table.

4   *More compact program documentation.* Several pages of flowcharting may be condensed into one small table. And, of course, it is easier to follow a particular flow path down one column than it is to follow the same path through several flowchart pages.

5   *Direct conversion into computer programs.* It is possible for the contents of a decision table to be coded directly into a language that the computer understands.

Although decision tables appear to have an edge over flowcharts in expressing complex decision logic, they do have limitations and are not as widely used as flowcharts because (1) many problems are simple, have few branches, and lend themselves to charting; (2) charts are able to express the *total sequence* of events better; and (3) charts are familiar to, and preferred by, many programmers who resist changing to the use of tables.

SUMMARY   Once system design specifications have been determined, the programming process may begin. The first step in programming is to break the

[5] These rules contain the following entries:

| (1) | (2) | (3) | (4) | (5) | (6) | (7) | (8) |
|-----|-----|-----|-----|-----|-----|-----|-----|
| Y | Y | Y | N | Y | N | N | N |
| Y | Y | N | Y | N | Y | N | N |
| Y | N | Y | Y | N | N | Y | N |

specifications down into specific arithmetic and logic operations. The remaining steps are to (1) prepare programs in a form that the processor can accept, (2) test the new programs, and (3) implement and maintain them as needed. These remaining steps will be considered in the next chapters.

The basic tools of programming analysis are flowcharts and decision tables. System flowcharts provide the broad overview required for programming analysis to begin. Program flowcharts evolve from the system charts. A set of standardized charting symbols is presented in Fig. 10-2. Compared with pages of written notes, flowcharts help the programmer obtain a quicker grasp of relationships. Charts also aid in communication, provide valuable documentation support, and contribute to more efficient coding and program maintenance.

A decision table is an excellent means of defining complex program logic. In this respect it has an edge over flowcharts. A table is easy to construct and change. It is more compact, provides excellent program documentation, and is an aid in communication.

## REVIEW AND DISCUSSION QUESTIONS

**1** (**a**) What is the purpose of a program flowchart? (**b**) How does it differ from a system flowchart?

**2** (**a**) What symbols are used in a program flowchart to represent input and output, processing, decision, terminal, and connector? (**b**) Construct a flowchart on a problem of your choice using these symbols.

**3** What is a subroutine?

**4** Discuss the benefits and limitations of flowcharts.

**5** Why is proper documentation required?

**6** (**a**) What is a decision table? (**b**) Explain the basic parts of the decision table. (**c**) What is a rule?

**7** What benefits may be obtained from the use of decision tables?

## SELECTED REFERENCES

American National Standards Institute: *Flowchart Symbols and Their Usage in Information Processing* (ANSI X3.5-1970), New York, 1970.

Chapin, Ned: "Flowcharting with the ANSI Standard: A tutorial," *Computing Surveys,* June 1970, pp. 119–146.

Chesebrough, Wilfred C.: "Decision Tables as a Systems Technique," *Computers and Automation,* April 1970, pp. 30–33.

Farina, Mario V.: *Flowcharting,* Prentice-Hall, Inc., Englewood Cliffs, N.J., 1970.

Honeywell Information Systems, Inc.: *An Introduction to Decision Tables,* Wellesley Hills, Mass., 1969.

Pollack, S., H. Hicks, Jr., and W. Harrison: *Decision Tables: Theory and Practice,* Wiley-Interscience, New York, 1971.

# program preparation and programming languages

LEARNING OBJECTIVES   After studying this chapter and answering the discussion questions, you should be able to: ☐ Identify the types of instructions that may be executed by a computer ☐ Explain the differences between machine, symbolic, and high-level programming languages ☐ Discuss the factors that should be considered in the selection of a programming language ☐ Identify and discuss a number of aids and techniques that have been developed to (a) assist programmers in the initial preparation of application programs, and (b) make it possible to convert existing programs so that they can be used on new hardware ☐ Outline some of the characteristics and some of the strengths and weaknesses of FORTRAN, COBOL, PL/I, BASIC, and RPG

**B**y now, you may be tired of being reminded that the programming process begins with the system design specifications. The programmer analyzes these specifications in terms of (1) the *output solution* needed, (2) the *input data* that are necessary to produce the output, and (3) the *operations and procedures* required to achieve the necessary output.

In connection with this analysis, the programmer develops a programming plan and prepares program flowcharts and/or decision tables which detail the procedures for converting input data into output information. Once the programming analysis phase is completed, the next step is to prepare the written instructions that will control the computer during the processing. These instructions are generally coded in a higher-level translatable language according to a specific set of rules. And as we saw in Chapter 2, higher-level source program statements must then be converted into the machine language object program that the computer can accept. If this conversion is successful, the object program must still be tested before it is used on a routine basis; if the conversion is not successful, or if difficulties arise during program testing, the program must be debugged to correct mistakes and errors. Finally, all supporting documents pertaining to the problem and the program solution must be assembled and put in good order, and the program must be maintained as required. Figure 11-1 summarizes this brief review of the programming process.

The purpose of this chapter is to give you an idea of what a programming language is and what is involved in expressing problems in a language that is acceptable to a computer. Therefore, in the following pages we shall look at (1) *computer instructions,* (2) *languages for computers,* (3) *program preparation aids and techniques,* and (4) *program coding with popular languages.* The subject of program debugging, testing, documentation, maintenance, and other topics necessary to the implementation of programs and systems are considered in the next chapter.

**COMPUTER INSTRUCTIONS**

A program, we know, is a complete set of written instructions that enables the computer to process a particular application. Thus, the instruction is the fundamental component in program preparation.

### formats of basic instructions

Like a sentence, a machine instruction prepared in a *basic form* consists of a subject and a predicate. The subject, however, is usually *not* specifically mentioned; it is, instead, some *implied* part of the computer system that is directed to execute the command that is given. For example, if a teacher tells a student to "read the book," the student will interpret this instruction correctly even though the subject "you" is omitted. Similarly, if the machine is told to "ADD 0184," the control unit may interpret this to mean that the arithmetic-logic unit is to add the contents of address 0184 to the contents of the accumulator.

In addition to an implied subject, every basic computer instruction has an explicit predicate consisting of at least two parts. The *first* part is referred to as the *command,* or *operation;* it answers the question "what?"; i.e., it tells the computer what operation it is to perform. Each machine has a limited number of built-in operations that it is capable of executing. An *operation code* is used to communicate the programmer's intent to the machine. Operation codes vary from one machine line to another. In the IBM System/360 and /370 lines, for example, the machine "op codes" for ADD, LOAD, and STORE are 5A, 58, and 50.

The *second* explicit part of the instruction, known as the *operand,* names the object of the operation. In general terms, the operand answers the question "where?"; i.e., it tells the computer where to find or store the data or other instructions that are to be manipulated. Thus, an operand may indicate:

1   The location where data to be processed are to be found.

**2** The location where the result of processing is to be stored.

**3** The location where the next instruction to be executed is to be found. (When this type of operand is not specified, the instructions are taken in sequence.)

The *number* of operands and therefore the structure or format of the instruction *vary* from one computer to another. Up to this point we have dealt only with instructions having a *single* operand. But in addition to the *single-address* format there are also *two-* and *three-address* command structures.[1]

Several instructions may be required to complete an arithmetic operation when a single-address format is used. For example, Fig. 11-2a shows the procedure that may be required to add two numbers and store the result. Figure 11-2b shows one way in which an addition may be handled in a two-address machine, while Fig. 11-2c demonstrates a three-address instruction format. Newer computers frequently have the ability to vary the length of the instruction word just as they have the ability to deal effectively with both fixed- and variable-length data words.

### types of computer instructions

The number of basic commands that may be executed varies from less than 50 to more than 200 depending on the computer make and model. Regardless of the number of built-in operations found in the repertoire of a specific machine, however, the instruction set of every computer (and of every programming language used with computers) can be classified into just a few categories that will permit the computer system to perform the necessary input-processing-output activities. *These categories are*

**1** *Input/output instructions.* Required to permit communication between I/O devices and the central processor, these instructions provide details on the type of input or output operation to be performed and the storage locations to be used during the operation. For example, one or more operations to control the reading of data from a punched card into a storage area or to control the printing of the data held in an output storage area would be included in this category.

**2** *Data movement and manipulation instructions.* These instructions are used to copy data from one storage location to another and to rearrange and change data elements in some prescribed manner during processing. An example of a *data movement* instruction is shown in Fig. 11-2b. If a programmer is using the basic instruction set of a two-address processor and wishes to preserve the number in address 0184 for future use, he or she may need to copy the number in another location prior to the add

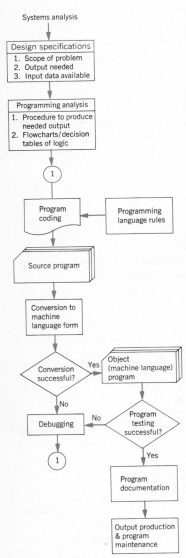

FIGURE 11-1

**Programming process.**

---

[1] The single-address format is popular in microcomputers; the two-address structure is likely to be available in most other computers.

## Command

| Code | Meaning | Operand | Explanation |
|------|---------|---------|-------------|
| (1) XX | (CLA) | 0184 | Three steps are used to perform an addition and a storage operation. The accumulator is cleared of previous data, and the number in address 0184 is then put in that register (1). The number in address 8672 is added to the first number. The result is now in the accumulator (2). The result in the accumulator is stored in address 1273 (3). |
| (2) XX | (ADD) | 8672 | |
| (3) XX | (STO) | 1273 | |

(a)

## Command

| Code | Meaning | First Operand | Second Operand | Explanation |
|------|---------|---------------|----------------|-------------|
| (1) XX | (ADD) | 0184 | 8672 | The number in address 8672 is added to the number in location 0184. The result may automatically be stored in address 0184 by the computer circuitry. Of course, this erases the original number contained in 0184, so if that number is to be saved, it must be duplicated elsewhere *prior* to the add instruction. Instructions (2) and (3) show how this could be done. Instruction (2) duplicates the contents of 0184 in 0185 prior to the addition order (3). |
| (2) XX | (MOVE) | 0184 | 0185 | |
| (3) XX | (ADD) | 0184 | 8672 | |

(b)

## Command

| Code | Meaning | First Operand | Second Operand | Third Operand | Explanation |
|------|---------|---------------|----------------|---------------|-------------|
| (1) XX | (ADD) | 0184 | 8672 | 1273 | The number in address 8672 is added to the number in 0184, and the result is stored in address 1273. |

(c)

FIGURE 11-2

Instruction formats: (a) single-address, (b) two-address, (c) three-address.

instruction. *Manipulation commands* may also be provided to refine or *edit* stored data—e.g., to remove lead zeros from a data item—and to combine several processing operations in a single instruction for the convenience of the programmer. A LOAD AND TEST command, for example, may combine data movement and logical operations.

3  *Arithmetic instructions.* Instructions to permit addition, subtraction, multiplication, and division during processing are, of course, common in all digital computers.

4  *Logic and transfer of control instructions.* During processing, two data items may be *compared* as a result of the execution of a *logic* instruction. The computer is able to determine the relationship that exists between the two items (A has a greater numerical value than B; C comes before D in an alphabetic sequence). *Transfer of control* instructions may then be used to branch or change the sequence of program control, depending on the outcome of the comparison. Of course, some transfer instructions are not based on the outcome of comparisons. As you saw in Chapter 6, transfer commands may be *conditional* or *unconditional*. If the change in

sequence is based on the outcome of a test or comparison, then it is a conditional transfer; if not, it is an unconditional branch.

Figure 11-3 presents a small sample of the command repertoire for IBM System/370 computers (the complete repertoire has about 200 commands). Instruction sets for several other lines have similarities. The operation codes are shown for each instruction. A symbolic code used by programmers to represent each instruction is also presented in Fig. 11-3.

| Command Name | OP Code | Symbolic Code | Type* of Command |
|---|---|---|---|
| **Input/Output Commands** | | | |
| Start I/O | 9C | SIO | SI |
| Halt I/O | 9E-O | HIO | SI |
| **Data Movement/Manipulation Commands** | | | |
| Load Register | 18 | LR | RR |
| Load | 58 | L | RX |
| Load and Test | 12 | LTR | RR |
| Move Characters | D2 | MVC | SS |
| Move Numerics | D1 | MVN | SS |
| Shift Left Single | 8B | SLA | RS |
| Shift Right Single | 8A | SRA | RS |
| Store | 50 | ST | RX |
| Store Character | 42 | STC | RX |
| Edit | DE | ED | SS |
| **Arithmetic Commands** | | | |
| Add | 5A | A | RX |
| Subtract | 5B | S | RX |
| Multiply | 5C | M | RX |
| Divide | 5D | D | RX |
| **Logic and Transfer of Control Commands** | | | |
| Compare Register | 19 | CR | RR |
| Compare | 59 | C | RX |
| Compare Logical Character | D5 | CLC | SS |
| Branch on Condition Register | 07 | BCR | RR |
| Branch on Condition | 47 | BC | RX |
| Branch on Count Register | 06 | BCTR | RR |
| Branch on Count | 46 | BCT | RX |

* You will recall that computers such as the System/360 and /370 models may be used for both business and scientific applications. As we saw in Chap. 6, scientific applications using fixed-length data words make use of registers; business applications using variable-length words use a storage-to-storage approach during processing. Instructions are classified in this table into types on the basis of register and storage usage: Some are normally used in one type of application but not in the other. Thus, RR indicates an instruction which is used in a register-to-register operation; RS and RX instructions deal with situations where one operand is in a register and another is in primary storage; SS commands involve storage-to-storage operations; and SI commands deal with instruction-to-storage situations. For further details, see Ned Chapin, *360/370 Programming in Assembly Language*, 2d ed., McGraw-Hill Book Company, New York, 1973.

**FIGURE 11-3**

Partial command repertoire, IBM System/370 computers.

**LANGUAGES FOR COMPUTERS**

We know that in writing program instructions, the programmer must use a language that can be understood by the computer. One awkward approach to human-machine communication is to have the programmer laboriously code instructions directly into the machine language form. Another approach, as we saw in Chapter 2, is to employ translation software that enables the computer to convert the instructions written in the programmer's language into its own machine code. The programmer finds this approach much more desirable; the machine—being a machine—has no objection.[2] Let us now look at the language categories that have been developed.[3]

### machine languages

Early computers were quite intolerant. Programmers had to translate instructions directly into the machine language form that computers understood—a form consisting of a string of numbers that represented the command code and operand address. To compound the difficulty for programmers, the string of numbers was often not even in decimal form. For example, the instruction to ADD 0184 looks like this in the IBM 7040 machine language:[4]

000100000000000000000000000010111000

In addition to remembering the dozens of code numbers for the commands in the machine's repertoire, a programmer was also forced to keep track of the storage locations of data and instructions. The initial coding often took months, was therefore quite expensive, and often resulted in error. Checking instructions to locate errors was about as tedious as writing them initially. And if a program had to be modified at a later date, the work involved could take weeks to finish.

---

[2] A third approach, and a most desirable one from the human point of view, is for the machine to accept and interpret instructions written (without constraints) in everyday English terms. The semantic problems involved in this approach, however, are formidable. John Pfeiffer points out that while the sentence "Time flies like an arrow" may seem clear to people, it is subject to several machine interpretations. One incorrect translation, for example, might be: "Time the speed of flies as quickly as you can." ("Time" is considered a verb.) Another false interpretation might be that "certain flies enjoy an arrow." ("Time" is now considered an adjective, while "like" is interpreted as a verb.) And once the machine has been straightened out about the interpretation of "Time flies like an arrow," how will it interpret "Fruit flies like a banana"?

[3] We shall deal primarily with categories in this section rather than with specific languages. Some of the characteristics of the most popular business programming languages are discussed later in the chapter. There are probably more than 1,000 programming languages in existence, and some of these languages have dozens of dialects!

[4] In this case, the last 8 bits represent 0184.

### symbolic languages

To ease the programmer's burden, *mnemonic* command codes and *symbolic* addresses were developed in the early 1950s. The word *mnemonic* (pronounced *ne-mon-ik*) refers to a memory aid. One of the first steps in improving the program preparation process was to substitute letter symbols for basic machine language command codes. Figure 11-3 shows both the mnemonic (symbolic) and machine operation codes used in IBM System/370 computers. Each computer now has a mnemonic code, although, of course, the actual symbols vary among makes and models.[5] Machine language is *still* used by the computer in the actual processing of the data, but it first translates the specified command code symbol into its machine language equivalent.

The improvement in the writing of command codes set the stage for further advances. It was reasoned that if the computer could be used to translate convenient symbols into basic commands, why couldn't it also be used to perform other clerical coding functions such as assigning storage addresses to data? This question led to *symbolic addressing;* i.e., it led to the practice of expressing an address, not in terms of its absolute numerical location, but rather in terms of symbols convenient to the programmer.

In the early stages of symbolic addressing, the programmer initially assigned a symbolic name and an actual address to a data item. For example, the total value of merchandise purchased during a month by a department store customer might be assigned to address 0063 by the programmer and given the symbolic name of TOTAL. Also, the value of merchandise returned unused during the month might be assigned to address 2047 and given the symbolic name of CREDIT. Then, for the remainder of the program, the programmer would refer to the *symbolic names rather than to the addresses* when such items were to be processed. Thus, an instruction might be written "S CREDIT, TOTAL" to subtract the value of returned goods from the total amount purchased to find the amount of the customer's monthly bill. The computer might then translate this symbolic instruction into the following machine language string of bits:[6]

| 011111 | 011111111111 | 000000111111 |
|:------:|:------------:|:------------:|
| Operation or command code | 2047 | 0063 |
| (S) | (CREDIT) | (TOTAL) |

---

[5] For example, erasing old data in the accumulator and then adding the contents of an address to it is a common command. The mnemonic code used in some computers is ZA (Zero and Add). In other machines the symbol for the same operation may be CLA (Clear

Another improvement was that the programmer turned the task of assigning and keeping track of instruction addresses over to the computer. The programmer merely told the machine the storage address number of the *first* program instruction, and then all others were automatically stored in sequence from that point by the processor. If another instruction were to be added later to the program, it was not then necessary to modify the addresses of all instructions that followed the point of insertion (as would have to be done in the case of programs written in machine language). In such a case, the processor automatically adjusted storage locations the next time the program was used.

Programmers no longer assign actual address numbers to symbolic data items as they did initially. Rather, they merely specify where they want the first location in the program to be, and an assembly program then takes it from there, allocating locations for instructions and data. The *assembly program* translates the programmer's symbolic language instructions into the machine code of the computer. The following steps (numbered in Fig. 11-4) may take place during the *assembly* and *production* runs:[7]

1   The *assembly program* is read into the computer, where it has complete control over the translating procedure. This program is generally supplied by the manufacturer of the machine as part of the total hardware/software package.

2   The *source program* written by the programmer in the symbolic language of the machine is recorded on an input medium such as punched cards.

3   During the assembly the source program is treated as data and is read into the CPU an instruction at a time under the control of the assembly program.

4   The assembly program translates the source program into a machine language *object program,* which is recorded on tapes or cards as the output of the assembly run. It is important to remember that *during the assembly run no problem data are processed.* That is, the source program is not *being executed;* it is merely being converted into a form in which it can be executed. After the assembly run, the assembly program is filed for future use.

5   The object program is read into the CPU as the first step in the *production run.*

6   Problem data, recorded on a suitable input medium, are read into the CPU under object program control.

---

accumulator and <u>A</u>dd) or RAD (<u>R</u>eset accumulator and <u>AD</u>d). Some examples of symbolic programming languages are IBM's Basic Assembly Language and Honeywell's Easycoder.

[6] This example uses a format and machine language of the Honeywell 200 computer.

[7] Assembly programs and frequently used object programs are often stored in online storage devices rather than on secondary storage media.

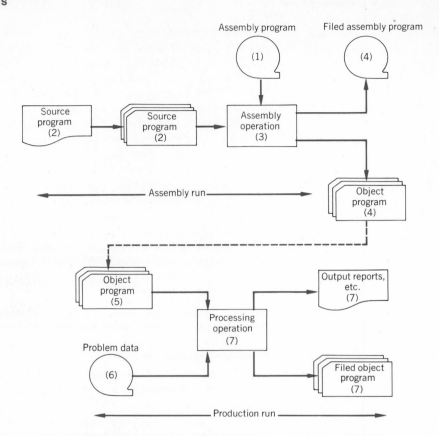

**FIGURE 11-4**

Converting symbolic language to machine language.

7   The application is processed, the information output is properly received, and the object program is filed for future repetitive use.

Symbolic languages possess *advantages over machine languages*. Much time is saved; detail is reduced; fewer errors are made (and those that are made are easier to find); and programs are easier to modify. But there are *limitations*. Coding in symbolic language is still time-consuming. Also, symbolic languages are *machine oriented;* i.e., they are designed for the specific make and model of processor being used. Programs might have to be recoded if the organization acquired a different machine. Furthermore, the programmer writing instructions in a machine's symbolic language must have an intimate knowledge of the workings of that processor. Finally, the earlier assembly programs produced only *one* machine instruction for each source program instruction.

**high-level languages**

To speed up coding, assembly programs were developed that could produce a *variable* amount of machine language code for *each* source program instruction. In other words, a single *macro instruction* might produce *several* lines of machine language code. For example, the programmer might write "READ FILE," and the translating software might then automatically provide a detailed series of previously prepared machine language instructions which would copy a record into primary storage from the file of data being read by the input device. Thus, the programmer was relieved of the task of writing an instruction for every machine operation performed. Input/output control systems (IOCS) employing macro instruction routines were developed to (1) handle the complex programming problems associated with overlap operations, (2) schedule operations, (3) identify errors, and (4) provide greater efficiency in reading and writing records. In spite of significant advances, however, assembly programs were still machine oriented; they were still written to meet the requirements of a specific equipment line.

The development of mnemonic techniques and macro instructions led, in turn, to the development of *high-level languages* that are often oriented toward a particular class of processing problems. For example, a number of languages have been designed to process problems of a scientific-mathematic nature, and other languages have appeared that emphasize the processing of business applications.

Unlike symbolic programs, high-level language programs may be used with *different makes of computers* with little modification. Thus, reprogramming expense may be greatly reduced when new equipment is acquired. *Other advantages of high-level languages are* (1) they are easier to learn than symbolic languages; (2) they require less time to write; (3) they provide better documentation; and (4) they are easier to maintain. Also, a programmer skilled in writing programs in such a language is not restricted to using a single machine.

Naturally, a source program written in a high-level language must also be translated into a machine-usable code. The translating program that performs this operation is called a *compiler*. Compilers, like advanced assembly programs, may generate many lines of machine code for each source program statement.[8] A *compiling run* is required before problem data can be processed. With the exception that a compiler program is substituted for an assembly program, the procedures are the same as those shown in Fig. 11-4. The production run follows the compiling run.

**which language to use?**

As you have concluded by now, a number of languages are generally available that will permit the programmer to write instructions to control

---

[8] Some use the word *statement* to refer to a line of code in a high-level language and the word *instruction* to refer to a line of machine or symbolic language code that will produce a single machine operation.

the computer during the processing of an application. Which of these languages should be used? Obviously, a selection must be made prior to program coding, but several factors may combine to make language selection difficult. However, obtaining answers to the following questions will generally help in the selection process:

1 *Are company programmers familiar with the language?* In many cases, the language used is simply the one that is best known to the programmers. If a language is not familiar, can it be learned quickly? Is it easy to use?

2 *What is the nature of the application?* Does the language perform well in applications of this type?

3 *Is satisfactory translating software available?* There is an important distinction, for example, between a language and a compiler. A language is a humanly convenient set of rules, conventions, and representations used to convey information from human to machine; a compiler is a translator written by one or more programmers. It is entirely possible that a good language, when used with an inefficient compiler, will yield unsatisfactory results.

4 *How frequently will the application be processed?* A symbolic language program written by a clever programmer usually has a shorter production run time and takes less storage space than does a program of the same application written in a high-level language. If the job is run frequently enough, the value of the operating time saved may be more than enough to offset the cost of additional time spent in program preparation. For limited-life jobs, however, the faster the possible programming time is (with high-level languages), the more economical the approach.

5 *Will the program be changed frequently?* The ease of program modification varies with different languages. A high-level language is typically easier to modify than a symbolic language.

6 *Is a hardware change anticipated during the life of the application?* Conversion of high-level language programs is easier and faster; machine-oriented programs may have to be completely rewritten.

7 *Is the language being supported, improved, and updated?* Are resources being committed to the support of the language? Will new computers continue to accept the language source programs? Who is sponsoring the language, and what is their commitment to it?

## PROGRAM PREPARATION AIDS AND TECHNIQUES

The above pages have shown that considerable improvement has been made in programming languages since the early days of computers. And, although programming is still a time-consuming and expensive process, a number of aids and techniques have been developed to assist programmers in the *initial preparation* of applications programs. In addition, there have also been developments that make it possible to *convert existing programs* so that they can be used on new hardware without the necessity for extensive reprogramming. Let us briefly look at each of these topics.

### initial preparation aids

A listing of the aids that have improved programming performance in the initial preparation of applications would include the following:

1   *Programming standards.*[9] We have seen that standards are needed in an organization to guide those involved in the analysis and design stages of the system development process. The availability of similar guidelines is a particularly important aid in program preparation. In addition to the guidelines that must be followed in using the programming language selected, programmers also need standards that outline such things as *(a)* the procedures followed in the organization to carry out the program design task; *(b)* the standard names and definitions of key data items that are frequently used; *(c)* the documentation rules to be followed during program preparation; *(d)* the conventions followed in the organization in filling out the program coding sheets—e.g., the rules on program identification, explanatory comments, indentation of code sections, the formation of characters, the numbering of the lines and pages of code; and *(e)* the procedures to follow in planning and conducting program tests and in implementing tested programs.

2   *Translating and operating system software.* We have already seen how these aids improve program-preparation time while reducing error.

3   *Library of subroutines.* We have also already seen how the maintenance of a library of commonly used computational procedures that may be spliced into new programs can reduce the time and cost of program preparation.

4   *Packaged programs.* The issue of making or buying programs was discussed in Chapter 9. A growing inventory of tested applications packages now makes it possible for more and more organizations to bypass many of the problems associated with initial software preparation.

5   *User groups.*[10] Users of similar machines and software packages have formed associations to share experiences and to exchange information and programs. In 1955, for example, a number of organizations using *large-scale* IBM machines met to form a user group known as SHARE, an acronym said to mean the Society to Help Alleviate Redundant Effort. Meetings are held biannually, with IBM paying part of the expenses.

---

[9] For more details on this topic, see Susan Wooldridge, *Systems and Programming Standards,* Petrocelli/Charter, New York, 1977, pp. 81–124. See, also, The Diebold Group, Inc., *Automatic Data Processing Handbook,* McGraw-Hill Book Company, New York, 1977, pp. 2-303 to 2-323.

[10] For the names and addresses of several hardware/software user groups, see ''Associations Provide Pragmatic Information Exchange,'' *Infosystems,* December 1977, pp. 60ff.

Members of the group have access to a library of contributed programs. The users of smaller IBM equipment may belong to a group known as COMMON. Other manufacturers help sponsor groups that use their equipment, and software vendors sponsor their own user groups. University Computing Co., for example, sponsors a 250-member group of users of its Financial Control System (FCS) package.

6  *Software consultants.* A number of independent software consulting companies have been formed to help businesses with their programming and implementation problems. The better firms can often provide their clients with specialized software that is not available from the manufacturer or that is more efficient than the software provided by the manufacturer. Consultants, for a fee, can supplement a firm's own programming staff during overload periods created by conversion to a new machine or by preparation of complex new system programs.

### initial preparation techniques

In addition to the program-preparation aids mentioned above, a number of techniques have been devised to facilitate the development of applications programs. Some of these techniques may be used for *organizing programmers;* others may be used in *program construction.*

Techniques for organizing programmers    How should the programmers assigned to a particular system development project be organized in order to achieve an effective product at an economical price? The following organizing techniques are commonly used:

1  *Traditional hierarchical grouping.* In this approach, a programming manager assigns tasks to one or more levels of subordinates and exercises overall control over the project. The manager may be responsible for several projects running concurrently, but he or she is not an active participant in the actual program designs or coding efforts. Individual programmers are expected to design, code, test, and document the programs to which they are assigned. The manager may consider programmers in the same pay grade to be "interchangeable" entities, and may shift them from project to project as the workload dictates.

2  *Chief programmer teams.*[11] When this approach is used, each programming project is assigned to a team consisting of a senior-level *chief programmer,* a skilled *backup programmer,* and a *librarian.* One or more *applications programmers* and other specialists are added to this nucleus as needed. In many ways a chief programmer team is like a surgical team in a hospital. The chief programmer (surgeon) has complete technical responsibility for the project and is the principal architect and key coder of the program(s) being prepared. The backup programmer (assisting

[11] For an account of an early application of this organizing technique, see F. Terry Baker and Harlan D. Mills, "Chief Programmer Teams," *Datamation,* December 1973, pp. 58–61.

doctor) supports the chief programmer, is ready to take the chief programmer's place if necessary, and is often called on to develop important elements of the system. The other members of the team perform special tasks under the guidance of the chief programmer (just as the anesthesiologist and the nurses on a surgical team perform special tasks under the guidance of the surgeon). The librarian, for example, relieves the chief programmer of much of the clerical work by gathering, organizing, and maintaining the records and documents associated with the project, while the applications programmers assigned to the team code specific tasks that have been mapped out by the chief programmer. Chief programmer teams are typically found in organizations that employ the top-down approach to system analysis and design discussed in Chapters 8 and 9. It is thus the chief programmer's job to *(a)* write the control code for the top-level system functions (refer back to Fig. 9-7, page 245), *(b)* define the ways in which the various lower-level system modules and components will interface with each other and with the top-level functions, and *(c)* assign other programmers to code specific lower-level procedures. The chief programmer team organization is similar to the traditional hierarchical approach in that there is a single manager who assigns jobs, monitors performance, and decides if corrective action is required. Also, applications programmers are added to the project as needed to code program modules. However, the manager of a chief programmer team is a very active participant in the design and coding effort.

3    *Egoless programming team.*[12] In the traditional organizational setting we have seen, the individual programmer is responsible for a program from design to implementation. If errors are then discovered in a program after it is implemented (and they often are), the programmer may then assume a defensive posture and treat the discovery as a personal attack. In short, the close and exclusive association of the programmer with a specific program may serve to make the program an extension of the programmer's ego. To avoid this situation, the egoless programming approach calls for the assignment of a close-knit team of programmers to a project. Membership in the team seldom changes from project to project, and there is no designated chief programmer. Rather, assignments and leadership roles are determined in a democratic way with each team member doing that part of the work for which he or she is best suited. For example, a member who excells in program design would lead in that phase of the project while one who is particularly good at program testing would be in charge during that period. During coding, team members are expected to check the work of others to learn what they are doing and to locate errors so that they can be corrected. (Since the team is like a close-knit family, members should not feel threatened by this peer review.) The completed code is then *not* the responsibility of a single person but is rather the product of the entire team.

[12] Gerald M. Weinberg originated the phrase "egoless programming." For a detailed discussion of the concept of egoless programming teams, see Weinberg's influential book entitled *The Psychology of Computer Programming,* Van Nostrand Reinhold, New York, 1971.

Each of the above approaches for organizing programmers differs in significant ways from the others. Obviously, there is no agreement as to which approach is best. A number of businesses are currently seeking to develop organizing techniques that combine some of the best features of more than one approach.

Techniques for program construction    Several program construction techniques have received a lot of attention in recent years. Some of the objectives of these techniques are to (1) create programs that better serve the needs of users, (2) reduce the time and money spent in development and implementation, (3) produce programs that have fewer errors and better error-detection controls, and (4) produce programs that are structured in such a way as to make them easier to maintain and easier to convert to another computer system. Some of the methods currently being used in an attempt to achieve these goals are

1    *The use of modular program design.* Programs may be prepared in such a way that there is a *main-control module* that specifies the order in which each of the *other* modules (or *subroutines*) in the program will be used. (A subroutine, you will remember, is a well-defined set of instructions that performs a specific program function.) In the modular programming approach, an instruction in the main-control module branches program control to a subordinate module. When the specific processing operation performed by the module is completed, another branch instruction may transfer program control to another module or return it to the main-flow program. Thus, the modules or subroutines are really programs within a program. (Each module typically has only one entry point and only one exit point. Many programmers believe that modules should be limited in size to about 50 lines of code—the amount that can be placed on one page of printer output.) Figure 11-5 summarizes the modular design concept. Some of the advantages of modular program design are *(a)* complex programs may be divided into simpler and more manageable elements; *(b)* simultaneous coding of modules by several programmers is possible; *(c)* a *library* of modules may be created, and these modules may be used in other programs as needed; *(d)* the location of program errors may be more easily traced to a particular module, and thus debugging and maintenance may be simplified; and *(e)* effective use can be made of tested subroutines prepared by equipment manufacturers and furnished to their customers. Although modular concepts are used in the traditional bottom-up approach to system development where the lower-level modules are coded first and then an effort is made to integrate these modules with higher-level control coding,[13] the modular approach is particularly suited to *top-down program construction.* The main-con-

---

[13] The difficulty with this approach, as we have seen, is that when it comes time to write the higher-level control code to integrate the modules, interface problems are then discovered. These problems are often subtle and difficult to detect, but the result often is that the modules must be reworked. And this reworking frequently leads to project delays and cost overruns.

Main-control
module

Subordinate program
modules

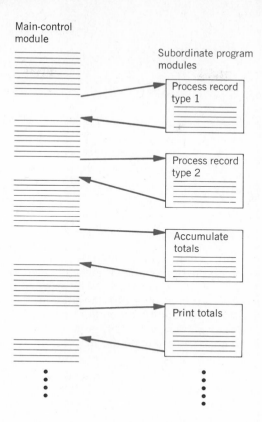

**FIGURE 11-5**

Modular programming approach.

trol module represents the control code for the top-level system functions
and is prepared first. The subordinate program modules that represent the
lower-level system modules and components are then written. Chief
programmer teams, as noted earlier, make use of this top-down modular
program design approach.

**2**   *The use of basic coding structures.* Only three basic coding structures
are needed to prepare any computer program. Each of these structures
has a single entry and exit point, and, like the page of a book, each is
readable from the top to the bottom—a feature that may make it easier to
check and maintain a program that is prepared using only these structures. What are these basic structures? I thought you would never ask. The
basic patterns are shown in Fig. 11-6. The *simple sequence* pattern (Fig.
11-6a) merely consists of one step followed by another. The *selection*
structure (Fig. 11-6b) typically involves a test for some condition followed by two alternative control paths. The path selected depends, of
course, on the results of the test. This pattern is sometimes referred to as
an IF-THEN-ELSE structure. The *loop or repetition* structure involves the
repeating of one or more operations until a condition is found to be *false*
(Fig. 11-6c) at which time the looping process is terminated. If the
condition is initially false, the operation(s) found in this DO WHILE

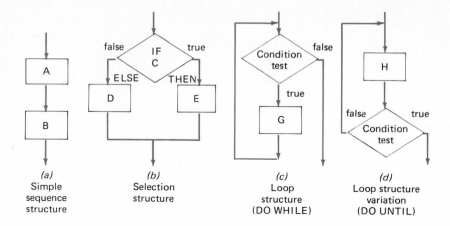

FIGURE 11-6

Basic coding structures.

*(a)*
Simple
sequence
structure

*(b)*
Selection
structure

*(c)*
Loop
structure
(DO WHILE)

*(d)*
Loop structure
variation
(DO UNTIL)

structure will not be executed. A variation of this third basic pattern is one in which the operation(s) is (are) repeated until a condition is found to be *true* (Fig. 11-6*d*) after which the exit path is followed. This variation is referred to as a DO UNTIL structure.[14] Although these basic coding structures are combined and/or "nested" in actual practice (see Fig. 11-7), their inherent simplicity may lead to more understandable program logic and may facilitate the maintenance of programs.

**3**    *The use of structured walkthroughs.* The technique of holding a series of peer reviews during the program development cycle to detect software errors is called a *structured walkthrough.* Each review is typically organized and scheduled by the programmer whose work is to be checked. Materials are handed out in advance of the review session, and the objectives of the session are spelled out to those who will participate. (Programmer managers are not invited.) The role of the session participants is to detect errors, but no attempt is made during the session to correct any errors that are discovered. A walkthrough session will typically include, in addition to the programmer whose work is being reviewed, three to five of the programmer's colleagues. (These colleagues will have their own work reviewed in other similar sessions.) During the session, the reviewee will walk through, step by step, the logic of the work. One participant will keep a record of any errors, discrepancies, or inconsistencies that are uncovered so that proper corrective action can be taken by the reviewee. The tone of the session should be relaxed, and there should be no personal attacks. The possible *advantages of the structured walkthrough technique are (a)* fewer errors are likely to get through the development process; *(b)* faster implementation, a reduction in development costs, and greater user satisfaction may then be possible; *(c)* better program documentation may be obtained; *(d)* later program maintenance efforts may be easier and less expensive; and *(e)* higher programmer morale may result from the spirit of cooperation that can

---

[14] You will notice in Fig. 11-6*c* that operation G will never be executed so long as the condition test is false. In Fig. 11-6*d,* however, operation H will be executed at least once.

exist. These same advantages, of course, are possible when programmers
are organized into the egoless programming teams described earlier.

**4**   *The combining of techniques to create a structured programming
environment.* The term "structured programming" has been compared to
a snowman after a day in the warm sun—both may originally have been
distinctly formed, but both are now rather vaguely defined. Originally,
the term "structured programming" was applied to the disciplined use of
the three basic coding structures described above. Care was taken to
allow only one entrance and one exit from a structure and to minimize

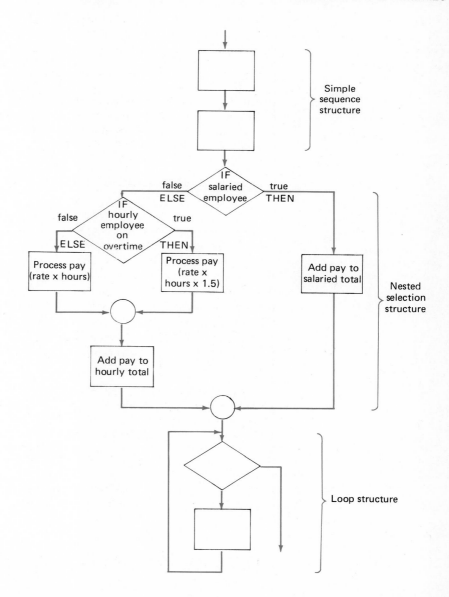

FIGURE 11-7

Partial payroll program showing
structure combinations.

the use of branching instructions such as GO TO. Rules on indenting the coding structures on the coding sheets were also established to give a clearer picture of the coding logic. Since this original use of the term, however, a number of the *other* techniques that we have now studied have also been added under the structured programming banner. Thus, many now expand the definition of structured programming to include the use of *(a)* "structured analysis and design"—i.e., the use of the top-down approach of identifying a main function and then breaking it down into lower-level components for system analysis, system design, and modular program design purposes; *(b)* structured walkthroughs; and *(c)* chief programmer teams. Combining these program construction and programmer organizing techniques into a disciplined structured programming environment can lead to improvements in programming efficiency and in software quality. But an organization must carefully weigh the possible benefits to be obtained from the use of structured programming techniques against its own needs and resources. To recklessly abandon traditional program preparation methods that may have yielded good results in a particular setting in favor of new techniques that may not live up to expectations (but may, instead, produce organizational shock) would, of course, be foolish.

### program/system conversion techniques

We saw in Chapter 9 that the development of compatibility and modularity concepts has served to ease system transition problems. But is there any alternative to completely rewriting proved and satisfactory programs before a new computer can be utilized if the existing computer system (1) is no longer adequate, (2) is not compatible with other models, and (3) does not have modular units to extend its capabilities? Considering the tremendous investment in such programs, the answer, fortunately, is yes. The transition from an old system (computer O) to a new one (computer N) can be made less painful by the use of the following techniques, which permit existing programs to run on computer N without the necessity for initial reprogramming.[15]

1   *Writing programs in a machine-independent language.* As discussed earlier, if computer O programs have been prepared in a high-level standardized language that is essentially machine independent, computer N will have translating software available to accept existing programs directly with a minimum of reprogramming needed.

2   *Using translation techniques.* The machine-level language of a particular computer is a collection of all the acceptable instructions it can understand and execute. The machine-level languages of different computers may vary because of design and technology changes. Several special programs have been developed to translate the "foreign"

---

[15] On frequently used programs some subsequent reprogramming will likely be necessary to realize the full potential of computer N, but the conversion pace need not be so frantic.

"... How big of a system do you want?"

© DATAMATION ®

machine language of machine O into the machine language of computer N. The new machine language program produced can be used thereafter without reference to the original program.

3   *Using emulation techniques.* Emulation involves the use of microprograms stored in a special-purpose read-only memory device. Computer O program instructions are channeled through the microprograms in this *emulator* where they are interpreted, converted into computer N equivalent instructions, and then executed by computer N. This process (see Fig. 11-8) is repeated each time the program is run. Computer N is thus made

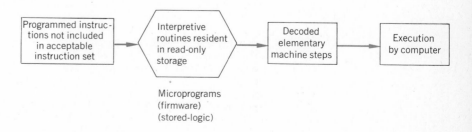

FIGURE 11-8

to act like Computer O. System/370 machines will emulate second-generation IBM models such as those in the 1400 and 7000 series, a UNIVAC 9700 will emulate the computers acquired by UNIVAC from RCA in the early 1970s so that former RCA customers can conveniently shift over to UNIVAC equipment, and the Burroughs B1700 systems will emulate earlier B200, B300, and B500 machines.

4  *Using simulation techniques.* A *simulator* is software that performs the same functions as an emulator. Under the direction of the simulator, instructions from the old program are fed into computer N where they are interpreted, converted into computer N equivalent instructions, and executed. Simulation is generally slower than emulation.

## PROGRAM CODING WITH HIGH-LEVEL LANGUAGES

The initial work on high-level languages is credited to UNIVAC's Dr. Grace M. Hopper who developed a compiler (named "A-2") in 1952. In 1956, UNIVAC also produced an early high-level language to solve mathematical problems (MATHMATIC) and one to process commercial problems (FLOW-MATIC). Most popular high-level languages have emphasized one of these two paths. Slightly later, the IT (Internal Translator) was developed, which could be used by both the IBM 650 and the Burroughs 205 Datatron. This marked the first time that a compiler was used with equipment produced by different manufacturers.

In the next few pages, we shall present a brief overview of the five most popular high-level languages *used in business.*[16] Our treatment of these languages will obviously be little more than a bare outline since entire volumes are available on each. Nevertheless, the material presented here will acquaint you with (1) the *development* of each language, (2) the *coding forms* that may be needed,[17] and (3) some of the *basic characteristics* of each language. In addition, you have seen that all programming languages must have an instruction set that makes it possible for (1) I/O, (2) data movement/manipulation, (3) arithmetic, and (4) logic and transfer of control operations to be performed. Therefore, examples of some of the approaches used in each of these languages to perform these operations are also noted.

### FORTRAN

In 1954, an IBM-sponsored committee headed by John Backus began work on a scientific-mathematic language. The result of this effort was

---

[16] At least, these are the five most popular high-level languages identified by name in a study published in December 1977. However, that study shows that symbolic languages are also popular in business applications. See Andreas S. Philippakis, "A Popularity Contest for Languages," *Datamation,* December 1977, pp. 81ff.

[17] Special *coding forms* are used with several languages to (1) help the programmer comply with language rules, (2) help reduce clerical errors, and (3) make the job of card punching easier.

FORTRAN Coding Form    X28-7327-6 U/M050
Printed in U.S.A.

| PROGRAM | AVERAGE OF TEST SCORES | | | | | | |
| PROGRAMMER | JOHN Q. PROGRAMMER | DATE 1/26/7— | PUNCHING INSTRUCTIONS | GRAPHIC | | PAGE 1 OF 1 | |
| | | | | PUNCH | | CARD ELECTRO NUMBER | |

```
      READ  (1,10)N,ANAME1,ANAME2
 10   FORMAT(I2,2X,2A10)
      IF(N)100,100,20
 20   ITOTAL=0
      WRITE (3,30)ANAME1,ANAME2
 30   FORMAT(10X,4HNAME,2X,2A10/)
      WRITE (3,40)
 40   FORMAT(21X,12HTEST RESULTS)
      DO 70 I=1,N,1
      READ  (1,50)ISCORE
 50   FORMAT(I3)
      WRITE (3,60)ISCORE
 60   FORMAT(23X,I4)
      ITOTAL=ITOTAL+ISCORE
 70   CONTINUE
      IAVE=(ITOTAL+(N+1)/2)/N
      WRITE (3,80)ITOTAL
 80   FORMAT(12 2X,I5/)
      WRITE (3,90)IAVE
 90   FORMAT(5X,7HAVERAGE,11X,I4)
 100  STOP
      END
```

FIGURE 11-9

FORTRAN (FORmula TRANslator), which was introduced in 1957 for the IBM 704 computer. It has been estimated that the cost of producing the 25,000 lines of detailed machine instructions that went into the first FORTRAN compiler was $2.5 million. Since its introduction, FORTRAN has been widely accepted and has been revised a number of times.

The overwhelming majority of all computers now in use have FORTRAN capability. Because of this widespread acceptance, the forerunner of the American National Standards Institute (ANSI) began work in 1962 on FORTRAN standard languages. These standards were approved in 1966.[18] In 1977, proposed revisions of these FORTRAN standards were circulated for study and comment. The proposed revisions add some features and make some minor changes to the 1966 standards.

A FORTRAN source program (like programs written in other high-level languages) is composed of *statements* that will direct the computer to *read the input data, process* (i.e., perform calculations, move, and manipulate) *the data, compare values, transfer program control, repeat the input/processing operations* as needed, and *transmit the output results.* The example program in Fig. 11-9 shows the coding required (and the

INFOSYSTEMS

"Am I familiar with FORTRAN? I may be—what's his first name?"

[18] There are two published standards. The ANSI Basic FORTRAN version is a subset of the "full" FORTRAN standard and does not have some of the additional features of the more extensive version. They do not differ, however, in their structure. The ANSI Basic FORTRAN standard is similar to FORTRAN II; ANSI FORTRAN corresponds to FORTRAN IV.

NAME  A.V.  STUDENT

TEST RESULTS

| | |
|---|---|
| | 75 |
| | 50 |
| | 55 |
| | 0 |
| | 100 |
| | 100 |
| | 75 |
| | 100 |
| | 100 |
| | 50 |
| | 0 |
| | 75 |
| | 100 |
| | 67 |
| | 63 |
| | 97 |
| | 63 |
| | 93 |
| | 57 |
| | 67 |
| | 83 |
| | 0 |
| | 100 |
| | 100 |
| | 72 |
| | 75 |
| | 63 |
| | 87 |
| | 93 |
| | 75 |
| | 100 |
| | 100 |
| | 100 |
| | 100 |
| | 90 |

2,625

AVERAGE          75

FIGURE 11-10

coding sheet used) to process Professor Shirley A. Meany's grade-averaging application discussed in the last chapter and presented in a flowchart in Fig. 10-5. This program accepts as input the grade scores of a student (in our example, the student is A. Valiant Student, the sole survivor of Professor Meany's course). Each grade is punched into a card and read into a computer under program control. The output of this FORTRAN program (and of the COBOL, PL/I, and BASIC language programs that follow) will have the appearance of Fig. 11-10. The input grade data for Mr. Student are also indicated in Fig. 11-10.

This FORTRAN program, of course, utilizes statements from the basic categories. The first line of code in Fig. 11-9, for example, is a READ statement that is used to enter *input* data from an input device into primary storage, and the fifth line of code is a WRITE statement that is used to transfer *output* information from primary storage to an output device. Input and output statements are accompanied by FORMAT statements (lines 2 and 6 in Fig. 11-9) that supply *data movement/manipulation* information to the processor. The *arithmetic assignment* statement found in Fig. 11-9 that computes a student's average grade[19] for the 35 exams is IAVE = (ITOTAL + (N + 1)/2)/N. When this statement is executed, the average grade will be assigned to a storage area that the programmer has identified by the *variable name* IAVE.

FORTRAN programs are executed sequentially until the sequence is altered by a *transfer of control* statement. An example of a *conditional* branch statement is found on the third line of Fig. 11-9. *If* N (the number of exams taken) is mistakenly entered as a *negative* value or as *zero*, program control will be transferred to statement number 100 (STOP); if N is a *positive* value, control branches to statement 20.[20] An additional program-control arrangement that sets up a *loop* to permit a *repetitive input/processing operation* to continue as long as necessary is found on lines 9–15 of Fig. 11-9. The DO statement on line 9 determines the number of times the steps in the operation will be performed.

FORTRAN has the *advantage* of being a compact language that serves the needs of scientists, engineers, and business statisticians very well. It is available for use with the smallest minicomputers or the largest number-crunchers. Because there are established FORTRAN standards, programs written in the standard dialect for one computer are usually easily converted for use with another processor. *However,* it may be more

[19] Since Shirley Meany wants a rounded average grade, the purpose of (N + 1)/2 is to round off computations to the nearest whole value. In FORTRAN, the slash symbol (/) represents division; one asterisk (*) represents multiplication; and two asterisks (**) indicate exponentiation.

[20] One example of an acceptable FORTRAN *unconditional* branching statement is GO TO 100, where 100 refers to a statement number in the program. Although the use of the GO TO statement is discouraged in a structured programming environment, it is difficult to prepare long FORTRAN programs without making use of this branching statement.

difficult to trace program logic in FORTRAN code than in some other
high-level languages, and it is not as well suited for processing large
business files as COBOL.

### COBOL

As its name indicates, COBOL (COmmon Business Oriented Language)
was designed specifically for business-type data processing applications.
The group that designed the language gathered at the Pentagon in
Washington, D.C. in May 1959, with the official sanction of the U.S.
Department of Defense—the world's largest single user of computers.
Members of the COnference of DAta SYstems Languages (CODASYL)
represented computer manufacturers, government agencies, user organizations, and universities. The CODASYL Short-Range Committee, which
prepared the COBOL framework, consisted of representatives from federal government agencies (the Air Material Command, the Bureau of
Ships, and the Bureau of Standards) and from computer manufacturers
(IBM, Honeywell, Burroughs, RCA, UNIVAC Division of Sperry Rand,
and Sylvania). From June to December 1959, this committee worked on
the language specifications. Its final report was approved in January
1960, and the language specifications were published a few months later
by the Government Printing Office.

Since 1961, COBOL compilers have been prepared for all but the
smallest commercial processors. Other CODASYL committees have continued to maintain, revise, and extend the initial specifications. An ANSI
COBOL standard was first published in 1968, and a later version was
approved in 1974.

COBOL is structured much like this chapter. *Sentences* (analogous to
statements in FORTRAN) are written to direct the processor in performing
the necessary operations. A varying number of sentences dealing with the
same operation are grouped to form a *paragraph*. Related paragraphs
may then be organized into a *section,* sections are grouped into a
*division,* and *four* divisions complete the structural hierarchy of a
COBOL program. Figure 11-11 shows the COBOL coding (and the
coding forms used) to process the grade-averaging application discussed
in the preceding FORTRAN section.

The first entry in Fig. 11-11 (page 001, line 010) is IDENTIFICATION
DIVISION—the *first* of the COBOL divisions. A required paragraph
identifies the program (001, 020), and additional optional paragraphs are
included for documentation purposes. The *second* division is the ENVI-
RONMENT DIVISION (001, 060), which consists of two required sections that describe the specific hardware to use when the program is run.
If the application is to be processed on different equipment, this division
will have to be rewritten, but the rewriting usually presents no problem.

# IBM

## COBOL Coding Form

| SYSTEM | | | |
|---|---|---|---|
| PROGRAM | AVERAGE GRADE | PUNCHING INSTRUCTIONS | PAGE 1 OF 4 |
| PROGRAMMER | BAL SHEET | GRAPHIC / PUNCH / CARD FORM # | |

DATE 10/13/1999

| SEQUENCE | CONT | COBOL STATEMENT | IDENTIFICATION |
|---|---|---|---|
| 010 | | IDENTIFICATION DIVISION. | AVERAGES |
| 020 | | PROGRAM-ID. 'AVERAGES'. | |
| 030 | | AUTHOR. BAL SHEET. | |
| 040 | | DATE-WRITTEN. OCTOBER 13, 1999. | |
| 050 | | DATE-COMPILED. OCTOBER 13, 1999. | |
| 060 | | ENVIRONMENT DIVISION. | |
| 070 | | CONFIGURATION SECTION. | |
| 080 | | SOURCE-COMPUTER. IBM-360 F30. | |
| 090 | | OBJECT-COMPUTER. IBM-360 F30. | |
| 100 | | INPUT-OUTPUT SECTION. | |
| 110 | | FILE-CONTROL. | |
| 120 | | SELECT GRADE-CARDS ASSIGN TO UNIT-RECORD 2540R. | |
| 130 | | SELECT REPORT ASSIGN TO UNIT-RECORD 1403. | |
| 140 | | DATA DIVISION. | |
| 150 | | FILE SECTION. | |
| 160 | FD | GRADE-CARDS, DATA RECORD IS GRADE-RECORD | |
| 170 | | LABEL RECORDS ARE OMITTED. | |
| 180 | 01 | GRADE-RECORD. | |
| 190 | | 02 INITIALS-1 PICTURE IS A. | |
| 200 | | 02 INITIALS-2 PICTURE IS A. | |
| 210 | | 02 LAST-NAME PICTURE IS A(12). | |
| 220 | | 02 SCORE PICTURE IS 999. | |
| 230 | | 02 FILLER PICTURE IS X(63). | |

* A standard card form, IBM Electro C61897, is available for punching source statements from this form.
Instructions for using this form are given in any IBM COBOL reference manual.
Address comments concerning this form to IBM Corporation, Programming Publications, 1271 Avenue of the Americas, New York, New York 10020.

GX28-1464-5 U/M 050
Printed in U.S.A.

FIGURE 11-11

SYSTEM
PROGRAM
PROGRAMMER
DATE

PUNCHING INSTRUCTIONS
GRAPHIC
PUNCH
CARD FORM # ___ *

```
SEQUENCE
(PAGE) (SERIAL) CONT A B        COBOL STATEMENT

002010        FD  REPORT, DATA RECORD IS PRINT-LINE
   020            LABEL RECORDS ARE OMITTED.
   030        01  PRINT-LINE  PICTURE IS X(132).
   040        WORKING-STORAGE SECTION.
   050        77  ONE  PICTURE IS 9  USAGE IS COMPUTATIONAL-3  VALUE IS 1.
   060        77  ACCUMULATOR  PICTURE IS S9999  USAGE IS COMPUTATIONAL-3
   061            VALUE IS ZERO.
   070        77  NO-GRADES  PICTURE IS 99  USAGE IS COMPUTATIONAL-3
   071            VALUE IS ZERO.
   080        77  AVERAGE  PICTURE IS 999  USAGE IS COMPUTATIONAL-3
   081            VALUE IS ZERO.
   090        01  HEADING-LINE.
   100        02  FILLER  PICTURE IS X(10)  VALUE IS SPACES.
   110        02  FILLER  PICTURE IS X(6)  VALUE IS 'NAME'.
   120        02  INITIAL-P1  PICTURE IS A.
   130        02  FILLER  PICTURE IS X  VALUE IS '.'.
   140        02  INITIAL-P2  PICTURE IS A.
   150        02  FILLER  PICTURE IS XX  VALUE IS '.'.
   160        02  LAST-NAME-P  PICTURE IS A(12).
   170        02  FILLER  PICTURE IS X(99)  VALUE IS SPACES.
   180        01  HEAD-LINE-2.
   190        02  FILLER  PICTURE IS X(21)  VALUE IS SPACES.
   200        02  FILLER  PICTURE IS X(12)  VALUE IS 'TEST RESULTS'.
   210        02  FILLER  PICTURE IS X(99)  VALUE IS SPACES.
```

*A standard card form, IBM Electro C61897, is available for punching source statements from this form.
Instructions for using this form are given in any IBM COBOL reference manual.
Address comments concerning this form to IBM Corporation, Programming Publications, 1271 Avenue of the Americas, New York, New York 10020.

GX28-1464-5 U/M 050
Printed in U.S.A.

**FIGURE 11-11** (continued)

# IBM

## COBOL Coding Form

| SYSTEM | | | |
|---|---|---|---|
| PROGRAM | | PUNCHING INSTRUCTIONS | |
| PROGRAMMER | DATE | GRAPHIC | PUNCH | CARD FORM # | * |

| SEQUENCE (PAGE) (SERIAL) | CONT | A | B | COBOL STATEMENT | IDENTIFICATION |
|---|---|---|---|---|---|
| 003 010 | | 01 | DATA-LINE. | | AVERAGES |
| 020 | | | 02 FILLER | PICTURE IS X(5) VALUE IS SPACES. | |
| 030 | | | 02 LABEL | PICTURE IS X(7) VALUE IS SPACES. | |
| 040 | | | 02 FILLER | PICTURE IS X(9) VALUE IS SPACES. | |
| 050 | | | 02 SCORE | PICTURE IS ZZ,ZZ9. | |
| 060 | | | 02 FILLER | PICTURE IS X(105) VALUE IS SPACES. | |
| 070 | | | PROCEDURE DIVISION. | | |
| 080 | | | OPEN-PARA. | | |
| 090 | | | OPEN INPUT GRADE-CARDS OUTPUT REPORT- | | |
| 091 | | | READ GRADE-CARDS AT END GO TO TOTAL-PARA. | | |
| 100 | | | INITIALIZ-PARA. | | |
| 110 | | | PERFORM HEADING-ROUTINE. | | |
| 111 | | | GO TO A1. | | |
| 120 | | | PROCESS-PARA. | | |
| 130 | | | READ GRADE-CARDS AT END GO TO TOTAL-PARA. | | |
| 140 | | | A1. ADD SCORE OF GRADE-RECORD TO ACCUMULATOR. | | |
| 150 | | | ADD ONE TO NO-GRADES. | | |
| 160 | | | MOVE SCORE OF GRADE-RECORD TO SCORE OF DATA-LINE. | | |
| 170 | | | WRITE REPORT FROM DATA-LINE AFTER ADVANCING 1 LINES. | | |
| 180 | | | GO TO PROCESS-PARA. | | |
| 190 | | | TOTAL-PARA. | | |
| 200 | | | MOVE ACCUMULATOR TO SCORE OF DATA-LINE. | | |
| 210 | | | WRITE REPORT FROM DATA-LINE AFTER ADVANCING 2 LINES. | | |
| 220 | | | DIVIDE NO-GRADES INTO ACCUMULATOR GIVING AVERAGE ROUNDED. | | |

*A standard card form, IBM Electro C61897, is available for punching source statements from this form.
Instructions for using this form are given in any IBM COBOL reference manual.
Address comments concerning this form to IBM Corporation, Programming Publications, 1271 Avenue of the Americas, New York, New York 10020.

GX28-1464-5 U/M 050
Printed in U.S.A.

FIGURE 11-11 (continued)

# IBM

## COBOL Coding Form

| SYSTEM | | |
|---|---|---|
| PROGRAM | | CARD FORM # |
| PROGRAMMER | DATE | |

PUNCHING INSTRUCTIONS

| GRAPHIC | | | |
|---|---|---|---|
| PUNCH | | | |

| SEQUENCE | | | |
|---|---|---|---|
| (PAGE) | (SERIAL) | CONT A | B |
| 3 4 | 6 7 8 | | 12 16 ... COBOL STATEMENT |

```
004 010    MOVE AVERAGE TO SCORE OF DATA-LINE.
    020    MOVE 'AVERAGE' TO LABEL.
    030    WRITE REPORT FROM DATA-LINE AFTER ADVANCING 2 LINES.
    040    CLOSE GRADE-CARDS REPORT. STOP RUN.
    050 HEADING-ROUTINE.
    060    MOVE INITIALS-1 TO INITIAL-P1.
    070    MOVE INITIALS-2 TO INITIAL-P2.
    080    MOVE LAST-NAME TO LAST-NAME-D.
    090    WRITE REPORT FROM HEADING-LINE AFTER ADVANCING 0 LINES.
    100    WRITE REPORT FROM HEAD-LINE-2 AFTER ADVANCING 2 LINES.
```

IDENTIFICATION
72        76        80
A V E R A G E S

*A standard card form, IBM Electro C61897, is available for punching source statements from this form.
Instructions for using this form are given in any IBM COBOL reference manual.
Address comments concerning this form to IBM Corporation, Programming Publication, 1271 Avenue of the Americas, New York, New York 10020.

GX28-1464-5 U/M 050
Printed in U.S.A.

**FIGURE 11-11** (continued)

The DATA DIVISION (001, 140), the *third* of the four divisions, is divided into two sections. The purpose of this division is to present in detail a description and layout of (1) all the *input* data items in a record, and all the records in each file that is to be processed (lines 001, 150 and 001, 230); (2) all *storage locations* that are needed during processing to hold intermediate results and other independent values needed for processing (lines 002, 040 to 002, 081); and (3) the format to be used for the *output* results (lines 002, 090 to 003, 060).

The *last* COBOL division, the PROCEDURE DIVISION, contains the sentences and paragraphs that the computer follows in executing the program. In this division, *input* (e.g., 003, 091), *data movement and manipulation* (003, 160), *arithmetic* (003, 220), *transfer of control* (003, 180), and *output* (004, 090) operations are performed to solve the problem.

One advantage of COBOL is that it can be written in a quasi-English form that may employ commonly used business terms. Because of this fact, the logic of COBOL programs may be followed more easily by the nonprogrammers in business. Thus, there may be less documentation required for COBOL programs. Also, COBOL is better able to manipulate alphabetic characters than FORTRAN, and this is important in business processing where names, addresses, part descriptions, etc., are frequently reproduced. Finally, a standard version exists; the language is relatively machine independent; and it is maintained, updated, and supported by its users. A *limitation* of COBOL, however, is that it is obviously not a compact language. (The 22 lines of FORTRAN code in Fig. 11-9 will produce the same output as the 81 lines of code in Fig. 11-11.) It is not the easiest high-level language for most of us to learn, and it is not as well suited for complex mathematical computations as FORTRAN. In spite of these drawbacks, however, "COBOL is the most widely used language in the world by a very wide margin, and it will stay that way at least a decade."[21]

### PL/I

Developed in the mid-1960s by IBM and a committee of users for the IBM System/360 family of computers, PL/I (Programming Language I, where I stands for one) has been promoted as a universal language because it can be used to solve all types of business and scientific problems efficiently. As a scientific language, PL/I appears to be an extension of FORTRAN; however, COBOL-type data description is also used.

The measure of success of a language, of course, is determined by its use. Although the ultimate success of PL/I remains to be determined, it is

[21] Daniel D. McCracken, "Let's Hear It for COBOL," *Datamation*, May 1976, p. 242.

expected that its use will increase in the future because of its suitability
for use in a *structured programming* environment.

The PL/I coding for Shirley Meany's grade-averaging problem is shown
in Fig. 11-12. Although a general-purpose coding form is used, PL/I
programs may be written in a rather *free-form* way. The basic element in
PL/I is the *statement* which is concluded with a semicolon. Statements
are combined into *procedures*. A procedure may represent an entire
small program (as in Fig. 11-12) or a "building block" or module of a
more complex program. Of course, *input* (e.g., page 1, line 15 of Fig. 11-
12), *arithmetic* (2, 6), *transfer of control* (2, 4), *repetition of input/
processing* (from lines, 1, 15 to 2, 4), and *output* (2, 5) operations may be
performed in any PL/I program.

PL/I has the *advantage* of being a flexible and sophisticated language
with features found in both FORTRAN and COBOL. Because of its
modular structure, a novice programmer need only learn a *small part* of
the language in order to prepare applications programs of a particular
type. Also, modular procedure blocks facilitate the use of structured
programming concepts and are efficiently handled by a processor operating in a multiprogramming environment. Finally, programmers have
considerable latitude in the way they write statements, and the PL/I
compiler has built-in features—called *default options*—that can detect
and correct common programming errors. A *limitation* of PL/I, however,
is that it is more difficult to learn in its entirety than either FORTRAN or
COBOL. There is no ANSI standard version of PL/I at this writing, but
efforts are underway to develop such a standard.

## BASIC

BASIC (Beginner's All-purpose Symbolic Instruction Code) is a popular
*timesharing* or interactive language that has wide appeal because of its
ease of usage.[22] A problem solver with little or no knowledge of computers or programming can learn to write BASIC programs at a remote
terminal in a short period of time. Because of its simplicity, BASIC is also
by far the most popular high-level language used in microcomputer
systems. (A number of recreational and educational programs are published in each issue of such magazines as *Creative Computing* and *Byte*
that cater to individual users of microcomputers, and these programs are
usually documented in BASIC.)

BASIC was developed in 1963–1964 at Dartmouth College under the
direction of Professors John Kemeny and Thomas Kurtz. The purpose of

[22] Another interactive language that is gaining in popularity is APL (A Programming Language). Complex algorithms can be expressed in a very concise way from a special
keyboard that has a large and rather unusual set of characters.

GENERAL PURPOSE CARD PUNCHING FORM

PUNCHING INSTRUCTIONS

| JOB | AVERAGE OF TEST SCORES | | WRITTEN AS: |
|-----|------------------------|--|-------------|
| BY  | JOHN Q PROGRAMMER | DATE 1/26/99 | PUNCH AS: |

NOTES: PL/I

FIELD IDENTIFICATION

Column guide: 1-10 | 11-20 | 21-30 | 31-40 | 41-50 | 51-60 | 61-70 | 71-80

```
1   AVERAGE: PROCEDURE OPTIONS (MAIN);
2   DECLARE
3     N FIXED (2),
4     NAME CHARACTER (15),
5     SCORE FIXED (3),
6     TOTAL FIXED (4),
7     AVE FIXED (3),
8     SWT FIXED (1),
9     WORK FILE,
10    NWORK FILE PRINT;
11    TOTAL = 0;
12    N = 0;
13    SWT = 0;
14    OPEN FILE (WORK) INPUT, FILE (NWORK) OUTPUT;
15    READ: GET FILE (WORK) EDIT (NAME, SCORE) (X(60),A(15),X(2),F(3));
16    ON ENDFILE (WORK) GO TO OUTPUT;
17    IF SWT = 1 THEN GO TO CONTINUE;
18    SWT = 1;
19    PUT FILE (NWORK) EDIT ('NAME     ,NAME) (PAGE,X(10),A(6),A(15));
20    PUT FILE (NWORK) EDIT ('TEST RESULTS') (SKIP(2),X(21),A(12));
```

PAGE 1 OF 2

FIGURE 11-12

GENERAL PURPOSE CARD PUNCHING FORM

PUNCHING INSTRUCTIONS

| | |
| --- | --- |
| JOB AVERAGE OF TEST SCORES | WRITTEN AS: |
| BY JOHN Q. PROGRAMMER  DATE 1/26/99 | PUNCH AS: |

NOTES: PL/1

FIELD IDENTIFICATION

```
1  CONTINUE: PUT FILE (NWORK) EDIT (SCORE) (SKIP(1),X(24),P'ZZ9');
2  N = N + 1;
3  TOTAL = TOTAL + SCORE;
4  GO TO READ;
5  OUTPUT: PUT FILE (NWORK) EDIT (TOTAL) (SKIP(2),X(22),P'9,999');
6  AVE = TOTAL / N;
7  PUT FILE (NWORK) EDIT ('AVERAGE',AVE) (SKIP(2),X(5),A(7),X(12),P'Z99');
8  CLOSE FILE (WORK), FILE (NWORK);
9  END AVERAGE;
10
11
12
13
14
15
16
17
18
19
20
```

FIGURE 11-12  (continued)

this effort was to produce a language that undergraduate students in all fields of study (1) would find easy to learn and (2) would thus be encouraged to use on a regular basis. BASIC was a success at Dartmouth on both counts. The Dartmouth timesharing system was implemented on General Electric equipment with the assistance of GE engineers. Recognizing the advantages of BASIC, GE quickly made the language available for the use of commercial timesharing customers. BASIC is now offered in some form by virtually every major computer manufacturer and by almost every independent supplier of timesharing. Users of BASIC range from public school students to aerospace engineers.

The BASIC program for Shirley Meany's grade-averaging problem is presented in Fig. 11-13. As you may notice, BASIC is similar to FORTRAN. A series of statements make up a program. These program statements are all identified by a line number and are typically entered into the computer from an online terminal keyboard. The data needed to solve the problem are also entered via the terminal (see the 35 test grades scored by a Mr. A. Valiant Student in Shirley's class in line numbers 180 through 240). Processing is initiated by the system command RUN, and the output results are then transmitted back to the terminal as soon as the

```
010 READ A,N$
020 IF A<=0 THEN 250
030 LET T=0
040 PRINT TAB(11);"NAME";TAB(17);N$
050 PRINT
060 PRINT TAB(22);"TEST RESULTS"
070 FOR I=1 TO A
080 READ S1
090 PRINT USING 95,S1
095:                              ####
100 LET T=T+S1
110 NEXT I
120 LET M1=T/A
130 PRINT
140 PRINT TAB(23);T
150 PRINT
160 PRINT TAB(6);"AVERAGE";TAB(25);M1
170 DATA 35,A.V. STUDENT
180 DATA 075,050,055,000,100,
190 DATA 100,075,100,100,050,
200 DATA 000,075,100,067,063,
210 DATA 097,063,093,057,067,
220 DATA 083,000,100,100,072,
230 DATA 075,063,087,093,075,
240 DATA 100,100,100,100,090
250 END
```

FIGURE 11-13                RUN

NAME   A.V. STUDENT

TEST RESULTS

| |
|---|
| 75 |
| 50 |
| 55 |
| 0 |
| 100 |
| 100 |
| 75 |
| 100 |
| 100 |
| 50 |
| 0 |
| 75 |
| 100 |
| 67 |
| 63 |
| 97 |
| 63 |
| 93 |
| 57 |
| 67 |
| 83 |
| 0 |
| 100 |
| 100 |
| 72 |
| 75 |
| 63 |
| 87 |
| 93 |
| 75 |
| 100 |
| 100 |
| 100 |
| 100 |
| 90 |
| |
| 2625 |

AVERAGE     75

FIGURE 11-14

program has been executed. The result of processing the program shown in Fig. 11-13 is presented in Fig. 11-14. Statements that perform *input* (e.g., line numbers 010, 080, and 170–240 of Fig. 11-13), *arithmetic* (100), *transfer of control* (020), *repetition of input/processing* (070–110), and *output* (040, 060, 090–095, 130–160) operations are, of course, likely to be found in any BASIC program.

BASIC has the *advantage* of being the easiest to learn of any of the languages discussed in this chapter. Entering data is easy, and the problem solver need not be confused about output formats because a usable format may be automatically provided. And if revisions are to be made in a BASIC program, it is only necessary to retype the line number(s) of the statement(s) to be changed and then supply the revised statement(s). Additions can easily be inserted into existing programs in much the same way. Libraries of BASIC programs may be stored in direct-access devices for immediate call-up by users working at terminals. By interacting with the program by following directions written into the program, the user need only know how to correctly enter the data in order to receive processed output information. BASIC is thus a "friendly" language for nonprogrammers. Finally, BASIC is available for even the smallest processors. Unfortunately, however, it is *limited* in its ability to handle large file processing applications. And there is as yet no ANSI standard version of the language.

## RPG

First introduced for widespread use on the IBM 1400 series computers as a language that could readily duplicate the processing approach used with punched card equipment, RPG (Report Program Generator) is now used primarily on the small card-oriented business computers produced by IBM (e.g., the System/3 line) and by other manufacturers. As the name suggests, RPG is designed to generate the output reports resulting from the processing of such business applications as accounts receivable and accounts payable. But RPG can also be used to periodically update accounts-receivable and accounts-payable files.

In spite of its file-updating capabilities, however, RPG is a *limited-purpose* language because *every* object program generated from source programs by the RPG compiler follows a basic processing cycle from which it *never* deviates. (The general form of this cycle is shown in Fig. 11-15.) Since the processing logic never varies, the RPG programmer is concerned only with *file description* and with specifications about *input, calculations,* and *output.* Very detailed specification sheets are used for coding purposes. Figure 11-16 shows the coding sheets required to process the accounts-receivable penalty procedure outlined in the last chapter in Fig. 10-6 (flowchart) and 10-8 (decision table). For illustration

purposes, let us assume that the following input data are punched into
cards:

| Days Overdue | Unpaid Balance | Customer Name |
|---|---|---|
| 25 | $150.00 | John Smith |
| 45 | 200.00 | A. V. Student |
| 65 | 250.00 | Randy Johnson |
| 30 | 300.00 | Beverly Bivens |
| 60 | 350.00 | Alexandre Dumas |

A computer under the control of the RPG program shown in Fig. 11-16
would then produce the output result shown in Fig. 11-17. (An IBM
version of RPG is used here.)

One *advantage* of RPG is that it is relatively easy to learn and use.
Since program logic is fixed, there are fewer formal rules to remember
than with many other languages. RPG is well-suited for applications
where large files are read, few calculations are performed, and output
reports are created. It has been an important language of small business-
oriented computers for several years. Of course, the limited purpose for
which it was designed is also a *disadvantage* of the language since it
therefore has restricted mathematical capability and cannot be used for
scientific applications. Finally, RPG is not a standardized language and so
programs written for one processor may require extensive modification
before they will run on a different make of machine.

### executing coded programs

We have seen how the system command RUN is used in BASIC to cause
a program to be executed. But how are programs in languages such as
FORTRAN and COBOL executed? Thank you for your interest (?). You
may recall from Chapter 2 that one of the functions of an operating
system is to control the loading of programs for processing. A group of
programs awaiting processing may be assembled into a *job stream* by the
computer operator and fed into some input device such as a card reader.
*Job control cards* are used to supply the operating system with such
information as the name of the job, the user's name and account number,
and the language compiler to be used. After the source program has been
compiled, additional job control cards signal the end of the program and
the beginning of the data to be processed by the program (Fig. 11-18).
The codes used on these job control cards differ from one installation to
another.

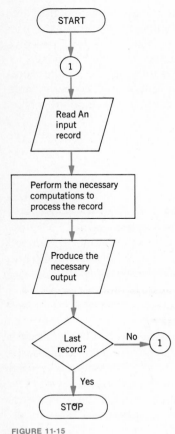

FIGURE 11-15

RPG object program processing
logic.

**IBM**

INTERNATIONAL BUSINESS MACHINES CORPORATION
**REPORT PROGRAM GENERATOR FILE DESCRIPTION SPECIFICATIONS**
IBM System 360

Form X24-3347-3
Printed in U.S.A.

Date 1/26/99

Program ACCOUNTING PENALTY PROCEDURE

Programmer JOHN Q PROGRAMMER

Punching Instruction — Graphic / Punch

Page 01

Program Identification 75 76 77 78 79 80

| Line | Form Type | Filename | File Type | File Designation | End of File | Sequence | File Format | Block Length | Record Length | Mode of Processing | Length of Key Field | Record Address Type | Type of File Organization | Overflow Indicator | Key Field Starting Location | Extension Code | Device | Symbolic Device | Labels | Name of Label Exit | Extent Exit for DAM | No. of Extents | Tape Rewind |
|---|---|---|---|---|---|---|---|---|---|---|---|---|---|---|---|---|---|---|---|---|---|---|
| 0 1 0 | F | CARD | I P | | | | | | | | | | | | | | | | | | | |
| 0 2 0 | F | OUTPUT | O | | | | | | | | | | | | | MFCM1 | | | | | | |
| 0 3 | F | | | | | | | | | | | | | | | PRINTER | | | | | | |
| 0 4 | F | | | | | | | | | | | | | | | | | | | | | |
| 0 5 | F | | | | | | | | | | | | | | | | | | | | | |
| 0 6 | F | | | | | | | | | | | | | | | | | | | | | |
| 0 7 | F | | | | | | | | | | | | | | | | | | | | | |
| 0 8 | F | | | | | | | | | | | | | | | | | | | | | |
| 0 9 | F | | | | | | | | | | | | | | | | | | | | | |

**IBM**

INTERNATIONAL BUSINESS MACHINES CORPORATION
**REPORT PROGRAM GENERATOR    INPUT SPECIFICATIONS**
IBM System/360

Form X24-3350-1 U/M025
Printed in U.S.A.

Date 1/26/99

Program ACCOUNTING PENALTY PROCEDURE

Programmer JOHN Q. PROGRAMMER

Punching Instruction — Graphic / Punch

Page 02

Program Identification 75 76 77 78 79 80

| Line | Form Type | Filename | Sequence | Number (1-N) | Option (O) | Resulting Indicator | Record Identification Codes Position 1 | Not (N) | C/Z/D | Character | Position 2 | Not (N) | C/Z/D | Character | Position 3 | Not (N) | C/Z/D | Character | Stacker Select | Packed (P) | From | To | Decimal Positions | Field Name | Control Level (L1-L9) | Matching Fields or Chaining Fields | Field-Record Relation | Plus | Minus | Zero or Blank | Sterling Sign Position |
|---|---|---|---|---|---|---|---|---|---|---|---|---|---|---|---|---|---|---|---|---|---|---|---|---|---|---|---|---|---|---|---|
| 0 1 0 | I | CARD | A A | | | 0 1 | 2 | N | C | | | | | | | | | | | | | | | | | | | | | | |
| 0 2 0 | I | | | | | | | | | | | | | | | | | | | 1 | 2 0 | | NDAYS | | | | | | | |
| 0 3 0 | I | | | | | | | | | | | | | | | | | | | 3 | 1 0 | 2 | UNBAL | | | | | | | |
| 0 4 0 | I | | | | | | | | | | | | | | | | | | | 1 1 | 2 5 | | NAME | | | | | | | |
| 0 5 | I | | | | | | | | | | | | | | | | | | | | | | | | | | | | | |
| 0 6 | I | | | | | | | | | | | | | | | | | | | | | | | | | | | | | |
| 0 7 | I | | | | | | | | | | | | | | | | | | | | | | | | | | | | | |
| 0 8 | I | | | | | | | | | | | | | | | | | | | | | | | | | | | | | |
| 0 9 | I | | | | | | | | | | | | | | | | | | | | | | | | | | | | | |
| 1 0 | I | | | | | | | | | | | | | | | | | | | | | | | | | | | | | |

FIGURE 11-16

INTERNATIONAL BUSINESS MACHINES CORPORATION

# REPORT PROGRAM GENERATOR  CALCULATION SPECIFICATIONS
## IBM System/360

Date 1/26/99

Program ACCOUNTING PENALTY PROCEDURE

Programmer JOHN Q. PROGRAMMER

Page 03

Program Identification [ ][ ][ ][ ][ ][ ]

| Line | Form Type | Control Level | Indicators And/Not | | | Factor 1 | Operation | Factor 2 | Result Field | Field Length | Decimal Positions | Half Adjust (H) | Plus 1>2 | Minus 1<2 | Zero or Blank 1=2 | Comments |
|------|-----------|---------------|---|---|---|----------|-----------|----------|--------------|--------------|-------------------|-----------------|------|-------|-------|----------|
| 0 1 0 | C | | | | | | SETOF | | | | | | 02 | 03 | 04 | |
| 0 2 0 | C | | | | | | SETOF | | | | | | 05 | | | |
| 0 3 0 | C | | | | | NDAYS | COMP | 30 | | | | | | 02 | | |
| 0 4 0 | C | | | 02 | | | GOTO | COMPUT | | | | | | | | |
| 0 5 0 | C | | | | | UNBAL | COMP | 200. | | | | | 03 | | | |
| 0 6 0 | C | | | 03 | | UNBAL | MULT | 0.03 | PENLTY | 5 | 2 | | | | | |
| 0 7 0 | C | | | 03 | | | GOTO | PNLIZE | | | | | | | | |
| 0 8 0 | C | | | | | UNBAL | MULT | 0.02 | PENLTY | 5 | 2 | | | | | |
| 0 9 0 | C | | | | | PNLIZE | TAG | | | | | | | | | |
| 1 0 0 | C | | | | | UNBAL | ADD | PENLTY | CACCNT | 5 | 2 | | | | | |
| 1 1 0 | C | | | | | | SETON | | | | | | 04 | | | |
| 1 2 0 | C | | | | | NDAYS | COMP | 60 | | | | | 05 | | 05 | |
| 1 3 0 | C | | | | | COMPUT | TAG | | | | | | | | | |
| 1 4 | C | | | | | | | | | | | | | | | |
| 1 5 | C | | | | | | | | | | | | | | | |
| | C | | | | | | | | | | | | | | | |
| | C | | | | | | | | | | | | | | | |
| | C | | | | | | | | | | | | | | | |

**IBM**

INTERNATIONAL BUSINESS MACHINES CORPORATION

# REPORT PROGRAM GENERATOR OUTPUT-FORMAT SPECIFICATIONS
## IBM System/360

Form X24-3352-1 U/M 025
Printed in U.S.A.

Date 1/26/99

Program ACCOUNTING PENALTY PROCEDURE

Programmer JOHN Q. PROGRAMMER

Page 04

Program Identification [ ][ ][ ][ ][ ][ ]

| Line | Form Type | Filename | Type (H/D/T) | Stacker Select | Space Before | Space After | Skip Before | Skip After | Output Indicators And/Not | | | Field Name | Zero Suppress (Z) Blank After (B) | End Position in Output Record | Packed Field (P) | Constant or Edit Word | Sterling Sign Position |
|------|-----------|----------|--------------|----------------|--------------|-------------|-------------|------------|---|---|---|------------|-----------------------------------|-------------------------------|------------------|-----------------------|------------------------|
| 0 1 0 | O | OUTPUT | D | | 2 | | | | 01 | | | | | | | | |
| 0 2 0 | O | | | | | | | | | | | | | 24 | | 'CUSTOMER STATEMENT FOR ' | |
| 0 3 0 | O | | | | | | | | | | | NAME | | 39 | | | |
| 0 4 0 | O | | D | | 3 | | | | 02 | | | | | | | | |
| 0 5 0 | O | | | | | | | | | | | | | 21 | | 'ACCOUNT NOT INCLUDED' | |
| 0 6 0 | O | | D | | 1 | | | | 02 | | | | | | | | |
| 0 7 0 | O | | | | | | | | | | | | | 2 | | ' ' | |
| 0 8 0 | O | | D | | 2 | | | | 04 | | | | | | | | |
| 0 9 0 | O | | | | | | | | | | | | | 19 | | 'BALANCE DUE $ ' | |
| 1 0 0 | O | | | | | | | | | | | CACCNT | | 25 | | ' 0. ' | |
| 1 1 0 | O | | D | | 2 | | | | N05 | N02 | | | | | | | |
| 1 2 0 | O | | | | | | | | | | | | | 2 | | ' ' | |
| 1 3 0 | O | | D | | 3 | | | | 05 | | | | | | | | |
| 1 4 0 | O | | | | | | | | | | | | | 12 | | 'ACCOUNT IS ' | |
| 1 5 0 | O | | | | | | | | | | | NDAYS | Z | 14 | | | |
| 1 6 0 | O | | | | | | | | | | | | | 27 | | ' DAYS OVERDUE' | |
| 1 7 0 | O | | D | | 1 | | | | 05 | | | | | | | | |
| 1 8 0 | O | | | | | | | | | | | | | 2 | | ' ' | |
| | O | | | | | | | | | | | | | | | | |
| | O | | | | | | | | | | | | | | | | |

Card Electro Number _____

```
CUSTOMER STATEMENT FOR JOHN SMITH
ACCOUNT NOT INCLUDED


CUSTOMER STATEMENT FOR A.V. STUDENT
BALANCE DUE       $ 204.00


CUSTOMER STATEMENT FOR RANDY JOHNSON
BALANCE DUE       $ 257.50
ACCOUNT IS 65 DAYS OVERDUE


CUSTOMER STATEMENT FOR BEVERLY BIVENS
BALANCE DUE       $ 309.00


CUSTOMER STATEMENT FOR ALEXANDRE DUMAS
BALANCE DUE       $ 360.50
ACCOUNT IS 60 DAYS OVERDUE
```

FIGURE 11-17

**SUMMARY**    Although computers vary with respect to the number of commands that they can execute, they are all similar in the sense that their instruction sets can be classified into (1) I/O, (2) data movement/manipulation, (3) arithmetic, and (4) logic and transfer of control categories. All computers are also similar in that they must ultimately receive their instructions in a machine language form. Early programmers had to code instructions laboriously into this machine language.

To ease the programmer's burden, mnemonic operation codes and symbolic addresses were developed in the early 1950s. The development of machine-oriented symbolic languages led to further programming improvement, first in the form of macro instructions and then in the form of high-level languages. Most computers will now accept programs written in a number of languages.

A number of program preparation aids and techniques have also been developed to assist programmers in the initial preparation of applications programs. A listing of some of the aids that have improved programming performance is presented in the chapter. In addition, several techniques for organizing programmers (e.g., chief programmer teams) and for constructing programs (e.g., the use of modular program design and basic coding structures) have been discussed. Techniques that may be used to permit existing programs to run on new equipment without the need for initial reprogramming have also been presented.

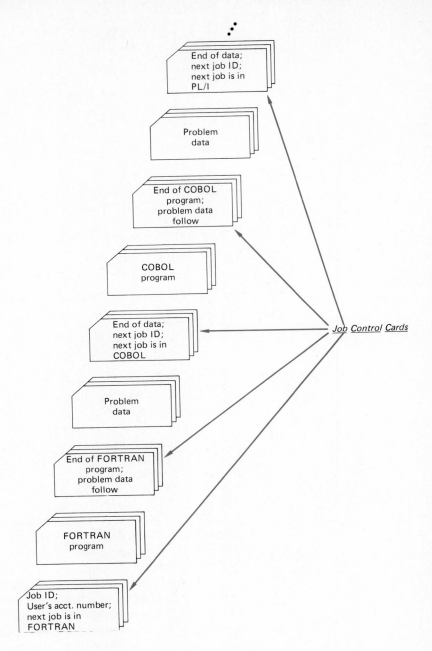

FIGURE 11-18

Job control cards in a job stream.

Many high-level languages are directed toward either scientific or commercial problems. Some languages, e.g., PL/I, are used with both types of applications. The selection of a language, like the selection of hardware, is a complex task. Among the most popular high-level languages are FORTRAN, COBOL, PL/I, BASIC, and RPG. A brief overview of these languages has been presented in this chapter to acquaint you with the general structure of each and to introduce you to some of their characteristics. Each language has strengths and weaknesses.

**REVIEW AND DISCUSSION QUESTIONS**

1   Identify the steps in the programming process.

2   "Every computer instruction has an explicit predicate consisting of at least two parts." Identify and explain these two parts.

3   Compare the command structures of single-, two-, and three-address machines.

4   What types of instructions are found in a computer's repertoire?

5   What are the differences among machine, symbolic, and high-level languages?

6   (a) What is an assembly program? (b) What is a source program?   (c) What is an object program? (d) Explain the relationship among these three programs.

7   Discuss the factors to consider in language selection.

8   Identify and discuss the aids that have improved programming performance in the initial preparation of applications.

9   (a) Identify and discuss the approaches that may be used to organize the programmers that are assigned to a particular development project. (b) What are the strengths and weaknesses of each organizing approach?

10   "Several program construction techniques have received a lot of attention in recent years." (a) What are the objectives of these techniques? (b) What techniques are currently being used in an attempt to achieve these goals?

11   (a) What is the modular program design approach to program construction? (b) What are the advantages of this approach? (c) How can chief programmer teams make use of this approach?

12   (a) Identify the three basic coding structures that can be used to prepare any program. (b) What might be the advantage of using only these basic structures in coding?

13   (a) What is a structured walkthrough? (b) What are the possible advantages of this technique? (c) How is "egoless programming" enhanced by the use of this technique?

14   "Combining program construction and programmer organizing techniques into a disciplined structured programming environment can lead to improvements in programming efficiency and in software quality." Discuss this comment.

**15** What techniques may be used to permit existing programs to run on new equipment without the need for initial reprogramming?

**16** Differentiate between emulation and simulation.

**17** (**a**) What is FORTRAN? (**b**) For what type of problems was FORTRAN designed?

**18** (**a**) What is COBOL? (**b**) How did it originate? (**c**) For what purpose was COBOL designed?

**19** (**a** What is PL/I? (**b**) How did it originate? (**c**) Why is it suitable for use in a structured programming environment?

**20** (**a**) What is BASIC? (**b**) Where did it originate? (**c**) For what purpose was BASIC designed?

**21** (**a**) What is RPG? (**b**) For what is it used?

**22** (**a**) What are job control cards? (**b**) How are they used?

**SELECTED REFERENCES** In addition to the references suggested in the chapter footnotes, you might also be interested in the following sources:

Canning, Richard G.: "The Search for Software Reliability," *EDP Analyzer,* May 1974, pp. 1–13.

Casey, William: "Hard Facts about Software Transferability," *Government Data Systems,* May-June 1977, pp. 44–45.

Chapin, Ned, Roger House, Ned McDaniel, and Robert Wachtel: "Structured Programming Simplified," *Computer Decisions,* June 1974, pp. 28–31.

Paretta, Robert L., and Stephen A. Clark: "Management of Software Development," *Journal of Systems Management,* April 1976, pp. 21–27.

Structured programming topics—see the December 1973 issue of *Datamation* for a number of articles on this subject.

Weinberg, Gerald M.: "The Psychology of Improved Programming Performance," *Datamation,* November 1972, pp. 82–85.

# system/ program implementation

# 12

**LEARNING OBJECTIVES**    After studying this chapter and answering the discussion questions, you should be able to: ☐ Identify some earlier decisions that may reduce the time and effort required to implement a system ☐ Outline the purpose of, and some of the techniques used during, the debugging and testing period ☐ Discuss some of the actions to be taken during a system conversion and changeover ☐ Identify information that should be included in a program documentation package ☐ Point out some of the topics that will have to be taken into account in implementing new computing hardware ☐ Think of some questions that should be answered during a follow-up audit of an implemented system or program

For the last few chapters, we have been following several steps or stages in the *system development/programming life cycle*. Assuming that (1) the problem has been analyzed (Chapter 8), (2) a feasible system or application solution has been designed (Chapter 9), (3) the system specifications have been analyzed and broken down into the detailed arithmetic and logic operations required to solve the problem (Chapter 10), and (4) the written instructions that will control the computer during processing have been coded in a source program form (Chapter 11), the final steps remaining in the life cycle dealing with the *implementation* of programs and systems may now be considered. Of course, you should realize that *the steps in this life cycle do not necessarily follow a rigid chronological order*. Questions arising during programming analysis may make it necessary for the study team to gather additional facts and redesign the problem solution; and, as you may have noticed in Fig. 11-1, an unsuccessful program test may send the programmer back to the coding sheets. In short, many of the steps that we have rather arbitrarily assigned to this chapter may have been performed concurrently with earlier phases of the system development/programming process. Certainly, for example, the program debugging, testing, and documentation of some parts of a new system may be occurring simultaneously with the coding of other parts of the same system.

It is often a hectic time for those who are installing a new application or system (and for those awaiting the results!) even when existing hardware is available to handle the job(s). But when new hardware must be acquired to implement the system, the number of details that must be considered is magnified. In later sections we shall discuss the *debugging, testing, conversion, documentation, maintenance,* and *follow-up* activities needed to properly install any new application. Brief comments are also made about some of the details that cannot be overlooked if a *new*

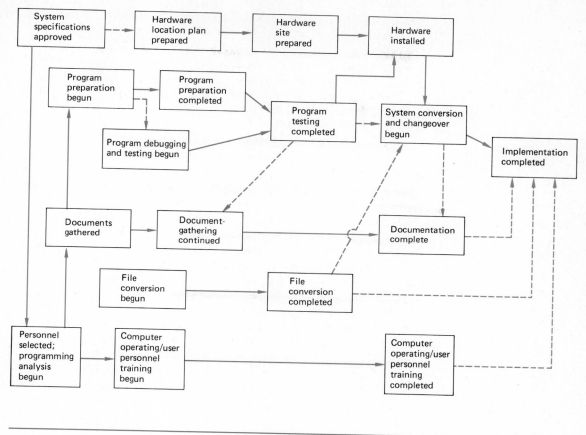

Time—in months (years?)

------→ Necessary sequence not involving time usage.

FIGURE 12-1

Implementation considerations.

computer system is needed. Figure 12-1 summarizes implementation activities and shows the overlapping nature of many of these tasks.

**EARLIER DECISIONS AFFECTING IMPLEMENTATION EFFORTS**   Many of the actions that may have been taken by thoughtful system analysts and programmers during the system design and initial program preparation stages may now pay dividends by reducing the time and effort required to implement the system. Some of these preinstallation decisions that may now prove beneficial are

1   *Decision to follow standard rules and procedures.* The job of testing and maintaining systems and programs is much easier if coding proce-

dures are consistently applied, if data items are consistently defined, and if documentation rules are consistently followed.

2   *Decision to use modular program design.* We saw in the last chapter that modular design could be used to divide complex programs into simpler and more manageable elements so that (a) errors could be more easily traced, (b) program debugging, testing, and maintenance could thus be simplified, and (c) tested and proven subroutine modules could be easily inserted as needed.

3   *Decision to use tested applications packages.* Buying proven software, when appropriate, may make it possible to bypass many implementation problems.

4   *Decision to call on user groups and/or software consultants for assistance.* The advice of others who have worked on similar problems can obviously be helpful during implementation.

5   *Decision to use basic coding structures.* Programs constructed with the three basic coding patterns discussed in the last chapter may be easier to understand, and this can lead to programs that are easier to test and maintain.

6   *Decision to use structured walkthroughs.* We have seen that fewer errors, faster testing and conversion, better documentation, and easier maintenance are some of the benefits that may result when structured walkthroughs are conducted during program preparation.

7   *Decision to put top priority on satisfying user needs.* The best standards and modular design approach; the most effective use of packaged programs, basic coding structures, structured walkthroughs, etc.; and the most judicious use of user groups and consultants to solve problems are of little value if the solutions do not satisfy the needs of the end-users of the processed information. It will be very expensive if it is discovered during the implementation stage that the efficient programs that have been coded or acquired have to be completely revised. Although these may seem to you to be obvious points, they have sometimes been overlooked in practice!

## PROGRAM DEBUGGING AND TESTING

A COBOL programmer named Mays
Had careless programming ways.
By a slip of the hand he wrote an "or" for an "and."
Now his program has run for 3 days!

W. I. Jordan

Clerical mistakes, and errors caused by faulty logic, are inelegantly referred to as *bugs*. Eliminating these mistakes and errors that prevent the program from running and producing correct results is appropriately called *debugging*.

**debugging**

> It is a tale
> Told by an idiot, full of sound and fury,
> Signifying nothing.
>
> William Shakespeare
> (A possible description of the first attempt to run a program.)

There are days when things never seem to go quite right. Such days may be more common for programmers than for other mortals because program bugs (or "glitches") just seem to occur even under the best of circumstances and even when matters are not being helped along by our natural human tendency to screw things up. [Of course, Murphy's laws—which state, among other things, that (1) anything that can go wrong will go wrong, (2) when left to themselves, things will always go from bad to worse, and (3) if there is the possibility that several things can go wrong, the one that will go wrong is the one that will do the most damage—may account for the distressing frequency with which bugs appear.]

It is unusual for complex programs to run to completion in the first attempt. In fact, the time spent in debugging and testing often equals or exceeds the time spent in program coding.[1] Failure to provide for a possible program path, or branch, keypunching errors, mistakes in coding punctuation, incorrect operation codes, transposed characters—these are but a few of the bugs that can thwart the programmer.

To reduce the number of clerical and logical errors, the programmer should carefully check the coding sheets before they are turned over to the keypunch operator. When structured walkthroughs and/or egoless programming teams are used, the review of the code at this time by a programmer's colleagues can be very helpful in spotting errors that the programmer has overlooked. This *desk-checking* process should include an examination of program logic and program completeness; furthermore, typical input data should be manually traced through the program processing paths to identify possible errors. In short, the programmer (and, perhaps, the programmer's peers) attempts to play the role of the computer.

After program cards are punched and again desk-checked for accuracy, an attempt is made to assemble or compile the source program into object program form. Assembly and compiler programs contain error diagnostic features, which detect (and print messages about) mistakes caused by the incorrect application of the programming language used to

---

[1] See Frederick P. Brooks, Jr., "The Mythical Man-Month," *Datamation*, December 1974, pp. 45–52. Professor Brooks estimates that *half* the total time of a programming project is likely to be spent in debugging and testing.

prepare the source program (e.g., undefined symbols and incorrect operation codes). These detected *syntax errors,* of course, must be remedied by the programmer. But compiler or assembly diagnostic checks will not detect the presence of *logical errors* in the program. Thus, an error-free pass of the program through the assembly or compiler run *does not* mean that the program is perfected or that all bugs have been eliminated. It usually does mean, however, that the program is ready for testing.

**testing**

> All real programs contain errors until proved
> otherwise—which is impossible.
>
> Tom Gilb

A program to be tested has generally demonstrated that it will run and produce results. The purpose of *testing* is to determine if the results are correct. The testing procedure involves using the program to process input test data that will produce known results. Since users are the ones who receive and utilize the output results, they should participate in developing the data that will be processed during testing. Auditors should also be active participants during the testing phase to ensure that the controls that have been built into the program are operating effectively. The items developed for testing should include (1) typical data, which will test the generally used program paths; (2) unusual but valid data which will test the program paths used to handle exceptions; and (3) incorrect, incomplete, or inappropriate data, which will test the program error-handling capabilities. Both hypothetical data and actual data supplied by users, auditors, and programmers may be processed during these tests.[2]

*If the program passes the tests* and is accepted by users, it will be released for implementation. It should be noted here, however, that bugs may still remain undetected. In complex programs there may be tens of thousands of different possible paths through the program. It simply is not practical (and maybe not even possible) to trace through all the different paths during testing. For example, the flowchart in Fig. 12-2 looks rather simple, but the number of different possible paths is an astounding $10^{20}$.

---

[2] This does not mean, of course, that an untested program should be given access to current real files. Rather, the actual input data could be a duplicate set of facts that have already been used to update real files. Actual transactions should be combined with hypothetical data, however, because the probability is high that unusual but valid data would not be included in the actual transactions. For more details on the testing function, see Laura L. Scharer, "Improving System Testing Techniques," *Datamation,* September 1977, pp. 115ff. See also The Diebold Group, Inc., *Automatic Data Processing Handbook,* McGraw-Hill Book Company, New York, 1977, pp. 3–168 to 3–185.

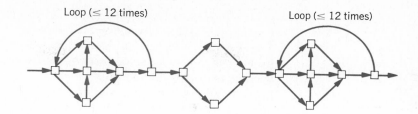

FIGURE 12-2

(Adapted from B. W. Boehm, "Software and Its Impact: A Quantative Assessment," *Datamation*, May, 1973, p. 58).

As Dr. Barry Boehm has observed, if we could somehow check out one path per nanosecond, and if we had started our testing in the year 1, we would only be about half done at the present time! This example explains why programs may suddenly produce nonsense months after they have been released for production use. Some unique and unanticipated series of events has produced input or circumstances that turn up a bug for the first time. The error was always there; it simply remained undetected. Very complex systems are considered to be *undebuggable* by professional programmers.

*If the program does not pass the test,* the programmer may do the following:

**1**   Trace through the program, a step at a time, at the computer console. Errors may be discovered by noting register contents after each program operation. Such an approach may be permissible with microcomputers and with a few minicomputer and small business systems, but it is hardly appropriate to tie up an expensive large computer for such purposes.

**2**   Call for a *trace program* run. The trace program prints out the status of registers after each operation and thus is comparable with console checking. However, less machine time is required.

**3**   Call for a *storage dump* when the program "hangs up" during a test run, i.e., obtain a printout of the contents of primary storage and registers at the time of the hangup. The programmer can then study this listing for possible clues to the cause of the programming error(s).

## SYSTEM CONVERSION AND CHANGEOVER

After the program(s) appears to be running properly and producing correct results, the system conversion and changeover may begin. This conversion period is almost always a period of personnel and organizational strain. Data processing employees may work long hours and be subjected to pressure to complete the conversion. Unforeseen problems, last-minute corrections, and the disruption of data processing services to using departments, customers, suppliers, etc., may contribute to these pressures. It is at this time that cooperation is badly needed between data processing specialists and personnel of affected departments. Yet it is precisely at this time that cooperation frequently breaks down because of managerial preoccupation with technical conversion matters at the expense of proper personnel preparation.

Everyone who will be affected by the new program(s) or system should have been receiving some training prior to the conversion period to become familiar with the nature of the expected changes. This training is likely to become more intense during the conversion period, however, as new procedures are phased into operation, as old forms are replaced by new ones, as old input devices are retired in favor of new hardware, and as last-minute changes are made in manual methods and personnel assignments.

During system conversion, current files must be changed into a form acceptable to the processor. This can be a tremendous task, and it is one that is often underestimated. Files should be consolidated and duplicate records eliminated; errors in current files must be detected and removed; and file inconsistencies must be found *before* the changeover rather than later when they can cause system malfunctions.

There is frequently a transitional changeover or shakedown period during which applications are processed by both currently used and new procedures as a final check before the cutover to the new system occurs. A *parallel running conversion* involves the processing of *current* input data by old and new methods. If a significant difference appears, the cause must be located. Various *pilot testing* approaches may also be used during conversion. For example, input data for a *previous* month's operations may be processed using new methods, and the results may be compared with the results obtained from existing operations. If new hardware is being acquired to implement the new system, preliminary pilot tests can be run on the vendor's equipment prior to delivery of the user's hardware. Thus, debugging and testing may be facilitated through the use of actual input data, and it may be possible to reduce the time (and costs) associated with maintaining two different systems at a later date. Also, a pilot conversion approach is often used when a system is to be installed in a number of different locations over a period of time. One location—say, a regional warehouse— may be selected for the initial conversion effort. Once the start-up problems have been solved and the system has been proven under actual operating conditions, the organization can then convert other regional warehouses to the new procedures. A full-scale conversion of all warehouses at the same time would, of course, run a higher risk of failure.

Regardless of the conversion approach, final changeover to computer production runs comes from satisfactory performance during this shakedown period.

## DOCUMENTATION AND MAINTENANCE

Consider that two wrongs never make a right but that three do. Whenever possible, put people on hold. Be comforted that in the face of all the aridity

and disillusionment and despite the changing
fortunes of time, there is always a big fortune in
computer maintenance

*Anonymous in* Deteriorata

Documentation, as we have seen, is the process of collecting, organizing, storing, and otherwise maintaining on paper (or on some relatively permanent medium) a complete record of *why* applications were developed, *what* functions they perform, *how* these functions are carried out, *who* the applications are to serve, and *how* they are to be used. In other words, documentation should be available to give users, system analysts/designers, programmers, computer operators, and auditors a clear understanding of all aspects of an application or system.

*The documentation package for each applications program should include:*

1   *A definition of the problem.* Why was the program prepared? What were the objectives? Who requested the program and who approved it? Questions such as these should be answered.

2   *A description of the system.* The system or subsystem environment in which the program functions should be described; system flowcharts should be included. Broad system specifications outlining the scope of the problem, the form and type of input data to be used, the form and type of records and files to be processed, the form and type of output required, and the audit trails and other controls to be followed should be clearly stated. A *user's manual* should be prepared.

3   *A description of the program.* Program flowcharts, decision tables, program listings, test decks and test results, storage dumps, trace program printouts—these and other documents that describe the program and give an historical record of difficulties and/or changes should be available to allow accurate and efficient maintenance and modification operations to take place after conversion. Program change request forms should be prepared and filled out when any subsequent changes are made.

4   *A recitation of operating instructions.* Among the items covered should be instructions on the preparation of input data, computer switch settings, loading and unloading procedures, and starting, running, and terminating procedures. Restart and recovery methods to follow after production difficulties have been encountered should be spelled out. And procedures to ensure the adequate backup, retention, and control of sensitive programs and data should also be listed.

5   *A description of program controls.* Controls may be incorporated in a program in a number of ways. For example, programmed controls may be used to check on the reasonableness and propriety of input data. A description of such controls should be a part of the documentation.

If schedules begin to slip during program preparation and debugging (and they often do), there is often a tendency on the part of data processing specialists to slight the documentation activity. But time made up at the expense of good documentation is likely to be a very temporary gain; it will be lost at high cost in a later period when programs must be tested and when program corrections and changes must be made.

Realizing this fact, some organizations have found that it is to their advantage to support documentation preparation activities by acquiring package software aids that make use of the computer to produce necessary documentation elements. System and program analyzer packages, for example, will accept an applications program as input and will then produce an overview of the entire application including both graphic (flowchart) and cross-referenced information.[3] And IBM has produced a package called HIPODRAW that uses a number of input statements to produce an output HIPO documentation package consisting of a series of charts and supporting text.

Production-run programs are continually being *maintained,* modified, and improved. Sometimes the object program can be patched to include small modifications so that a compiling run is not necessary. (A danger of this approach, however, is that the small changes may not be incorporated in the supporting documents.) Program maintenance is an important duty of programmers and may involve all steps from problem definition through analysis, design, and program preparation. It is not unusual to find programmers spending the bulk of their time on this activity. In some installations there are programmers who do nothing but maintain production programs.

When an organization first acquires a computer (and usually for several years thereafter), much of the programming effort goes into the development of new applications and systems. But as the number of installed programs and systems in the organization grows, it is not unusual to find that more programming time is being spent on maintenance than on development work.[4] And it has been estimated that over the life cycle of a typical system, the maintenance and enhancement costs that are incurred may be 2 to 4 times larger than the initial development costs (see Fig. 12-3).[5]

**EQUIPMENT IMPLEMENTATION CONSIDERATIONS**

It is sometimes necessary to acquire new hardware or to upgrade existing equipment in order to implement a new system. If only a few new I/O devices are needed, or if it is only necessary to plug in one or two

[3] For more details on such packages, and for further information about available packaged products, see Richard A. Moore, Jr., Benjamin F. Rose III, and Thomas J. Koger, "Computer-generated Documentation," *The Journal of Accountancy,* June 1975, pp. 82–90.

[4] Two consultants with Booz, Allen & Hamilton, Inc., have reported that in their dealings with clients they have observed that "over the past five years, the ratio of overall maintenance to development work has flip-flopped from about 40 percent to 60 percent to about 60 percent to 40 percent." See G. H. Hoxie and D. M. Shea, "Ten Hot Buttons Facing Management," *Infosystems,* September 1977, p. 100.

[5] See Douglas T. Ross, "Homilies for Humble Standards," *Communications of the ACM,* November 1976, p. 599.

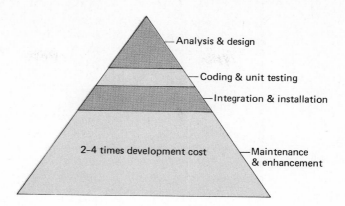

FIGURE 12-3

System life-cycle cost pyramid.

additional storage units, then little time or effort may be required for the equipment changeover. If, on the other hand, a completely new computer system will be needed, then a great deal of planning may be necessary in preparing a suitable site to receive the new installation.[6] Of course, the cost of site preparation can range from a very modest figure for a minicomputer to hundreds of thousands of dollars for a large system. *Some of the factors that must be considered during site planning and preparation are:*

1   *Location.* From an economic standpoint, the computer location should probably be chosen for its accessibility to those company departments that will be closely associated with computer operations. Consideration must also be given to the *physical security* of the hardware/software in determining the proper location. Other factors, such as soundproofing and the structure's ability to support the weight of the hardware, must also be taken into account.

2   *Space and layout.* The physical dimensions of the equipment to be housed; the location and length of power and connecting cables; the space needed to allow service access to this hardware; the data movement patterns; the storage room needed for input/output media, supplies, spare parts, and maintenance equipment; and the number and size of work areas, offices, and conference rooms—all these factors must be considered in determining the space requirements and the layout of the site. Future expansion needs should also be taken into account.

3   *Air conditioning.* Air conditioning is needed for employee productivity and for dust, temperature, and humidity control.

4   *Power and lighting.* Hardware electrical requirements must be met. If rewiring is called for (and it is usually needed), the job should be done by

---

[6] Vendors are of considerable help in site preparation. They have had extensive experience in this matter, and in this case their interests and the interests of the customer are usually the same. Both are interested in efficiency, safety, ease of maintenance, and attractiveness. Vendor engineers, of course, install the hardware and make the necessary tests to be sure it is operating properly before it is turned over to the user.

qualified electricians in accordance with building codes and fire insurance rules. Adequate illumination of the site is a detail which should not be overlooked. Since the power supplied to a computer site from an electric utility company is subject to a number of common faults that can cause computer problems (e.g., a "spike" or sudden surge of voltage of very brief duration, a momentary interruption or dip in voltage lasting a few microseconds, and/or a blackout or brownout lasting minutes or hours); since enough of these power faults have occurred to teach data processing managers that power can no longer be taken for granted; and since computer systems may employ volatile semiconductor storage devices that may be erased when a power failure occurs, some organizations have installed *uninterruptible power supplies* (UPS) to eliminate these power-related problems. A UPS is installed between the utility company power source and the computer (Fig. 12-4). Under normal operation, alternating current (ac) is fed from the utility line through a rectifier/charger system where the ac current is changed into direct current (dc). Part of this dc power may be used to keep a full charge on the UPS battery power system, while the rest is fed through an inverter where it is converted back into ac, filtered, and supplied to the computer system. Should there be a momentary or longer loss of utility power, the battery system would automatically cut in to provide the needed power. If the UPS system should be down for maintenance or for some other reason, a static switch would be tripped to supply utility power directly to the computer through a bypass line.

5   *Cable protection.* Numerous cables interconnect hardware units and supply electric power. Yet attractive sites have no distasteful cables lying around on the floor to impair safety. The usual practice is to install a raised or false floor and then run the cables beneath this floor.

6   *Fire protection.* Since much of the data stored on cards and tapes may be irreplaceable, fireproof materials should be used wherever possible in the site preparation. Hardware and media fire insurance protection is available. A fireproof vault to store vital records, programs, etc., might be

"Don't just stand there gawking . . . Sharpen pencils!"

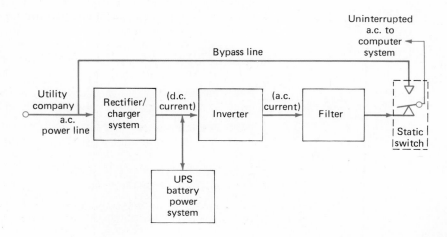

FIGURE 12-4
UPS operation.

a wise investment. Adequate fire, heat, and smoke detectors should be installed, emergency power cutoffs should be provided, and fire prevention systems using Halon gas, $CO_2$, and water sprinklers should be placed in appropriate areas.

**OPERATIONAL CONSIDERATIONS**

It was noted earlier that personnel and organizational strain is likely to be experienced during the system/program conversion period. A number of changes are usually taking place during this period that involve technical, economic, and scheduling considerations. But, although it may be understandable that managers and specialists tend to be preoccupied with these pressing matters in the short run, in the long run the success of the new system or program depends on how well it is accepted by the people in the organization.

It is therefore necessary during all phases of the system development effort (and especially during the conversion period) that the human needs of users and other affected personnel be given careful attention. Changes in information systems can bring about changes in compatible work groups, changes in job duties, and even changes in employment status. Unless careful plans are made to minimize employee resistance to such changes, the new system or program may be doomed to ultimate failure regardless of its technical and economic strengths.

Since the impact of computer-based information systems on organizational structure and on people is too important to be dismissed here with a few sentences, we will consider these topics in more detail in the next few chapters.

**FOLLOW-UP ON SYSTEM DECISIONS**

Once the system has been implemented and is in operation, a thorough appraisal or audit should be made. This follow-up is commonly conducted by internal auditors and others who have an independent viewpoint and are not responsible for the development and maintenance of the system. *Some of the questions that should be considered in the audit are:*

1  How useful is the system to decision makers? How enthusiastic are they about the service they receive? Do they receive reports in time to take action?

2  Are planned processing procedures being followed? Are all new procedures being processed on the computer? Have old procedures been eliminated? If not, why not?

3  Are responsibilities of data processing personnel defined and understood? Are training programs of acceptable quality?

4  Have adequate debugging and testing procedures been established?

5  Are system controls being observed? Is documentation complete? Have procedures to control program changes been established? Are these

control procedures being enforced? Are any modifications or refinements indicated as a result of operating experience? If so, are they being made? How are they being controlled?

6   How do operating results compare with original goals and expectations? Are economic benefits being obtained? If variations exist, what is the cause? What can be done to achieve expected results.

**SUMMARY**   Among the earlier decisions that may reduce the time and effort required to implement a problem solution are those to (1) follow standard rules and procedures, (2) use modular program design, (3) use tested applications packages, (4) call on user groups and/or software consultants for assistance, (5) use basic coding structures, (6) use structured walk-throughs, and (7) put top priority on user needs. But in spite of these decisions, it is still often a hectic and frustrating time for those who are implementing a new computer application or system.

A major cause of slippage in the implementation schedule is the clerical mistakes and logical errrors that crop up in coded programs. Of course, a program must be debugged as much as possible and tested before it can be used. These activities often take as much time as is required to perform the initial coding; sometimes they can take much longer. After programs appear to be running properly, the system conversion and changeover begins. Parallel running or pilot testing approaches are often used in the final check before the cutover to the new system occurs. The implementation phase cannot be considered complete, however, until the total documentation package is put in good order. Later maintenance of production-run programs will depend heavily on this package. Implementing programs and systems may also require changes in hardware, and, once the problem solution has been implemented, a follow-up audit should be made.

**REVIEW AND DISCUSSION
QUESTIONS**

1   What decisions may be made by system analysts and programmers during the system/program design and initial program preparation stages that may reduce the time and effort required to implement the system/ program?

2   "The steps in the system/program development cycle do not necessarily follow a rigid chronological order." Discuss this statement.

3   (a) What is the purpose of the debugging stage? (b) What techniques may be employed during debugging?

4   What steps can be taken during program testing to locate and remove errors?

5   What information should be included in a program documentation package?

6   "Very complex systems are considered to be undebuggable by professional programmers." Discuss this statement.

7   Why is the system conversion and changeover period likely to result in personnel and organizational strain?

8   What factors should be considered during computer site preparation?

9   What questions should be considered during a follow-up audit of an implemented system?

10   Why would an organization want to install a UPS?

**SELECTED REFERENCES**

Canning, Richard G.: "The Internal Auditor and the Computer," *EDP Analyzer,* March 1975, pp. 1–13.

Fitzpatrick, Richard C.: "Making Documentation Painless," *Datamation,* August 1977, pp. 62–64ff.

Jinks, Daniel W.: "System Documentation," *Journal of Systems Management,* June 1977, pp. 24–33.

Kelley, Neil D.: "Living with Power Failures," *Infosystems,* September 1977, pp. 36ff.

Liu, Chester C.: "A Look at Software Maintenance," *Datamation,* November 1976, pp. 51–55.

Moore, Richard A., Jr., Benjamin F. Rose III, and Thomas J. Koger: "Computer-generated Documentation," *The Journal of Accountancy,* June 1975, pp. 82–90.

Morgan, D. E., and D. J. Taylor: A Survey of Methods of Achieving Reliable Software," *Computer,* February 1977, pp. 44–51.

Scharer, Laura L.: "Improving System Testing Techniques," *Datamation,* September 1977, pp. 115ff.

The three principal goals of this book were identified in Chapter 1. Two of these three goals have now been discussed in the preceding chapters. In the remaining pages of this book we shall concentrate on the third goal, which is to give you an insight into the broad impact that computers have had, are having, and may be expected to have on managers, on the environment in which managers and employees work, and on the society in which we live.

In Chapters 13 and 14, the emphasis is placed on examining some of the effects which computer usage may have had on the managerial functions of planning, organizing, staffing, and controlling. Chapter 15 then looks at some of the broader social implications of the business use of computers. Finally, Chapter 16 deals with the factors that must be considered in managing the computer facility in an organization.

The chapters included in Part IV are:

# IV

# COMPUTER IMPLICATIONS FOR MANAGEMENT

# the computer's impact on planning and organizational structure

## 13

LEARNING OBJECTIVES    After studying this chapter and answering the discussion questions, you should be able to: ☐ Identify and explain the basic activities performed by managers ☐ Discuss the use and impact of computer information systems in business planning and decision making ☐ Outline why computer usage will support both centralization and decentralization of authority ☐ Summarize the advantages of both the centralized and the decentralized approaches to the processing of data and to the storage of data ☐ Point out some of the factors to be considered in determining the organizational location of computing resources

A number of changes have occurred in recent years in the structure, policies, and operations of many organizations as a direct result of their use of computers. The purpose of this chapter and the one that follows is to show you some of the ways in which computer systems have affected the activities performed by managers. After briefly *reviewing these activities* at the beginning of this chapter, we shall then outline some of the effects of computer usage on the *planning and decision-making* and *organizing* activities *within* an organization. In the next chapter, we shall examine the implications of computer systems for the *staffing* and *controlling* activities *within* a company. Then, in Chapter 15, we will consider some of the important *external* or *social* issues that have emerged, in part, as a result of the increased use of business computer systems. Finally, in Chapter 16, we conclude this Part of the text by looking at the planning, organizing, staffing, and controlling activities that must be carried out in order to *manage the computing resources* in the organization.

**MANAGERIAL ACTIVITIES**   As we saw in Chapter 1, *planning, organizing, staffing,* and *controlling* are important activities because the successful achievement of organizational goals depends on how well they are performed. All managers must engage in these activities although, of course, the goals pursued vary according to the particular manager's mission.

### planning

The *planning* activity looks to the future; to plan is to decide in advance on a future course of action. Thus, *planning* involves making decisions with regard to (1) the selection of both short- and long-run strategies and goals, (2) the development of policies and procedures that will help accomplish objectives or counter threats, (3) the establishment of operating standards that serve as the basis for control, and (4) the revision of earlier plans in the light of changing conditions. *The steps followed in planning and in arriving at rational decisions* are about the same as those followed in conducting a system study—i.e., the steps are

1   *Identifying the problem or opportunity.* Meaningful planning may begin when a manager understands and has correctly defined the problem or opportunity that he or she faces. Information is needed to bring about awareness.

2   *Gathering and analyzing relevant facts.* To plan and make decisions, managers must have information that possesses the desirable characteristics outlined in Chapter 1. As Sherlock Holmes noted in *The Adventure of the Copper Beeches:* "Data! Data! Data!" [Holmes] cried impatiently. "I can't make bricks without clay."

3   *Determining suitable alternatives.* The manager must seek out the most attractive possible courses of action. The appropriateness of the options selected is determined by the manager's skill and the quality of the available information.

4   *Evaluating and selecting the most appropriate alternative.* The manager must weigh the options in light of established goals and then arrive at the plan or decision that best meets the needs. Again, the correctness of this choice depends upon managerial skill and information quality.

5   *Following up on the decision(s).* Broad plans may require supporting supplementary plans.

### organizing

The *organizing* function involves the grouping of work teams into logical and efficient units in order to carry out plans and achieve goals. In a manufacturing company, for example, employees may be grouped by *type of work* (production, marketing), by *geographic area* (district sales offices), and by *product line* produced or sold. Managers at each organizational level receive formal authority to assign goal-directed tasks; they then must motivate and coordinate employee efforts if goals are to be achieved. The formal organizational (or authority) structure clarifies the formal lines of authority and the assigned role of a work group in the overall structure.

### staffing

Although one aspect of the *staffing* function consists of selecting people to fill the positions that exist in the organizational structure of the business, the staffing activity also includes (1) training employees to meet initial or changing job requirements, (2) preparing employees for changing conditions, and (3) reassigning or removing employees if such action is required.

### controlling

Unlike planning, which looks to the future, the *control* function looks at the past and the present. It is a follow-up to planning; it is the check on past and current performance to see if planned goals are being achieved. *The steps in the control function are*

1   *Setting standards.* Proper control requires that predetermined goals be established by planners. These standards may be expressed in *physical terms* (e.g., units produced, quantities sold, or machined tolerances permitted) or in *monetary terms* (e.g., operating-cost budgets or sales-revenue quotas). The setting of realistic standards requires quality information.

2   *Measuring actual performance.* Timely and accurate performance information is essential to control.

3   *Comparing actual performance with standards.* Comparison information is action oriented. Computers can provide this information to managers on an *exception basis only* when performance variations are outside certain specified limits.

4   *Taking appropriate control action.* If performance is *under control,* the manager's decision may be to do nothing. However, if actual performance is not up to the standard, it may be because the standard is unrealistic. Therefore, replanning may be necessary to revise the standard. Unfavorable performance may have to be corrected by reorganizing work groups or adding more employees. Thus, the control actions taken may require further planning, organizing, and staffing activities. If outstanding performance is noted, the appropriate action may be to reward the individuals or groups responsible.

The *order* of the activities presented here is a logical one, and we shall use this order to present material in the following pages. In practice, however, managers carry out these activities simultaneously, and it is unrealistic to insist on a particular sequence in all situations.

**PLANNING, DECISION MAKING, AND COMPUTER USAGE**

We can look at this broad topic from at least two viewpoints. *First,* we can examine the implications of *planning with computers,* and second, we can consider some computer-oriented *decision-making techniques* that are now being used.

### planning with computers

As businesses have expanded in recent years within this country and across national borders; as separate firms have merged in order to expand markets and product lines; as the complexity of operations of such firms has increased; and as governments have increased the reporting requirements of organizations to include such things as occupational safety and health programs, affirmative action programs, and pension plans, the need for better planning tools and techniques has become critical. Gener-

©CREATIVE COMPUTING

"About our prospects for that merger, it says: 'you have a snowball's chance in . . . .' "

ally speaking, *the use of computers can have an impact on planning
activities by*

1   *Causing faster awareness of problems and opportunities.* Computers
can quickly signal out-of-control conditions requiring corrective action
when actual performance deviates from what was planned. Masses of
current and historical internal and external data can be analyzed by the
use of statistical methods, including trend analyses and correlation techniques, in order to detect opportunities and challenges. Planning data
stored online may permit managers to probe and query files and receive
quick replies to their questions (see Fig. 5-16, page 147).

2   *Enabling managers to devote more time to planning.* Use of the
computer can free the manager of clerical data-gathering tasks so that
more attention may be given to analytical and intellectual matters.

3   *Permitting managers to give timely consideration to more complex
relationships.* The computer gives the manager the ability to evaluate
more possible alternatives (and to consider *more of the internal and
external variables* that may have a bearing on the outcome of these
alternatives). It makes it possible for managers to do a better job of
identifying and assessing the probable economic and social effects of
different courses of action. The awareness of such effects, of course,
influences the ultimate decision. In the past, oversimplified assumptions
would have to be made if resulting decisions were to be timely. More
complex relationships can now be considered and scheduled. In short,
computers can furnish managers with planning information that could
not have been produced at all a few years ago or that could not have been
produced in time to be of any value.

4   *Assisting in decision implementation.* When decisions have been
made, the computer can assist in the development of subordinate plans
that will be needed to implement these decisions. Computer-based techniques to schedule project activities have been developed and are now
widely used. Through the use of such techniques, business resources can
be utilized and controlled effectively.

Computer information systems now regularly support the planning and
decision-making activities of managers in a number of business areas (see
Fig. 13-1)[1] In *marketing,* for example, data may be gathered that show
consumer preferences from consumer surveys, results of market testing in
limited geographic areas, and past sales data on similar products in an
industry (obtained from the company's own past sales records and from
subscriptions to data-gathering services). These facts may subsequently

---

[1] For more information on computer-based planning and decision-support systems, see
Steven L. Alter, "How Effective Managers Use Information Systems," *Harvard Business
Review,* November–December 1976, pp. 97–104; Eric D. Carlson, "Decision Support
Systems: Personal Computing Services for Managers," *Management Review,* January 1977,
pp. 4–11; "Management Gets the Picture," *Infosystems,* April 1977, pp. 37–38ff.

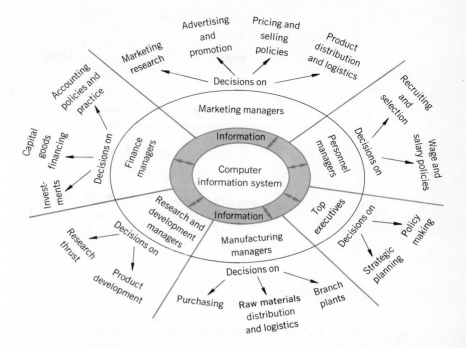

FIGURE 13-1

be processed by a computer to produce summary statistical measures (market percentages, arithmetic means, product rankings, etc.). These summary measures may then be analyzed by managers or by computer programs. These analyses, in turn, can be used as input to computerized statistical forecasting procedures that may be used to project sales volume into the future, given assumptions about pricing, economic trends, promotional effort, competitive reactions, and so on. Armed with this information, managers may be able to do a better job of planning marketing strategies. And in many companies, market plans become the basis for *inventory acquisition plans* and *production plans*.

Of course, provisions must also be made in a business to have adequate *financial* resources available to carry out marketing and production plans. The costs and revenues associated with alternative estimates of promotion plans and prices, and sales and production volumes must be analyzed to determine the financial implications. To evaluate these implications (and to determine the expected profitability of various alternatives), financial managers frequently use computer programs to make cash flow analyses, time-series financial forecasts, and loan and interest rate projections. Decisions about the advisability of making investments in new plants and equipment are often made with the help of a computer.

### decision-making techniques[2]

A number of quantitative managerial aids have been introduced which utilize computers to provide the framework for decision-producing analyses. These techniques (which are often classified under the heading of *operations research or management science*) can be used to (1) speed up problem or opportunity awareness, (2) permit more timely consideration of increasingly complex relationships, and (3) assist in decision implementation. In particular, the computer-based techniques of *network analysis, linear programming,* and *simulation* have decision-making implications.

Network analysis Both PERT (Program Evaluation and Review Technique) and CPM (Critical Path Method) are network models which are used to plan, schedule, and control complex projects. The basic concepts of PERT and CPM are similar. The following procedure is used to set up a network model:

1 *All* the individual *activities* to be performed in the project must be identified.

2 The sequence of each activity must be determined; i.e., it must be known what elements have to be completed prior to the start of a particular activity and what tasks cannot commence until after its completion.

3 The *time interval* required to complete each activity must be estimated.

4 The *longest sequence* of events in the project must be identified. The sum of the individual activity times in this sequence becomes the total project time, and this sequence of activities is known as the *critical path*.

The use of such a model in a construction project, for example, improves the *planning* function because it forces managers to identify *all the project activities that must be performed. Control* is also improved because attention can be focused on the sequence of activities in the critical path. Managers quickly become aware of potential problems. If a critical activity begins to slip behind schedule, steps can be quickly taken to correct the situation. By trading project cost against project time, several alternative paths can initially be computed to help in planning. By

---

[2] For more details on the decision-making techniques that follow, see Gerald Adkins and Udo W. Pooch, "Computer Simulation: A Tutorial," *Computer,* April 1977, pp. 12–16; George A. W. Boehm, "Shaping Decisions with Systems Analysis," *Harvard Business Review,* September–October 1976, pp. 91–99; William G. Browne, "Techniques of Operations Research," *Journal of Systems Management,* September 1972, pp. 8–13; P. L. Kingston, "Concepts of Financial Models," *IBM Systems Journal,* vol. 12, no. 2, 1973, pp. 113–123; Thomas H. Naylor and Daniel R. Gattis, "Corporate Planning Models," *California Management Review,* Summer 1976, pp. 69–78.

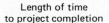

Length of time
to project completion

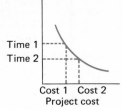

Time 1
Time 2

Cost 1  Cost 2
Project cost

FIGURE 13-2

Reducing of project time may be
possible if greater costs are
acceptable.

a greater commitment of resources, managers can often reduce the time required to complete certain activities in the critical path (and thus reduce total project time). The effect of a greater resource commitment, however, is often higher project cost (see Fig. 13-2). Network models can simulate the effects on time and cost of a varying resource mix. Computations for small networks can be produced manually, but a computer is needed with networks of any significant size. Most computer manufacturers have PERT and CPM packaged programs available, and they are also available in the online program libraries of many timesharing services.

Linear programming   Linear programming models are used to find the *best combination* of limited resources to achieve a specified objective (which is, typically, to maximize profit or minimize cost). One important class of linear programming applications is in blending operations, where the objective is often to minimize the cost involved in the production of a given amount of blended product. For example, cattle feed may be a mixture of minerals, grains, and fish and meat products. The prices of these ingredients are subject to change, so the least expensive blend required to achieve specified nutritional requirements is subject to variation. Linear programming can help managers quickly determine the correct blend to use to minimize cost while meeting product specifications.

In addition to blending, linear programming is being used for such diverse purposes as preparing work schedules, selecting media for advertising purposes, determining minimum transportation costs from given supply points to specified points of delivery, and determining the most profitable product mix that may be manufactured in a given plant with given equipment. Practically all linear programming applications require the use of a computer (Fig. 13-3). As a powerful *planning* tool, linear programming enables a manager to select the most appropriate alternative from a large number of options. It is also a technique that may aid the manager in carrying out his other functions. Its use in preparing work schedules, for example, has definite staffing implications.

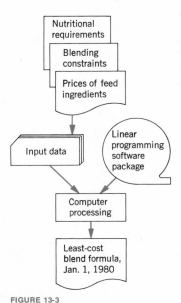

Nutritional
requirements

Blending
constraints

Prices of feed
ingredients

Input data

Linear
programming
software
package

Computer
processing

Least-cost
blend formula,
Jan. 1, 1980

FIGURE 13-3

Simulation   In the physical sciences, experiments may be performed in a laboratory using small models of a process or an operation. Many complex variations may be possible in these tests, and the results show the scientist what happens under certain controlled conditions. Simulation is similar to scientific experimentation. Perhaps Fig. 13-4 will clarify the meaning of simulation. At its base, Fig. 13-4 rests on reality or fact. In complex situations, few people (if any) fully understand all aspects of the situation; therefore, theories are developed which may focus attention on only part of the complex whole. In some situations models may be built or conceived in order to test or represent a theory. Finally, *simulation* is

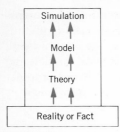

FIGURE 13-4

the use of a model in the attempt to identify and/or reflect the behavior of
a real person, process, or system.[3]

In organizations, administrators may evaluate proposed projects or
strategies by constructing theoretical models. They can then determine
what happens to these models when certain conditions are given or when
certain assumptions are tested. Simulation is thus a trial-and-error problem-solving *approach;* it is also a *planning aid* that may be of considerable value to organizations.

Simulation models have helped *top executives* decide, for example,
whether or not to expand operations by acquiring a new plant. Among
the dozens of complicating variables that would have to be incorporated
into such models are facts and assumptions about (1) present and potential size of the total market, (2) present and potential company share of
this total market, (3) product selling prices, and (4) investment required to
achieve various production levels. Thus, simulation has helped top executives in their strategic planning and decision-making activities.

Simulation may also be helpful to *middle-level managers* in tactical
planning and decision making. For example, simulation models are used
to improve inventory management. The problem of managing inventories
is complicated because there are conflicting desires among organizational units and what is best for one department may not be best for the
entire firm. To illustrate, the purchasing department may prefer to buy
large quantities of supplies and raw materials in order to get lower prices;
the production department also likes to have large inventories on hand to
eliminate shortages and make possible long—and efficient—production
runs; and the sales department prefers large finished-goods inventories so
that sales will not be lost because of out-of-stock conditions. The finance
department, on the other hand, views with concern large inventory levels
since storage expense is increased, risk of spoilage and deterioration is
increased, and funds are tied up for longer periods of time. Through the
use of simulated inventory amounts and simulated assumptions about
such factors as reorder lead times and cost of being out of stock, middle-
level managers can experiment with various approaches to arrive at more
profitable inventory levels.

Finally, simulation models serving managers at different levels may be
integrated into an *overall corporate modeling approach* to planning and
decision making. For example, Potlatch Forests, Inc., a producer of
lumber and wood pulp products, has a corporate planning staff that has
developed an overall corporate financial model. Given assumptions from
top executives about economic conditions, capital expenditures, etc., for
a 5-year future period, simulation runs produce estimated financial statements for each of the 5 years. Executives then analyze the simulated

---

[3] Several programming languages have been developed for the special purpose of preparing
simulation programs. Some of these languages are SIMSCRIPT, GPSS, GASP, and
DYNAMO.

financial statements. If results are judged to be disappointing, executives may change variables in the model that are under their control—e.g., future capital expenditures—and the simulations are repeated. When acceptable financial results are obtained, they become the targets for planning at lower levels in the company. When feasible, lower-level plans are formulated (again, simulation models are used), and they are assembled into an overall corporate plan.

Of course, the output of simulation models is only as good as the facts and assumptions that go into the computer.[4] National economic data and assumptions about the national economy are usually an integral part of a corporate simulation model. Several organizations such as Lionel D. Edie, Data Resources, Inc., and the National Bureau of Economic Research provide extensive national economic data bases that are available to subscribers to their services. General Electric's MAP system is one that was originally developed for internal use by that organization but is now available to timesharing customers. When combined with a firm's internal information, the national economic data provided by these services may enable managers to more accurately model a firm's future.

To summarize several of the points that have now been made, the planning and decision process followed by many business executives may resemble the one shown in Fig. 13-5. The strategies, goals, eco-

[4] The U.S. Geological Survey uses a complex computer-based model to come up with estimates of the oil and gas reserves that might be found in the government's offshore tracts that oil companies bid on. In one area 50 miles off New Jersey's shore, the model "estimates that reserves in the area range from 400 million to 1.4 billion barrels of crude oil and from 2.6 trillion to 9.4 trillion cubic feet of natural gas. But oilmen in Houston irreverently call this computerized approach SWAG—for 'Scientific Wild-Ass Guess.'" See *Business Week*, Sept. 20, 1976, p. 116.

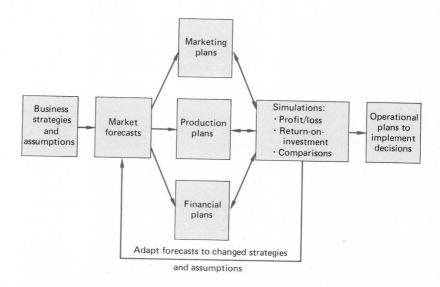

FIGURE 13-5

nomic assumptions, etc., of these executives serve as the basis for market forecasts. This expectation of *how many* items can be sold then becomes the basis for determining (1) how and when to acquire materials and make the items (the production plans), (2) how and when to have the money on hand to pay for the acquired materials and produced items (the financial plans), and (3) how and when to promote and distribute the items (the marketing plans). And these plans are then used in simulations to estimate such variables as profit and return on investment. Of course, the results of these simulations may bring about changes in established plans and/or the results may cause changes in strategies and assumptions. Once initial simulations have been concluded and high-level plans have been made, operational plans at lower levels are often needed to implement the decisions.

From this brief overview, we can see that *computer simulation offers such advantages as* (1) controlled experimentation involving alternative policies and the consideration of many variables, (2) the ability to enhance operational understanding, and (3) the means of providing effective managerial training in decision making. However, *simulation disadvantages may include* (1) the time and cost required to develop the model, (2) the use of oversimplified or incorrect assumptions hidden in the model, and (3) the possible lack of enthusiastic support for the model from managers who may be expected to use it.

## ORGANIZATIONAL STRUCTURE AND COMPUTER USAGE

It was pointed out in Chapter 2 that when it is possible to introduce a new technological development into a business to improve on a process or to do something that was previously not feasible, then there will usually be those who will seek to take advantage of the new opportunity even though changes in the ways individuals and groups are organized may then be necessary. Certainly the introduction of computer technology into businesses has often resulted in such organizational changes.

When a computer is installed, for example, it may take over a large part of the work of several departments. If there is then no longer any valid reason for some units to continue to exist, changes are likely to be made in the organizational structure to avoid duplication and waste.[5] In other words, as computer-based management information systems are designed and implemented, there is often a need to reconsider the answers to several important and interrelated organizing questions. Included in these questions are (1) *Where will decision making occur?* (2) *Where will data be processed?* (3) *Where will data be stored?* and (4) *Where will computing resources be located?* As is so often the case, the "right" answers to these questions in one situation may be very wrong in

---

[5] Unless careful planning precedes such changes, however, they are likely to produce efficiency-robbing employee resistance in the affected departments.

another. Thus, all we will do in the following sections is look at some of the general implications of these issues.

### where will decision making occur?

The concept of *centralization of authority*[6] refers to a concentration of the important decision-making powers in the hands of a relatively few top executives. *Decentralization of authority,* on the other hand, refers to the extent to which significant decisions are made at lower levels. In very small organizations, *all* decision-making power is likely to be centralized in the hands of the owner-manager; in larger firms, the question of centralization or decentralization *is a matter of degree*—i.e., it is a question of how much authority is held at different levels. The extent to which authority is delegated to lower levels depends, in part, on such factors as: (1) the managerial philosophy of top executives; (2) the availability of qualified subordinates; and (3) the availability of good operating controls. Since all these factors may change, it is apparent that the degree of authority centralization is subject to revision.

Before computers came along, the general trend was toward *greater decentralization* of authority. To some top managers decentralization was more a matter of necessity than of choice. They often found themselves in a position where they could (1) wait for the necessary supporting information to arrive from lower levels before making a decision (in which case company reaction time suffered and opportunities were lost); (2) place their trust in experience, intuition, and their horoscope and make the decision without proper supporting information; or (3) delegate the authority to make the decision to a lower-level manager who was closer to the situation calling for the decision and who could thus be expected to react in a prompt and more informed manner. Given these alternatives, it is understandable that as businesses grew in complexity, the third path was frequently chosen.

With the introduction of quick-response computer systems, however, information may be processed and communicated to top executives at electronic speeds; reaction time may be sharply reduced; and thus the *need* for decentralization of authority may be lessened. But although new systems may make it possible to reconcentrate at the upper echelons authority and control previously held at lower levels, there *no reason* why the information output cannot be disseminated via online terminals to lower-level managers to provide them with better support for decision-making purposes. In fact, if an organization implements the distributed processing concepts that were discussed in Chapters 2 and 5, the lower-

---

[6] *Authority* is defined here as the right to give orders and the power to see that they are carried out.

level managers may have access to an entire hierarchy of processors that can supply them with decision-making information. Thus, the degree to which authority and decision-making powers are centralized or decentralized in an organization is now often determined more by managerial philosophy and judgment than by necessity. But the implications of the path selected for the organizational structure and for middle-level managers may be great.

### where will data be processed?

Prior to the introduction of computers, data processing activities were generally handled by manufacturing, marketing, and finance departments on a separate and thus decentralized basis. When computers first appeared, however, the tendency was to maximize the use of the expensive hardware by establishing one or more central processing centers to serve the company's needs. But in recent years, such developments as (1) the rapid reduction in hardware costs and (2) the arrangement of intelligent terminals, minicomputers, and larger processors into distributed processing systems have made it feasible for businesses to use either a centralized or a decentralized approach to data *processing*. Thus, many firms must now decide to what extent (if any) they will centralize their data processing operations. Should small computers be used by individual organization units, or should these units furnish input to (and receive output from) one or more central computer centers which can process data originating at many points? (See Fig. 13-6.)

*The possible considerations in favor of the centralized approach are*

1   *It may permit economies of scale.* With adequate processing volume, the use of larger and more powerful computing equipment may result in reduced operating costs. Also, duplication in record storage and program preparation may be eliminated; less expensive standardized forms can be used; and site preparation costs may be reduced since fewer sites are involved.

2   *It may facilitate necessary systems integration.* For example, achieving companywide standards on customer code numbers is a necessary step in integrating the procedures required to process customer orders. Such agreement is more likely to occur for efficiency reasons when order processing is handled at a central point. It may also be easier to establish and enforce the use of consistent corporate standards and controls at a central site.

3   *It has certain personnel advantages.* It may be possible to concenrate fewer skilled programmers at a centralized site and thus make more effective use of their talents. A sizable operation may offer more appeal to highly qualified computer specialists. Thus, recruiting may be simplified and a professional group will be available to help train new personnel.

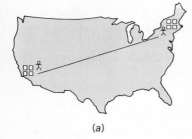

(a)

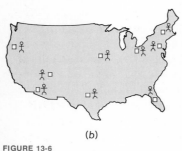

(b)

FIGURE 13-6

(a) Centralization or (b) decentralization of data processing activities.

**4** *It may permit better utilization of processing capability.* With a centralized operation, *companywide* priorities can be assigned to processing tasks. Those jobs that are of greatest importance are, of course, completed first. With a decentralized approach, however, low-priority work may be processed in one division with excess capacity while in another division a higher-priority application may be left unfinished because of inadequate processing capability.

*Disadvantage Decent* →

In view of these benefits, it might seem that a decision to follow a centralized approach would be automatic. Yet there are limiting factors in centralization, which may cause a company to follow a more decentralized path. These limitations are implicit in the following discussion of the advantages of decentralization.

*Included among the possible advantages of decentralization are the following:*

**1** *Greater interest and motivation at divison levels.* Division managers in control of their own computers may be more likely to *(a)* maintain the accuracy of input data and *(b)* use the equipment in ways that best meet their particular operating needs. Greater interest and motivation, combined with greater knowledge of division conditions, may produce information of higher quality and value.

*Disadvantage of central.* →

**2** *Better response to user needs.* The system standardization typically required for centralized processing may not be equally suitable for all divisions. With decentralization, special programs can be prepared to meet exact divisional needs. In addition, although a smaller machine will probably be slower than the centralized equipment, it should be remembered that central machine time must be allocated to several users. Information considered important by one division may be delayed because higher priority is given to other processing tasks. Thus, the fact that a smaller machine allows for prompt attention to a given job may lead to faster processing at the division level.

**3** *Reduced downtime risks.* A breakdown in the centralized equipment or the communications links may leave the entire system inoperative. A similar breakdown in one division, however, does not affect other decentralized operations.

There is no general answer to the question of where *should* data be processed. Small organizations have usually opted for central computers because their departments often do not have sufficient volume to justify separate machines. Large organizations following the centralization approach have generally not created single huge installations. Rather, they have often achieved a greater degree of centralization by establishing several regional data centers. Some executives who have chosen to follow the *centralized processing* route have retained a *decentralized decision-making structure* by giving operating managers online terminals with which to obtain the necessary support information.

Firms with centralized hardware may also achieve greater interest and

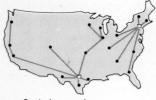

□ Central processing
  complex

• Intelligent terminal/satellite
  minicomputer

FIGURE 13-7

Distributed processing compromise
approach.

motivation at operating levels by maintaining some system-analysis operations on a more decentralized basis. This can be a logical arrangement
because (1) divisional system analysts may have a better understanding of
the information needs of the division, and (2) this approach can effectively counter the argument from division managers that since system
design is beyond their control, they cannot be held accountable for
design results.

Finally, other organizations are following a *distributed processing
compromise approach* to the centralization-decentralization issue by
combining larger central computers (and centralized data files) with small
processors, minicomputers, and intelligent terminals at operating levels.
The central processor(s) serves the local processors by managing large
data bases and by executing those jobs that require extensive computations (see Fig. 13-7).

### where will data be stored?

Before computers came along, data were typically stored at the using
departments, although some summary facts needed to prepare companywide reports were maintained at centralized sites in large organizations.
When computers first appeared, however, we have seen that the tendency was to maximize the use of expensive hardware by setting up
centralized computer centers. Not surprisingly, the tendency was also to
establish and store large centralized data bases at these central sites on
such media as magnetic tape and disks.

In most cases, data with corporatewide significance will continue to be
stored at a central site. But with the reduction in hardware costs, with the
increase in data communications facilities, and with the development of
distributed computing networks using intelligent terminals, minicomputers, and larger processors, there is no technical reason why applications-
oriented files with local significance cannot be returned to the outlying
user departments for storage and maintenance. Thus, many firms are now
in the process of deciding to what extent (if any) they will relocate the
storage of previously centralized computer-based data to using
departments.

*A decision to distribute some data-base files from a central site to local
levels might be made in the following circumstances:*

1   When large volumes of data are produced at many local sites and
quick access to the data is needed by local users. In a chain of retail
stores, for example, local accounts-receivable and customer credit records could be maintained at each store. Such records, of course, would
be of little value to other stores in the chain.

2   When data are produced both centrally and at remote sites, when quick access to the data is needed by a number of remote locations, and when records can be updated from any site. For example, an organization may maintain regional warehouses to distribute a number of common inventory items. One or more inventory files containing records of these items may be updated centrally to reflect additions to inventory, while shipment transactions from each warehouse may be used to reduce inventory levels. To answer inquiries from salespersons about available items, warehouse personnel may need access to records showing local inventory levels as well as access to information about the inventory available at other warehouse locations.

In the *first* circumstance just described, a decision might be made to *partition* a centralized accounts-receivable file and distribute the data to the local stores. However, summary data from all store files could be transmitted to a central site in a timely manner for use in the preparation of periodic reports. In the *second* circumstance, a decision might be made to have *duplicate* or *replicated* copies of the inventory file(s) stored centrally *and* at each warehouse location. Updating of inventory records might be controlled by a central or host computer facility in a hierarchical computing network, or distributed processors at each warehouse location might communicate directly in a ring network structure.

There are *possible advantages to the centralized storage approach* in those situations where (1) unified control and strict adherence to standards is desired, (2) the partitioning or replication of files adds system security problems, (3) file sizes are large and many transactions do not originate at local levels, and (4) the application is too critical to run the risk of having data updated at one location and not at another.

On the other hand, however, there are also *possible advantages to a distributed data storage approach* in those situations where (1) data communication costs between central and local sites can be substantially reduced by moving frequently accessed records to the user's location; (2) the performance of data communications facilities and/or the central computing center presents system reliability problems for users; (3) user interest and motivation is improved through faster access to, and better control over, records that are locally stored; and (4) the redundancy found in replicated files can add storage backup and a degree of added data security to the system.

In summary, there is no general answer to the question of where *should* data be stored, just as there was no general answer to the question of where should data be processed. Some organizations may find it best to store and maintain data at a central site; some may prefer to use a partitioned approach to data storage; some may choose to use a replicated approach in order to distribute data-base files; and many organizations may elect to use a combination of these basic data storage approaches.

### where will computing resources be located?

Each business must determine the proper location for its main computer department. What is "proper" depends, in part, on the size of the company, the jobs to be processed, the degree of systems integration achieved and sought, and the importance attached to information systems by top executives. Three possible locations for the main computer department are designated in Fig. 13-8. Let us look at each of these arrangements.

Location number one  Historically, the accounting department was often the first to see that a computer could be used to process large-volume applications such as customer billing. Since most of the early applications were of a financial nature, the computer was most often placed under the control of financial managers. It still remains in this location in many businesses. But there may be several possible drawbacks associated with this finance-area location:

1  *Possible lack of objectivity in setting job priorities.* Computer-department personnel may tend to concentrate on accounting applications at the expense of important nonfinancial jobs.

2  *Possible limited viewpoint.* The computer department may continue to be staffed and managed by people whose viewpoint is limited primarily to accounting.

3  *Possible lack of organizational status.* Organizational status and authority are lacking when the top computer executive is interred several echelons down in one functional area of the business.

Location number two  One approach which can avoid the lack of objectivity in setting job priorities is to establish a company "service

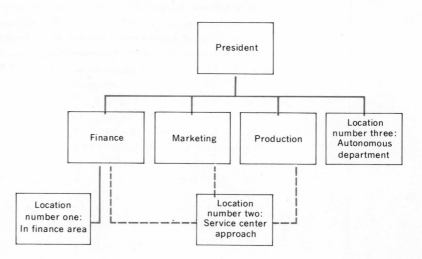

FIGURE 13-8

Alternative computer department locations.

center'' to handle the various tasks. Each department may be charged its proportionate share of center costs. While the center manager may report to a neutral top-level executive or an executive committee, the service center basically occupies a position that is on the periphery of or outside the main organizational structure.

The main limitation of this type of organizational arrangement for business data processing is that the center manager generally has little status or authority outside his or her own department. Thus, little attempt is made to initiate system improvements or develop integrated systems; a fragmented, every-department-for-itself approach may be expected.

Location number three   In order to realize the full potential of the computer a large number of managers have established an independent computer department as shown in location three of Fig. 13-8. Their reasoning is that this location:

1   *Reflects the broad scope of information.* Independent status is needed to give impartial service to all organizational units that receive processed information. An interdepartmental viewpoint is required of data processing personnel.

2   *Confers organizational status.* The top computer executive should have a strong voice in determining the suitability of new and existing applications, should probably set processing priorities, and should study and make necessary changes in corporatewide systems and procedures in order to achieve better integration. To perform these duties, the information manager must have the cooperation of executives at the highest operating levels. In the event of significant change, such cooperation may not be received unless the information manager occupies a position that is no lower in the organization than the highest information-using department. Furthermore, in the event of a dispute, the information manager should report to an executive who is at a higher level than any of the disputing parties.

3   *Encourages innovation.* Personnel of an independent department can be encouraged to recommend improvement and change whenever and wherever the opportunity arises. They may also be encouraged to introduce, for the greatest total benefit, fresh ideas that may upset certain conventional approaches.

SUMMARY   To achieve organizational goals, managers must perform the activities of planning, organizing, staffing, and controlling. The information produced by a computer-based system can have an impact on *planning* by (1) quickly identifying problems and opportunities, (2) supporting problem analysis and selection of alternatives, (3) influencing the choice of the most appropriate option, and (4) supporting decision implementation. Computers can also be used to apply decision-making techniques such as PERT/CPM, linear programming, and simulation to problems.

In addition to these planning implications, computer usage also raises a number of questions which have organizing implications. Although there are no general right or wrong answers that apply in every situation, executives must consider such questions as: (1) Where will decision making occur—i.e., will decision making be centralized or decentralized? (2) Will the data processing be centralized or decentralized? (3) Will the storage of data be centralized or distributed? and (4) Where will the computing resource(s) be located within the organization?

1   (a) What is involved in the planning function? (b) What steps must be followed in planning?

2   Explain what is involved in (a) the organizing function and (b) the staffing function.

3   Identify and discuss the steps in the control function.

4   (a) How may computer usage have an impact on the planning activities of managers? (b) Give examples of the use of computers for planning and decision making.

5   (a) Identify and explain the purpose of three computer-based decision-making techniques. (b) What are the managerial implications of these techniques?

6   (a) What is meant by centralization of authority? (b) What factors determine the extent to which authority is delegated to lower management levels?

7   "An organization may be centralized in one sense of the term and not in others." Discuss this statement.

8   (a) What developments have made it possible to centralize data processing activities? (b) What are the possible advantages of centralized data processing? (c) What are the possible advantages of decentralized data processing?

9   (a) What developments have made it possible to decentralize or distribute the storage of computer-based data files from central sites to outlying user departments? (b) What approaches might be used to distribute or relocate these files? (c) What are the possible advantages of a centralized storage approach? (d) What are the possible advantages of a distributed data storage approach?

10   (a) Identify and discuss three possible organizational locations for the computer department. (b) What reasons can be given to justify the establishment of an independent computer department?

In addition to the sources cited in the chapter footnotes, you might wish to examine the following references:

Champine, G. A.: "Six Approaches to Distributed Data Bases," *Datamation*, May 1977, pp. 69–72.

Hannan, James, and Louis Fried: "Should you Decentralize?" *Computer Decisions,* February 1977, pp. 40–42.

Hunter, John J.: "Distributing a Database," *Computer Decisons,* June 1976, pp. 36ff.

Keider, Stephen P.: "Once Again—Centralize or Decentralize," *Infosystems,* December 1976, pp. 40ff.

Kim, Chai, and Hal Cheney: "Tailor-made Records Management Program," *Journal of Systems Management,* January 1977, pp. 12–16.

Reynolds, Carl H.: "Issues in Centralization," *Datamation,* March 1977, pp. 91–93ff.

Smith, Walton E.: "Centralization vs. Decentralizaton," *Data Management,* January 1977, pp. 24–25.

# the computer's impact on staffing and management control

LEARNING OBJECTIVES    After studying this chapter and answering the discussion questions, you should be able to: ☐ Discuss the possible implications of computer usage on noncomputer personnel in terms of the effects on job duties and employment status ☐ Explain the forms that resistance to information system changes may take, the reasons for this resistance, and some guidelines that may be used to reduce this resistance ☐ Describe how computer systems help managers control business operations ☐ Explain what is meant by internal control and what information system failures may result from poor internal control □ Outline some of the effects of computer usage on auditors and auditing

In this chapter we continue our study of the *internal* effects of computer usage on business organizations by examining some of the *personnel/ staffing* and *controlling* implications of computer-based information systems. In the next chapter, we shall consider some of the important ways in which business computer systems may be exerting an influence on society *as a whole.*

**SOME PERSONNEL/ STAFFING IMPLICATIONS OF COMPUTER USAGE**

We saw in the last chapter how computers may change the organizational structure of a business. And as computers change an organization, they are bound to touch the lives of its members. The nature of this influence will depend on decisions consciously made, and on the indirect and perhaps unintentional effects of the application of computing tools. In this chapter we will look at some of the possible effects of computer usage on *noncomputer personnel;* in Chapter 16 (which deals with the management of computing resources), we will then consider some of the issues related to the staffing of the computer department(s) in an organization.

Computer-based systems can affect noncomputer personnel by changing their *job duties* and/or their *employment status*. Naturally, employees may be expected to offer *resistance to some of these possible changes.*

### changes in job duties

Both *managers* and *employees* may *benefit* from changes in job duties brought about by their organizations' use of computers. *High-level executives* have, in some cases, been able to use better and more timely information in order to reassume some of the decision-making powers previously delegated to subordinates. In other cases, executives have, with a greater feeling of confidence in their ability to monitor performance through computer-produced reports, delegated additional authority to subordinates. However, the primary role of top executives lies in formulating objectives and policies and planning and guiding overall organizational strategy. Computer-based systems should, through the use of improved simulation techniques, help remove some of the uncertainties from the usually unique and ill-structured problems that top administrators face. But substantial changes in the top executive role have not occurred, nor are they expected in the near future.

A most important role of *lower-level supervisors* is to provide face-to-face communication, direction, and leadership to operating employees. But these administrators have, in the past, been caught in a squeeze between rising personnel and materials costs on the one hand and the need to maintain cost controls and remain within budget limits on the other. Computer usage has benefited supervisors by permitting them to (1) schedule operations more efficiently, (2) maintain better control over economic resources, and (3) cope with a generally increasing level of paperwork. By relieving supervisors of many of their clerical duties, computers have thus made it possible for them to give more attention to the important personnel administration aspects of their work.

Administrators occupying *middle-level positions* in an organization,[1] like all managers, must perform the activities of planning, organizing, staffing, and controlling. As a result of computer information systems, some middle managers no longer need to spend as much time in controlling, because the computer can take over many of the clerical control activities—e.g., it can signal with a "triggered" report whenever actual performance varies from what was planned. Time saved in controlling has enabled some middle-level administrators to devote more attention to

---

[1] *Middle managers* may be defined as those who are above the lowest level of supervison and below the highest level of a self-contained operating organization; i.e., they occupy positions between foremen and first-rung supervisors, on the one hand, and company presidents, executive vice presidents, and division managers of larger corporations, on the other. Thus, the term *middle manager* is rather nebulous and is applied to a number of levels. The difficulties of generalizing about such a wide range of positions should be recognized.

planning and directing the work of subordinates. More accurate and timely organizationwide information supplied by the computer has given some administrators the opportunity to spend more time identifying problems, recognizing opportunities, and planning alternate courses of action. In this respect, then, their jobs have become more challenging and more nearly resemble those of chief executives. With more time to devote to departmental employee matters, improved morale may be expected; furthermore, the more timely information that is now available to some middle managers puts them in a position to be able to react more rapidly to external changes.

And *operations research employees* using the techniques of linear programming, simulation, etc.; *scientists* conducting research into complex problem areas that could not be considered without computers; *design engineers* and *architects* using computers to simplify design work and increase the alternatives that can be considered; *structural engineers* using computer models to predict the effect of stresses on different structural configurations; *sales personnel* who receive more timely information about customers and product inventories and who are able to promise more efficient handling of sales orders in order to serve their customers better and thus improve their own sales performance; *clerical employees* whose job duties have changed from routine, repetitive operations to more varied and appealing tasks—all these individuals are among the beneficiaries of the use of computers in organizations.

In short, computer usage has often made it possible for people to eliminate routine procedures and to use their creative abilities in more challenging and rewarding ways.

Unfortunately, however, some company personnel have been the *victims* of computer usage. *Top-level executives* are the ones who approve the installation of computer systems. In giving their approval, they obviously do not expect to be victimized. And yet, in a sense, a number of top administrators have been computer victims. Many have been disappointed in the economic effects of their installations; some have discovered too late that poor security provisions in the computer center have left their organizations *more* vulnerable to theft, espionage, and sabotage; and more than a few have been disappointed because their new information systems have not given them the service and support for decision making they were led to believe would be provided. Some top administrators also feel more constrained because they are now more dependent on their systems staff for information.

Some *administrators below the top levels* whose decisions were highly structured and repetitive have found that those decisions were programmable on a computer. The information systems have therefore taken over those duties, and the need for as many to perform the remainder of the job duties has been reduced. In some organizations, those who were not displaced found their jobs less challenging because, although they retained the duties that required less judgment and skill, their other tasks that required the skilled interpretation of systems information were moved upward in the organization or were taken over by the information system staff. And in some cases, managers are finding that they have little voice in determining the information they will receive or in the design of the new systems which will be used to monitor their performance. (In one retail chain, store managers dread Monday mornings because they may receive a critical telephone call from their boss if the previous week's sales are down since the boss has a report prepared by the computer over the weekend while the store managers do not receive the figures until later in the week.) Managers caught in this type of situation have experienced the same frustrations as many employees whose duties and performance have been put under the microscope of a time-and-motion study engineer. Many administrators, of course, have not meekly accepted new system changes which they perceive to be a threat, as we shall see in a later section on resistance to change.

Many *lower-level clerical supervisors* and their *employees* have suffered because their departments have been eliminated, merged with others, or reduced in scope and status as the result of the installation of computer information systems. When such changes occur, they can lead to changes in the employement status of individuals.

### changes in employment status

The use of computers has created hundreds of thousands of new jobs, and many of these employees are currently working in challenging and satisfying positions. But computer usage has also been responsible for the elimination of jobs and the displacement of employees.[2] On balance, then, what is likely to be the net effect of computer usage on employment? Will the net result be greater unemployment or increased job opportunities? Printed sources can be found to support each position.

Nature of the controversy  To some extent the employment controversy is fed by a failure on the part of some writers to make a distinction between unemployment and displacement. Those who are optimistic about the effects of computers on employment are generally looking at the effect of technological change on the *total employment* picture; i.e., they are looking at the effect on the *total number of jobs* in the labor market. Those who view the picture pessimistically are frequently looking at the short-run effects of *displacement* on *specific occupational cate-*

---

[2] New York's Citibank has established a distributed processing network of hundreds of small computers in recent years. "In the process, the bank's staff for the activities involved has been cut from 10,500 in 1970 to about 5,000 now. In almost all cases, the work force was cut through normal attrition." See, "New Trends in Data Processing," *Dun's Review*, July 1977, p. 96.

*gories;* i.e., they are looking at the reduction in the number of jobs in a specific segment of the labor force.

*Unemployment and displacement are not the same. Unemployment* refers to the total number of people involuntarily out of work. *Displacement* occurs when the jobs of individual workers are eliminated as a result of technological change. *If* these displaced workers cannot find similar jobs elsewhere and *if* they cannot find work in other occupations, then there is, indeed, an increase in the unemployment figures. But has the use of computers caused a larger number of people to be unemployed than would otherwise have been the case? In other words, have computers reduced the total number of jobs available in the total labor market? Many economists are of the opinion that, although computers do cause displacement and some displaced workers become unemployed, unemployment may not be created in the sense that more people are out of jobs than would have been if computers had not been used. Why? Because there are those who owe their jobs to computer usage, and there are probably many more who might have joined the jobless if new technology had not been used to maintain a competitive level of productivity with other countries of the world.

Regardless of the ultimate effects of computers on total employment, to the employee being displaced today the future consequences are of secondary importance. The displaced victim is likely to be in sympathy with the famous economist who noted wryly that "in the long run we are all dead."

Business displacement experience    The extent to which displacement has actually occurred in business, and the significance of the problem in particular cases, has depended in large measure on the following factors:

1    *The rate of growth of the firm and the economy.* If the company is growing so rapidly that more work must be done to handle the expanding business, then there may be little or no effect on the number of clerical workers employed. The use of a computer enables workers to be more productive, but increases in the demand for a company's output can prevent a layoff problem. Reassignment of surplus workers to different departments may, of course, be required. If workers must be laid off, they will have greater opportunity to find employment elsewhere if the economy is in a period of prosperity. It is fortunate that most computer installations have occurred during relatively prosperous periods.

2    *The objectives sought.* Is the company introducing a computer system for processing purposes that could not otherwise be considered? Is the goal to do more work with present employees? Or is it to save money by eliminating existing jobs? Objectives obviously play a part in determining the degree of displacement.

3    *The care in planning and preparation.* Business executives should give careful thought to the displacement problems that they are likely to

encounter. It should be noted that fear of displacement is a cause of resistance to change. If displacement is not expected, employees should be so informed; if jobs are to be eliminated, plans should be made to protect present employees as much as possible. Employees in departments where reductions are expected can be given the first chance to fill vacancies occurring elsewhere in the company.

4    *The type of occupations threatened.* Up to the present time, most of the jobs that have been eliminated have been of a clerical nature and have usually been held by young women who can be transferred to other departments without too much difficulty. In the past, few clerical workers were laid off in larger businesses when job reductions occurred.[3] This was possible because those workers in affected departments who quit during the many months between the time the computer order was placed and the time the conversion was completed were simply not replaced. Thus, a potentially serious layoff problem often has not developed. When the affected jobs are *not* of the clerical type, the displacement problem is likely to be much more severe. Attrition and turnover in these situations may not be of much help. The affected workers may be older employees or lower-level managers whose skills are no longer needed. They are not likely to quit, but they may find it difficult to retrain for jobs at an appropriate level. In some *production-oriented occupations,* for example, displacement is occurring as a result of the installation of computer-controlled machines (e.g., certain machine tools and typesetting machines). Employees in these occupations are protected to some extent by union contract agreements, but the demand for their skills is declining.

### personnel resistance to systems change

It was observed early in Chapter 8 that "If people in the operational areas that prepare the data input and use the information output are not sold on the new system and do not want to make it work, it is likely to fail to achieve its goals." In too many cases, however, company personnel *have not been convinced* of the merits of the changes taking place and no attempt has been made to counter this attitude. Why not? One reason is that executives and data processing specialists have too frequently become so preoccupied with system problems of a technical nature that they have ignored the human factors involved in the transition. In short, the emphasis has too often been placed on work rather than on workers.

Personnel preparations should receive considerable attention during the system-study period and at the same time that technical preparations are being made so that employees will accept changes with a minimum of resistance.

---

[3] Small firms have not been as successful in preventing layoffs, possibly because there may not have been other departments to which surplus workers could be reassigned.

Forms of resistance   Resistance to change is the rule rather than the exception, and it may appear in many forms. At one extreme employees may temporarily feel threatened by a change, but after a brief adjustment period they resume their previous behavior. At the other extreme, reaction may be evidenced by open opposition and even destruction. Between these extremes may be found a number of other symptoms, including the following:

1   *Withholding data and information.* It is not uncommon during the system study for employees to withhold information about current operations.

2   *Providing inaccurate information.* Input data containing known inaccuracies are submitted to sabotage processing results.

3   *Distrusting computer output.* Some employees continue to maintain old methods after the conversion is made.

4   *Showing lowered morale.* A general lowering of employee morale may result in lack of cooperation, sullen hostility, sloppy effort, an attitude of indifference, jealousy among workers, etc.

Although employee reaction to change depends, of course, on the individual, it also depends on answers to such questions as: (1) What are the nature and magnitude of the changes? (2) Why are they being made? (3) Who is backing them? (4) Who will administer them? (5) When will they take place? (6) In what departments will they be felt? (7) What has been the extent of personnel preparation? (8) Does the firm have a history of good personnel relations? (9) Does the firm have a reputation for innovation and change?

Reasons for resistance   We have seen that there are likely to be those in an organization who are motivated to seek change because of their dissatisfaction with the status quo, and because of their desire to create and be a leader in the use of new techniques. But the changes sought by some may appear to others to be a threat—a threat that may take one or more of the following paths:

1   *The threat to security.* Computers have a reputation for replacing people; therefore, there is the understandable fear of loss of employment and/or of reduction in salary.

2   *The reduction in social satisfaction.* The introduction of a computer system often calls for a reorganization of departments and work groups. When change causes a breaking up of compatible human relationships and a realigning of personnel, it also causes a reduction in social-need satisfaction. Resistance to such a proposed change may be anticipated.

3   *The reduction in self-esteem and reputation.* Individuals need to feel self-confident; but self-confidence may be shaken by the lack of knowledge about and experience with a computer system. The equipment is strange to them, and they may fear that they will be unable to acquire the

skills necessary to work with it. In short, their self-esteem may suffer as a result of the change; therefore, the change may be resisted. Egoistic needs relating to the reputation of the individual are also threatened by change. Fear of loss of status and/or prestige is an important reason for resistance by both managers and employees. Department managers, for example, may oppose a change because to admit that the change is needed may imply that they have tolerated inefficiency—an admission that can hardly enhance their reputations. And employees knowledgeable in the ways of the old system may also suffer a loss of prestige because when new procedures are installed they may no longer be looked to for information.

Employees who resist   In summary, then, *nonsupervisory employees* may resist change because they fear they will (1) lose their jobs or be downgraded, (2) be transferred away from their friends, (3) be unable to acquire the needed new skills, and/or (4) lose status and prestige. A greater obstacle to successful computer operations, however, may be *managerial* resistance to change.[4] Although managers may suffer economic loss because of the change to computer processing, the more usual motivating force behind their resistance is the threat of a reduction in ego-need satisfaction. Many managers feel that their positions are being threatened (and indeed this is sometimes the case). In a very real sense, those who may be most affected by the change are being asked to help plan and implement it. But it is unrealistic to expect a manager to be enthusiastic about changes that threaten his or her position. Proper personnel preparation must include managers as well as nonsupervisory employees.

Suggestions for reducing resistance   Although there is no simple formula that prevents resistance and ensures successful computer usage, *there are some guidelines*—developed as a result of practical experience and social research—*which may, when used with care, help to reduce the level of organizational resistance*. Included in these guidelines are suggestions to:

1   *Keep employees informed.* Information relating to the effects of the change on their jobs should be periodically presented to personnel at all

---

[4] Of course, there are some managers who don't fear change because of an outlook which may be summarized as follows:

> Yea, though I walk through the valley
> Of the shadow of death
> I shall fear no evil.
> Because I'm the meanest son-of-a-bitch in the organization.

See Thomas L. Martin, Jr., *Malice in Blunderland,* McGraw-Hill Book Company, New York, 1973, p. 109.

levels. Topics discussed should include loss of jobs, transfers, the extent of necessary retraining, the reasons for (and the benefits of) the change, the effect on various departments, and what is being done to alleviate employee hardships. Basic company objectives should be reviewed; the motives behind these objectives should be identified; and the contribution that the change makes to goal achievement should be explained. When possible, employees should be assured that the change will not interfere with the satisfaction of their personal needs.

**2**  *Seek employee participation.* Employees are more likely to support and accept changes that they have a hand in creating. In addition to yielding valuable information during the system study, requirements and review sessions also help reduce later resistance by allowing managers to have a say in the planning of the project. Psychologists tell us that *participation has three beneficial effects. First,* it helps the employee satisfy ego and self-fulfillment needs. *Second,* it gives the employee some degree of control over the change and thus contributes to a greater feeling of security. And *third,* the fear of the unknown is removed. The *participation of supervisors and informal group leaders* may greatly reduce the level of resistance. But participation is not a gimmick to manipulate people. Employees asked to participate must be respected and treated with dignity, and their suggestions must be carefully considered.

**3**  *Use managerial evaluation.* Make their ability to handle change one of the criteria for evaluating supervisors' managerial capability. Let them know that this criterion has been established.

**4**  *Consider the timing of the change.* Do not set unreasonable conversion deadlines. Give personnel time to get used to one major change before another is initiated.

## MANAGERIAL CONTROL, INTERNAL CONTROL, AND COMPUTER USAGE

There are numerous controlling implications associated with the use of computer-based information systems that are of concern to managers and auditors in business organizations.[5] A primary concern of managers, of course, is that they have ready access to a good information system in order to control the business operations for which they are responsible. In addition to this *managerial control* consideration, however, executives and auditors are also vitally interest in—and responsible for—maintaining the necessary *internal control over the information system itself* so that the system is operating efficiently, and so that the integrity and security of data, records, and other business assets are preserved. Let us now look at a few of the implications of computer usage for these managerial and internal control responsibilities.

---

[5] Our emphasis in this chapter is on the *general control interests of managers and auditors.* The *specific methods and procedures* designed by auditors and computer personnel to control the accuracy, integrity, and security of the data processed by the computer facility are discussed in Chapter 16.

## managerial control implications

You will recall that the general control procedure consists of several steps: (1) the establishment of predetermined goals or standards, (2) the measurement of performance, (3) the comparison of actual performance with the standards, and (4) the making of appropriate control decisions.

The information output of the computer can help the manager carry out this procedure in many ways. First of all, better information can lead to better planning and the creation of *more realistic standards.* Computer simulation can assist managers in setting goals by showing them the effects of various alternative decisions when certain conditions are assumed; and computer-based network models such as PERT and CPM can improve planning (and therefore control) by forcing managers to identify all project activities that must be performed.

Computer processing systems can also help managers control by gathering, classifying, calculating, and summarizing *actual performance data* promptly and accurately. Once performance data are read into the computer, it is possible for the machine to *compare* the actual performance with the established standards. Periodic reports showing this comparison can be prepared. In some systems, triggered reports, based on the *principle of exception,*[6] may be furnished to the manager only when variations are outside certain specified limits.

It is also possible to program the computer so that it signals when *predetermined decisions* should be carried out. For example, a program may specifiy that when the inventory of a certain basic part falls below a given level, an output message signals the need to reorder and indicates the reorder quantity. By thus relieving people of many of the routine operational control tasks, the computer frees them to devote more time to (1) planning future moves and (2) leading the all-important human resources of the organization. Such a human/machine relationship, in other words, makes it possible for people to concentrate more of their attention on the heuristic area of intellectual work—an area in which they are far superior to the machine—while the machine is permitted to take over the well-structured control tasks. Figure 14-1 illustrates the place of a computer system in the overall managerial control process.

## internal control implications

Managers and auditors are responsible for *internal control:* that is, they are responsible for the controls needed to (1) safeguard assets against theft

---

[6] In chapter 18 of Exodus, Jethro gives good advice when he tells Moses to delegate some of his routine leadership duties to subordinates and concentrate his attention on the more important exceptions, which the subordinates are unable to handle. This idea is called *the principle of exception* in management literature.

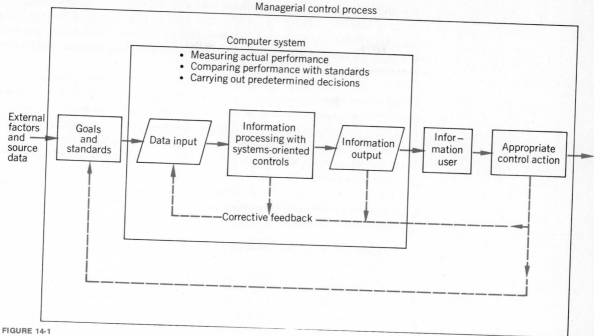

**FIGURE 14-1**

Managerial control and the
computer.

and destruction, (2) check on and maintain the accuracy and security of company data, (3) promote operating efficiency, and (4) encourage compliance with company policies and procedures.

**Need for internal control**   Some managers have been surprised to learn that the introduction of a computer system often requires a reexamination of internal control procedures. Why? How thoughtful of you to ask. A review is required because in noncomputer systems the data processing activities are typically separated into several departments, with a number of employees being responsible for some portion of the total activity. For example, in the processing of a customer order, credit approval may come from one location, control of the inventory of ordered items may reside in another department, customer billing may be handled by a third department, and receipt of payment for items shipped may be in a fourth location. Thus, the organizational structure separates those who authorize and initiate the order from those who record and carry out the transaction. And both of these groups are separated from those who receive payment for the order. Such a division of data processing activities makes it difficult for fraud to go undetected since several people from different departments would have to be a party to any deception. Also, personnel in each organizational unit can check on the accuracy of others in the course of their routine operations. Thus, internal control has been achieved by the reviews and cross-checks made by people at separate points in the company. In other words, *internal control was employee-oriented.*

But computer usage may make it possible for processing steps to be consolidated and integrated so that these steps may all be performed by only one or two departments. With fewer departments involved, however, and with the likelihood that fewer poeple are cross-checking data, it *may appear* that, even though source documents originate outside the computer department, the use of computer systems results in a reduction of internal control. Responsible managers have sometimes been distressed to learn that such a reduction *can occur* in an *inadequately controlled* computer department and can produce the following related and unhappy results:

**1**   *Failure to safeguard assets.* Knowledgeable employees (or even a skilled outsider) can steal data and/or programs and sell them; they can acquire and use them intact to support an ongoing fraud or embezzlement; they can add, subtract, or substitute transactions in the data for fraud or embezzlement purposes; and they can do these things at the computer site or at a remote terminal hundreds of miles away.[7] Thieves have become interested in computerized financial records because the job of accounting for the assets of many organizations has now been entrusted to computer systems, and the moves by the banking industry in the direction of EFTS will simply hasten this trend. In the past, paper money was introduced and thieves used presses; now, plastic money (credit cards) and magnetic money (money cards with magnetic strips, computer tapes and disks) are used and thieves are using embossers and computers. And they are making big "hauls." The average computer embezzlement loss suffered by organizations is reported to be between $500,000 and $1 million—5 to 10 times higher than the average manual system loss. A widely discussed example of a "computer crime" is the case involving the chief teller at a Union Dime Savings Bank branch in New York City who was charged with stealing about $1.5 million from

---

[7] Computer science students and computer hobbyists have discovered that outsmarting a computer system can be an entertaining and challenging "game." It is reported that computer science students at one university reached a skill level that allowed them to write programs whose sole purpose was to "crash" the operating system of the school's computer. "There was keen competition among the best students to crash it elegantly, irreparably, frequently, and undetectably. . . . The computer, of course, spent most of its time being crashed or initialized. . . . The solution was a purely political one: every Thursday morning was set aside as "crash time" and students could run their programs from the operator's console and reinitialize the system themselves." (See Peter G. W. Keen and E. M. Gerson, "The Politics of Software System Design," *Datamation,* November 1977, p. 84). And a computer hobbyist from Florida claims to be able to get into anybody's system with a few telephone calls. He has obtained over $100,000 from a Canadian department store, has managed to acquire credit cards against which nothing is ever billed, and has received credit from airlines for tickets he did not buy. (See *Creative Computing,* July–August 1977, p. 128.)

the bank's accounts. Hundreds of legitimate accounts were manipulated; money was transferred to fraudulent accounts and then withdrawn; and false information was fed into the bank's computer so that when quarterly interest payments were due the legitimate accounts appeared intact. And all this was done by a person who did not have direct access to the computer. Other techniques used by computer-wise thieves include *(a)* deducting a few cents in excess service charges, interest, taxes, or dividends from thousands of accounts and writing themselves a check for the total amount of the excess deductions and *(b)* reporting inventory items as broken or lost and then transferring the items to accomplices.[8] In short, it has been estimated that losses suffered by organizations as a result of fraud and embezzlement now exceed those caused by robbery, loss, and shoplifting—and the computer is playing an active part in an increasing number of theft cases.

**2** *Failure to maintain the physical security of the computer site.* The very existence of some organizations would be threatened by the physical destruction of the files and software that may now be concentrated at a *single* site. Among the possible hazards are *fire, flood,* and *sabotage.* Thousands of military records were destroyed by fire at the Army Records Center in St. Louis; numerous computer centers were flooded in the mid-Atlantic states by the rains that accompanied tropical storm Agnes; and cases of disgruntled employees changing programs to sabotage records and using magnets to ruin tapes containing programs and data have been reported. Several computer centers were also destroyed by bombs during the antiwar period of the late 1960s and early 1970s.

**3** *Failure to maintain data integrity.* If input data are accurate and complete when they *enter* the computer system; if they are *classified, sorted,* and *updated* properly when necessary; if they do not become inaccurate through subsequent errors of omission or *calculation;* and if they are not distorted or lost through system malfunctions or operating mistakes, then a manager can be confident about the *integrity* of the data. Unfortunately, the internal control procedures in many businesses have sometimes failed to maintain a high degree of data integrity.

**4** *Failure to maintain data security.* As Fig. 14-2 indicates a modern computer system is vulnerable to attack and penetration at many points and from many people both inside and outside the organization. Programmers, operators, and maintenance personnel usually have the opportunity to penetrate systems security, and they may do so for per-

"Dawson, is there any truth in the rumor that you used company computers to work out a Vegas system?"

---

[8] For additonal techniques and examples, see Brandt Allen, "The Biggest Computer Frauds: Lessons for CPAs," *The Journal of Accountancy,* May 1977, pp. 52–62; Brandt Allen, "Embezzler's Guide to the Computer," *Harvard Business Review,* July–August 1975, pp. 79–89; Richard G. Canning, "The Importance of EDP Audit and Control," *EDP Analyzer,* June 1977, pp. 1–13, Hal Lancaster, "Rise of Minicomputers, Ease of Running Them Facilitates New Frauds," *Wall Street Journal,* Oct. 15, 1977, pp. 1ff.; Laton McCortney, "Is Paper Products Case Tip of the Iceberg?" *Datamation,* March 1977, pp. 148–149; Donn B. Parker, *Crime by Computer,* Charles Scribner's Sons, New York, 1976; Marshall Romney, "Detection and Deterrence: A Double Barreled Attack on Computer Fraud," *Financial Executive,* July 1977, pp. 36–41; K. S. Shankar, "The Total Computer Security Problem: An Overview," *Computer,* June 1977, pp. 50–61.

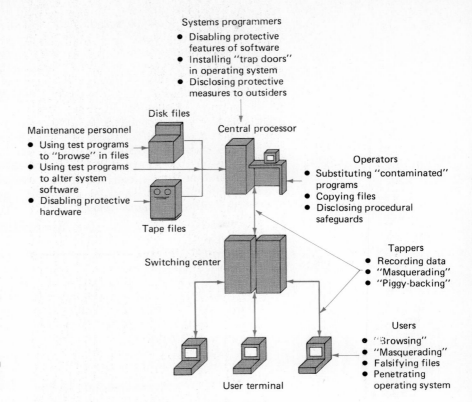

Systems programmers
- Disabling protective features of software
- Installing "trap doors" in operating system
- Disclosing protective measures to outsiders

Disk files

Central processor

Maintenance personnel
- Using test programs to "browse" in files
- Using test programs to alter system software
- Disabling protective hardware

Operators
- Substituting "contaminated" programs
- Copying files
- Disclosing procedural safeguards

Tape files

Switching center

Tappers
- Recording data
- "Masquerading"
- "Piggy-backing"

Users
- "Browsing"
- "Masquerading"
- Falsifying files
- Penetrating operating system

User terminal

FIGURE 14-2

(*Source:* Tom Alexander, "Waiting for the Great Computer Rip-off," *Fortune*, p. 144, July 1974.)

sonal grudges or for personal gain—e.g., for a bribe from an outsider. Operators, for example, can make duplicate copies of master tapes for outsiders in a few minutes, and programmers can insert code into an operating system in such a way that it provides a "trap door" for penetration at any convenient time in the future.[9] But even without help from within an organization, unscrupulous outsiders may gain access to the secrets and confidential records stored in an organization's computer system. Among the techniques employed against online systems are "masquerading" and "piggybacking." Penetrators obtain the passwords of legitimate users by wiretapping or other means and then use these passwords to masquerade as authorized users in order to get access to the system and to other people's files. The piggybacking approach is similar in that a small computer or "bootleg" terminal is attached to a tapped communications line where it may intercept and modify legitimate messages. In summary, then, those with motivation, financial resources, and access to computer skills may find that, as one authority has stated, penetrating today's computer system is about as difficult as solving the crossword puzzle in a Sunday paper.

[9] For further information on this penetration technique, see Richard G. Canning, "Protecting Valuable Data—Part 2." *EDP Analyzer*, January 1974, pp. 1–3.

**5**   *Failure to protect privacy rights of individuals.* Unlike the information stored in older systems, files maintained in large, integrated computer data banks may be more complete, less subject to deterioration, and therefore more worthy targets for unscrupulous persons bent on ferreting out information of a private and confidential nature. Seemingly innocent data recorded and stored at one time may be retrieved and correlated quickly and inexpensively by the computer (perhaps through the use of social security numbers) with other data collected from different sources and at different times to reveal information about individuals that might be damaging to them. It has only been in recent years that some managers have recognized the importance of safeguarding the privacy rights of those whose records are stored in their computer systems.

In spite of the possible dangers inherent in an inadequately controlled computer system, however, *there is no reason why a company should have less internal control because of computer usage.* On the contrary, there is no reason why *system-oriented controls,* in the form of computer programs, cannot be substituted for the employee-oriented controls of manual systems. Also, there is no reason why the separation of duties and responsibilities cannot be maintained *within* the computer department to safeguard the integrity of the system-oriented controls. In fact, there is no reason why a firm cannot achieve better control because of (1) the computer's ability to follow policies and execute processing procedures uniformly, (2) the difficulty of changing and manipulating, without detection, proper programmed systems controls, and (3) the computer's inherent accuracy advantage when given correct input data. Of course, top executives expect auditors to be sensitive to, and knowledgeable about, internal control arrangements that will avoid negative consequences.

**Auditors, auditing, and internal control[10]**   Auditors may either be employees of the organization *(internal auditors)* or be independent certified public accountants employed by the board of directors *(external auditors).* Periodic examinations or *audits* are performed by these auditors to evaluate the existing internal control arrangements. In studying these arrangements, auditors check to see if there is an *organizational separation of activities* within the computer department between those who design and prepare the new systems and those who prepare the input data and operate the equipment. In other words, analysts and

[10] For additional information on the effects of computer usage on auditors, auditing, and internal control, see Richard G. Canning, "The Importance of EDP Audit and Control," *EDP Analyzer,* June 1977, pp. 1–13; "Data Processing Audit Practices Report," and "Executive Report," *Systems Auditability and Control Study,* Institute of Internal Auditors, Inc., Altamonte Springs, Fla., 1977; Elise G. Jancura and Fred L. Lilly, "SAS No. 3 and the Evaluation of Internal Control," *The Journal of Accountancy,* March 1977, pp. 69–74; John B. Wardlaw, "Security, Control, and Auditing in a Dispersed Data Processing Environment," *The Internal Auditor,* June 1977, pp. 66–73; Bryan Wilkinson, "An Application Audit," *Datamation,* August 1977, pp. 51–55; and Edward K. Yasaki, "Who Is the DP Auditor?" *Datamation,* August 1977, pp. 55–58.

programmers should design, maintain, and make necessary changes (according to specified procedures) to programs, but they *should not* be involved with day-to-day production runs; equipment operators, on the other hand, should not have unrestricted access to completed computer programs, nor should they be involved with making changes in data or programs.

In addition to their concern about a proper separation of duties that can help safeguard assets, auditors are also concerned about whether adequate controls have been created to maintain data integrity and security. Thus, during the audit attention is turned to the *audit trail* to monitor systems activity, and to determine if security and integrity controls are effective. The audit trail begins with the recording of all transactions, winds through the processing steps and through any intermediate records which may exist and be affected, and ends with the production of output reports and records. By selecting a representative sample of previously processed source documents and following the audit trail, the auditor can trace these documents through the data processing systems to their final report or record destinations as a means of testing the adequacy of systems procedures and controls.

In a manual system, a visible and readily traceable paper trail is created from the time source documents are prepared until output reports are produced. With the introduction of computer systems, however, the form of the trail has changed. Of course, *it cannot be eliminated* because of the desire for good internal control and because of tax and legal requirements. The Internal Revenue Service (IRS), in a report on the use of EDP equipment, has said that the audit trail, or the ability of a system to trace a transaction from summary totals back to its source document, must not be eliminated. Nevertheless, intermediate steps in the information systems that were previously visible have *seemed to vanish* into magnetizeable and erasable media.

Nor will the audit trail become more visible in the future. The increased use of online direct-access storage devices to hold intermediate data and the substitution of online processing techniques for batch processing will result in an even greater decrease in the visible portion of the trail. For example, source documents may be replaced by machine language recordings made with transaction recording equipment; input data will originate from widely dispersed locations through the use of remote terminals (again, no paper documents need be involved); and a reorder message for a basic part may be transmitted by the computer to the supplier through the use of data communications facilities, with no paper documents being prepared. In examining such systems, the auditor must be satisfied that adequate controls are incorporated to prevent unintentional or deliberate damage to "invisible" files and records stored in an erasable medium. To comply with IRS requirements, for example, source data originating from online terminals may have to be "logged," or collected, in a separate operation by the system as they are processed.

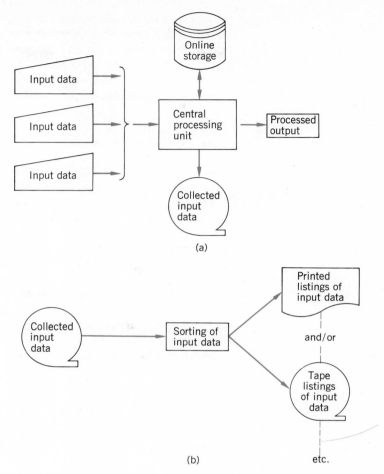

FIGURE 14-3

Preserving audit trail in online
processing environment. (*a*)
Collecting source data originating at
online terminals, (*b*) periodic sorting,
listing, and storing of collected
source data.

At prescribed intervals, the collected input data may then be sorted, listed, and stored in a suitable form so that the audit trail is preserved (see Fig. 14-3).

*Test data* may be used in the examination by the auditor. Just as the programmer uses simulated input data to check programs during the debugging and testing stage, so, too, may an auditor use test decks to check on program integrity and security controls. Both valid and invalid transactions are included in the test data. Of course, the fact that a program passes the auditor's test does not mean that the tested program always receives accurate input data or is always the one that is used during processing. Reasonable but incorrect input data may be supplied, and a fraudulent patch may be inserted into the program during subsequent processing runs.

The *function* of the auditor will probably not change in the future, but his or her *techniques* will certainly be subject to revision as a result of computer usage. One of the greatest challenges facing the systems designer and the auditor will be to devise ways of preserving an audit trail that (although it may seem to be nearly invisible) must be readily retrace-able. Furthermore, this trail must be kept as simple as possible, and it must not require great masses of supporting printed detail.

### a final note on management responsibility

We have now seen that the inadequate control of a computer system can lead to a lack of data integrity/data security and to a failure to safeguard vital assets (including the computer system itself). Furthermore, a lack of control can compromise the legitimate privacy rights of those whose records are stored in an organization's computer files.

Since poorly controlled computer systems are, at best, likely to pro-duce unreliable information for management decision-making purposes, and since, at worst, such systems can endanger the very existence of the organization, the *primary responsibility* for establishing overall internal control policies and procedures must reside with top-level executives. Furthermore, the *operational responsibility* for the accuracy and com-pleteness of input data and output information should reside with the managers of using departments. With proper management support, audi-tors *should* be expected to design appropriate controls into new systems and to perform periodic audits to ensure that these controls are reliable and efficient. but auditors *cannot* be expected to function effectively in an environment where top managers and users have simply assumed that data processing specialists will provide whatever controls are needed.

SUMMARY     Some of the implications for staffing and controlling that result from the use of computer-based information systems have been presented in this chapter. In the personnel/staffing area, we have seen that computer systems have changed the job duties of many managers and employees. In some cases these people have benefited from changes in job duties brought about by their organization's use of computers; in other cases, however, company personnel have been the victims of computer usage. The reorganization of work groups resulting from the installation of computer information systems can also lead to changes in the employ-ment status of individuals. Since some changes in employment status have threatened or damaged employees, it is not surprising that resistance to system change has been common.

Several controlling implications associated with the use of computer systems that are of concern to managers and auditors have also been presented in the preceding pages. We have seen, for example, that information produced by computer systems can help improve managerial control over business operations. But we have also seen that the introduction of a computer can have a significant effect on the internal control of the information system itself. In some cases, the control procedures that have replaced the numerous employee-oriented checks used in a manual system have been poorly designed. Several system failures resulting from poor internal controls were presented in the chapter. Of course, managers and auditors are concerned about these failures and are working to develop and preserve system-oriented controls and auditing procedures that will safeguard assets and maintain the integrity and security of the system. (Several of these specific control procedures are discussed in Chapter 16.)

**REVIEW AND DISCUSSION QUESTIONS**

1  (**a**) How may individuals benefit from changes in job duties resulting from computer usage? (**b**) How may their job duties be adversely affected?

2  What changes in employment status may result from computer usage?

3  (**a**) What is the distinction between displacement and unemployment? (**b**) What factors influence the significance of the displacement problem when computer systems are introduced into businesses?

4  (**a**) Identify an industry that has come into existence in the last 10 years. (**b**) What factors account for the creation of this industry? (**c**) Did the creation of this industry cause displacement elsewhere? (**d**) Would jobs have been lost to foreign producers if the industry had not been created? (**e**) What is your estimate of the net effect of this industry on total employment?

5  (**a**) Why do managers resist change? (**b**) Why do employees resist? (**c**) How may resistance to change be reduced?

6  How can computer systems help managers control business operations?

7  (**a**) What is internal control? (**b**) Why is it needed?

8  Identify and discuss the types of information system failures that can result from poor internal control.

9  Of what significance is organizational structure in maintaining internal control?

10  (**a**) What is the audit trail? (**b**) Why is it needed?

11  "Data integrity, data security, and personal privacy are interrelated." Define these terms and discuss this statement.

12  Why must the primary responsibility for internal control reside with top-level executives?

**SELECTED REFERENCES**

A number of good sources for additional information on topics discussed in this chapter have been presented in the chapter footnotes. In addition, you might find material of interest in the following references:

Bullard, Elmer W.: "A Data Processing View of Computer Auditing," *The Internal Auditor,* February 1977, pp. 69–73.

Feeney, William, and Frea Sladek: "The Systems Analyst as a Change Agent," *Datamation,* November 1977, pp. 85–88.

Menkus, Belden: "Management's Responsibilities for Safeguarding Information." *Journal of Systems Management,* December 1976, pp. 32–38.

Perry, William E.: "Internal Auditing of DP," *Infosystems,* August 1977, pp. 44ff.

Sterling, Theodor D., and Kenneth Landon: "Humanizing Information Systems," *Datamation,* December 1976, pp. 53–56ff.

# social
# implications
# of the
# business use
# of computers

# 15

LEARNING OBJECTIVES   After studying this chapter and answering the discussion questions, you should be able to: ☐ Describe some additional ways in which business computer usage may benefit society ☐ Outline how a lack of control over data integrity can lead to undesirable consequences for individuals in society ☐ Discuss how a lack of control over data security can have an adverse effect on individuals ☐ Explain why the creation of integrated computer data banks can threaten an individual's right to privacy

CHAPTER OUTLINE
Possible social benefits of business computer usage: Benefits to Nonbusiness Organizations / Benefits to Private Individuals
Possible negative implications of business computer

usage: Data Integrity Issues / Data Security Issues /
The Privacy Issue
Summary
Review and discussion questions
Selected references

In addition to affecting the planning, organizing, staffing, and controlling activities *within* an organization, computer usage in business is also exerting a significant influence *outside* the business community on society as a whole. Of course, it is not possible to present a full discussion of the social impact of computer usage.[1] But it is also not possible to discuss the "computer implications for management" in this Part of the text without considering some of the effects that the business use of computers is having on customers and others that a business firm must serve if it is to continue to exist. Therefore, in the pages that follow, we shall first look at some of the possible *beneficial social implications of business computer usage*. Some of the possible *negative influences that business computers may have* on our changing society are then examined.

**POSSIBLE SOCIAL BENEFITS OF BUSINESS COMPUTER USAGE**

We should never lose sight of the important fact that business computer usage has already had a positive influence on (and will continue to offer countless benefits to) *nonbusiness organizations* and *private individuals*.

### benefits to nonbusiness organizations

Much of the work involved in developing and/or improving (1) sophisticated software products and (2) computer-based decision-making tools and techniques has been sponsored by computer-using businesses. And these tools, techniques, and software products have then been adapted for the use and benefit of numerous nonbusiness entities—e.g., government units and hospitals, to name just two categories.

To briefly illustrate, some of the management science tools and techniques used to tackle industrial management problems have been applied

[1] For more information on this general topic, see Donald H. Sanders, *Computers in Society*, 2d ed., McGraw-Hill Book Company, New York, 1977.

in the attempt to solve public problems at the federal, state, and local levels. The state of California, for example, has called on aerospace firms to conduct systems studies on such problems as police protection and waste management.[2] And inventory control techniques and software developed by businesses have been used by military leaders for planning and controlling logistics—i.e., for managing the procurement, storage, and transportation of needed supplies and equipment. Finally, hospitals (and educational institutions) are also the beneficiaries of business computer experience. Accumulating patient charges, keeping track of health insurance coverages, ordering and then controlling supplies and medicines, preparing patient bills, accounting and paying for services and supplies purchased, preparing personnel payrolls—these are but a few of the businesstype applications that a hospital must process.

### benefits to private individuals

We all know that the federal government provides certain services to individuals that require the use of computers. Without computers, for example, the Social Security Administration could not keep up with the payment of benefits to widows, orphans, and retired persons, and the Federal Aviation Administration could not effectively control the aircraft traffic in congested areas. But we sometimes fail to realize the extent to which we benefit from the business use of computers.

Some (but certainly not all) of the possible benefits that private individuals may receive from their dealings with computer-using business organizations are

1  *The benefits of greater efficiency.* Most of us have probably been disturbed by the way prices have increased for many of the goods and services that we buy. However, what we may perhaps fail to realize is that, to the extent that businesses have avoided waste and improved efficiency and productivity through the use of computers, the prices we now pay may be less than they would otherwise have been. Edmund Berkeley, editor of *Computers and People,* has estimated that "the use of computers on a large scale has made prices lower by 10 to 30 percent and often much more, than they would be without computers."[3] For

---

[2] It should be noted, however, that the decision-making approaches developed for industrial applications have not always been appropriate for the social problems to which they have been applied. In some cases, precise computer-generated analyses of the behavior of complex humanistic systems have simply not been relevant to the real-world social, political, and economic problems that face individuals and groups.
For more information on the limitations of using these techniques to solve social problems, see Ida R. Hoos, "Can Systems Analysis Solve Social Problems?" *Datamation,* pp. 82–83ff, June 1974; and C. C. Gotlieb and A. Borodin, *Social Issues in Computing,* Academic Press, New York, 1973, pp. 126–137.

[3] Edmund C. Berkeley, "How Do Computers Affect People?" *Computers and People,* April 1975, p. 6.

example, industrial engineers are using computers extensively for *production planning and scheduling* purposes. The amount of planning and scheduling required varies from one production process to another. An assembly line which produces a standard item with little or no variation requires less in the way of planning and scheduling than does the operation of a machine shop where nonstandard items are produced every day and where different jobs require different raw materials and different machine operations. Such a *job shop* is typically organized by types of machines used (i.e., lathes may be at one location, stamping machines at another, etc.). The *sequence* of operations *varies* in a job shop from one product to another. Not surprisingly, the planning and scheduling is more difficult because each job may require completely different raw materials and a completely different production sequence. In one job, for example, drill presses may be required near the end of the project, and in another job the same machinery may be needed at an early stage. Engineers must attempt to plan and schedule operations to minimize bottlenecks at one location and slack periods at another. In short, planners must seek to minimize waiting times for raw materials, maximize the use of expensive machinery, and complete the jobs on the dates promised the customers. Computers are used in this complex environment to help planners obtain maximum total performance at the lowest possible cost.[4] And as we saw in Chapter 5 (and in Fig. 5-12), data collection stations tied to computers may be used to transmit such facts as the time spent on an operation, the status of a machine tool, or the size of a queue requiring work. The computer may then be used to compare the actual conditions against the production plan in order to determine if appropriate *control* action is required. In addition to controlling the overall production process, computers may also be used to control individual production tools and to thus increase efficiency. For example, numerically controlled machine tools, directed by computer-produced tapes, can be used to automatically produce precision parts meeting blueprint specifications. Finally, to the extent that these computer applications significantly improve productivity—i.e., the amount of goods or services possessing economic value that individuals and machines can produce in a given time period—these productivity gains can lead to (*a*) a stronger competitive position in the world for United States firms, and (*b*) higher levels of real income for an increased number of individuals.

**2** *The benefits of higher-quality products.* In addition to possibly having an impact on the prices we pay *to* businesses, computers may also play a role in improving the quality of the products we receive *from* them. For example, computerized process-control systems are being used to monitor such continuously operating facilities as oil refineries, chemical plants, and steel and paper mills. These processes are similar in that they convert input materials and energy into output materials, products, converted energy, and waste. During the process, instruments measure such variables as pressure, temperature, flow, and so on. If the process is

---

[4] An example of a production planning and scheduling system is found in Jerome P. Rickert, "On-Line Support for Manufacturing," *Datamation*, July 1975, pp. 46–48.

deviating from an acceptable quality standard, regulating devices are adjusted to bring the process back into control. In an *open-loop* operation, the computer records instrument readings, compares the readings against quality standards, and notifies process-control personnel of needed manual adjustments in regulating devices; in a more complex *closed-loop* operation (Fig. 15-1), the computer receives measurements, makes comparisons, and, *in addition,* sends signals to the regulatory devices to make the necessary changes. Of course, human operators may monitor the overall process and instruct the computer to make occasional changes in control parameters in particular situations. But the control operation is essentially automatic. Use of the computer in this way permits quicker-responding and more accurate quality control than would otherwise be possible. The use of minicomputers for process-control applications is expanding rapidly in business.

**3**   *The benefits of better service.* Businesses also use computers to improve the services they provide to customers. Computer processing techniques, for example, make possible the shortening of customer waiting lines at airline ticket offices and at the reservation desks of hotels, motels, and car-rental agencies; the use of credit cards as a convenient means of handling purchase transactions; and the efficient control of inventory in retail outlets so that popular items are reordered in time to

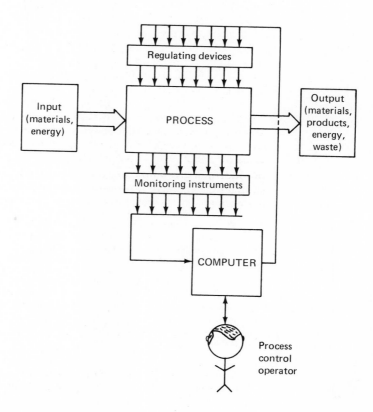

**FIGURE 15-1**

Process and quality control.

avoid many of the out-of-stock situations that frustrate consumers. Other examples that involve the use of computers to improve customer service include the monitoring of electricity-generating networks so that power failures can be minimized,[5] and the controlling of automobile tire records so that tire buyers can be quickly notified if flaws are suspected. In this latter example, federal regulations require that tire manufacturers maintain, for at least 3 years, records of those who purchased new tires. Tires are identified by a serial number that includes the manufacturer's code number, size of the tire, and the week it was produced. Should a tire be found defective, all other tires produced by the manufacturer during the week may have to be recalled. With annual sales of 300 million tires, the task of keeping buyer records is obviously a formidable one. Axicom Systems, Inc., of Paramus, New Jersey, has established a Tire Safety Registry system to handle the entire record-keeping problem. Tire dealers, at the time of purchase, fill out forms giving the necessary information (buyer's name, address, tire, numbers, etc.). These forms are then sent to Paramus, where the information is kept in online storage devices. If a recall is necessary, the computer retrieves from the batch in question the names and addresses of all purchasers of tires. Buyers are then notified by certified mail of the recall and are instructed to return the tires to a dealer for replacement.

4   *The possible benefits of EFTS.* We have seen in earlier chapters (e.g., Chapter 5, page 144) that financial and retailing organizations are very interested in the use of electronic funds transfer systems (EFTS). But how

---

[5] The following hypothetical narrative shows how computers can help maintain electrical service to customers (the facts are true; only the names have been changed to protect the innocent).

It was Tuesday, September 22, 197X. It was hot in Philadelphia. I was working the day watch in the control room of PJM—the Pennsylvania–New Jersey–Maryland Interconnection—an electric power pool that coordinates power distribution to 20 million people from the 500 generating units belonging to PJM's 12 participating companies. My partners' names are Wednesday and Saturday. My name is Thursday. Every 2 seconds our computer monitors generation and transmission-line power flow. If deviations from preselected standards are detected on the nearly 4,000 miles of transmission lines, the computer runs a check to give me details on system conditions. In addition, every 5 minutes the computer simulates the effect of unexpected breakdowns in selected generators and transmission lines. In spite of the heat wave and the peak use of electricity for air conditioning, it looked like it would be a routine day at the control room. Then, at 8 a.m., the Oyster Creek Number One generator in New Jersey went out of service. Quick computations showed that PJM would not have enough generating capacity in the afternoon unless output levels were increased. I tried to buy power from neighboring power networks but none was available (one smart aleck offered to sell me a D-cell battery). Anyway, by increasing output, PJM was meeting the demand. But then, at 2:29 p.m., the Number Two generator at the Keystone complex in western Pennsylvania overheated, tripped its circuit breaker, took 750 megawatts of power out of the network—and ruined my coffee break. Fortunately, the computer had already simulated the loss of Keystone Number Two. To relieve overloaded lines, generation had to be shifted throughout the network. Generators serving overloaded lines had to be curtailed; those serving safe lines had to be speeded up. The computer evaluated alternative ways of meeting needs and we were somehow able to prevent a major power failure by optimizing the use of the network.

can these systems benefit individuals in our society? (Once again you have asked the right question!) Although EFTS are still in the formative stages and the fully developed version(s) will be shaped by intense competition and government regulation, their general shape is clear enough for us to identify certain advantages for individuals. In a *check-less payment system,* for example, authorized credits to specified individuals from an employer, pension fund, etc., are recorded on magnetic tape along with the name of the recipient's bank and his or her bank account number. The tape is delivered to the paying organization's bank. This bank sorts out its own customers, deposits the payment amounts to their accounts, and then transfers the remaining names to an *automated clearing house* (ACH) facility. An ACH computer sorts the remaining names according to their banks and then notifies these banks of the amounts to be deposited in the specified accounts. A benefit of this EFTS approach is that it eliminates the fear of theft of checks. Millions of people are now receiving direct-deposit Social Security payments in lieu of mailed checks. As one recipient living on Chicago's South Side has noted, "It's better for [the check] to be in the bank than to take the chance of having it in your mailbox."[6] Another way in which EFTS may benefit individuals will involve the use of terminals conveniently located anywhere that substantial numbers of nontrivial financial transactions occur. Point-of-sale *cash terminal systems,* for example, have been tested and found to be technologically feasible. When such systems are fully developed, you might present your plastic "currency" or "debit" card (which uses, perhaps, a magnetic stripe to supply the necessary account information) to make a request at a store's terminal for an electronic transfer of funds to pay for a purchase. The terminal would then send a message to your bank asking for approval of the transfer. If your account has the necessary funds (or if you are eligible for sufficient credit), the bank's computer would (1) send a message approving the transaction to the merchant's terminal, and (2) see to the transfer of the payment funds to the merchant's account. This EFTS approach would give individuals the benefits associated with completing transactions for cash (speed, lack of "red tape," etc.) without the possible dangers associated with carrying large amounts of cash. Of course, you and the merchant may use different banks and so one or more ACH facilities would be used in the transaction to switch and process messages. Fully developed cash terminal systems will depend on a strong national network of ACHs. But a National Automated Clearing House Association (NACHA) has been formed, and other ACH facilities are being developed (Fig. 15-2).

**5** *The possible benefits of UPC.* Merchants selling products coded with the Universal Product Code (UPC) symbols discussed in Chapter 4 expect to receive the benefits of greater efficiency and reduced costs. But their customers may also find that a UPC system (1) reduces their waiting time and gives them faster service at checkout counters, (2) reduces the chances for human error at checkouts, and (3) provides them with an *itemized* sales receipt rather than just a tape with a column of numbers.

---

[6] *Wall Street Journal,* Nov. 18, 1975, p. 15.

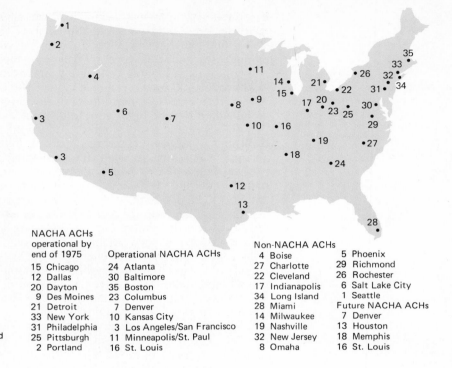

FIGURE 15-2

Operational and planned automated
clearinghouses.

| NACHA ACHs operational by end of 1975 | Operational NACHA ACHs | Non-NACHA ACHs | |
| --- | --- | --- | --- |
| 15 Chicago | 24 Atlanta | 4 Boise | 5 Phoenix |
| 12 Dallas | 30 Baltimore | 27 Charlotte | 29 Richmond |
| 20 Dayton | 35 Boston | 22 Cleveland | 26 Rochester |
| 9 Des Moines | 23 Columbus | 17 Indianapolis | 6 Salt Lake City |
| 21 Detroit | 7 Denver | 34 Long Island | 1 Seattle |
| 33 New York | 10 Kansas City | 28 Miami | Future NACHA ACHs |
| 31 Philadelphia | 3 Los Angeles/San Francisco | 14 Milwaukee | 7 Denver |
| 25 Pittsburgh | 11 Minneapolis/St. Paul | 19 Nashville | 13 Houston |
| 2 Portland | 16 St. Louis | 32 New Jersey | 18 Memphis |
| | | 8 Omaha | 16 St. Louis |

**6** *The possible recreational benefits.* Some organizations are using
computers for the sole purpose of amusing and entertaining individuals.
For example, the computer of Recreational Computer Systems, Inc.,
Atlanta, Georgia, is used for just this purpose. In one application, image
enhancement technology developed for the Mariner spacecraft project
has been used to convert a small customer photograph into a 12- by 12-
inch mosaic of computer printer characters (Fig. 15-3).[7] In addition to
those organizations that are using computers to entertain customers, there
are other concerns that are manufacturing sophisticated games containing microprocessors that may be attached to television sets. The possibilities in this area are discussed in the last chapter.

## POSSIBLE NEGATIVE IMPLICATIONS OF BUSINESS COMPUTER USAGE

It should be apparent by now that computer systems have taken on
increasingly responsible tasks in many organizations and are now performing vital functions in our society. Thus, it is essential that in the data
processing steps performed by business computers *vital and relevant data
are not lost or stolen, errors are not introduced into the data, and data are*

[7] The original 12- by 12-inch mosaic in Fig. 15-3 obviously had to be reduced to fit on the
page. Unfortunately, the computer could do nothing to enhance the features of the subject
of the photograph.

FIGURE 15-3

Computer-produced mosaic from customer photograph. *(Courtesy Recreational Computer Systems, Inc.)*

*not stored, retrieved, modified, or communicated without proper authorization.* In other words, as Fig. 15-4 shows, it is essential that the interrelated issues of *data integrity, data security,* and *personal privacy* be given careful consideration in the design and use of business computer systems. Unfortunately, however, some businesses have used questionable data processing practices that have tended to ignore some of these issues and that have thus had adverse effects on the private lives of individuals.

### data integrity issues

The data processing steps that must be carried out properly if data integrity is to be maintained are *originating-recording, classifying, sorting,* and *calculating.* Let's now look at some of the possible ways in which the insensitive and/or thoughtless performance of these steps may lead to undesirable social results.

**Data originating-recording matters**    A staggering volume of information of a highly personal nature has been (and is being) gathered and recorded by businesses (e.g., credit bureaus, insurance companies, etc.) as well as

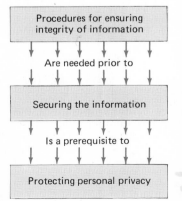

by governmental agencies. One fear arising from this development is that an unscrupulous person could be tempted by existing technology and the availability of mounds of computer-accessible data on individuals to misuse the data in ways not originally intended. Facts about age, sex, income, marital status, health, spending habits, life-style, etc., could be analyzed in a trial-and-error fashion just to see what might happen. In summary, as Frank T. Cary, chairman of the board of IBM, has observed:

In the past you had to be famous or infamous to have a dossier. Today there can be a dossier on anyone. Information systems, with seemingly limitless capacity for storing and sorting information, have made it practical to record and transfer a wealth of data on just about anyone. The result is that we now retain too much information. The ambiguous and unverified are retained along with legitimate data. . . . One way of preventing misuse of personal information is to discourage its collection in the first place.[8]

In addition to the widespread general concern about the seemingly uncontrolled collection of personal information on individuals, some more specific problems associated with the originating-recording step are

**1**  *Gathering data without a valid need to know.* When he was Vice President, Gerald Ford wrote that it was the responsibility of all who use computers to "assure that information is not fed into the computer unless it is relevant. Even if it is relevant, there is still a need for discretion. A determination must be made if the social harm done from some data outweighs its usefulness."[9]

**2**  *Using gathered data in ways not originally intended.* It was brought out during the Watergate scandal that the Nixon administration had tried to obtain printouts from IRS computers in order to possibly use the tax information against its political opponents. Although abuses of this magnitude have not been reported in business, any temptation to use personal data gathered for some legitimate purpose in ways not originally planned or approved should be resisted.

**3**  *Gathering inaccurate and incomplete data.* More "computer errors" may be attributed to inaccurate and incomplete data input than to either hardware failure or incorrect software. *Unintentional mistakes* in filling out input forms, keying records, coding accounts, etc., are common enough in any record-keeping system. But the consequences may be more serious in a computer-based system because there may be fewer individuals to catch errors and the speed with which inaccurate information is made available to system users may be much faster than the speed with which errors are detected and corrected. The author, for example, had a check to a major oil company "bounce" because that particular check had been encoded with an incorrect account number by a clerk at

[8] Quoted by Hanna Shields and Mae Churchill in "The Fraudulent War on Crime," *The Nation,* Dec. 21, 1974, p. 655.

[9] Gerald R. Ford, "Individual Privacy and Databanks," *The Internal Auditor,* July/August 1974, p. 14.

his bank. Although in time the bank wrote letters of apology and a new check was issued to the oil company, there is still the possibility that in some credit bureau data bank there may be a negative entry in his dossier that has not been corrected. In another example, a keypunching mistake resulted in an electric bill (and subsequent warnings about nonpayment) being sent to the wrong address. You have probably already guessed the outcome: One cold night the electricity was cut off as a result of a computer-prepared disconnect message, and the household was without power until the error could be corrected. Additional problems can result from cases of *mistaken identity*. Good, bad, and indifferent input data prepared by grantors of credit usually find their way into credit bureau data banks. If your name is not keyed correctly, if your address has changed, if you have a common name, or if you are not consistent in the way you use your first name and initials, you may be confused with some other individual (and with your luck it would be a "deadbeat" rather than a millionaire). Thus, as Robert L. Patrick has observed:

Despite all the programming done by all the clearing-houses to date, these mistaken identities do occur, they are troublesome, and they are one of the primary reasons why credit reporting agencies treat individuals unfairly.[10]

Unfortunately, in addition to the unintentional mistakes that occur in credit bureau input data, *deliberate* errors have also been introduced into these data banks that are so important to individuals. "In one credit bureau, investigators have admitted to falsifying computer input data because they feel their case loads are too heavy to allow them time to gather all the details called for by the system."[11]

**4**  *Problems of confusion and bewilderment associated with data gathering.* There have been several verified cases of frustrated individuals actually firing bullets into computers. And the number of such incidents would probably be much larger if individuals confused and bewildered by computer data input procedures had followed their initial impulses. A significant cause of this confusion, of course, is that people affected by an information system are often not informed of what the system does or how it works. And the result of this confusion may be the belief on the part of individuals that they have been tricked or deceived by the system. Credit application forms, for example, may not indicate that the supplied data are going to be entered into third-party data banks and used in rather secretive ways. Innocent errors in filling out one form may be considered as highly suspicious discrepancies in a consolidated data bank. Another potential source of confusion lies in the pricing of products in supermarkets using scanning equipment to read UPC symbols. As originally designed, the UPC system would save time and money for stores by eliminating the need to mark the price on *each* item; rather, a *single*

[10] Robert L. Patrick, "Privacy, People, and Credit Services," *Datamation,* January 1974, p. 49.

[11] Frederic G. Withington, "Five Generations of Computers," *Harvard Business Review,* July–August 1974, p. 107.

price would be posted on the shelf containing the item. (The computer, of course, would store the current prices of all products in the store for checkout purposes.) However, consumers are concerned about price confusion that may result in their knowing less and paying more. At this writing legislation has been introduced in Congress and in dozens of state and local governments to require that the price be stamped on every item. Individuals may also find it confusing to operate the computer input devices that are replacing more familiar forms and procedures. Automated voting systems, for example, have confused voters and have produced questionable tallys. Finally, people have been bewildered by the use of the deposit slips with magnetically encoded account numbers that banks supply to customers. It is reported that in at least one case a man distributed his encoded deposit slips about the lobby of a bank where they were used by bewildered depositors who wrote their names and account numbers on the slips. Since the names and handwritten numbers were ignored by the bank's MICR equipment, however, the deposits were credited to the account number encoded on the slips. The following morning our resourceful swindler closed out his $67,000 account and proceeded on his way.

Classification-sorting matters     Classifying and sorting input data according to some commonly defined and consistently organized coding scheme can lead to more *standardized* information systems. And the standardization now taking place in organizations may result in economies and increased efficiency. But standardization may also lead to unwanted *depersonalization.* As an individual comes in contact with an increasing number of computer systems, the use of numerical codes for identification purposes may also be expected to increase. Although individuals may understand that their being treated as numbers can lead to standardized and efficient computer usage by organizations, they may wish that it were not so. Instead of being numerically coded and molded to meet the computer's needs, they might prefer that the computer systems be designed so that they would be treated as persons rather than as numbers. *This is not likely to happen.* Depersonalization is something that individuals are likely to have to submit to more often in the future. Of course, as standardization spreads, individuals may need to remember fewer code numbers—e.g., their Social Security numbers may be substituted for several different codes. In fact, the Social Security number is now being used as the personal identifier in a number of large data systems. The Internal Revenue Service, the U.S. Army, colleges and universities, state driver's license departments, insurance companies, banks, credit bureaus—these and many other organizations may know you as 353-27-4765. The threat of an eventual "universal identifier," of course, is that the separate data records you have established for particular purposes can easily be consolidated through the use of the common number, and the combined data can be merged into a large personal dossier.

"Sorry, but I'll have to check on you. What is your Social Security number?"

© DATAMATION ®

In addition to treating individuals as numbers, standardized procedures, once established, tend to become inflexible.[12] Thus, if an individual's needs do not conform to the "norms" of the system, there may be difficulty in getting the system to deal properly with the exception. This tendency to try to force everyone into the same mold may naturally give the individual a feeling of helplessness in trying to cope with a cold, impersonal, and remote organization. A Mr. D'Unger, for example, wrote several organizations asking them to spell his name correctly. He received several replies, all telling him that it was impossible because of the equipment employed by the systems. A computer expert then looked into the matter and found that the line printers involved had the apostrophe available, but the systems did not bother to use it.

---

[12] This tendency toward inflexibility is *not* an inherent flaw of computer usage. Actually, computerized systems can make individual treatment possible and can cater to individuality for less cost than manual systems. But uniform and rigid treatment costs even less to provide and is thus the approach too often used by system designers.

System miscalculations   Miscalculations are primarily due to human errors in preparing input data, in designing and preparing programs, and in operating the hardware. Thus, when the computer itself is blamed for some foul-up, it is frequently being used as a convenient "scapegoat" to cover up human error, carelessness, or indifference. Or, perhaps, it is being used to add credibility to false claims. For example, the Allen Piano and Organ Company of Phoenix, Arizona, advertised on a radio broadcast that its computer had made a mistake and as a result the firm was overstocked with furniture which it was now offering at bargain prices. When a local computer professional, on behalf of the Association for Computing Machinery, contacted the firm and offered to repair any malfunctioning computer hardware free of charge, he found that the company did not have a computer and did not use any computing service!

Of course, the unfortunate fact remains that people may believe such false advertising because they are aware of computer system miscalculations that actually have occurred. Since we have already seen some examples of business system miscalculations in Chapter 3, we need not belabor the point here. But perhaps it might be appropriate to conclude this section with a few pitiful examples of nonbusiness computer system "atrocities" that have had a negative impact on individuals.

1   A New York City employee failed to get his check for three pay periods after a computer payroll system was installed. Finally, after the employee had initiated legal action against the City, a program bug was discovered, removed, and Mr. Void was at last paid.

2   Individuals have been arrested for "stealing" their own cars. The sequence of events goes something like this: The car is stolen, the theft is reported to a law enforcement data bank, the car is recovered (perhaps in another jurisdiction) and returned to its owner, the recovery is *not* entered into the data bank, and the owner is then picked up while driving the recovered property. Since the arrest may also be entered into the data bank, but the final disposition may not be, the owner may wind up with an arrest record for "grand theft-auto." If you do not think this can be serious, you should consider the plight of the ex-Marine from Illinois who has been jailed several times for desertion because of incorrect information stored in the FBI's computerized National Crime Information Center.

### data security issues

In addition to the need to maintain data integrity, businesses must also maintain the security of the data if adverse effects are to be eliminated. In other words, the data processing steps of *summarizing, communicating, storing, retrieving,* and *reproducing* must also be controlled if negative consequences for organizations and for people are to be avoided. It does not help an organization if its secret product data that fall into the hands of a competitor are accurate. And it does not help much for people to know that the information relevant to them that has been summarized and stored in a data bank is accurate and complete if they also know that the information is *not secured* and protected against theft, fraud, accidental or malicious scrutiny, manipulation, and/or destruction.

Problems with the security of information systems existed before and during the time that computers first began to replace file cabinets. But the vulnerability of computer systems has increased substantially in recent years, and so the security issue has become much more important. Early computers were generally located in self-contained installations, were accessible to a relatively small number of specialists, and were employed to process batches of data in a single stream. As computer systems increased in number and became more sophisticated, however, multiprogramming and multiprocessing concepts became available, many more individuals had access to information systems, the use of shared resources and jointly used data became common, and remote access to direct interaction with a distant computer became a routine operation for even casual users. Such an environment has obviously increased the difficulty of maintaining security. But in addition to the security difficulties caused by easy systems access by many people, the vulnerability of systems has also increased because (1) the information to be found in a relatively complete and up-to-date data bank may be of sufficient value to provide the incentive for outsiders to seek access to it, and (2) an increased number of individuals have now been trained in computer science and in the skills required to program, penetrate, and manipulate computer systems.[13]

Since the security of computer systems was recognized as a significant problem only in recent years, the computer *hardware* in general use today was not designed with security provisions in mind. Thus, the security provisions that do exist are found in the software and in the organizational policies, administrative procedures, and data processing controls that may exist in the particular system.

When it comes to security, existing *software* is indeed soft. Clever individuals have had no difficulty in breaking through the security provisions of those computer operating system programs that they have sought to penetrate. In fact, a favorite activity of some bright students on college campuses has been to successfully infiltrate the college computer system. For example, two students—one a theology major!—at little Southern Missionary College in Collegedale, Tennessee, "broke through" the file-security system used in the Hewlett-Packard 2000 series timeshared computers and devised programs that decoded protected files.

[13] For example, a few years ago, as part of their rehabilitation programs to provide inmates with marketable skills, several penitentiaries began offering courses in computer programming. For one example of such a program, see Derek Reveron, "Computer Enterprise behind Prison Walls Wins Outside Clients," *Wall Street Journal*, Oct. 19, 1977, pp. 1ff.

Whether the invaders be theology majors who doth covet their neighbor's files for the challenge presented, or whether they be thieves, criminal manipulators, saboteurs, or spies, they have found that the computer center of an organization may be its nerve center, that it usually contains sensitive information, and that it is often vulnerable to attack. Without adequate computer security provisions, a business, as we have seen, may be exposed to danger through theft, through careless handling of records, through espionage, and/or through sabotage. But a lack of control over data security has also led to *undesirable consequences for individuals in society.*

Individuals as well as organizations *lose money* to the computer thief. In one instance, a computer was used to send out phony invoices to individuals. The thief knew that some people pay authentic-looking bills automatically, without questioning their validity. When a phony bill was questioned, however, the thief would merely send back a form letter saying, "Sorry. Our computer made an error." In another instance, bank customers have found that several times a year small errors in favor of the bank have occurred in their statements. Some customers have complained, but since the losses are small, most people probably have not bothered. At this writing, the bank in question does not know what is happening. It is estimated, however, that the mysterious thief may be realizing about $300,000 each year from individuals. A person's finances could also become fouled up as a result of the penetration of an EFTS by an enemy or an unethical competitor. Invalid charges from organizations selected by the penetrator—e.g., insurance companies, utilities, department stores—could be entered against the individual's accounts. At best, the resulting mess would probably involve long delays and great *inconvenience* to straighten out; at worst, it could result in financial ruin.

Finally, our society expects that confidential data on individuals be preserved and used only by authorized persons for approved purposes. But a lack of control over data security can lead to the invasion of an individual's legitimate *right to privacy.* Since this is the subject of the next section, we will not dwell on it here. It should be pointed out here, however, that the majority of computer systems installed in the nation today are *not* secure enough to meet the personal data confidentiality conditions required by existing laws; nor are they secure enough to protect the privacy rights which existing laws give to individuals.

### the privacy issue

As every man goes through life, he fills in a number
of forms for the record, each containing a number of
questions. There are thus hundreds of little threads
radiating from each man, millions of threads in all. If

these threads were suddenly to become visible,
people would lose all ability to move.

Alexander Solzhenitsyn

As we saw in Fig. 15-4, both data integrity and security are needed to protect an individual's legitimate *right to privacy*—i.e., to protect the right of an individual to limit the access to personal and often sensitive information to persons authorized to use it in the individual's best interests.

For years, private and public organizations have been building separate files containing "threads" of information about those with whom they come in contact. We know that the use of these files has led to past abuses of individuals' legitimate right to keep to themselves (or to have kept on a confidential basis) those facts, beliefs, thoughts, and feelings that they do not wish to divulge publicly. But, many of these older files are incomplete and poorly maintained. Thus, the value of their contents may be such that unauthorized persons have little incentive to snoop. But as we saw in the last chapter, *the development of computer data banks has changed the situation.* Up-to-date personal information files stored on readily accessible media and devices in large consolidated data banks may now be worthy targets for unscrupulous persons. Thoughtful opponents of consolidated data banks are therefore concerned about the threat that they might eventually present to an individual. This concern is perhaps best summarized in a *Saturday Review* cartoon which shows a distressed executive listening to a telephone message. The message is: "This is the Computer Data Bank. Leave $100,000 in small bills in Locker 287 at the Port Authority Bus Terminal or I'll print out your complete dossier and send it to your wife."

There are several possible negative implications of business computer usage that are linked to the subject of individual privacy. The following examples and speculations should be sufficient to demonstrate how a computer system or network could be used for *surveillance activities,* for *list-compiling abuses,* and for the creation of a *climate that can restrict individual freedom.*

EFTS surveillance possibilities   Although the EFTS being designed and implemented by banks and other financial institutions are not intended for surveillance, they may be easily adapted to this purpose in the future. If all your nontrivial financial transactions were normally to be processed through EFTS computers, a *daily record* of much of *what* you do and *where* you do it could be prepared. Thus, the situation illustrated in a *New Yorker* magazine cartoon of a husband and wife trying to decide what movie to see and the wife asking her husband "What would look good on our dossier?" could become less amusing and more possible in the future. Furthermore, if you were to decide to use cash for a transaction that you wished to keep private, the cash acquisition might be quite conspicuous (and suspicious?). In 1971, a group of computer, communication, and surveillance experts was gathered and given the following hypothetical problem: As advisers to the head of the KGB (the Russian Secret Police), they were to design an *unobtrusive* surveillance system to monitor the activities of all citizens and visitors inside the USSR. As Paul Armer testified in congressional hearings:

That exercise . . . was only a two-day effort. I am sure we could add some bells and whistles to increase its effectiveness somewhat. But the fact remains that this group decided that if you wanted to build an unobtrusive system for surveillance, you couldn't do much better than an EFTS.[14]

Of course, EFTS proponents in the financial community maintain that adequate laws can be passed to prevent surveillance abuse. But critics are not so sure. They point out that existing check authorization systems, and systems such as BankAmericard, Master Charge, and American Express, can "flag" individual accounts so that if a "flagged" individual tries to cash a check or make a purchase someone (police perhaps?) can be notified of the individual's exact location. And they are fearful that future operators of EFTS networks would be unable to resist the pressures from government organizations to allow the EFTS to be used for surveillance purposes.

List-compiling abuses   Mailing lists giving details about individuals are regularly compiled and sold by both private and public organizations. State auto licensing agencies, for example, sell lists to auto equipment suppliers. There is probably not much harm in this if it results only in your receiving literature that tries to persuade you to buy seat covers a few weeks after you have registered your new car. But what about the case of the computer dating service that sold its list of female clients to a publishing organization that printed and sold through local newsstands lists of "Girls Who Want Dates"? Try and tell one of those women that her privacy hasn't been invaded!

Freedom restrictions   Consider the following facts:

1   At this time, thousands of bank, employment agency, and credit company employees have access to law-enforcement and other data-gathering networks that contain information on millions of people. It is possible that employees without any real "need to know" may while away the time browsing through the records of friends and acquaintances just to see what they can uncover.

2   In at least one state, insurance companies have access to records

---

[14] See Paul Armer, "Computer Technology and Surveillance," *Computers and People,* September 1975, p. 11.

"I wrote to the FBI for my personal file. They say they never heard of me and I should stop bothering them."

© DATAMATION ●

containing the name, Social Security number, and diagnosis of patients hospitalized for psychiatric treatment.

3   Most categories of personal information gathered for legitimate research purposes by reputable social and behavioral scientists do not enjoy any statutory protection. Thus, sensitive personal information gathered by well-intentioned researchers may be obtained through a subpoena issued by a court, legislative committee, or other government body and put into data banks for future use. If the researchers, who may have assured the respondents that their replies would be kept in strictest confidence, refuse to honor the subpoena and turn over the data, they may be cited for contempt and be made to suffer the consequences. Given that alternative, the data are generally surrendered.

The awareness of such facts and such uses of large computerized data banks tends to have a sobering effect on individuals—it tends to restrict their freedom, and it tends to have a chilling effect on their actions even when the data are accurate, even when the use of the data is authorized by law, and even when controls on the use of the data are imposed. You may agree, for example, that credit bureau data banks play important roles in a modern society, but you may also resent being listed in an unsecured system that makes your financial records available to thousands of people; you may be in favor of mental health departments keeping records on psychiatric patients, but you may question the wisdom of possibly recommending to disturbed friends that they seek professional help when their records might then fall into the hands of an insurance industry data network; and you may believe that a market researcher (or a university professor) should conduct a study that requires the gathering and analyzing of personal data, but you may not feel free to personally participate in that study. In short, you may now tend to behave differently (and less freely) than you once would have because of your increasing awareness that what you say and do may become part of some computer record.[15]

**SUMMARY**

Business computer usage has had a positive influence on (and will continue to offer benefits to) large segments of society in general and many individuals in particular. For example, greater efficiency resulting from computer usage may keep prices lower than they would otherwise have been, and individuals may also benefit from the higher-quality products and better service received from businesses. Also, the possible benefits of EFTS and UPC would not have been feasible without computers. Furthermore, in nonbusiness areas governmental agencies use computers to control air and water pollution, prepare better weather forecasts, and provide more efficient law enforcement; and health care organizations use computers to provide faster and more thorough testing to detect and identify disease.

Unfortunately, however, some businesses have used questionable data processing practices that have had adverse effects on the private lives and records of individuals. Data are sometimes gathered without a valid reason and are too often inaccurate and/or incomplete. Also, some people have felt themselves to be the relatively helpless vitims of a cold, impersonal, and remote system that classifies, sorts, and treats them as depersonalized numbers. And we have probably all read accounts in newspapers of people being victimized by computer system errors and miscalculations.

A lack of control over data security in some business information systems has also led to undesirable consequences for individuals in

[15] If you think the privacy issue has been exaggerated here, see Robert E. Smith, "Take the Privacy Initiative," *Computer Decisions*, January 1977, pp. 35–36; and "Striking Back at the Super Snoops," *Time*, July 18, 1977, pp. 15ff.

society. And this lack of security, combined with the development of large integrated data banks, has raised serious questions about the possible threat to an individual's right to privacy.

Fortunately, the possible negative implications discussed in the chapter are now receiving thoughtful study. A few of the approaches used to control the negative impact are outlined in the next chapter.

**REVIEW AND DISCUSSION QUESTIONS**

1   How may business computer usage benefit nonbusiness organizations?

2   (**a**) How can computer usage result in greater operating efficiency in a business? (**b**) How may greater efficiency benefit individuals in society?

3   "Computers can play a role in improving the quality of the products we receive from businesses." Discuss this statement.

4   How may computer-using firms provide better service to customers?

5   (**a**) What are the possible benefits of EFTS for individuals? (**b**) What are the possible benefits of UPC?

6   "Some businesses have used questionable data processing practices that have had adverse effects on the private lives and records of individuals." Discuss this statement.

7   (**a**) How may a lack of control over data originating-recording lead to undesirable social results? (**b**) How may computer system classifying and sorting practices lead to the same results?

8   What are the primary causes of computer system miscalculations?

9   How may a lack of control over data security lead to undesirable consequences for individuals in society?

10   Why has the creation of integrated computer data banks increased the possible threat to an individual's right to privacy?

11   How may a computer system be used (**a**) for surveillance, and (**b**) to create a climate that can restrict individual freedom?

**SELECTED REFERENCES**

In addition to the references suggested in the chapter footnotes, you might be interested in the following sources:

Benton, John R: "Electronic Funds Transfer: Pitfalls and Payoffs," *Harvard Business Review,* July-August 1977, pp. 16–17ff.

Boche, Ray: "The Universal Product Code—A Defense," *Computers and People,* February 1976, pp. 16ff.

Carey, Frank T.: "IBM's Guidelines to Employee Privacy," *Harvard Business Review,* September-October 1976, pp. 82–90.

"Electronic Banking: A Retreat from the Cashless Society," *Business Week,* Apr. 18, 1977, pp. 80–83ff.

"The Growing Threat to Computer Security," *Business Week,* Aug. 1, 1977, pp. 44–45.

Myers, Edith: "Security: The Only Means to Privacy," *Datamation,* May 1977, pp. 240–242.

Sobczak, Thomas C.: "Universal Product Coding: Who Profits and Who Loses?" *Computers and People,* February 1976, pp. 17–19.

Ware, Willis H.: "Handling Personal Data," *Datamation,* October 1977, pp. 83–85ff.

# the management of computing resources

# 16

LEARNING OBJECTIVES   After studying this chapter and answering the discussion questions, you should be able to: □ Explain the roles of top-level executives and data processing managers in planning for computing resources □ Discuss some factors that have a bearing on the organizational structure of a computer department and the activities that may be grouped in such a department □ Identify the staffing considerations and procedures that are involved in selecting, training, and motivating computer department personnel □ Describe the steps and techniques that are used in controlling the operating efficiency, data integrity, and system security of a computer facility

CHAPTER OUTLINE
Planning for computing resources
Organizing the computer facility
Staffing the computer facility: The Selection Process / Training Selected Employees / Motivating Computer Personnel

Controlling the computer facility: Control of Operating Efficiency / Control of Data Integrity, System Security, and Personal Privacy
Summary
Review and discussion questions
Selected references

In the first two chapters of this Part of the book, which deals with computer implications for management, we took a broad overall look at the possible impact of computer usage on the general management functions of planning, organizing, staffing, and controlling. An additional computer-related matter that will likely have an impact on the management of an organization is whether or not the computing resources in a business are managed in an *effective* and *efficient* way.

A computer facility may be said to be *effective* if it is "doing the right things"—i.e., if it is producing relevant information that meets the real needs of decision makers in the organization. Of course, the primary responsibility for the effectiveness of the applications being processed by a computer department should reside with the system users. However, managers of computing resources can contribute to the effectiveness of present and proposed systems by (1) making suggestions for improvements in existing procedures, (2) recommending new applications that could employ the latest technology to support users in areas that would provide a payoff to the business, and (3) pointing out any problem areas that may exist in user system proposals.

Since much of the material in Chapters 8 and 9 was concerned with system effectiveness, however, we need not spend further time here on the subject. Rather, we shall be more concerned in parts of this chapter about the efficiency with which computing resources are being used. When a computer facility is described as being *efficient,* it is meant that the facility is "doing things right"—i.e., it is making economic use of such resources as people, time, money, hardware/software, and materials to produce output with a minimum of waste.

Managers of computing facilities, like all managers, must perform the functions of planning, organizing, staffing, and controlling. You should not be surprised, then, when you encounter such topics as (1) *planning for computing resources,* (2) *organizing the computer facility,* (3) *staffing the computer facility,* and (4) *controlling the computer facility* in the pages ahead.

**PLANNING FOR COMPUTING RESOURCES**

By now you know that (1) the acquisition and use of computing resources can cost millions of dollars in larger firms, and (2) the information output from computer operations may be depended on to support decisions involving many additional millions of dollars each year. Given the cost and significance of the information management function, then it is an important responsibility of *top-level executives* to establish long-term strategic plans for the management of information processing resources. That is, top executives (who are often organized into an information services steering committee) are responsible for setting the general guidelines and policies that will be followed by the manager(s) of the computer facility(ies), and they are responsible for defining the general scope of operations of the facilities.

In establishing these policies and guidelines, *top executives will typically consider such representative questions* as: (1) What is the mission of the computer department, and what problems should it be working on? (2) Which decisions are to be made at the top, which are to be made by users, and which are reserved for the computer department? (3) Who is expected to take the initiative in suggesting new applications? (4) What economic resources are available to support data processing, and what guidelines must be met before a new system will be approved? (5) Should users be allowed to go outside the facility to obtain computing services? (6) Will data processing be centralized or decentralized? What about data storage? (7) Where will computing resources be located in the organization? (8) What internal control guidelines must be followed? and (9) What guidelines must be followed in submitting budgets and requests for additional resources?

Of course, planning for computing resources does not end with the establishment of policies and guidelines by one or more top executives. Rather, these policies and decisions provide guidance to *data processing managers* as they prepare additional plans to manage computer department resources.[1] While top-level plans often deal with issues of effectiveness (doing the right things), department-level plans are often focused on the goal of improving efficiency (doing things right with the right resources). *Among the questions to be considered in preparing department-level plans are* (1) Do any of the existing systems need to be redesigned? (2) Are there any changes in user requirements, government

[1] For further information on computer department planning, see Richard G. Canning, "Do We Have the Right Resources?" *EDP Analyzer,* July 1975, pp. 1–12; and Benjamin Knowles, Jr., "Get Ready for Long Range DP Planning," *Computer Decisions,* January 1977, pp. 38–40ff.

regulations, etc., that may lead to new systems? (3) Would a conversion to new technology lead to greater efficiency and effectiveness? (4) Will changing existing systems or adding new projects require additional resources?[2] (5) What is the available budget to support computer activities? (6) Can future goals be reached with the existing staff, or will additional employees and/or new training programs be required? (7) Can the department be reorganized to improve efficiency? (8) Should new tools and techniques (e.g., those employed in structured programming) be employed to improve productivity? (9) Are existing department standards adequate, or should new standards be instituted to ensure better control? (10) Have appropriate procedures been established to measure overall hardware/software performance and to charge users for their hardware/software usage? and (11) Have adequate controls been set up to maintain data integrity, system security, and personal privacy?

The nature and extent of the plans made to organize, staff, and control the computer facility depend on the answers to the questions presented above. Obviously, much time and effort must be devoted to this planning activity.

**ORGANIZING THE
COMPUTER FACILITY**

In Chapter 13, we considered such important organizational questions as, "Where will the data be processed?" "Where will the data be stored?" and "Where will computing resources be located within the business?" In this section, we will now look at the organizational composition of the computer department itself. Of course, the decisions made in response to those earlier questions will have a direct bearing on the composition of a particular computer facility. For example, a facility located at the headquarters of a company that has elected to use a centralized data processing and storage approach would probably not be organized like the headquarters facility of a firm that has distributed most of the data processing and storage functions to outlying branches.

The composition of a computer facility thus depends on the scope and magnitude of the data processing work that must be performed and the extent to which this work is carried out by the particular department. It is usual, however, to include the activities of system analysis and design, program preparation, and computer operation in the department. Although other logical arrangements are possible, Fig. 16-1 provides us

---

[2] If changing existing systems or adding new projects is likely to require additional hardware and/or software, then planning decisions will have to be made on whether in-house or outside hardware resources will be employed, and on whether software will be developed internally or purchased from applications package vendors. Since some of the factors to be considered in using the hardware of remote computing services were discussed in Chapters 2 and 9, and since the issue of making or buying software was also considered in Chapters 2 and 9, we need not repeat these discussions here.

"It's a very new installation operating on a very small budget . . ."

with an organizational framework from which combinations or further subdivisions of activities may be made as needed.[3]

The _data-base administrator (DBA) function_ does not yet exist in many installations. The activities of this administrator are to (1) establish and control data definitions and standards, (2) act as a file-design and data-base consultant to others in the organization, and (3) design the data-base security system to guard against unauthorized use. Although the DBA function may be located at a lower level in the organization, a good case can be made for locating it as shown in Fig. 16-1 because of the departmental cooperation and compromise that is needed if the job activities described above are to be accomplished.

Because of the close cooperation that also must exist between programmers and system analysts, it is generally desirable that both groups report to the same executive to minimize friction. The _system-analysis section_ acts as the vital interface between outside operating departments and the other sections in the computer organization. As noted earlier, it

[3] For the pros and cons of this and other organizational possibilities, see Thomas R. Gildersleeve, "Organizing the Data Processing Function," _Datamation,_ November 1974, pp. 46–50.

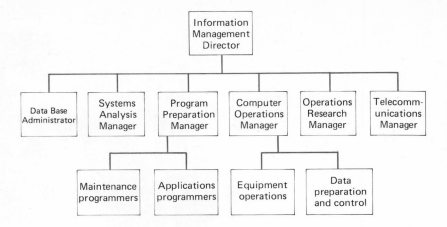

FIGURE 16-1

Possible functional organization of computer facility.

may be desirable to maintain system analysts in the operating divisions of large firms with centralized computer centers.

There is no reason why a single supervisor could not be in charge of both system analysis and program preparation. In medium-sized and large organizations, however, a separate supervisor is frequently found. The *programming function* is sometimes subdivided into (1) the preparation of new applications and (2) the maintenance of existing programs. Authority may also be given to one or more individuals to make sure that proper standards and documentation levels are maintained. In order to fix total responsibility for the design, implementation, and maintenance of a new system, it is often desirable to establish a *project group* of analysts and programmers. (Such a group might employ the chief programming team or egoless programming team concepts discussed in Chapter 11.) Under this type of *project organization* (Fig. 16-2), a project leader might report to a manager of new system development. There may be training and motivational benefits from this type of approach.

The function of the *computer-operations section* is to prepare the input data and produce the output information on a continuing production basis. Multiple shifts may be required. The control of equipment time and the scheduling of processing activities are an important part of the duties of the operations supervisor. Controls must also be established to make sure that input data are accurate. Computer operators, operators of peripheral equipment, keypunch operators, and media librarians are found in this section. The total number of employees may be large, and turnover is likely to be high; thus, personnel-management considerations may occupy a significant part of the operations supervisor's time.

The *operations-research section* may logically be assigned to some other corporate planning element concerned with the overall study of company operations. But since the use of computers and data files is required to support many of the mathematical models which operations-

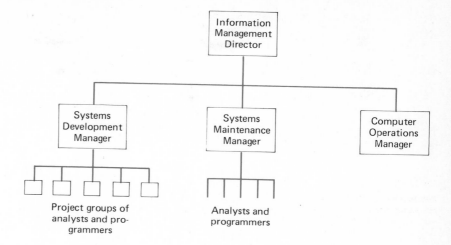

**FIGURE 16-2**

Possible project organization of computer facility.

Information Management Director

Systems Development Manager

Systems Maintenance Manager

Computer Operations Manager

Project groups of analysts and programmers

Analysts and programmers

research (OR) personnel create, there may be good reasons for assigning them to the computer department for coordination purposes. Certainly, the work of the OR and system-analysis groups should be closely coordinated. It makes little sense to develop a mathematical model if the system will not provide the necessary input data.

The *telecommunications function* may also logically be assigned to some other organizational unit. However, there is a growing tendency to place the responsibility for both computing and telecommunications services under a single information management executive. In some smaller firms, an analyst or programmer might be able to make the necessary telecommunications decisions. But as the distinctions between data processing and data communications become more blurred, as the knowledge needed to efficiently manage the complex communications networks that many organizations are now planning becomes more specialized, and as new techniques and services to carry voice, data, and facsimile messages between remote points are implemented, the need for a separate telecommunications function located as shown in Fig. 16-2 may become more acute.[4]

## STAFFING THE COMPUTER FACILITY

Since people are the most important resource in any computer facility (Fig. 16-3), the procedures that are followed in a facility to *select* and *train* employees, and the approaches that are used to *motivate* computer personnel, are of particular significance.

[4] For a survey of some of the rapid and radical changes taking place in the telecommunications field, see "The New New Telephone Industry," *Business Week,* Feb. 13, 1978, pp. 68–71ff.

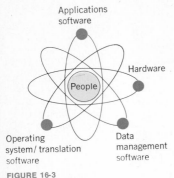

Applications
software

Hardware

People

Operating
system/ translation
software

Data
management
software

FIGURE 16-3

All elements of a computer-based
information system revolve around
the system's personnel.

## the selection process

The selection process consists of *determining the nature and number of positions to be filled, recruiting potential candidates for jobs,* and *selecting from among the job applicants.*

Personnel needed    A prerequisite to the selection process is the preparation of job descriptions and job specifications for any new positions to be filled. A *job description* defines the *duties that must be performed* and the equipment that is used, indicates the degree of supervision that is given and received, and describes the working conditions associated with the position. A *job specification* identifies the *qualifications that candidates for each job should possess.* Job specifications include the levels of education, experience, and training considered necessary to perform each job adequately. Also included is a statement outlining the physical and communication skills needed as well as the personality traits desired. These facts are useful for (1) staffing purposes (since both the recruiter and the candidate must know what is needed and expected) and (2) wage purposes (to determine the relative worth of the new job).

Most of the positions to be filled in a computer facility can be classified into the following occupational categories: *information system management, system analysis and design, program preparation, data-base administration,* and *computer operation.* Very brief descriptions and specifications for such positions might include the following points:

1   *Information system management. Information system managers,* like all managers, must perform the functions of planning, organizing, staffing, and controlling (i.e., the functions being discussed in this chapter). To be able to plan effectively and then control department activities, such managers should possess technical competence in addition to managerial ability. But too much emphasis on technical competence at the expense of managerial ability should be avoided. Too often in the past, the most skilled technician became the manager, only to demonstrate, very soon, incompetence in the techniques of management. It is likely, in fact, that the larger the data processing department, the more important managerial skills become in the total mix of skills required by the manager (Fig. 16-4). The manager selected should understand the company's business, its purpose and goals, and its data processing procedures; he or she should be able to communicate with and motivate people; and he or she should possess the poise, stature, and maturity to command the respect of other company executives as well as data processing employees. Increasingly, people planning to seek a career in information system management must first acquire a college degree. Courses in business administration, economics, data processing, and statistics are desirable.

2   *System analysis and design.* Although there are several grades of *system analyst* (lead, senior, junior), the job basically consists of (a) gathering facts about and analyzing the basic methods and procedures of

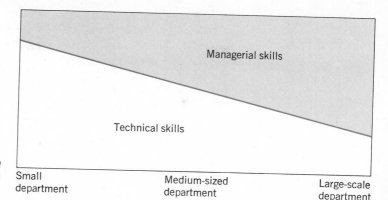

Managerial skills

Technical skills

Small department            Medium-sized department            Large-scale department

**FIGURE 16-4**

Total mix of skills required by the information systems manager (adapted from R. L. Nolan, "Plight of the EDP Manager," *Harvard Business Review*, May–June, 1973, p. 145).

current information systems, (*b*) determining information needs, and (*c*) modifying, redesigning, and integrating these existing procedures into new system specifications as required to provide the needed information. In addition to making the most effective use of existing data processing equipment, the analyst may also (as in the case of the system study) recommend justifiable equipment changes. Analysts must usually be very familiar with the objectives, personnel, products and services, industry, and special problems of the specific firms that employ them. They must also know the uses and limitations of computers as well as other types of data processing equipment, for they are the interpreters between managers and data processing specialists. They must understand programming basics; they must be able to determine which jobs are candidates for computer processing; they must have logical reasoning ability; they must have initiative and the ability to plan and organize their work since they will frequently be working on their own without much direct supervision; and they must be able to communicate with and secure the cooperation of operating employees and supervisors. Educational backgrounds vary, but a college degree or the equivalent is generally desired. Courses that have proven valuable to the types of system analysts described above are the same ones mentioned for data processing managers.

**3    *Program preparation*.** The job of the typical business *programmer* (as defined in this book) is to take the broad system designs of the analysts and transform these specifications into workable, coded machine instructions.[5] However, there are different programmer categories, and their duties vary in different organizations. In some companies, for example, a person with the title of "programmer" may perform *both* the system-

---

[5] We are referring here to *business applications programmers* for the most part. In scientific programming a strong mathematics background is required. *System programmers*—i.e., those who write the complex operating system software and translating programs discussed in Chapter 2—are also likely to have a more scientific background than business applications programmers.

analysis and programming functions.[6] And since job descriptions vary, there are also varying opinions about the educational background required of business programmers. Such factors as the duties of the programmer, the degree of separation between the system-analysis and programming functions, the complexity of the data processing systems, and the industry in which the business operates should probably be considered by the company in establishing educational standards. As the programmer's job is defined here, a college degree is not an absolute condition for employment in many organizations. What *is required*, however, is that the programmer have (a) analytical reasoning ability, (b) the ability to remember and concentrate on small details, (c) the drive and motivation to complete programs without direct supervision, (d) the patience and perseverance to search for small errors in programs, (e) the accuracy to minimize the number of such errors, and (f) the creativeness to develop new problem-solving techniques.

**4** *Data-base administration.* Three basic duties of the data-base administrator (DBA) were briefly outlined a few pages earlier. In addition, the DBA is responsible for (a) monitoring and auditing data-base operations in order to improve effectiveness and efficiency and (b) investigating new data management software packages that might also be used to increase effectiveness and efficiency. To perform these duties, a DBA must have a high degree of technical ability; furthermore, the DBA must also have the ability to communicate effectively with a large number of users with dissimilar backgrounds. It is not surprising then that the DBA has sometimes been referred to as the "superman" (superperson?) of the data processing community.[7] Educational backgrounds again vary, but a college degree or the equivalent is generally needed.

**5** *Computer operations.* The duties of the *computer operator* include setting up the processor and related equipment, starting the program run, checking to ensure proper operation, and unloading equipment at the end of a run. Some knowledge of programming is needed. *Keypunch* and/or *key-to-tape operators*, a media *librarian* who maintains control over master tape and card files, a *scheduler* who plans the daily flow of work to be accomplished and assigns the necessary personnel, and various other clerks and operators of peripheral equipment may be needed in the operations area.

**Recruiting potential candidates**   To fill the jobs described above, it is necessary to *recruit* potential candidates and then to *select* from among

---

[6] The degree of separation of system analysis and programming has depended upon the size and complexity of the company and its data processing systems, the ability of data processing personnel, and the desire of high-level executives to reduce communication problems and fix responsibility for each application on a single person. The lack of general agreement on the definition and description of system-analyst and programmer positions presents some personnel management problems for the data processing manager, who is expected to recruit, select, train, evaluate, and compensate the employees who occupy these positions.

[7] For more details on this emerging occupation, see Edward K. Yasaki, "The Many Faces of the DBA," *Datamation*, May 1977, pp. 75–79.

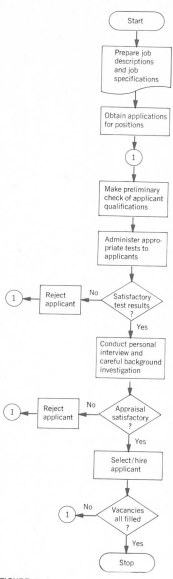

**FIGURE 16-5**

The selection process.

those candidates the right people for the jobs. Figure 16-5 summarizes the recruitment and selection steps in the selection process that are discussed in this section and in the section that follows.

Two general procedures are often used to *recruit* candidates for new jobs. *One procedure* is to review personnel records and supervisory recommendations (or application forms and references in the case of nonemployee candidates) to compile a selective list of people qualified. People on this screened list are then contacted to see if they might be interested. The main weakness of this approach is that qualified candidates may be overlooked. A *second "reserve pool" procedure* is to announce the openings to all employees and invite them to make application if interested. Those applicants who appear to possess the necessary qualifications join the pool from which initial and subsequent openings are filled. Printed advertisements, college placement offices, outside employment agencies, contacts made at professional meetings, the knowledge of vendor representatives—all these resources can be used to secure nonemployee applications.

The information system manager may sometimes be hired from an outside source to supervise an initial computer installation. The big disadvantage of this approach is that the person hired has little knowledge of the firm or of the people with whom he or she must work. Perhaps a preferable choice would be to appoint someone in the company who has the managerial qualifications and give her or him the required technical training. In staffing other vacancies, too, most firms prefer to select suitable candidates from within and to train them in the necessary skills. This approach is particularly valid in the case of system analysts who must be familiar with company operations.

Programmers are more likely to be recruited from outside than analysts and other data processing employees. This may be especially true when the programming job is considered to be basically coding and includes little in the way of system work. In staffing programming jobs requiring some degree of system analysis, a firm may give technical training to people possessing a knowledge of the business or it may hire experienced programmers (or programmer trainees) and school them in company policies, problems, and operations. Businesses have usually found that *when suitable candidates are available,* the first approach is preferable.[8] In spite of these considerations, however, hiring experienced programmers may help speed up a conversion to new hardware. Many organizations have found that programmers skilled in the use of the hardware

---

[8] There are several *advantages associated with internal selection:* (1) employees have a better understanding of the business; (2) their work habits and personality traits are easier to appraise; (3) having demonstrated some degree of company loyalty, they may be less inclined to leave the firm after they are trained; and (4) internal selection can improve employee morale. In some situations, too, union contract agreements may specify that selections be made internally.

ordered for a new system are a valuable complement to company trainees.[9]

Selection procedures    When possible candidates have been identified, it is then necessary to balance and compare their qualifications with those listed in the job specifications. Sorting out the "best" applicants is a difficult job. The screening process generally involves the use of such selection devices as *aptitude or skill tests, personal interviews,* and careful *examination of records* indicating the candidate's educational background, experience, and work habits. A frequently used approach in the selection of analyst and programmer *trainees* is to give candidates an aptitude test[10] and then to follow up with interviews and careful record examinations on all who receive satisfactory test scores. In the selection of *experienced* programmers, personal interviews and personal or telephone contacts with parties familiar with the work of the candidate are of particular importance. Proficiency tests are sometimes used to check on the ability of a candidate to program a test problem. Tests may also be used in the selection of computer-operations personnel. These tests measure manual dexterity, mechanical aptitude, clerical aptitude, etc., and they generally yield satisfactory results.

Selection decisions follow the testing, interviewing, and background-investigation phases. The chosen candidates must then be trained to prepare them for their new duties.

**training selected employees**

Extensive preliminary training is likely to be needed by those selected to be system analysts and programmers. Trainees selected from within the organization will need to master the necessary technical details, and experienced analysts and programmers hired from outside will have to learn a great deal about the business. Of course, in addition to having a *knowledge of the business and the industry,* the system analyst must also understand the *techniques of system-analysis and design.* There is lack of

---

[9] Of course, there is always the danger that they may select an "experienced" programmer who is interested in keeping one jump ahead of past mistakes.

[10] *Programmer aptitude tests* are math-oriented exams that *attempt* to measure the ability of trainees to acquire whatever skills are needed to become successful programmers. Although there is lack of agreement about the ability of these tests actually to measure what they claim to measure, when carefully used they may give an indication of a trainee's ability to reason in arithmetic and abstract terms. Since this ability is considered to be an important prerequisite for many data processing jobs, the test may serve as a screening aid. But good test performance alone does not necessarily mean that the candidate will be a successful programmer. The tests do not measure motivation, and they may not begin to measure all the other qualities that may be required.

uniformity at the present time in the methods used to train (*educate* is probably a better word) analysts to meet the latter requirement. A good grounding in the "core" courses found in collegiate schools of business combined with further emphasis on accounting systems, communication skills, mathematics, and statistics are felt by many to be prerequisites to more specialized systems training. Graduate and undergraduate programs for additional specialized work in system analysis and design have been proposed by the Association for Computing Machinery (ACM).[11]

Consulting firms, private institutes, and organizations such as the American Management Association conduct system-analysis seminars on a limited basis. Correspondence courses in systems work are offered by the Association of Systems Management and others. Also, an in-house system training program utilizing senior analysts as instructors has proved to be effective. For years, computer manufacturers have contracted to teach machine-dependent skills to their customer trainees. Their programs in formal systems training are newer since system-analysis is independent of machines; however, their systems representatives have provided some on-the-job-training in analysis and design techniques to customer personnel over the years.

Programmers must obviously possess *an understanding of computer hardware and software.* (The formal training given to analysts in this area may parallel or be identical with the formal training received by programmers.) One method employed to introduce those programmer students who have been selected from within the firm to hardware and software concepts is to enroll them in the vendor's programming classes. These classes introduce the students to the vendor's hardware and software that can be used. Such courses vary in length from 2 to 6 weeks, they are usually offered at the vendor's educational center, and they generally emphasize coding. Following satisfactory completion of the vendor's course, the students may receive additional on-the-job instruction from other experienced programmers who may be available. Alternatively, the students may receive all their training from in-house educational operations and/or from courses offered by independent training organizations.

Programmer training is a continued, lengthy, and expensive process. To the surprise (and dismay) of many executives, it has been found that *at least 6 months* is generally required before programmers attain a *minimum* level of proficiency. Training costs per programmer may run into the thousands of dollars. Of course, in addition to the training available from vendors and through in-house activities, programming skills are also

---

[11] Details about the graduate programs are found in R. L. Ashenhurst, ed., "Curriculum Recommendations for Graduate Professional Programs in Information Systems," *Communications of the ACM,* May 1972, pp. 363–398. The details on undergraduate programs are found in J. Daniel Couger, ed., "Curriculum Recommendations for Undergraduate Programs in Information Systems," *Communications of the ACM,* December 1973, pp. 727–749.

taught by consultants, professional organizations, colleges and universities, and vocational schools.[12]

Equipment manufacturers and vocational schools also offer brief courses to train operators of peripheral equipment. On-the-job training is often the only preparation required. Because of their need to know some programming, computer operators are often sent to the vendor's programming course or they receive the necessary in-house training.

Selecting and training employees for vacancies in the computer department are important aspects of staffing. But managers must also motivate computer personnel if they hope to achieve organizational goals.

**motivating computer personnel**

Although the problem of turnover among skilled employees in the computer department has been reduced somewhat in recent years, it has not disappeared. Locating and training replacements remains a time-consuming and expensive activity in many organizations. Furthermore, department productivity may suffer seriously because of the departure of key personnel. It is therefore important for computer managers to keep turn-

[12] More information on these training organizations (and on training approaches) may be found in a chapter by Gerald M. Weinberg and Daniel P. Freedman entitled "Training and Motivation of ADP Personnel" that appears on pages 5-23 to 5-31 of *Automatic Data Processing Handbook,* McGraw-Hill Book Company, New York, 1977.

© DATAMATION ®

"You think I **enjoy** working late, Alice?
Well, you're wrong."

over to a minimum. Psychologists have outlined the needs and factors that *influence* and *motivate* human behavior. Since motivated employees are less likely to leave an organization and are more likely to be highly productive members of a department, the manager should be aware of these important behavioral concepts.

What are the needs and factors that *influence* and *motivate* behavior? What is likely to cause job satisfaction and dissatisfaction among computer staff members? Behavioral scientists tell us that human needs may be classified into a series of ranks or levels as summarized in Fig. 16-6.

Professor Frederick Herzberg of the University of Utah has made a distinction between those factors that motivate and those that only influence behavior. The *motivating* factors are such high-level needs as (1) the need to *achieve* something useful, (2) the need to be *recognized* for such achievement, (3) the need to have the *work itself be meaningful,* (4) the need to be *responsible* for making decisions, and (5) the need to *grow and advance.* In short, job satisfaction, high production, and low employee turnover are related to the self-fulfillment of people on the job.

---

### Need Classification and Explanation

**1**   *Physiological needs.* Included in this lowest-level category are the needs for food, clothing, shelter, and sleep. They are necessary for survival and thus receive first priority. When thwarted, these needs override in importance all others in influencing behavior; when regularly satisfied, they cease to direct human behavior.

**2**   *Safety needs.* The needs for protection against danger, threat, or deprivation begin to dominate human behavior when the physiological needs are satisfied.

**3**   *Social needs.* When the above needs are satisfied, social needs, i.e., the need to belong to a group and to associate with and be accepted by others become important influencing factors.

**4**   *Ego needs.* When the first three need levels are reasonably satisfied, ego needs become important in behavior motivation. There are two kinds of egoistic needs: (*a*) those that relate to the *self-esteem* of an individual, e.g., the needs for self-confidence, achievement, and independence, and (*b*) those that relate to the *reputation* of an individual, e.g., the needs for status, recognition, and respect. Unlike the lower needs, these are rarely satisfied; people strive for more satisfaction of these needs once they have become important to them.

**5**   *Self-fulfillment needs.* The final level in the need hierarchy reflects the desire of individuals to realize their own potential, continue to develop, and be creative.

**FIGURE 16-6**

Needs that influence and motivate behavior.

The lower-level *physical, security, social,* and *status* needs are some-times called *maintenance* factors. According to Herzberg, the presence of these factors, along with economic and employee-orientation factors, does *not* necessarily motivate workers because such factors tend to be taken for granted. The absence of one or more of these factors, however, may have an *adverse influence* on employee behavior and may result in job dissatisfaction, low production, and high turnover.

The information systems manager must therefore look beyond the lower-level needs in motivating his or her staff. These needs *must* be satisified, of course, but frequent raises and private offices may not be enough to reduce turnover and produce motivated employees. What are likely to be more important in achieving these desirable ends are the promise of challenging work; the assignment of greater responsibility to staff members; the setting of realistic and carefully thought-out objec-tives; and the opportunity to grow and develop through such means as carefully planned training programs.[13]

## CONTROLLING THE COMPUTER FACILITY

The workload for a computer facility should be determined by decisions made by top-level executives and users relating to the facility's mission and the projects on which it *should* be working. In addition to having a keen interest in how effectively a facility is being used, however, execu-tives, users, and data processing managers are also intensely interested in the controls that may be used *to improve operating efficiency* (e.g., to reduce department costs or to permit more work to be done at the same cost), and *to avoid the problems that may result from failure to safeguard data integrity, system security, and personal privacy.* Let us look at these control topics in the remaining pages of this chapter.

### control of operating efficiency

The basic procedure to be followed to control the efficiency of computer department operations consists of the same steps used to control any other activity. That is, acceptable standards of performance for the department must first be established, actual operating performance must then be measured, the actual performance must next be compared against the standards, and, finally, the appropriate control actions must then be taken.

Establishing department standards of performance    The importance of *methods standards* (i.e., the procedural rules and instructions that are to be followed in performing specific tasks) were pointed out in several

---

[13] Most of these elements are likely to be found in the egoless programming team approach to organizing programmers discussed in Chapter 11.

earlier chapters. *Performance standards* are then used to specify *how well* the particular tasks are to be performed by both people and equipment. A methods standard, for example, might spell out the steps to be completed during the data-gathering phase of a system study; a corresponding performance standard might then specify, for a study of a given complexity, the length of time that should be needed to complete the data-gathering phase. Obviously, then, objective and realistic performance standards cannot exist in the absence of clearly defined methods standards.

A computer facility may establish standards of performance for both equipment and personnel. *Equipment performance standards* (which may be applied to each separately operated piece of hardware) may specify the time that should be spent on such activities as setup, testing, production, reruns, training, and scheduled and unscheduled maintenance. Such standards can be used in assigning processing tasks to facility hardware and in evaluating the performance of equipment operators.

Although *personnel performance standards* for equipment operators may be based on general equipment standards, it is usually much more difficult to establish realistic performance criteria for those engaged in the creative activities of system analysis/design and programming. To illustrate, the number of key strokes per hour at a data input device can be counted, and such counts can be used to establish keying performance standards. The number of lines of code (LOC) produced by programmers over a given period can also be counted, and LOC performance standards can then be established.[14] But it is quite possible for one programmer to prepare a flexible program with 200 LOC that is tested and ready on schedule, is straightforward and relatively easy to maintain, and is efficient in the use of machine time. Another programmer assigned to the same project might use 250 LOC to prepare a program that lacks many of the desirable qualities of the shorter program. Yet, if a rigid LOC performance standard were applied, the second programmer would likely receive a higher performance rating.[15] In spite of the hazards involved, however, many data processing managers are currently attempting to create system and programming performance standards by dividing each project into clearly defined tasks and deliverable outputs, evaluating the project in terms of its size and complexity, and estimating completion times on the basis of the past performance experience of the facility.[16]

---

[14] The case for using LOC as a measure of productivity is found in James R. Johnson, "A Working Measure of Productivity," *Datamation*, February 1977, pp. 106–107ff.

[15] In later periods, of course, the first programmer would likely produce code that was complex, voluminous, and redundant.

[16] For further discussion of this topic, see John Toellner, "Performance Measurement in Systems and Programming," *Infosystems*, Part 1, December 1977, pp. 34–36; and part 2, January 1978, pp. 60–62.

(The actual project performance is then measured and compared against the estimates. Subsequent project plans and controls are then influenced by this additional experience.)

Although departmental standards of performance are needed if managers are to control the operating efficiency of their computing resources, such performance standards do not exist at all in many organizations. And when performance criteria have been established, the emphasis has generally been on equipment usage.

Measuring department performance    Evaluating the performance of creative personnel is more of an art than a science, and the approaches currently vary from one facility to another. The success with which analysts and programmers perform the steps outlined in the chapters in Part III of this book, the satisfaction of users with the finished product, and the degree of success or failure detected in follow-up project performance reviews conducted by internal auditors are probably the best current indicators available to measure the performance of creative personnel.

The performance and efficiency of the computer system itself can suffer from such causes as the wrong hardware configuration, poorly written programs, and/or poor scheduling of the jobs to be processed. Unfortunately, both the causes and cures of inefficiency are seldom obvious. Thus, performance-measuring tools have been developed to break down computer usage time into productive and idle components. Included in these *computer performance evaluation (CPE) tools are:*[17]

**1**    *Hardware monitors.* A hardware monitor is an electronic data-gathering device that is usually connected by probes to the circuitry of the CPU. These probes collect timing and resource usage data from the processor during normal operation by sampling the electric pulses or signals that represent data flowing through the CPU. The data gathered by the monitor are recorded on magnetic tape for further analyses to determine system component utilization. These analyses may identify overworked components, bottleneck situations, and resource conflicts. An analysis

[17] A wealth of information is available on CPE tools. See, for example, Israel Borovits, and Phillip Ein-Dor, "Cost/Utilization: A Measure of System Performance," *Communications of the ACM,* March 1977, pp. 185–191; "Data Processing Audit Practices Report," *Systems Auditability and Control Study,* The Institute of Internal Auditors, Inc., Altamonte Springs, Fla., 1977, pp. 167–171; John R. Hansen, "Evaluating an Awesome Computer Facility," *Infosystems,* January 1978, pp. 66–67ff.; Thomas M. Hoger, "Monitors: How the Computer System Behaves!" *Infosystems,* October 1977, pp. 80ff.; "How to Squeeze More Out of a Computer," *Business Week,* Sept. 13, 1976, pp. 96ff; Phillip C. Howard, "Monitors and Merriment," *Computer Decisions,* September 1975, pp. 40–42ff.; John J. Hunter, "Measure for Measure," *Computer Decisions,* September 1976, pp. 54ff.; Neil D. Kelley, "Cutting DP Costs," *Infosystems,* June 1977, pp. 80–82; G. Jay Lipovich, "DP Manager and Performance Measurement," *Journal of Systems Management,* March 1977, pp. 22–27; and Barry Stevens, "Sharp Management Notes Performance," *Computer Decisions,* September 1975, pp. 27ff.

package supplied with the monitor may provide plots and graphical displays to aid the manager.

**2** *Software monitors.* These CPE tools are computer programs that are patched into the computer's operating system program. The status of system resources are periodically sampled and recorded on tapes or disks for subsequent analysis. An analysis software package may be provided with the monitor to produce reports on resource usage (e.g., on disk space utilization and on paging activity in a virtual storage environment) and on software performance. Unlike a hardware monitor which imposes no load on a system and does not interrupt normal operations, a software monitor does add a small additional burden on the system by taking up storage space and by periodically interrupting normal activities to gather data. The software monitor, however, is less expensive.

**3** *Job accounting packages.* Many operating systems contain routines to gather job accounting statistics as a byproduct during processing runs. These job accounting packages are supplied by computer manufacturers and by a number of independent software vendors. Two purposes may be served by the use of these packages: *first,* data dealing with such things as CPU usage, channel usage, elapsed times to process applications, peripheral device allocations, and storage utilization may be gathered to evaluate system performance; and *second,* the usage statistics may be converted into dollar figures by the operating system for user billing purposes.

**Comparing actual performance with standards and taking action**    These final control steps need little further discussion here. Significant variations of actual performance from established equipment usage standards, for example, would certainly call for an appropriate response. The response might be to institute an operator training program, consolidate underutilized resources, make hardware substitutions to alleviate bottlenecks, have equipment repaired, etc. Some examples of actions that have actually been taken to improve operating efficiency are:

**1**    American Airlines reduced its orders for CPUs and peripheral devices by 10 to 15 percent after monitors showed that program faults were misdirecting some of the 2.5 million reservation system messages processed each day.

**2**    INA Corporation sold one of its four large CPUs after performance measurement showed that the company's processing volume could easily be handled by the other three. The savings in annual maintenance costs alone amounted to about $40,000.

**3**    General Electric Company rescheduled the workflow of one computer—an action that resulted in the elimination of $140,000 worth of new equipment. Overall, GE has saved $1.5 million by measuring performance of existing systems and getting them to produce more work.

**Charging for computing resources**    In addition to performing the steps listed above to control the efficiency of computer department operations, the department manager should probably also establish some mechanism whereby computer users are "charged" a fair price for the computing resources that they use.[18] Although a *no-chargeout* approach that provides services to users on a no-charge basis and that treats all computer costs as a company overhead expense has the advantage of not requiring a user billing system, it also tends to encourage waste since users have little incentive to utilize computing resources in the most efficient manner. In the interest of promoting greater efficiency, then, the department manager may consider using one of the following *alternatives to the no-chargeout approach:*

1   *Full chargeout for resource usage.* In this approach, all operating expenses are absorbed by users, and the computer facility is run as a cost center. Chargeout computations are calculated frequently (e.g., weekly or monthly), and the chargeout rates can vary for the same application from period to period due to usage fluctuations. (If a system is fully loaded, the charge for processing the application will be lower because many users are sharing the total costs; if the system is underutilized during a period, however, the user's application must absorb a higher percentage of the total costs.) Since individual users have little or no control over these usage fluctuations, they also have little or no control over their charges from period to period. This lack of internal price stability often causes users to buy computing services outside the organization—an action that can result in further decreases in in-house computer utilization and higher charges to remaining in-house users! Of course, the advantages of a full-chargeout system are that (a) users realize that the computer is not a "free good," and (b) the computer department must offer rates competitive with outside facilities or risk losing user business.

2   *Partial chargeout for resource usage.* To overcome the disadvantage of charging fluctuating prices for the same tasks while retaining the advantage of giving users an incentive to make efficient use of computing resources, many organizations have settled on some form of partial-chargeout system. Typically, a constant rate based on some usage activity (e.g., seconds of CPU time used) is set at the beginning of a period and is then changed only infrequently. Some or all of the costs incurred to develop new applications may be charged to company overhead. Billing statistics are typically gathered by the job accounting packages discussed earlier. A computer chargeout program (which may charge less for jobs run during the evening hours and more for jobs that utilize those resources of the facility that are relatively scarce) then uses these statistics to prepare user bills.

---

[18] The following sources give further information on charging for computing resources: Richard G. Canning, "The Effects of Charge-Back Policies," *EDP Analyzer,* November 1973, pp. 1–13; John Dearden and Richard L. Nolan, "How to Control the Computer Resource," *Harvard Business Review,* November-December 1973, pp. 68–78; Richard L. Nolan, "Effects of Chargeout on User/Manager Attitudes," *Communications of the ACM,* March 1977, pp. 177–184; Carol Schaller, "Survey of Computer Cost Allocation Techniques," *The Journal of Accountancy,* June 1974, pp. 41–42ff.; J. J. Sobczak, "Pricing Computer Usage," *Datamation,* February 1974, pp. 61–64.

## control of data integrity, system security, and personal privacy

The unhappy managerial and social consequences of a lack of control over data integrity, system security, and personal privacy were discussed in Chapters 14 and 15. The purpose of this section is to briefly outline some of the integrity, security, and privacy controls that have been devised in the attempt to control the negative effects of computer usage.

Integrity controls[19]   To be assured that a computer department will provide accurate, complete, and reliable information, managers and auditors should periodically check to see that (1) all *input* data are correctly recorded; (2) the *processing* of all authorized transactions is accomplished without additions or omissions; and (3) the *output* of the system is distributed on a timely basis and only to those who are authorized to receive it.

The purpose of *input controls* is to make sure that *all* authorized input transactions are identified, these transactions are *accurately recorded* in a machine-usable form at the *right time,* and *all* these transactions are then sent to the processing station. *Among the input control techniques that may be adopted are:*

**1**   *The use of prenumbered forms.* Whenever possible, a simple and effective control is to use serially numbered forms so that documents may be accounted for. A missing number in the sequence signals a missing document.

**2**   *The use of control totals.* When batch processing is used, certain totals can be computed for each batch of source documents. For example, the total dollar-sales figure may be computed on a batch of sales invoices prior to, perhaps, keypunching. The same calculation can be made after keypunching to see if the figures compare. Control totals do not have to be expressed in dollars. They can be the totals obtained from adding figures in a data field that is included in all source documents being considered. A simple count of documents, cards, and other records is an effective control total. For example, the number of cards processed in the computer-operating department can be compared with the count of the number of cards that are delivered for processing. Similar comparisons between records read on magnetic tape and the number of input source documents may be possible.

**3**   *The use of transcription methods.* One means of controlling data

---

[19] A wealth of additional information on this topic may be found in Richard G. Canning, "The Importance of EDP Audit and Control," *EDP Analyzer,* June 1977, pp. 1–13; "Data Processing Control Practices Report," *Systems Auditability and Control Study,* The Institute of Internal Auditors, Inc., Altamonte Springs, Fla., 1977; William C. Mair, Donald R. Wood, and Keagle W. Davis, *Computer Control and Audit,* 2d ed., The Institute of Internal Auditors, Inc., Altamonte Springs, Fla., 1976; D. E. Morgan and D. J. Taylor, "A Survey of Methods of Achieving Reliable Software," *Computer,* Febraury 1977, pp. 44–51; and Robert L. Patrick, "Sixty Ingredients for Better Systems," *Datamation,* December 1977, pp. 171ff.

transcription is to have knowledgeable clerks conduct a preaudit of source documents prior to recording the transactions in a machine-usable form. If input is by means of punched cards, the card verifier can be used. Transaction recording devices are available that can reduce errors caused by recopying, keypunching, illegible records, and loss of documents.

**4** *The use of programmed checks on input.* Program instructions can be written to check on the reasonableness and propriety of data as they enter the processing operation. For example, program checks can be written to determine if (*a*) certain specified limits are exceeded, (*b*) the input is complete, and (*c*) a transaction code or identification number is active and reasonable. When online processing is used, lockwords or passwords may be required from remote stations before certain files can be made accessible.

*Processing controls* are established to determine when data are lost or not processed and to check on the accuracy of arithmetic calculations. These controls may be classified into hardware and software categories. Important *hardware processing controls include* parity checks (i.e., checks that test whether the number of digits in an array is odd or even) and the use of dual reading and writing heads in I/O equipment. *Software or programmed processing controls include:*

**1** *The use of record count.* As a check against a predetermined total, the computer can be instructed to count the number of records that it handles in a program run.

**2** *The use of tape labels.* The *external* labeling of magnetic tapes should be carefully controlled. These outside labels may give those interested such information as the tape contents, program identification number, and length of time the contents should be retained. *Internal* header and trailer control labels may also be recorded on the tapes themselves. The first (or *header*) record written on the tape gives the program identification number and other information. Before actual processing begins, then, a programmed comparison check may be made to make sure that the correct tape reel is being used. The last (or *trailer*) record contains a count of the number of other records on the tape.

**3** *The use of sequence check.* In batch processing, the records are in some kind of sequence, e.g., by employee number or stock number. Programmed checks to detect out-of-sequence and missing cards and records prevent a file from being processed in an incorrect order.

**4** *The use of structural check.* A test of the transactions to be processed can be made to determine whether the debits and credits called for represent acceptable combinations. Transactions with unacceptable debit and credit combinations are rejected.

*Output controls* are established as final checks on the accuracy and propriety of the processed information. *Among the output control methods that may be employed are*

**1** *The use of control totals.* How do the control totals of processed information compare with the input control totals? For example, is there agreement between the number of records that were delivered for processing and the number of records that were actually processed? A basic output control technique is to obtain satisfactory answers to such questions.

**2**  *The review of interested parties.* Feedback on a regular basis from input-initiating and output-using departments points out errors that slip through in spite of all precautions. Follow-up action must be taken to correct any file inaccuracies that may be revealed.

**3**  *The use of systematic sampling.* Auditors can check on output by tracing randomly selected transactions from source documents through the processing system to the output destination. This should be done on a regular and systematic basis.

**4**  *The use of prenumbered forms.* Certain output forms should be prenumbered and accounted for in the same manner as input documents. Blank payroll-check forms, for example, should be closely guarded.

System security controls[20]    Since easy access to the computer by people with the skills needed to manipulate the system is a primary reason for the difficulty in maintaining security, an important step in achieving a more secure system is to separate the activities of those working *within* the computer department as noted in Chapter 14. In addition, *system-design, programming, computer-operation,* and *retention* controls should be enforced.

*Systems should be designed* (and documented) with audit and control considerations in mind. (It is expensive to ignore control aspects and then have to revise and rework a designed system. The participation of a knowledgeable auditor in the design phase so that proper controls may be built in is thus a wise precaution.) One of the most important controls that can be exercised over system design is to assign authority to one or more individuals to make sure that system and program flowcharts, decision tables, manuals, etc., are correctly prepared *and maintained.* Specifically written control procedures should be established for this purpose.

*Programming controls* should be formulated to handle *program changes.* Changes should be made only after written approval is given by someone in a position of authority, e.g., the manager of the affected department. It is sometimes a good policy to postpone making a number of minor changes until the end of an accounting cycle so that data

---

[20] A number of the sources cited in the preceding footnote also provide information on system security. Additional references on this subject are: Richard G. Canning, "Integrity and Security of Personal Data," *EDP Analyzer,* April 1976, pp. 1–14; "Comprehensive EDP Security Guidelines," *The Australian Computer Journal,* March 1976, pp. 25–37; Lance J. Hoffman, *Modern Methods for Computer Security and Privacy,* Prentice-Hall, Inc., Englewood Cliffs, N.J., 1977; Jerome Lobel, "Planning a Secure System," *Journal of Systems Management,* July 1976, pp. 14–19; K. S. Shankar, "The Total Computer Security Problem: An Overview," *Computer,* June 1977, pp. 50–61; and August W. Smith, "Data Processing Security; A Common Sense Approach," *Data Management,* May 1977, pp. 7–8ff.

handling remains consistent throughout the accounting period. Changes in programs should be made by authorized programmers and not by computer-operating personnel. All changes should be charted and explained in writing; when completed, they should be reviewed and cleared· by someone other than a maintenance programmer. All documents related to the change should be made a part of the permanent program file.

Some of the *computer-operating controls that may be established are*

**1**    *Control over console intervention.* It is possible for computer operators to bypass program controls. They have the ability to interrupt a program run and introduce data manually into the processor through the console keyboard. With organizational separation of program preparation and computer operation and with operators having access to object programs and not source programs, it is unlikely that an operator will have enough knowledge of the program details to manipulate them successfully for improper purposes. But the possibility of unauthorized intervention should be reduced in a number of ways. Since, for example, the console typewriter may be used to print out a manual intervention, the paper sheets in the typewriter can be prenumbered and periodically checked. Other approaches using locked recording devices may be employed. Additional control techniques include rotating the duties of computer operators (or others in sensitive positions).[21]

**2**    *Control over physical security.* Definite controls should be established to safeguard programs and data from fire and water damage or destruction. Duplicate program and master file tapes may have to be kept at a location away from the computer site. A waste-disposal procedure to destroy carbon papers and other media containing sensitive information should be followed.[22] Only authorized personnel should be allowed access to the computer site.

**3**    *Control over terminal usage.* Control procedures to identify authorized users of the system should obviously be given special attention. Such identification is typically based on something that users *know* (e.g., a password), on something they *have* (e.g., a card with a magnetically coded identification number or a key such as is used in Fig. 16-7 to

---

[21] Managers should be alert to the risk inherent in having employees who never take vacations, who refuse promotion or rotation, who have access to the premises when no one else is present, and who are always around when the books are closed at the end of an accounting period.

[22] Almost $1 million in telephone equipment was stolen from Pacific Telephone & Telegraph Company by a clever thief who, at the age of 16, found in the telephone company trash cans information on Bell System operating procedures, manuals on "system instructions," and a guide book on "Ordering Material and Supplies." Catalogs and authority code numbers were also acquired from trash cans! The thief obtained a special input device and then accessed the Bell System computer to input coded order and authority numbers. The ordered equipment was then picked up by the thief at a company warehouse (he had also bought a used telephone company van for the purpose). See Leo Anderson, "This Man Stole Almost $1 Million from a Telephone Company," *Telephony*, Nov. 17, 1972, pp. 36–38. (After being caught and paying his debt to society, the thief started a consulting service called EDP Security, Inc.)

Security key lock

FIGURE 16-7

(Courtesy INCOTERM Corporation.)

unlock the terminal keyboard), on some *personal characteristic* they possess, or on some combination of these elements. Passwords are most commonly used, but when used frequently (and carelessly) these words lose their security value. A better approach, perhaps, would be to have the computer provide the user, each day, with a different word or code that the user could then modify by following a secret procedure in order to gain access to the system. For example, "the computer might send a five-digit password. The user then adds today's date to it, and then sends back the second and fourth digits of the sum."[23] Once an authorized user has been identified and has gained access to the system, various techniques employing cryptography—that is, "hidden writing"—are available to thwart those who would intercept the messages traveling between the computer and the remote terminal.

The security of records *retained or stored* in machine-readable form for extended periods of time must also be maintained. Such retention is often necessary in order to satisfy an IRS ruling that *requires* the preservation of certain machine-readable records by computer-using organizations for tax audit purposes. A second reason for retention control (although given the "persuasiveness" of the first reason, a second is not required) is that management decision making may be aided by having historical data readily available and easily incorporated into simulation models that might uncover possible trends and relationships.

Although punched paper media, microfilm, and magnetic disk packs may be used for long-term data storage, magnetic tape is by far the most popular retention medium. Thus, controls in most cases must be designed

[23] Richard G. Canning, "Protecting Valuable Data—Part 2," *EDP Analyzer*, January 1974, p. 8. This is a good source for further information on securing online terminals.

to protect archival magnetic tapes against dust, improper temperature and humidity fluctuations, and electromagnetic radiation.

Privacy controls[24]    An individual's "right" to privacy has been discussed at various times in this book, but privacy is not one of the rights specifically mentioned in the Bill of Rights of the Constitution. (In fact, the word "privacy" does not appear anywhere in the Constitution.) Furthermore, what one person may consider to be a privacy right may be in direct conflict with one of the rights that *is* explicitly mentioned in the Constitution. For example, if a newspaper reporter unearths the fact that a member of Congress has put a number of relatives on the government payroll for no good purpose, and if the reporter then reveals this fact and prints the names and salaries of the relatives, he or she has undoubtedly infringed on their privacy. But the reporter has also used rights guaranteed in the Bill of Rights (the First Amendment's freedom of speech and freedom of the press) to perform a public service. Thus, there may be legitimate rights operating against privacy in some situations. In short, since privacy is not one of the specific constitutional rights, and since a balance has to be struck between the need for privacy on the one hand and society's need for legitimate information on the other, *the extent to which individuals are given privacy protection must depend on judicial and legislative decisions.* That is, the *continuous* task of balancing human rights against basic freedoms in order to establish privacy controls is the responsibility of the judicial and legislative branches of government.

Recognizing that rapid advances in computer technology have given users of that technology the ability to gather and store information that goes beyond the legitimate information needs of society and can lead to excessive and unnecessary intrusions into an individual's personal privacy, lawmakers have been busy in recent years in the effort to restore some balance in favor of privacy. The result has been that federal statutes and dozens of state bills have been passed over a brief time span to control the invasion of privacy.

Some *examples of existing privacy laws* are:

1   *Fair Credit Reporting Act of 1970.* This federal law gives individuals the right to know what information is kept on them by credit bureaus and other credit investigation agencies. Individuals also have the right to

---

[24] Additional privacy control information may be found in several of the sources listed in footnotes 19 and 20 as well as in the following references: Paul B. Demitriades, "Administrative Secrecy and Data Privacy Legislation," *Journal of Systems Management.* October 1976, pp. 24–29; Jerome Lobel, "Computer Privacy States' Side: Seeking Cooperation amid Confusion," *Data Management,* April 1977, pp. 12–15ff.; *Personal Privacy in an Information Society.* U.S. Government Printing Office, Superintendent of Documents, stock no. 052-003-00395-3, July 1977; Willis H. Ware, "Handling Personal Data," *Datamation,* October 1977, pp. 83–85ff; and J. T. Westermeier, Jr., and Kenneth D. Polin, "Privacy Report to Alter Relation of Business to the Individual," *Data Management,* September 1977, pp. 30–33.

challenge information they consider to be inaccurate and to insert brief explanatory statements into the records in disputed cases.

**2** *State "Fair Information Practice" laws.* The California Fair Information Practice Act of 1974 spells out the rights of individuals when dealing with state government data banks. Individuals have the right (a) to know what information is kept on them in the various state computer data banks; (b) to contest the "accuracy, completeness, pertinence, and timeliness" of the stored data; (c) to force a reinvestigation of the current status of personal data, and (d) to resolve disputes in ways spelled out by the law. The Minnesota Privacy Act (and acts passed by other states) contains similar provisions.

**3** *Privacy Act of 1974.* This important privacy legislation was passed by Congress late in 1974 and signed into law by President Ford on January 1, 1975. It became effective late in September 1975. The act is aimed at some of the uses and abuses of *federal government* data banks. Some of the provisions of this law are (a) With the exception of classified files, Civil Service records, and law enforcement agency investigative files, individuals have the right to see their records in federal data banks; (b) they may point out errors in their records, and if these errors are not removed they may ask a federal judge to order the correction; (c) when federal agencies request personal information, they must tell individuals whether their cooperation in supplying the information is required by law; and (d) no federal, state, or local government agency can design a *new* information system based upon the use of the Social Security number. A Privacy Protection Study Commission was also established to monitor enforcement of the law and to study issues that will have to be resolved in the future. For example, the Commission was specifically given authority in the act to examine personal information activities in the medical, insurance, education, employment, credit and banking, credit reporting, cable television, telecommunications and other media, travel and hotel reservations, and EFTS areas. After a 2-year study the Commission issued a final published report in July 1977.[25] At this writing, it appears that additional laws will eventually be passed to incorporate the Commission's recommendations and to expand the scope of the Privacy Act to include the data banks maintained by federal, state, and local law enforcement agencies, state and local governments, and businesses.

**SUMMARY** In managing computing resources, the functions of planning, organizing, staffing, and controlling must be performed. It is the responsibility of top-level executives to define the mission of the computer department and to establish the general plans and policies that will provide guidance to data processing managers. It is then the responsibility of these managers to prepare additional plans to manage computer department resources. A

[25] The title of this report is *Personal Privacy in an Information Society.* See footnote 24 for further information.

number of questions that should be answered during the planning process have been presented in the chapter.

The organization of a computer facility depends on the scope and magnitude of the data processing work that must be performed and the extent to which this work is carried out by the particular department. The activities of system analysis and design, programming, and computer operation are typically found in the department. Data-base administration, operations research, and telecommunications functions may also be included in the organization of the computer facility.

The recruitment and selection of personnel to fill the positions that may exist in a computer department are one part of the staffing function. The selection process consists of (1) determining the nature and number of positions to be filled, (2) recruiting potential candidates for jobs, and (3) selecting from among the job applicants. Once employees have been selected, it is then usually necessary to train and motivate them if departmental goals are to be reached.

Controlling a computer facility usually involves making efforts to (1) improve operating efficiency, and (2) avoid the problems that may result from failure to safeguard data integrity, system security, and personal privacy. A number of control steps and techniques have been discussed in the chapter.

**REVIEW AND DISCUSSION QUESTIONS**

1  "Computing resources should be managed in an effective and efficient way." Discuss the meaning of "effective" and "efficient" in the context of this statement.

2  (a) What questions should be considered by top-level executives in planning for computing resources? (b) What questions should be considered by data processing managers?

3  (a) What activities may be performed by a data-base administrator? (b) Can you think of any reasons why the DBA function might be located outside the computer department?

4  What advantages might there be to organizing analysts and programmers into project groups?

5  (a) What steps are included in the process to select computer personnel? (b) What is a job description? (c) What is a job specification?

6  Give brief job descriptions and job specifications for the following positions: (a) Information systems manager (b) System analyst (c) Programmer (d) Data-base administrator (e) Computer operator.

7  (a) Discuss the possible procedures that may be used to recruit candidates for new jobs. (b) What selection procedures may be used to fill data processing positions?

8  What are the needs which influence and motivate human behavior?

9  (a) What is likely to cause job dissatisfaction among computer staff members? (b) What is likely to motivate employees?

**10** "The basic procedure to be followed to control the efficiency of computer department operations consists of the same steps used to control any other activity." Identify and discuss the use of these steps to control computer efficiency.

**11** (**a**) What is a performance standard? (**b**) Why is it difficult to establish realistic performance standards for system analysts and programmers?

**12** (**a**) What is the purpose of using computer performance evaluation tools? (**b**) Identify and discuss three CPE tools.

**13** (**a**) How may charging for computing resources lead to greater efficiency? (**b**) Compare the full-chargeout and partial-chargeout approaches to charging for computing resources.

**14** (**a**) What is the purpose of data integrity controls? (**b**) Into what three categories may integrity controls be classified? (**c**) Give some examples of integrity controls.

**15** (**a**) What is the purpose of system security controls? (**b**) Into what categories may security controls be classified? (**c**) Give some examples of security controls.

**16** "The extent to which individuals are given privacy protection must depend on judicial and legislative decision." Discuss this statement.

**SELECTED REFERENCES**    Over 40 references to specific topics may be found in the footnotes of this chapter.

In this final Part, we shall briefly consider the future outlook for computer technology and for information systems. In addition, we shall look at the future effects of computer systems on society. Are we about to enter the utopian period envisioned by optimists, or is George Orwell's *1984*, with its eerie visions of a society controlled by a fictional "Big Brother," just a few years away in fact as well as in fiction? Turn to Chapter 17 and make your own judgments.

The chapter included in Part V is

**V**

# EPILOGUE

# computers and the future 17

LEARNING OBJECTIVES Unlike preceding chapters that were primarily concerned with factual material and established procedures, this chapter deals with speculations about computer-related developments in the next few years. Nevertheless, after reading this chapter and answering the discussion questions, you should be able to: □ Describe how microprograms may be used □ Outline some developments in hardware, software, and information systems that you expect in the next 5 years □ Present the optimistic and pessimistic views about the future impact of computer systems

**I**n spite of the profound warning contained in an old proverb ("Prediction is difficult, particularly when it pertains to the future"), in this final chapter we shall attempt to summarize briefly some of the computer— and computer-related—developments that may be expected in the next few years. The topics to be considered can be classified as (1) the *technological outlook,* (2) the *information systems outlook,* and (3) the *outlook for society.*

## THE TECHNOLOGICAL OUTLOOK

### computer hardware

Numerous changes may be expected in the next few years in *I/O devices* and *central processors.*

I/O equipment   There will likely be little change in the performance of *punched card* equipment in the next several years. Efforts will be made to improve the reliability of card punches and readers, but the total demand for these devices will probably decline. In fact, Frost and Sullivan, a New York research organization, predicts that by 1984 keypunches will be supplanted by *keyboard-to-disk* storage devices for data entry purposes. *Impact printers* will not change significantly in speed or cost in the next few years, but new *nonimpact printers* using ink-jet and electrostatic technologies will likely appear, and these printers may offer higher speeds and better cost effectivenss than current nonimpact devices. There should also be some cost reduction in *magnetic tape* drives and their controllers, and there should be a doubling in transfer speeds as the amount of data packed in an inch of tape doubles. Substantial cost reductions (50 percent or more in some cases) are expected in *OCR readers,* and this reduction will increase their use. Significant price declines are also likely in *COM* technology.

   *Direct-access storage devices* will be developed to provide virtually unlimited online secondary storage at a very modest cost. *Storage hierarchies* will continue—i.e., the fastest auxiliary storage utilizing the latest technology will be more expensive and have less storage capacity than slower and less expensive alternatives. Mass storage approaches (in various stages of research and development) that are being considered by equipment designers include:[1]

**1**   *Higher-density direct-access systems.* Recording techniques using magnetic disk (and tape) surfaces that will significantly increase the density of data storage on a given surface are expected to be developed.

[1] For further information, see Douglas J. Theis, "An Overview of Memory Technologies," *Datamation,* January 1978, pp. 113–117ff.

**2**  *More efficient and reliable magnetic bubble systems.* Free of the mechanical motion required with disks and drums, bubble devices are expected to become more reliable and much lower in cost. Storage density will be very high (over a million characters may be stored on a square inch of positively magnetized film).

**3**  *Optical direct-access systems.* Information may be stored on a special light-sensitive plate by modulating electric pulses onto a *laser* light beam that is directed to a given area on the plate surface. A negative image of the varying light pattern—called a *hologram*—is etched on the plate surface and storage is thus accomplished. To retrieve information (without erasing it), a less intense laser beam is directed to the appropriate hologram to project the image onto sensors that will convert the light into electrical representations of the stored information. A single beam of light can cause the immediate transfer of a "page" of data. Theoretically, storage density and I/O speed is very high. Also, reliability is enhanced because of the absence of moving parts.

Sales of online *terminals* will more than double in the next few years, and terminals may represent over 25 percent of total hardware expenditures by 1984. Hundreds of thousands of *general-purpose typewriter* and *visual display* terminals will be installed each year in the 1980s, with visual display units being the most popular. In addition, hundreds of thousands of *special-purpose* terminals—e.g., POS and EFTS terminals—tailored specifically for a particular industry and/or application will be produced. The prices of the *intelligent terminals* discussed in Chapter 5 may rapidly decline as the costs of electronic components drop sharply. And as prices fall, increased demand for the intelligent devices will make possible an increase in production volumes which will further reduce costs and prices. By 1984, many more organizations will be (1) using stand-alone, intelligent terminals to carry out autonomous operations using the terminal's minicomputer, assorted peripherals, and secondary storage, and (2) utilizing a central computer to serve the terminals by managing large data bases and by executing those jobs that require extensive computations. In short, many more online terminals may be satellite minicomputers in a *distributed intelligence network* serviced by one or more central processing complexes.

Central processors    There will continue to be substantial reductions in the *size* of electronic circuits. The average number of components (transistors, resistors, etc.) packed on advanced integrated circuit chips has about doubled in every year since 1965, and this trend is expected to continue through 1985. Tiny chips capable of storing 16K bits will give way to chips of about the same size that may eventually have 100 times the storage capacity. Processors with more computing power than medium-sized and large machines of just a few years ago are already dwarfed by their peripherals, and they will become *much smaller* in the future.

"Have you noticed that as these things work faster and faster, we finish our day's work earlier and earlier?"

© DATAMATION ®

Along with further size reductions will come greater *speed*. Logic and storage circuits in 1984 will likely have switching speeds 10 to 50 times faster than those in use today; however, the total computer system may "only" be 5 times faster. Furthermore, circuits capable of performing at the same level as those in use today in larger systems may be available in just a few years at only one-twentieth the present cost. Even now, complete central processor kits are available with case, power supply, a variable amount of storage, and other features (including the ability to accept programs written in high-level programming languages) for just a few hundred dollars.[2]

[2] At a recent meeting of electronic engineers, Lester Hogan, an executive of Fairchild Camera & Instrument Co., displayed a Fairchild microprocessor chip that he claimed had the processing power of the IBM 701 that was valued at $1 million in 1953. Hogan then casually tossed 18 of the chips into the audience and thus threw away the 1953 equivalent of $18 million in computer processing power!

Semiconductor primary storage circuits will remain dominant during the late 1970s and early 1980s. Superconductive cryogenic devices operating at close to absolute zero temperatures have been found to be 100 times faster than any transistor circuit now in use, but such devices are not likely to appear in commercial equipment in the next few years.

In Chapters 7 and 11, and in Fig. 11-8, we saw that a special read-only storage unit in a CPU could be loaded with interpretative routines or *microprograms* that would permit one computer to interpret and execute instructions written for a different machine. In other words, the microprograms (also called *stored logic* and *firmware*) would analyze and decode foreign instructions into the elementary operations that the CPU is designed to execute. The usefulness of this concept extends beyond the emulation technique described in Chapter 11. It is also feasible to use various combinations of plug-in microprogrammed elements with *generalized* central processors to create custom-built systems for specific users. This "computer within a computer" approach can facilitate standardized CPU manufacturing and maintenance operations; it also makes it possible to convert critical, difficult, or lengthy software routines into microprograms that can be executed in a fraction of the time previously required. Furthermore, it is possible for vendors and users to *permanently* fuse their most important microprograms into read-only memory (ROM) chips and thus, in effect, convert important software into hardware.[3] Figure 17-1 illustrates how a computer manufacturer or user can create a customized computer system. Unlike the special-purpose computers of earlier years, however, the same processor can now be adapted to different functions by a simple change of microprograms. As Fig. 17-1 indicates, if nonpermanent microprograms are desired, they may be loaded into a writable storage device that can be plugged into the CPU, if permanent firmware is needed, it may be fused onto ROM chips by a special writing device.

Computer technology will likely make much greater use of firmware in the future. By converting functions currently being performed with software into circuit elements (which are becoming less expensive), the need for some of the detailed (and very expensive) programming currently being done may be reduced. For example, in performing its functions of scheduling, control, etc., the operating system (OS) software discussed in Chapter 2 uses storage space in and the time of the CPU—space and time resources that might otherwise have been used for mathematical or data processing tasks. To reduce this OS overhead, resident microprograms operating at hardware speeds may be substituted for some of the tasks currently being accomplished at relatively slow speeds with a series of OS program instructions. Also, specialized microprocessors and micro-

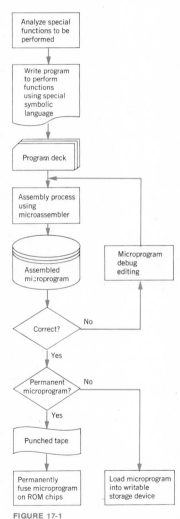

**FIGURE 17-1**

Procedure for customizing a computer with microprograms.

[3] It has been suggested that "ROM of the Month Clubs" may spring up in the 1980s to send subscribers new applications programs written in ROM chips that can be plugged into home microcomputers.

programs are likely to be used frequently in the future in place of software for language translation, data security, and data manipulation and control. We saw in Chapter 5 how "front-end" processors are used to relieve the host CPU of data communications functions. In the future, "back-end" processors may also be commonly used to handle data-base management functions and to control the movement of data between various storage elements in a storage hierarchy. Thus, the traditional and still very popular *uniprocessor* computer system that features single control, storage, and arithmetic-logic units will likely give way in the future to *multiprocessor* systems in all but the smallest installations. Of course, the component micro- and mini-sized processors dedicated to performing the specialized functions such as data-base management and security are likely to be smaller than those reserved to process user jobs in multiple and simultaneous streams. But future users—connected to such a multiprocessor system, perhaps, by intelligent terminals that further distribute and decentralize the computing power of the network—may expect faster, more reliable, and more secure service.

### computer software

There are numerous technical articles being published that predict with confidence the course of hardware development over the next decade. But this confidence is not found in the few articles dealing with the future of software development. Perhaps this is due to the fact that the development of software will continue to be slower, much more expensive, and more painful than hardware because the functions performed by software are now (and will continue to be) more complex than the operations performed by hardware. Of course, as we saw in the preceding section, many of the "normal" functions now being performed by operating system software may be taken over by future hardware elements. And the future use of multiprocessor systems may *reduce* the need for complex *multiprogramming* software that permits instructions from several programs to be interleaved and executed on a single processor. In short, the total-cost trends for information systems discussed in Chapter 2 (and shown in Fig. 2-6) will encourage the replacement of expensive software with cheap hardware whenever possible.

The comments just made in the preceding paragraph should not, however, be interpreted to mean that there will be no progress in software development. On the contrary, existing *languages* such as COBOL, PL/I, FORTRAN, etc., will be enhanced and improved to accommodate the *structured programming* approach discussed in earlier chapters. Subset dialects of these languages will also be developed for very small processors. Furthermore, new very-high-level languages may be developed to solve particular types of problems so that nonprogrammer users can conveniently make use of computing capabilities. Such languages may be *conversational*—i.e., the computer itself may keep track of the acceptable vocabulary of the language, and it may display permissible alternate terms and statements to users until the problem is satisfactorily formulated. The machine would then compute the answer to the problem. Thus, the users' major skill will be in their ability to state problems, and they will be assisted by a "dialogue" with the computer as it seeks to find out what they want to say.

Conversational programming is likely to be a feature of the *data-base management software* described in Chapter 2 (and in Fig. 2-21). In 1974, there were only about 1,500 true data-base management systems in worldwide use. By 1984, however, there will be tens of thousands of these software systems in operation, they will be more comprehensive, they will be large and may require up to a million characters of storage to operate effectively, and they will enable the end-user of the information to frequently bypass the services of applications programmers. Additional provisions to ensure the *integrity* and *security* of stored information will be incorporated into future data-base software as well as into future hardware.

Finally, *program development aids* such as structured programming will result in higher programmer productivity, shorter program development times, and more understandable and more error-free program modules. And the trend toward the greater use of packaged programs will accelerate rapidly. (It is expected that by 1985 the expenditures for applications packages will be 5 to 10 times the current level.)

## THE INFORMATION SYSTEM OUTLOOK

Although traditional batch processing computer installations are economical, are well suited to many types of applications, and are going to continue to account for a high percentage of the total processing work for some time, the trend is toward future systems that will be *quicker-responding* and *broader in scope* than these traditional installations.

### quick-response systems

As we have seen, emphasis is currently being given to the development of (1) distributed computer systems with logic and storage capability moved to the point of origin of transactions, (2) user-oriented interactive programming languages designed to enable operating personnel to get information quickly without having to wait for the help of an applications programmer, and (3) direct-access storage devices, online terminals, and multiprocessor computer configurations. And these developments, in turn, signal a definite trend in the direction of quick-response systems that will give remote users immediate access to very powerful computing facilities. (The number of firms operating such online systems in 1975 was about 9,500. By 1980, that number is expected to increase to 23,000.) *Real time processing* will become increasingly common in those applications where immediate updating of records is justifiable. When the time limitations are not so severe, *online processing,* with periodic updating of those records that affect other users of a distributed network, will be frequently used in place of traditional batch processing methods. Source data will frequently be keyed directly into the computer system, thus eliminating the need for cards and/or tapes in many applications.

With increased emphasis being placed on quick-response systems, there will obviously be greater use of *data communications* facilities. In fact, the transmission of data is expected to continue to increase by 35 percent *each year* between now and 1985. New data communications services will be established (satellites will be used), and the current services offered by data carrier organizations will be expanded to meet this demand. Data transmission line costs will be reduced by up to 50 percent by 1984.

### broader systems

Many of the quick-response systems that will be developed in the next few years will take a broader *data-base approach* to the needs of the organization. (Given the rapid growth expected in data-base management software, this is not a surprising prediction.) The data-base approach can be flexible; that is, it may be used by organizations combining large centralized computers (and a centralized data base) with nonintelligent terminals located at operating level, it may be used by organizations with a smaller central processor to maintain a centralized data base for a network of distributed minicomputers and outlying intelligent terminals, or it may be used by organizations adopting some other alternative.

Regardless of the technical approach used, the trend in many organizations will be to define, classify, and store certain types of basic data commonly so that better integration will be possible. The development efforts to produce data banks that will replace a multitude of the independent files maintained at the present time will probably continue at a more rapid pace in spite of the potential dangers to individual privacy. Why will this happen? It will likely happen because managers will have to respond to future changes that may occur at a much faster rate than in the past. Therefore, decision makers forced to make quicker choices involving greater risks will press for relatively complete information rather than settle for information in bits and pieces located in scattered files.

### the automated office

Many offices today have installed *word processing* equipment for the preparation of reports and letters. The widespread use of word processing devices began in 1964 when IBM announced the Magnetic Tape Selectric Typewriter (MTST). Frequently used form letters and paragraphs are typed once and the words are recorded on tape. The MTST may then be used to automatically prepare repetitive prerecorded letters or to compose letters and reports consisting of selected prerecorded paragraphs. Since the introduction of the MTST, IBM and many other vendors have brought out other stand-alone hard copy devices that use magnetic cards, cassettes, and internal belts as the recording media. In addition, word processors with visual display screens for text editing, with floppy disks for text storage, and with various kinds of hard copy printers have also been produced by dozens of vendors. The latest of these word processing devices are direct spinoffs from the intelligent terminal segment of the data processing industry.

At the present time, the word processing function is usually found in an "administrative services" department. But as word processors become virtually indistinguishable from online computer terminals, as they are connected to communications lines in a companywide network so that letters and reports need not be mailed but can be printed for the first time on the receiving word processor, and as they develop some data processing capability, it is likely that the word processing function will be merged with the computing and communications function in the "office of the future." In such an office, ordinary typewriters will incorporate electronic editing features that will permit a line of type to be corrected and justified before it is printed on paper, compact electronic files may replace additional rows of paper-filled file cabinets, and interoffice correspondence may travel (via satellite in many cases) through a companywide *electronic mail/message system* that may provide immediate delivery of words and pictures.

A computer-based electronic mail/message system, for example, could perform the following functions:

1   *Provide message distribution services.* Messages may be delivered *only* to specified individuals who use the message network: they may be transmitted to identified groups of people; or they may be sent to a combination of individuals and groups. Users with portable terminals can access the message network from any phone to enter or receive messages.

2   *Provide computerized conferences.* Conferences may be held at the convenience of the participants. Since the conference dialogue may be stored, it is not necessary for all participants to be online at the same time. Rather, a person may sit down at a terminal at a convenient time, call up

any conversations that he or she has not seen, make additional comments, respond to questions, etc., and then sign off. Phone call interruptions of other important work may thus be avoided, and a permanent history of all conference discussions may be recorded.[4]

**3**  *Provide message reception services.* The message system may provide services to help the message recipient take appropriate action. For example, the recipient may (a) reply to the sender of the message, (b) forward the message to others with or without further comments, (c) store the message in a "personal attention needed" electronic file, or (d) store the message in an electronic file so that a subordinate can then take appropriate action.

### additional possible applications of computer systems

The following applications seem to be *technically* possible during the 1980s; whether they are all *socially desirable,* however, is another matter. These few applications have not been included in earlier speculations, and they have been *arbitrarily* classified into those that may affect *businesses* and those that may have an impact on *individuals in society.* Of course, the development, for the home, of new computer-controlled products by some businesses will also affect the private lives of individuals in our society.

Applications affecting businesses    A few of the computer-related applications that may have an impact on businesses in the 1980s are:

**1**  *Computer-assisted manufacturing.* By 1984, the installation of tens of thousands of micro- and mini-sized computers to run machine tools will have resulted in an incredible gain in the efficiency and cost effectiveness of many manufacturing operations. Only 10 programmable manipulators, or robots, were installed during 1974; by 1984, however, it is predicted that 14,000 robots will be added *each year.* Since computer-controlled automatic machines can be switched from the production of one item to another simply by changing the program, it will be feasible to keep equipment busy by having it produce small quantities of a number of different items. Thus, small-lot manufacturing may become nearly as economical as mass production is today. In fact, "Nathan Cook of MIT predicts that computers and robots may reduce overall costs in small-lot

---

[4] For more information on this subject, see Richard G. Canning, "Computer Message Systems," *EDP Analyzer,* April 1977, pp. 1–13; Murray Turoff, "Computerized Conferencing: Present and Future," *Creative Computing,* September-October 1977, pp. 54–57; Ronald P. Uhlig, "Human Factors in Computer Message Systems," *Datamation,* May 1977, pp. 120ff.; and Jacques Vallee, Robert Johansen, and Kathleen Spangler, "The Computer Conference: An Altered State of Communication? *Creative Computing,* September-October 1977, pp. 58–59.

manufacturing by 80 to 90 percent."[5] And since the machines that will be used in future mass production operations will be produced in small lots, the net effect is that they will be relatively less expensive, and so may be the prices of the items they produce.

**2**   *Automatic meter reading.* At this writing, many telephone companies have installed computer-controlled testing equipment to check on the condition of telephone lines. In the 1980s, gas, electric, and water meters may be connected to these telephone lines so that as the system automatically tests line condition it will also read the meters for the utility companies.

**3**   *Attending meetings electronically.* Telephones and cable TV sets may be combined with computers to provide an integrated voice-data-picture communication system for some organizations. Ultimately (but probably not by 1984), it may be possible for many professionals such as managers, teachers, engineers, etc., to perform most of their job duties in offices located in their homes. Thus, the transmission of information may be substituted for the transportation and concentration of humans. The need to crowd together into cities may be reduced; communities of

[5] James S. Albus, "Automation and the Sleeping Nation," *Computer Decisions,* August 1975, p. 32.

© DATAMATION ®

"We'd rather look at something dumber than we are."

interest and interaction may be linked electronically rather than by geographic boundaries.[6]

Applications affecting individuals in society    Some of the computer-related applications that could affect the lives of people at home and at play in the 1980s are

1    *Home and hobby applications.*[7] Microprocessors on small chips will be used to control most home appliances in the 1980s. The electromechanical controls found on washers, dryers, food mixers, etc., will be replaced by more reliable microprocessors. Television sets may also have microprocessors to perform automatic tuning and color-regulating operations. Typewriters will incorporate tiny computers for control and duplication purposes. And a microcomputer could be added to the push-button telephone to convert it into a terminal suitable for requesting and receiving stock quotations, recorded information such as emergency first-aid procedures from voice libraries, mathematical computation procedures to assist in income tax preparation, and online banking (EFTS) services. Inexpensive computers with considerable power will also be widely used for *home recreation* and *education* purposes. When connected to a TV set, the computer will provide an almost unlimited number of games. For example, small children can play with a controllable TV puppet, they can do TV picture drawing, and they can play a simple electronic organ; older members of the family can play a target-shooting game, they can play a football game or go bowling, or they can trace through a maze or make a moon landing—the list of entertainment applications is virtually endless. The computer may be reprogrammed to play different games in just a few seconds by using preprogrammed tapes and an inexpensive audio-type cassette reader. In addition to recreational applications, this computer-TV system will also be used for educational purposes. Instead of games (which can be very educational in their own right), the preprogrammed tapes can provide all kinds of test and drill applications to bring the advantages of *computer-assisted instruction* right into the home.

In addition to computer systems using TV sets and preprogrammed tapes, there will also be, for the hobbyist, hundreds of thousands of home computer systems that can be programmed in high-level languages. Complete computer kits selling for less than $300 are now available. Much more powerful machines at the same cost will be available in the 1980s. Clubs of computer hobbyists are springing up across the nation to share programs and experiences.

---

[6] For more details on these intriguing possibilities, see Joseph Ferreira and Jack M. Nilles, "Five-Year Planning for Data Communications," *Datamation,* October, 1976, pp. 51–57.

[7] A wealth of information on home and hobby computer applications may be found in such periodicals as *Byte, Creative Computing, Dr. Dobb's Journal of Computer Calisthenics and Orthodontia, Interface Age, People's Computer Company,* and *SCCS Interface.* The March 1977 issue of *Computer,* and the July 1977 issue of *Datamation* also contain several articles of interest.

**2** *Opinion polling in the home.* In some parts of the country today, TV sets receive their signals from cable connections rather than from airwaves. Cable television may expand in the future to permit subscribers to choose from a wider selection of incoming programs. But the cable can also be used to communicate *outgoing* messages. A cable TV set might be equipped with a few buttons such as might be found on a pocket calculator. A broadcaster could then invite viewers to participate in a "personal response program." Questions could be asked, buttons could be pushed, and responses could be recorded and tabulated in computer systems. A national "town meeting" could be called in this way to provide political leaders with the electronic "votes" of citizens on important issues.

**3** *Automotive applications.* The family car in the 1980s will be equipped with microprocessors that will take over the functions now performed by electromechanical systems. Instruments, speed and skid control systems, ignition and fuel injection systems, engine analysis sensors, temperature control and antitheft devices, emission control and collision avoidance devices—all these components will be under computer control.

## THE OUTLOOK FOR SOCIETY

### the optimistic view

The optimistic view of the future is that *greater freedom and individuality* are encouraged by the use of computers. Optimists note the individual benefits, such as those mentioned in preceding sections and chapters, and they expand and project those benefits into the future. They foresee no insurmountable problems in society's adapting to the changes brought about by increased computer utilization. The greater productivity that results from computer usage, they contend, will lead to an increased standard of living, a shorter work week, and increased leisure time. Although it will be a challenge for human beings to put aside age-old attitudes toward work and learn to use creatively the free time that they will have in the future, the optimists believe that people can learn to use their leisure in ways that are contemplative and self-fulfilling.

Also, it is argued, people will be freed from the basic struggle to maintain their existence and will have the time and resources to pursue the activities of their choice. (Since individuality has been defined as the "freedom to exercise choice according to one's own scale of preference,"[8] it will thus be enhanced.) Aristotle's prophecy that "When looms weave by themselves, man's slavery will end" is cited by the optimists. Nonhuman slaves (computers and automated tools controlled by com-

---

[8] Robert M. Gordon, "Computers and Freedom, Individuality and Automation: Challenge and Opportunity," *Computer,* September-October 1971, p. 30.

puters) will liberate many people from the unpleasant working conditions that have evolved from Charles Dickens's England of the 1800s and Upton Sinclair's United States of the early 1900s. No longer will people have to spend long hours at an assembly line, for example, tightening a few bolts on the monotonous widgets passing by, when a computer-directed and uncomplaining robot can do the work accurately and inexpensively.

Optimists also believe that the sophisticated computer systems of the future will permit a *more human and personalized society* that will further reduce the need for individual conformity. They argue that the complexity of our present society, the millions of people crowded into it, and the inadequacy of our present information systems act to encourage conformity and thus to restrict personalization and human freedom of choice. However, when sophisticated information systems are developed and widely used to handle routine transactions, it will then be possible to focus greater personal attention on exceptional transactions. Therefore, more humanistic attitudes will emerge. Of course, these optimistic views do not go unchallenged.

### the pessimistic view

The pessimistic view of the future is that the effects of computer usage will *not* lead to greater freedom and individuality. On the contrary, pessimists can examine many of the same applications as optimists did and come to the opposite conclusion that computer usage will (1) dominate our lives as a society and as individuals and (2) sweep us along in a tide over which we—the harassed and exposed victims of a depersonalized and dehumanized process that places greater value on efficiency than on the more noble qualities of life—shall have little control.

Critics of the effects of computer usage have evidence to show that questionable practices in originating and recording data are common; that dossiers containing incorrect, ambiguous, and unverified data on individuals are produced; that correct personal data are misused; that systems miscalculations are frequent; that stored sensitive personal data are often not secured and protected against theft, manipulation, and malicious scrutiny; and that those facts, beliefs, thoughts, and feelings that people want to keep to themselves (or have kept on a confidential basis) are repeatedly revealed and disseminated. The net effect, pessimists contend, is that individual freedom will be severely threatened by computer-usage pressures leading to greater regimentation and conformity.

On the economic front, pessimists agree with optimists that computer-assisted manufacturing will result in enormous gains in productivity. But the pessimists argue that when humans must compete with programmable robots, the humans will lose—they will lose their jobs[9] and they will lose their personal dignity. And as jobs are eliminated by machines, purchasing power is certain to decline. A monumental economic depression may result from the overproduction of machines and the decline in demand, and this could lead to a severe political upheaval and a change in our form of government.

The fears expressed in the above summary of the pessimistic view are not all new, nor are they all related solely to the future impact on individuals of computers alone. For at least 100 years people have feared that automatic machines might develop consciousness and turn on their creators. In 1872, for example, a science fiction work entitled *Erewhon* was published by Samuel Butler. Residents of Erewhon, fearing that people would some day stand in the same relation to machines as "the beasts of the field" now stand to people, attacked and destroyed nearly all the machines in Erewhon.

### a final note

> There comes a time when one asks even of
>   Shakespeare,
> even of Beethoven, "Is this all?"
>
> *Aldous Huxley*

Is it possible in this last section to draw any conclusions from the dozens of different viewpoints that have so often been presented in the pages of this book? Perhaps. We can conclude, for example, that there are at least three different contemporary views of computers and technological change:

**1** *Computers and technology are an unblemished blessing.* This uncritical optimistic view holds that technology is the source of all progress for the individual and society, that social problems will inevitably be solved through the application of technology, and that every new technological possibility will automatically be beneficial.

**2** *Computers and technology are an unbridled curse.* This pessimistic view holds that technology increases unemployment, leads to depersonalization and bewilderment, threatens an individual's right to dignity and privacy, and threatens to pollute and/or blow up the world.

**3** *Computers and technology are undeserving of special attention.* This unconcerned view is that technology has been with us for decades, and

---

[9] A recent Associated Press news item quoted Bernard Sallot, executive director of the Robot Institute of America, as saying that a new programmable robot would soon replace thousands of semiskilled workers—perhaps hundreds of thousands of them—in factory jobs. A "tremendous backlog of orders" for robots now exists, Sallot added.

we are now better educated and more able than ever before to adapt to the new ideas and changes which it has brought (and will bring):

Each of these views is deficient although each probably contains an element of truth. The optimists are correct when they conclude that new technology often creates new opportunities for society; the pessimists are correct when they conclude that new problems are often created by new tools; and the unconcerned are correct when they conclude that social institutions (e.g., schools) can, and often do, play an important role in tempering the effects of technology.

The predictions of optimists or pessimists will become facts or fables if people make them so. We cannot know what people *will* do in the future. They *could* achieve the optimistic vision. But if in using computers they choose procedures that are impersonal and coldly efficient, they should not be surprised if the results are inhumane and inflexible. Thus, in the years ahead it will be up to concerned and informed managers and citizens who have an awareness of the potential dangers to see that the optimistic view prevails. I am confident that you will succeed.

SUMMARY

Significant developments are expected in the next few years in computer hardware and software. Some of the likely changes have been outlined in this chapter.

Future information systems will be quicker-responding and broader in scope than the average installation in operation today. Data communications services will have to be expanded to handle the rapid increase in data transmission. A network of distributed processors and a broader data-base approach will be frequently used to respond to the needs of organizations and decision makers.

The future uses of computers are viewed by some people with optimism while others believe that computers and technology are likely to be the curse of humanity. Which view—optimism or pessimism—will prevail? No one knows. Predictions of each group will become facts or fables only if people make them so. An enlightened citizenry, aware of the dangers, can help bring about the optimistic version.

REVIEW AND DISCUSSION QUESTIONS

1  (a) What future hardware developments would support the development of distributed computer networks? (b) Of the "office of the future"?

2  How are microprograms used?

3  Why might the development of multiprocessor systems reduce the need for multiprogramming software?

4  (a) What is conversational programming? (b) What is the purpose of data-base management software?

5   "Future information systems will be quicker-responding and broader in scope than traditional installations." Discuss this statement.

6   (a) Are you an optimist or a pessimist about the future impact of computer systems on society? (b) Defend your answer to 6(a).

7   (a) What is a word processor? (b) What role would word processing devices play in an electronic mail/message system?

# appendix A
## card punch operation

The purpose of this supplement is to acquaint you with some of the fundamentals of keypunch operation so that you may prepare the necessary cards to run short programs or make changes in existing program or data cards. The purpose is *not* to make you a highly skilled keypunch operator. Thus, only the most basic uses of the card punch are discussed here.

A card punch commonly encountered is the IBM model 29 (Fig. A-1). The keyboard and functional control switches for this machine are shown in Fig. A-2.

The *shaded* keys on the keyboard are used to control certain machine operations; the *unshaded* keys are used to punch the indicated characters. Depressing the NUMERIC shift key causes the character indicated on the upper portion of the key to be punched. As you will note, the alphabetic keys are located just where they would be on a typewriter.

**TYPICAL OPERATION TO PREPARE SHORT PROGRAMS**

The operating steps in punching a typical student program may be outlined as follows:

1   Turn on the *main line switch,* shown in Fig. A-1.

2   Load blank cards into the *card hopper* face forward with the 9-edge down.

3   Turn on the AUTO FEED and PRINT functional control switches, shown in Fig. A-2, and switch the *program control lever* (located right below the program unit shown in Fig. A-1) to the right.

4   By depressing the FEED key, you will move a card from the hopper to the entrance to the *punching station.* Pressing the FEED button a second time will drop a second card and properly align the first card at the punching station.

5   Punch the necessary data into the card.

6   If the last column punched is column 80, the completed card will be automatically advanced to the *reading station,* and a new blank card will be positioned at the punching station. If the last column punched is *not* column 80, the card may be advanced by pressing the REL key.

7   The punched card advanced to the reading station and the following

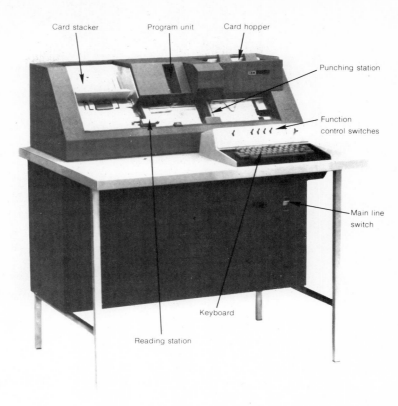

Card stacker    Program unit    Card hopper

Punching station

Function
control switches

Main line
switch

Keyboard

Reading station

**FIGURE A-1**

Model 29 Card punch (courtesy IBM
Corporation).

card positioned at the punching station move together—i.e., as columns
1, 2, 3, etc., of the completed card pass under the reading station, the
*same columns* of the following card are being positioned under the
punching station. This synchronization feature permits data to be duplicated in the second card. If the DUP key is depressed, data sensed in the
completed card will be automatically reproduced in the same columns of
the following card.

**8**    When the last card has been punched, the CLEAR function switch on
the model 29 may be used to move it to the *card stacker*.

**9**    Turn off the main line switch.

**SINGLE-CARD
PREPARATION**

It is often necessary to add one or two cards to a deck or to replace an
existing card with a corrected or undamaged one. The operating steps to
follow in these situations are:

**1**    Turn on the main line switch.

**2**    Turn off the AUTO FEED switch, turn on the PRINT switch, and
switch the program control lever to the right to disengage the program
unit.

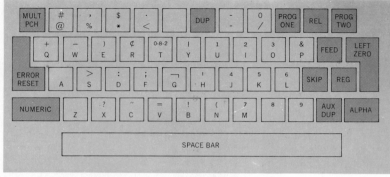

(a)

FIGURE A-2

(a) Card punch keyboard, (b) functional control switches.

(b)

3   Put a blank card into the *card hopper* and press the FEED key to move the card to the *punching station.* Then press the REG key to align the card under the punches.

4   Punch the card as required and then press the REL key to release it from the punching station.

5   The card can be cleared to the stacker by depressing the CLEAR switch.

6   Turn off the main line switch.

# appendix B
## glossary

The communication of facts and ideas in any field is dependent on a mutual understanding of the words used. The purpose of this appendix, then, is to present definitions for some of the terms that are often used in the field of information processing.

**Absolute address**   A machine-language address assigned to a specific location in storage.

**Access**   See *direct-access, random-access, remote-access, serial-access.*

**Access time**   The elapsed time between the instant when data are called for from a storage device and the instant when the delivery operation begins.

**Accumulator**   A register or storage location that forms the result of an arithmetic or logic operation.

**Address**   An identification (e.g., a label, name, or number) that designates a particular location in storage or any other data destination or source. Also, a part of an instruction that specifies the location of an operand for the instruction.

**ADP**   Automatic Data Processing.

**ALGOL (ALGOrithmic Language)**   An algebraic, procedure-oriented language similar to FORTRAN that is widely used in Europe.

**Algorithm**   A set of well-defined rules for solving a problem in a finite number of operations.

**Alphanumeric**   Pertaining to a character set that includes letters, digits, and, usually, other special punctuation character marks.

**Analog computer**   A device that operates on data in the form of continuously variable physical quantities.

**ANSI (American National Standards Institute)**   Formerly ASA and USASI.

**APL (A Programming Language)**   A mathematically-oriented language frequently used in timesharing.

**Arithmetic unit**   The part of a computing system containing the circuitry that does the adding, subtracting, multiplying, dividing, and comparing.

**Assembly program**   A computer program that takes nonmachine-language instructions prepared by a programmer and converts them into a form that may be used by the computer.

**Auxiliary storage**    A storage that supplements the primary internal storage of a computer.

**Background processing**    The execution of lower-priority computer programs during periods when the system resources are not required to process higher-priority programs.

**BASIC (Beginners All-purpose Symbolic Instruction Code)**    A terminal-oriented programming language frequently used in timesharing.

**Batch processing**    A technique in which a number of similar items or transactions to be processed are grouped (batched) for sequential processing during a machine run.

**BCD (Binary-Coded Decimal)**    A method of representing the decimal digits zero through nine by a pattern of binary ones and zeros (e.g., the decimal number 23 is represented by 0010 0101 in 8-4-2-1 BCD notation).

**Binary digit**    Either of the characters 0 or 1. Abbreviated "bit."

**Binary number system**    A number system with a base or radix of two.

**Bit**    See *binary digit.*

**Block**    Related records, characters, or digits that are grouped and handled as a unit during input and output.

**Branch**    An instruction that transfers program control to one or more possible paths.

**Buffer**    A storage device used to compensate for the difference in rates of flow of data from one device to another—e.g., from an IO device to the CPU.

**Byte**    A group of adjacent bits operated upon as a unit.

**Call**    A transfer of program control to a subroutine.

**Cathode ray tube (CRT)**    An electronic tube with a screen upon which information may be displayed.

**Central processing unit (CPU)**    The component of a computer system with the circuitry to control the interpretation and execution of instructions. Also called the *main frame.*

**Channel**    (1) A path for carrying signals between a source and a destination. (2) A track on a magnetic tape or a band on a magnetic drum.

**COBOL (COmmon Business-Oriented Language)**    A high-level language developed for business data processing applications.

**Code**    A set of rules outlining the way in which data may be represented; also, rules used to convert data from one representation to another. To write a program or routine.

**Collate**    To combine items from two or more sequenced files into a single sequenced file.

**COM**    Computer-Output Microfilm.

**Compiler**    A computer program that produces a machine-language program from a source program that is usually written in a high-level language by a programmer. The compiler is capable of replacing single source program statements with a series of machine language instructions or with a subroutine.

**Computer network**   A processing complex consisting of two or more interconnected computers.

**Conditional transfer**   An instruction that may cause a departure from the sequence of instructions being followed, depending upon the result of an operation, the contents of a register, or the setting of an indicator.

**Console**   The part of a computer system that enables human operators to communicate with the computer.

**Counter**   A device (e.g., a register) used to represent the number of occurrences of an event.

**CPU**   See *central processing unit.*

**CRT**   See *cathode ray tube.*

**Cybernetics**   The branch of learning which seeks to integrate the theories and studies of communication and control in machines and living organisms.

**DASD**   Direct-Access Storage Device.

**Data administrator**   The one responsible for defining, updating, and controlling access to a data base.

**Data bank**   See *data base.*

**Data base**   A stored collection of the libraries of data that are needed by an organization to meet its information processing and retrieval requirements.

**Data-base management system**   The comprehensive software system that builds, maintains, and provides access to a data base.

**Data processing**   One or more operations performed on data to achieve a desired objective.

**Debug**   To detect, locate, and remove errors in programs and/or malfunctions in equipment.

**Decision table**   A table giving all the conditions to be considered in the description of a problem, together with the actions to be taken.

**Density**   The number of characters that can be stored in a given physical space—e.g., an inch of magnetic tape.

**Digital computer**   A device that manipulates discrete data and performs arithmetic and logic operations on these data. Contrast with *analog computer.*

**Direct-access**   Pertaining to storage devices where the time required to retrieve data is independent of the physical location of the data.

**Documentation**   The preparation of documents, during system analysis and subsequent programming, that describe such things as the system, the programs prepared, and the changes made at later dates.

**Downtime**   The length of time a computer system is inoperative due to a malfunction.

**EBCDIC**   An 8-bit code used to represent data in modern computers.

**Edit**   To correct, rearrange, and validate input data. To modify the form of output information by inserting blank spaces, special characters where needed, etc.

**EDP**   Electronic Data Processing.

**Emulator**   A stored logic device or program that permits one computer to execute the machine-language instructions of another computer of different design.

**Executive routine**   A master program that controls the execution of other programs. Often used synonymously with *executive, monitor,* and *supervisory routines.*

**Field**   A group of related characters treated as a unit—e.g., a group of adjacent card columns used to represent an hourly wage rate. An item in a record.

**File**   A collection of related records treated as a unit.

**Flowchart**   A diagram that uses symbols and interconnecting lines to show (1) a system of processing to achieve objectives (system flowchart) or (2) the logic and sequence of specific program operations (program flowchart).

**FORTRAN (FORmula TRANslator)**   A high-level language used to perform mathematical computations.

**Generator**   A computer program that constructs other programs to perform a particular type of operation—e.g., a report program generator.

**Hardware**   Physical equipment such as electronic, magnetic, and mechanical devices. Contrast with *software.*

**Heuristic**   A problem-solving method in which solutions are discovered by evaluating the progress made toward the end result. A directed trial-and-error approach. Contrast with *algorithm.*

**HIPO charts (Hierarchy plus Input-Process-Output charts)**   Charts used in the analysis, design, and programming of computer applications.

**Hollerith code**   A particular type of code used to represent alphanumeric data on punched cards.

**Hybrid computer**   A data processing device using both analog and discrete data representation.

**Information**   Meaning assigned to data by humans.

**Information retrieval**   The methods used to recover specific information from stored data.

**Input/output (I/O)**   Pertaining to the techinques, media, and devices used to achieve human/machine communication.

**Instruction**   A set of characters used to direct a data processing system in the performance of an operation—i.e., an operation is signaled and the values or locations of the instruction operands are specified.

**Interface**   A shared boundary—e.g., the boundary between two systems or devices.

**Internal storage**   The addressable storage in a digital computer directly under the control of the central processing unit.

**Interpreter**   A computer program that translates each source language statement into a sequence of machine instructions and then executes these machine instructions before translating the next source language statement. A device that prints on a punched card the data already punched in the card.

**I/O** See *input/output.*

**ISAM (Index Sequential Access Method)** A method whereby records organized in a sequential order can be referenced directly through the use of an index based on some key or characteristic.

**Item** A group of related characters treated as a unit. (A record is a group of related items, and a file is a group of related records.)

**Job** A collection of specified tasks constituting a unit of work for a computer.

**Jump** A departure from sequence in executing instructions in a computer. See *conditional transfer.*

**K** An abbreviation for kilo or 1,000 in decimal notation.

**Key** An item that is used to identify a record.

**Label** One or more characters used to identify a program statement or a data item.

**Language** A set of rules and conventions used to convey information.

**Library routine** A tested routine maintained in a library of programs.

**Loop** A sequence of instructions in a program that can be executed repetitively until certain specified conditions are satisfied.

**Machine language** A language used directly by a computer.

**Macro instruction** A source language instruction that is equivalent to a specified number of machine language instructions.

**Magnetic ink character recognition (MICR)** The recognition of characters printed with a special magnetic ink by machines.

**Magnetic storage** Utilizing the magnetic properties of materials to store data on such devices and media as disks, drums, cards, cores, tapes, and films.

**Main frame** Same as *central processing unit.*

**Management information** An information system designed to supply organizational managers with the necessary information needed to plan, organize, staff, direct, and control the operations of the organization.

**Memory** Same as *storage.*

**MICR** See *magnetic ink character recognition.*

**Microprocessor** The basic arithmetic, logic, and storage elements required for processing (generally on one or a few integrated circuit chips).

**Microprogram** A sequence of elementary instructions that is translated by a micrologic subsystem residing in the CPU.

**Microsecond** One-millionth of a second.

**Millisecond** One-thousandth of a second.

**Minicomputer** A relatively fast but small and inexpensive computer with somewhat limited input and output capabilities.

**MIS** See *management information system.*

**Mnemonic**   Pertaining to a technique used to aid human memory.

**Monitor routine**   See *executive routine*.

**Multiplex**   To simultaneously transmit messages over a single channel or other communications facility.

**Multiprocessing**   The simultaneous execution of two or more sequences of instructions by a single computer network.

**Multiprocessor**   A computer network consisting of two or more central processors under a common control.

**Multiprogramming**   The simultaneous handling of multiple independent programs by interleaving or overlapping their execution.

**Nanosecond**   One-billionth of a second.

**Natural language**   A human language such as English, French, German, etc.

**Object language**   The output of a translation process. Contrast with *source language*. Synonymous with *target language*.

**Object program**   A fully compiled or assembled program that is ready to be loaded into the computer. Contrast with *source program*.

**OCR (Optical Character Recognition)**   The recognition of printed characters through the use of light-sensitive optical machines.

**Offline**   A term describing persons, equipment, or devices not in direct communication with the central processing unit of a computer.

**Online**   A term describing persons, equipment, or devices that are in direct communication with the central processing unit of a computer.

**Operand**   The data unit or equipment item that is operated upon. An operand is usually identified by an address in an instruction.

**Operating system**   An organized collection of software that controls the overall operations of a computer.

**Operation code**   The instruction code used to specify the operations a computer is to perform.

**Patch**   The modification of a routine in an expedient way.

**Peripheral equipment**   The input/output devices and auxiliary storage units of a computer system.

**Picosecond**   One-thousandth of a nanosecond.

**PL/I (Programming Language I)**   A high-level language designed to process both scientific and file-manipulating applications.

**Pointer**   A data item in one record that contains the location address of another logically related record.

**Procedure-oriented language**   A programming language designed to conveniently express procedures used to solve a particular class of problems.

**Program**   (1) A plan to achieve a problem solution; (2) to design, write, and test one or more routines; (3) a set of sequenced instructions to cause a computer to perform particular operations.

**Program flowchart**   See *flowchart*.

**Program library**   A collection of programs and routines.

**Programmer** One who designs, writes, tests, and maintains computer programs.

**Programming language** A language used to express programs.

**Radix** The base number in a number system—e.g., the radix in the decimal system is 10. Synonymous with *base*.

**Random-access** Descriptive of storage devices where the time required to retrieve data is not significantly affected by the physical location of the data.

**Real time** Descriptive of online computer processing systems which receive and process data quickly enough to produce output to control, direct, or affect the outcome of an ongoing activity or process.

**Record** A collection of related items of data treated as a unit. See *item*.

**Register** A device capable of storing a specific amount of data.

**Remote access** Relating to the communication with a computer facility by a station (or stations) that is distant from the computer.

**Report program generator (RPG)** Software designed to construct programs that perform predictable report-writing operations.

**Routine** An ordered set of general-use instructions. See *program*.

**Secondary storage** See *auxiliary storage*.

**Serial-access** Descriptive of a storage device or medium where there is a sequential relationship between access time and data location in storage—i.e., the access time is dependent upon the location of the data. Contrast with *direct-access* and *random-access*.

**Simulation** To represent and analyze properties or behavior of a physical or hypothetical system by the behavior of a system model. (This model is often manipulated by means of computer operations.)

**Software** A set of programs, documents, procedures, and routines associated with the operation of a computer system. Contrast with *hardware*.

**Solid-state** Descriptive of electronic components whose operation depends on the control of electric or magnetic phenomena in solids, such as transistors and diodes.

**Source language** The language that is an input for statement translation.

**Source program** A computer program written in a source language such as FORTRAN, BASIC, COBOL, etc.

**Statement** In programming, an expression or generalized instruction in a source language.

**Storage** Descriptive of a device or medium that can accept data, hold them, and deliver them on demand at a later time. Synonymous with *memory*.

**Structured programming** An approach or discipline used in the design and coding of computer programs. The approach generally assumes the disciplined use of a few basic coding structures and the use of top-down concepts to decompose main functions into lower-level components for modular coding purposes.

**Subroutine** A routine that can be a part of another routine or program.

**Supervisory routine**  See *executive routine.*

**System**  (1) A grouping of integrated methods and procedures united to form an organized entity; (2) an organized grouping of people, methods, machines, and materials collected together to accomplish a set of specific objectives.

**System flowchart**  See *flowchart.*

**System analyst**  One who studies the activities, methods, procedures, and techniques of organizational systems in order to determine what actions need to be taken and how these actions can best be accomplished.

**Throughput**  The total amount of useful work performed by a computer system during a given time period.

**Timesharing**  The use of specific hardware by a number of other devices, programs, or people simultaneously in such a way as to provide quick response to each of the users. The interleaved use of the time of a device.

**Top-down methodology**  A disciplined approach to organizing complexity by identifying the top-level functions in a system and then decomposing these functions into a hierarchy of understandable lower-level modules.

**Unconditional transfer**  An instruction that always causes a branch in program control away from the normal sequence of executing instructions.

**Utility routine**  Software used to perform some frequently required process in the operation of a computer system—e.g., sorting, merging, etc.

**Virtual storage**  Descriptive of the capability to use online secondary storage devices and specialized software to divide programs into smaller segments for transmission to and from internal storage in order to significantly increase the effective size of the available internal storage.

**Word**  A group of bits or characters considered as an entity and capable of being stored in one storage location.

**Word length**  The number of characters or bits in a word.

# index